AMERICAN
SWORDMAKERS

To my wife Judy, who has put up with my obsession with antique swords and cheered me on during the many years of study and research for this book.

"Chronicles"

First made of wood or stone . . . to poke, probe, and pierce. So man might live, perhaps another day upon the Earth. Then came the great destroyer, made of bronze then later steel. Chopping, thrusting, slashing! Follow its path through forests, fields, and hills. Upon which are strewn legions of dead. Corpses clad in red or blue or grey! Upon whose ground, empires were built or else destroyed.

—Robert Gramberg

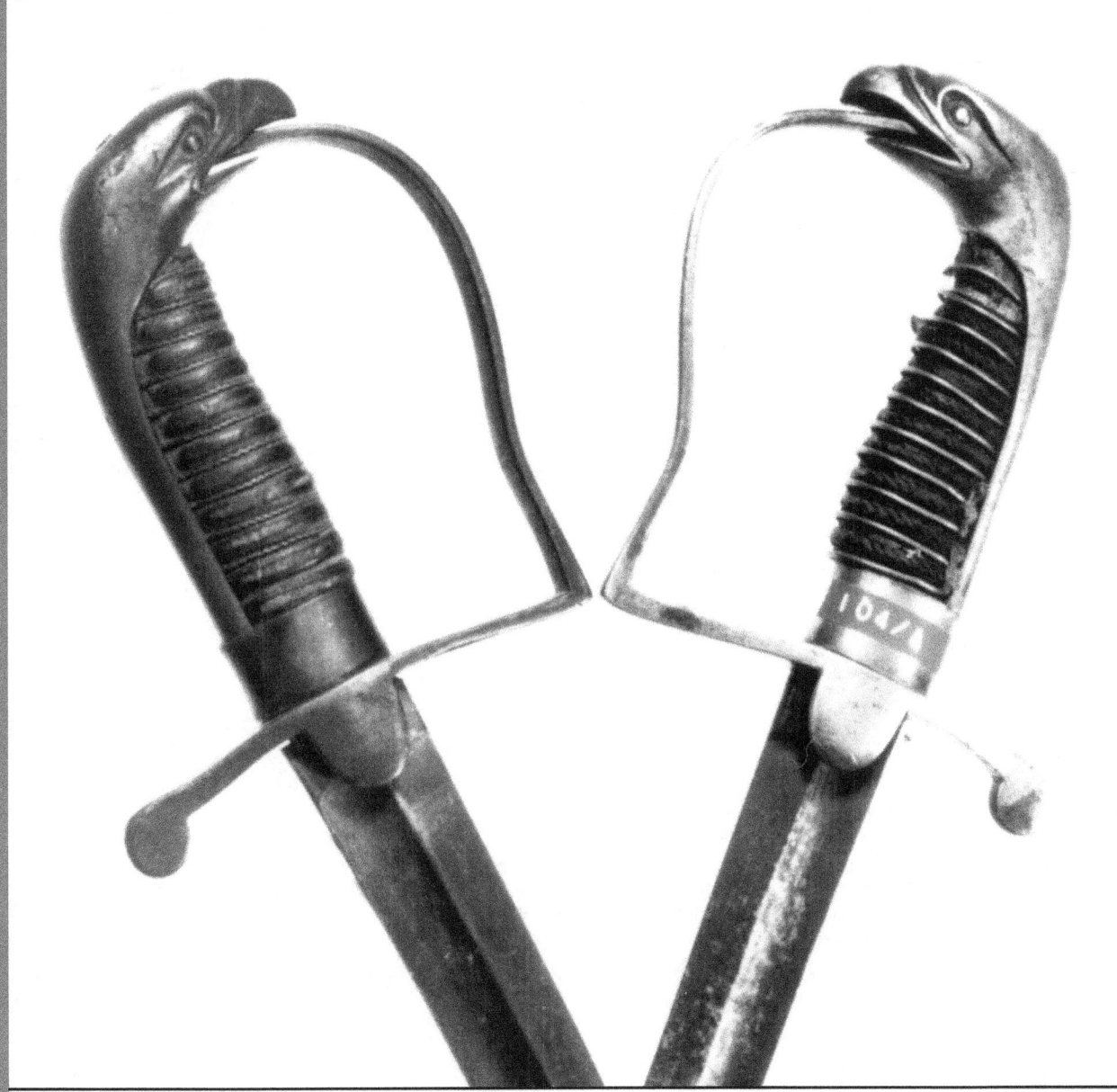

Richard H. Bezdek

American Swordmakers

American Swordmakers
Revised Edition
by Richard H. Bezdek

ISBN: 978-1-7321930-0-0

Copyright © 2018 Redd INK Press

"Chronicles" copyright © 1994 by Robert Gramberg
  c. 1835 (from the Leonard J. Garigliano collection).

Front cover photo: Eagle-head mounted artillery officer sabers with brass hilts made by F.W. Widmann,
Back cover photos: (top) Union Model 1875 Marine Corps officer sabers (from the Alan Jay Rice collection);
  (bottom) Confederate cavalry sword made by Memphis Novelty Works (Leech & Rigdon, from the
  Virginia Historical Society collection).

Contents

Contributors • vii

Illustrations • xiii

Preface • xix

Introduction • 1

CHAPTER 1
U.S. Armories and Arsenals Fabricating Swords and Edged Weapons • 3

CHAPTER 2
State Armories and Arsenals Fabricating Swords and Edged Weapons • 15

CHAPTER 3
U.S. Sword Makers • 21

CHAPTER 4
European Sword Makers and Dealers Who Exported to Union Dealers during the Civil War • 185

CHAPTER 5
U.S. Sword Dealers • 187

CHAPTER 6
U.S. Silversmiths Who Mounted Swords • 271

CHAPTER 7
Confederate Armories and Arsenals Making, Repairing, or Storing Edged Weapons • 315

CHAPTER 8
Confederate Sword Makers • 321

CHAPTER 9
European Sword Makers and Dealers Who Exported Swords to
Confederate Dealers during the Civil War • 377

CHAPTER 10
Confederate Sword Dealers • 379

APPENDIX A
Sword Markings • 385
U.S. Arms Inspectors and Their Initials

APPENDIX B
Armorers to the Pennsylvania Revolutionary War Navy
(Made and Repaired Ordnance and Edged Weapons) • 399

APPENDIX C
U.S. Cavalry Practice Swords • 401

Contributors

This book could not have been completed without the help of many, many people. I have been assisted by sword and edged weapon collectors and dealers, gun and military goods collectors and dealers, contemporary authors of books and articles about swords, curators and staffs of museums and historical societies, library personnel, owners of regalia and sword-making companies, as well as historical and geneological researchers. Many have become good friends. It is impossible to thank everybody who helped, but it is only right and fitting that I extend my special thanks to as many as I can and mention their special contributions.

Hampton B. Allen Library, Wadesboro, NC
Barbara Wheeler, Director
Contributed important information on Confederate sword maker Arnold & Cooley.

The Ancient and Honorable Artillery Company Museum, Boston, MA
John F. McCauley, Curator
Provided a brief history of the company.

The Athens Regional Library, Heritage Room, Athens, GA
Provided information on local Civil War sword makers.

The Atlanta Historical Society, Atlanta, GA
Devon Goddard, Library Assistant
Provided information on Atlanta Civil War sword and edged weapon makers and dealers.

The Augusta-Richmond Public Library, Augusta, GA
Alice Walker, Local History Librarian
Provided information on local Civil War artisans.

Francis Bannerman Son, Bayport, NY
James F. Hogan, owner
Provided information, books, and catalogs on the famous Francis Bannerman Company.

James Batson
Provided important information on several sword and bowie knife makers.

Bruce S. Bazelon
Chief, Division of Collections Services for the Pennsylvania Historical and Museum Commission; coauthor of *A Directory of American Military Goods Dealers and Makers: 1785-1885* (William F. McGuinn, coauthor); editor for *Swords from the Public Collections in the Commonwealth of Pennsylvania*. Bruce has been very helpful in providing suggestions concerning the technical aspects of this book.

The Ben West Library (Public Library of Nashville and Davidson County), Nashville, TN
Carol F. Kaplan, Librarian of the Nashville Room
Provided information on Civil War sword makers of Nashville.

Linda Berge
A very hard-working and helpful young lady who typed up this book on her personal computer. Many thanks for all your help.

Boston Public Library, Boston, MA
Charles S. Longley, Curator of Microtexts and Newspapers
Supplied important information on Boston sword makers and dealers.

Bradley Memorial Library, Columbus, GA
Joan Emens, Reference Department
Provided information on Columbus, GA, sword makers from the 1859-1860 Columbus Directory she had duplicated. A special thanks for all her efforts.

The Chelmsford Public Library, Chelmsford, MA
Kathy Cryan Hicks, Librarian
Provided some great information on Christopher Roby.

Fraternal Supplies Inc. (Successor to C.E. Ward Fraternal Supply Co.), New London, OH
Keith V. Bailey, owner
Provided unique information about his company, which can be traced all the way back to Nathan P. Ames Jr., who started sword production in 1829.

The Free Library of Philadelphia, Philadelphia, PA
Bernard F. Pasqualini, Database and Newspaper Center
Diane M. Calkins, Librarian II
Provided information on Philadelphia sword makers and dealers.

Leonard J. Garigliano
President, The Association of American Sword Collectors; prolific author of many articles on swords; author of *American Military Swords, An Annotated Bibliography* and *Abstract, Review and Notes Regarding Principal Sword Contractors During the American Civil War*. A true friend and fellow sword collector who helped me at every turn and provided me with copies of many rare articles on sword makers and dealers.

Bob Gramberg
Did some great illustrations for this book.

Greensboro Historical Museum, Greensboro, NC
William J. Moore, Director
Provided information on a Confederate saber by Arnold & Cooley.

Hagley Museum and Library
Marc Alan Lankin, Reference Librarian
A very special thanks goes to Marc and the museum staff—Barbara Hall, Marge McNinch, Lynn Catanese, Robert Howard, Debra Hughes, and Beth Parker Miller—for their marvelous cooperation in duplicating Civil War *Army and Navy Journal* newspapers, plus much other Civil War data, including information from Confederate periodicals.

John D. Hamilton
John is a well-known expert on swords and sword makers. He has written many articles for several magazines and is author of *The Ames Sword Company: 1829-1935*. As curator of collections and exhibits at the Museum of Our National Heritage, he has been instrumental in obtaining some very special information and material on sword and fraternal goods makers. He has my special thanks for his support and guidance in the writing of this book.

Ronald G. Hickox
Author of *U.S. Military Edged Weapons of the Second Seminole War (1835-1842)* and *Collectors Guide to Ames U.S. Contract Military Edged Weapons (1832-1906)* and many, many articles concerning American swords. A real friend whose help and encouragement over the years is highly valued. Ron provided invaluable data on William Horstmann and U.S. government sword purchases as well as several special articles on swords.

The Illinois State Historical Library, Springfield, IL
Kathryn M. Harris, Reference and Technical Services
Provided data on Chicago sword makers and dealers.

Darryl Kinnison
The late Mr. Kinnison was a supporter of this book from the first time I talked to him. He was not only a sword collector but wrote several articles on U.S. swords. Darryl also did extensive research for me on Mobile, Alabama, sword makers and dealers. The sword collecting fraternity has lost a very special member, and I personally will miss his wonderful enthusiasm and untiring efforts to assist me with this book.

Gordon A. Knapp
Gordon currently lives in the original home of D.J. Millard and provided extensive information on Millard and his family.

Madison County-Canton Public Library, Canton, MS
Paul C. Cartwright, Local History Librarian
Provided information on Canton sword makers.

Greg May
A friend and fellow collector.

The Memphis Shelby County Public Library, Memphis, TN
Patricia M. LaPointe, Reference Librarian
Provided data on Memphis Civil War sword makers.

The Museum of Our National Heritage, Lexington, MA
John D. Hamilton, Curator of Collections and Exhibits
Nola Skousen, Librarian-Archivist
Jennifer Barlow, Assistant Librarian
I am very grateful for all the assistance I received from this marvelous institution and its very capable staff. They provided an extensive list of fraternal and society goods makers and dealers, plus they duplicated several rare sword and fraternal goods catalogs.

The Newberry Library, Chicago, IL
Alexander E. Lucas, Reference Librarian
Provided information on city directories.

The New London Public Library, New London, OH
Carolyn Mench, Director
Provided extensive information on the C.E. Ward family and company.

The New Orleans Public Library, Louisiana Division, New Orleans, LA
Provided information on New Orleans sword makers.

The South Caroliniana Library, Columbia, SC (University of South Carolina)
Eleanor M. Richardson, Reference Librarian
Provided information on Columbia, SC, Civil War sword makers.

Kurt Stein
Editor of the Pennsylvania Antique Gun Collectors Association Inc. *Monthly Bugle*
Provided some special information on Philadelphia city directories and sword makers, and copies of *Bugle* articles on swords.

Donald R. Tharpe
Well-known collector of American swords.

The U.S. Cavalry Museum, Fort Riley, KS (Department of the Army)
William McKale, Museum Specialist
Provided copies of many great articles from the *Journal of the U.S. Cavalry Association*.

The Utica Public Library, Utica, NY
Barbara Brookes, Reference Department
Provided some excellent information on D.J. Millard, cavalry saber maker during the Civil War.

The Valentine Museum, Richmond, VA
Teresa Roane, Supervisor of Reference Services
Duplicated a complete 1860 Richmond, VA, directory, showing important information on sword makers and dealers.

Virginia Historical Society, Richmond, VA
Giles Cromwell, Registrar
AnnMarie F. Price, Museum Assistant Curator—Museum Programs. Provided information on Richmond, Virginia, edged-weapons makers.

The Washington Memorial Library, Macon, GA
Willard L. Rooker, Geneology Librarian
Provided some unique information on Confederate sword makers of Macon, GA.

Phillip M. Weber
A sword collector and expert on fraternal and society swords. Contributed an extensive list of fraternal and

society sword makers and dealers.

Dr. James B. Whisker
A leading expert on Pennsylvania gunsmiths, clock makers, and silversmiths. Jim has written over 50 articles on Pennsylvania artisans and gunsmiths. He has also written 15 books, including *Arms Makers of Philadelphia*, *Arms Makers of Pennsylvania*, *Arms Makers of Colonial America*, and *Arms Makers of Virginia and West Virginia*. Jim was a tremendous help by sending me an enormous amount of information on Pennsylvania sword and edged weapon makers. He has my very special thanks.

Illustrations

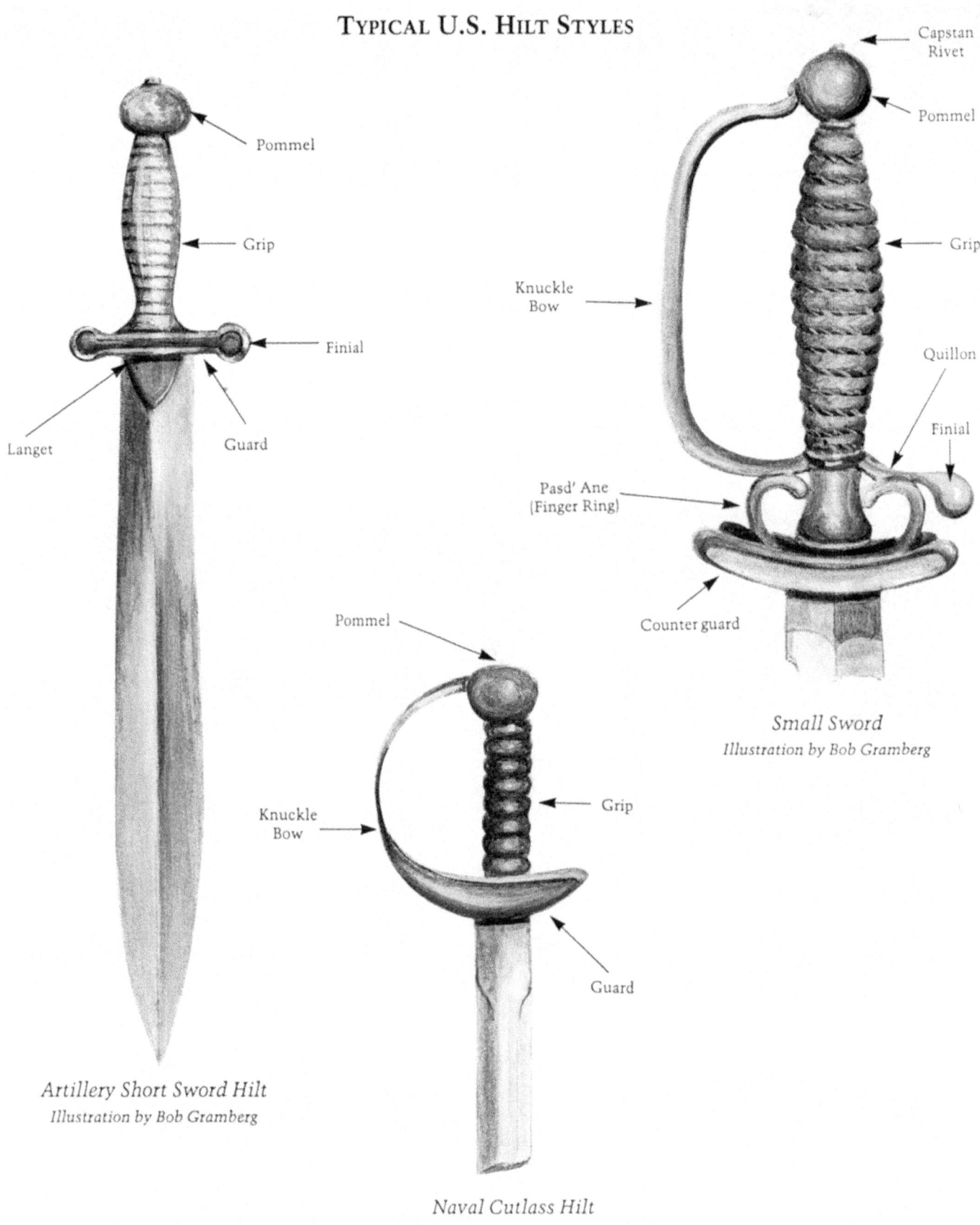

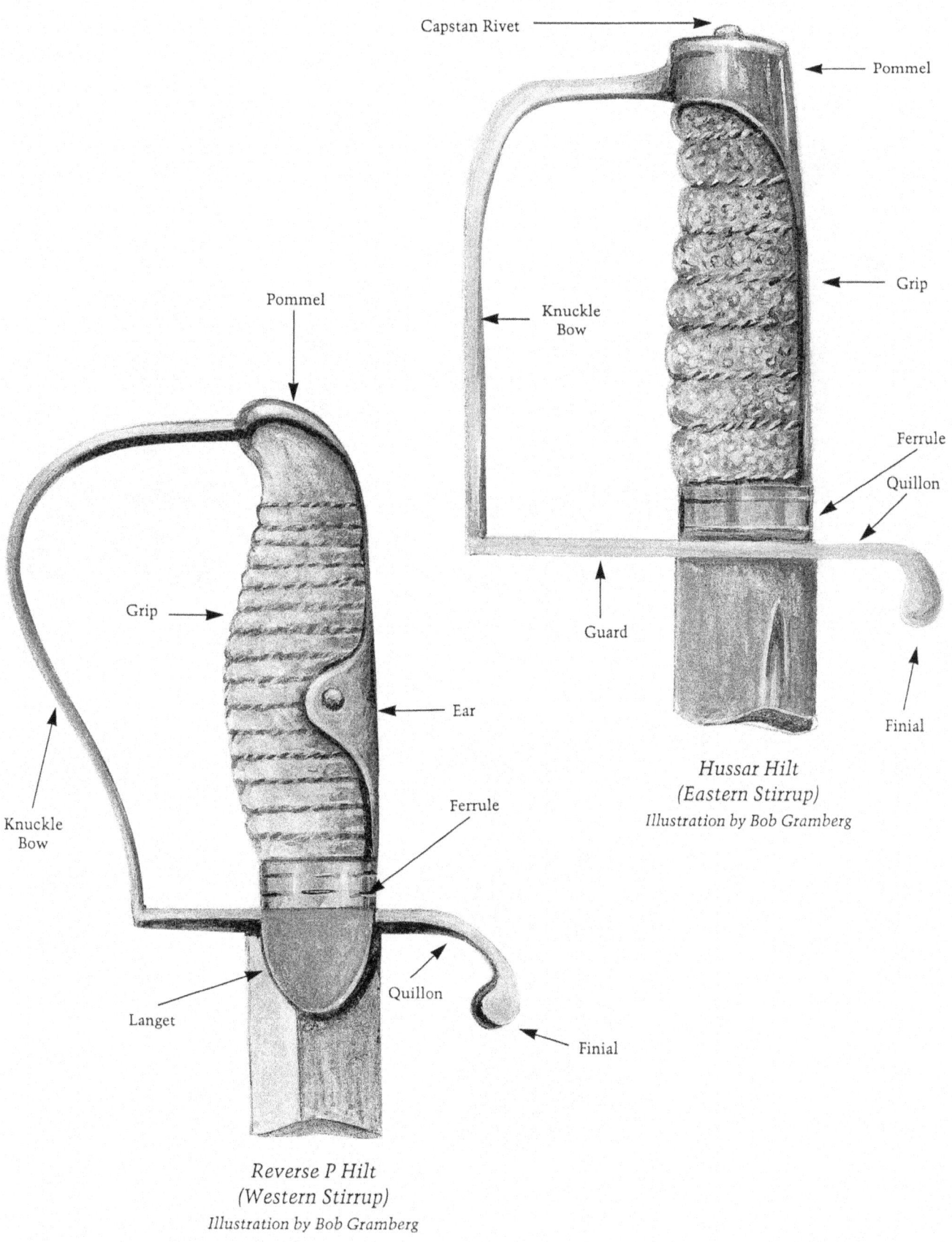

*Hussar Hilt
(Eastern Stirrup)*
Illustration by Bob Gramberg

*Reverse P Hilt
(Western Stirrup)*
Illustration by Bob Gramberg

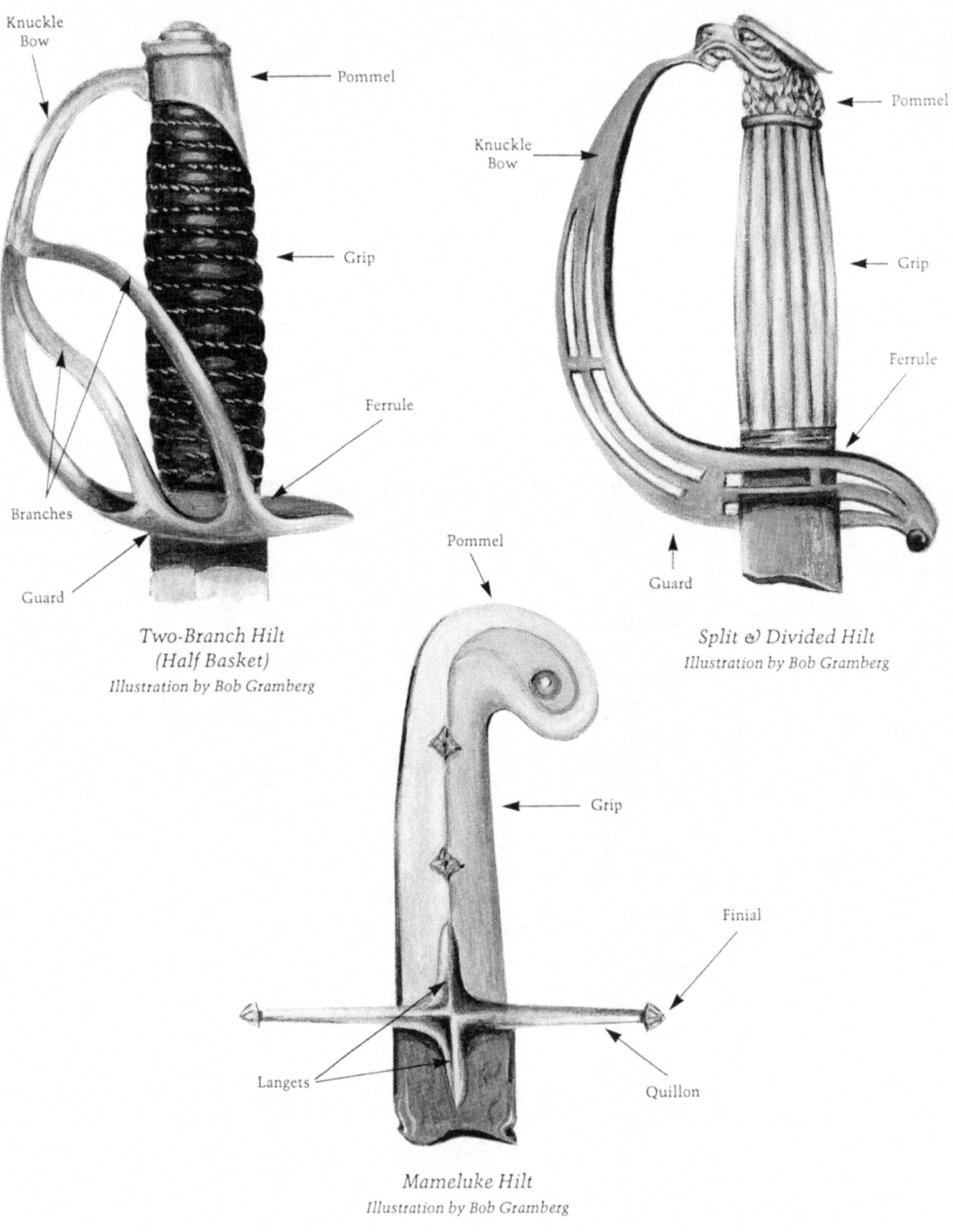

Two-Branch Hilt (Half Basket)
Illustration by Bob Gramberg

Split & Divided Hilt
Illustration by Bob Gramberg

Mameluke Hilt
Illustration by Bob Gramberg

U.S. Blade and Scabbard Types

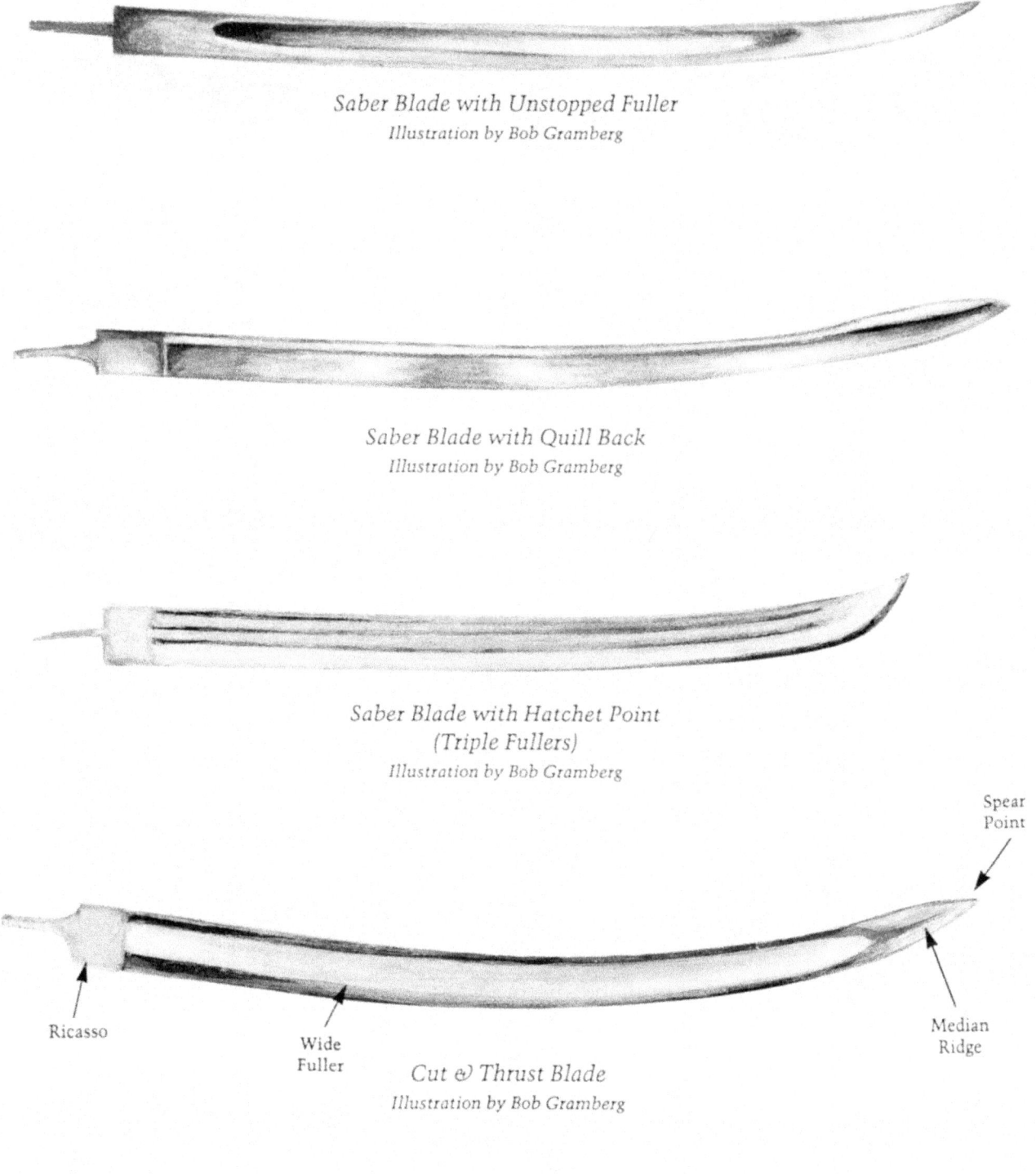

Saber Blade with Unstopped Fuller
Illustration by Bob Gramberg

Saber Blade with Quill Back
Illustration by Bob Gramberg

*Saber Blade with Hatchet Point
(Triple Fullers)*
Illustration by Bob Gramberg

Cut & Thrust Blade
Illustration by Bob Gramberg

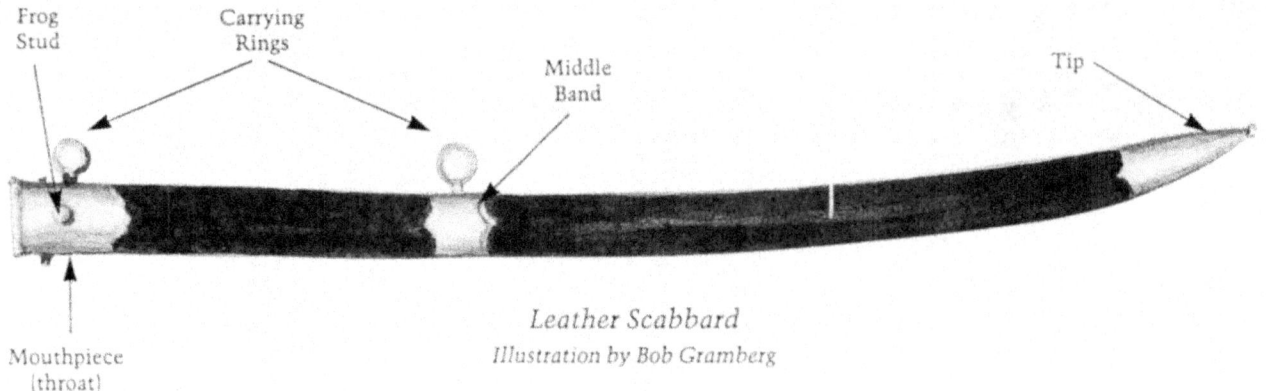

Leather Scabbard
Illustration by Bob Gramberg

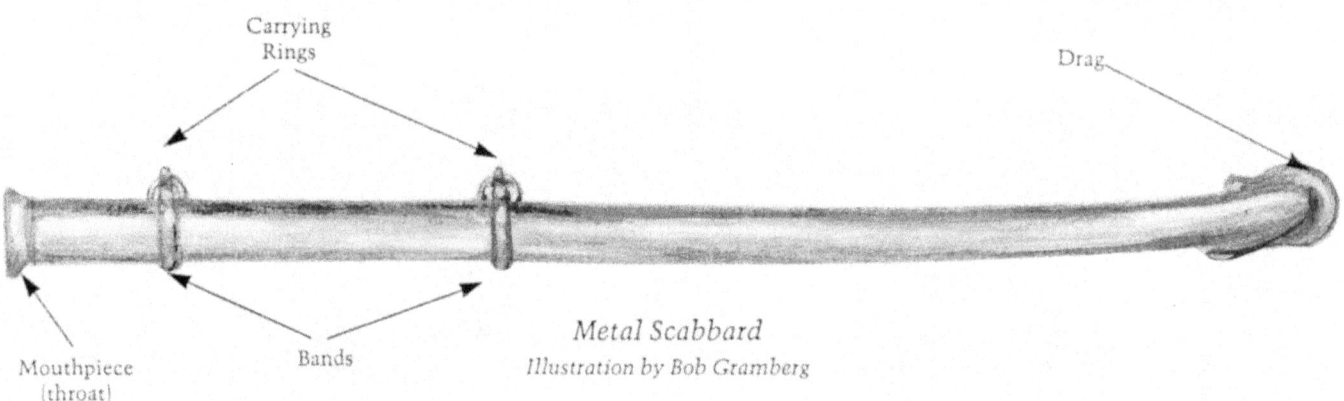

Metal Scabbard
Illustration by Bob Gramberg

Preface

This book is designed in such a way that any piece of information can be found easily and quickly. All sword makers' names are listed in alphabetical order. All occupations are listed. The town and/or location of the sword makers are shown. Where possible, the year of birth, years active, and the year of death are shown. A history of many of the sword makers is given, including changes of location.

All dates are based on my extensive research and the summing up of all available information. I must, therefore, say that they are as accurate as I could make them. The dates of birth and death should be 100-percent accurate. All other dates, although I have not used the word "circa," must be considered educated and well-researched approximations.

I have researched this book for more than 20 years. I obtained information by close examination of thousands of antique swords—swords obtained for my collection; in other collections; at antique, gun, and military shows; and in museums and historical societies. The research required the study of any written information I could find on sword makers, arms makers, silversmiths, and all other related professions. Federal, state, and city records and archives contained a tremendous amount of data. Old newspapers provided historical information as well as military goods, sword maker, and sword dealer advertisements. Census reports were also helpful. Tax records provided occupational information. Old tombstones provided birth, death, and family information. I read historical, biographical, and reference books. I examined government publications, such as the *Journal of the U.S. Cavalry Assocation*, old and new magazine articles and advertisements, sword maker and sword dealer catalogs, military society bulletins, city directories, museum catalogs, general military catalogs, and military auction catalogs. Much of the information also came from fellow collectors.

For information on identificaion and appraisal of American Swords, see my website (www.theswordman.com). My other sword books are also shown on this site. You can also contact me by e-mail at: theswordman@yahoo.com.

—Richard H. Bezdek

Introduction

ollecting antique swords is like collecting a piece of history. The sword has been used in every era since Stone Age man picked up a rock and sharpened a point on one end. The history of the sword parallels the history of man himself and his struggle for individual freedom and national sovereignty. There has been no war since before the birth of Christ until World War II in which the sword has not been used in one form or another.

The collecting of antique swords has grown tremendously in the last 20 years. The reference data on swords, however, has not kept up with the demand by collectors, expert or amateur. As with any antique collecting, there is a natural want and need by the collector to know who made the sword and when it was made. There is no book anywhere, out of print or current, that addresses this basic requirement—until now.

This book is not just a list of names and dates. It contains a huge amount of information about anyone who had anything to do with swords and edged weapons. First, there are the sword makers—the individual, company, or government manufactory that made the complete sword. Many sword makers started out making other metal products or made swords as part of their product lines. Examples would be general edged tool makers, gun makers, bayonet makers, knife makers, tinners, and so on. Many swords—such as officer, presentation, and hunting swords—were assembled and sold by jewelers, silversmiths, and goldsmiths. They bought blades and scabbards, then hilted the blades and decorated the scabbards. Then there were merchants, dealers, and retailers who imported and/or sold swords. Also, military outfitters and military goods dealers sold swords. Others—such as military ornamentors, tailors, hatters, and saddlers—sold swords as a sideline. Gun shops and gun dealers sold swords. Some artisans made only part of the swords. Brass founders made hilts and mountings. Many iron forges just made blades. Some made only scabbards. This book has documentation on all of these facets of the sword-making business.

During the eighteenth century (Colonial Period and Revolutionary War) and the early nineteenth century (War of 1812 and Mexican War), American arms makers were often multitalented. In many cases, the swordsmith made other edged weapons and edged tools. The gunsmith oftentimes made edged weapons and was a silversmith. Many silversmiths were also goldsmiths, watch makers, clock makers, and jewelers, as well as sword hiltors. Having many talents was, in many cases, a necessity in order to make a living.

The tradition of arms makers making many different types of weapons, an activity dating to the Middle Ages, was brought over to this country from Europe. They were called armorers (armourers). Immigrants from Germany were especially talented armorers.

Although many early American artisans and armorers were proficient in several trades, not all of their activities were necessarily documented. Information is continually being brought to light. Researchers, digging into local records, correspondence, archives, and similar sources, are still discovering much information showing swords and edged weapons being made by artisans specializing in other crafts. I have, therefore, decided to list all early edged weapon makers. Early clock, watch, musket, and bayonet makers are also listed. This information will be of great help to collectors of bayonets, knives, axes, hatchets, tomahawks, lances, pikes, poleaxes, surgical instruments, cutlery, and firearms. There is a complete section on silversmiths, goldsmiths, and jewelers who hilted swords.

In many cases, several family members or whole familes were involved in the same craft or related crafts. Arms making and metal working, in all their branches, were typical and much needed crafts in early America. I have, therefore, listed whole families of edged weapon makers living in the same town or area in the same time span.

CHAPTER 1

U.S. Armories and Arsenals Fabricating Swords and Edged Weapons

U.S. Carlisle, Pennsylvania, Revolutionary War Armory

- Made muskets, bayonets, and cannon.
- Military superintendants: Capt. John Orbison (1780-1781), Capt. John Jordon (1728-1729).
- Supervisor of blacksmiths: Valantine Hoffman (1779).

Artisan Code
Armorer—A
Artillery Artificer—AA
Blacksmith—B
Brass Founder—BF

John Barlow	AA	1779
Moses Boone	B-AA	1779-1782
William Chatwin	BF-AA	1777
William Curry	AA	1788-1780
William Duffield	AA	1780-1783
James Hadden	A	1778
Sylvester Holdcraft	AA	1779
J. Nathaniel Kirk	B-AA	1779

Daniel Reed	AA	1778
Timothy Shey	AA	1780
Frederick Stein	BF	1778
John Swindles	A-AA	1779-1782
William Wilson	B-AA	1778
Andrew Wilson	AA	1777-1781

U.S. Fort Pitt, Pennsylvania, Revolutionary War Armory

- Made muskets, bayonets, and cannon.
- Military superintendents: Capt. Nathaniel Irish, Major Craig.

John Harris	A	1778-1783
Conrad Hartman	A	1777-1782
Andrew McKinney	A	1779-1782
Jacob Peters	A	1779-1782
Jacob Stoner	A	1782
John Thomas	A	1779-1782
Jacob Judy	A	1775-1780

U.S. Lebanon, Pennsylvania, Revolutionary War Armory

- Made muskets, bayonets, and cannon.
- Ten miles from Hummelstown (location of Pennsylvania State Gunfactory).
- Commander: Col. Benjamin Flowers.

Military Superintendents:

Capt. Alexander Dow	1777-1782
Capt. James Gibson	1777-1782
Capt. John Jordan	1779-1783
Capt. Valantine Hoffmann	1777-1778
Capt. Theophilus Parke	1777-1780
Capt. Jesse Rowe	1777-1781
Capt. Thomas Wylie	1777-1782
Maj. Charles Lakens	1777-1782

John Adams	A	1777-1781
Samuel Adams	A	1777-1782
Adam Barger	A	1777-1781
Daniel Bitting	A	1777-1780
Daniel Blakley	A	1777-1780
James Bruce	A	1777-1781
John Cahill	A	1777-1782
Thomas Carothers	A	1777-1782
William Carr	A	1777-1781
John Clark	A	1777-1782
Edward Collins	A	1777-1781
John Dalton	A	1777-1781
John Diddy	A	1777-1781
James Dowdel	A	1777-1791
Michael Engles	A	1777-1781
Josiah Jenkins	A	1777-1781
John Kirker	A	1779-1780
William McCowing	A	1778-1780

Francis Miller	A	1777-1781
Christopher Roth	A	1777-1781
John Rowe	A	1777-1780
James Steel (Stahl)	A	1777-1781
Richard Thomas	A	1777-1781
Abraham Umstead	A	1777-1781
Patrick Wenn	A	1777-1781
George Yearhouse	A	1777-1781

U.S. Fishkill, New York, Armory and Depot

- Located near New York City, 5 miles east of the Hudson River.
- In operation during the Revolutionary War as a repair facility (ordnance and swords), ordnance depot, and marshalling area.
- The installation included:
    - Artillery field
    - Barracks
    - Blacksmith shop
    - Brass foundry
    - Parade grounds
    - Military storehouses
    - Guardhouse
    - Hospitals
    - Ammunition magazines
    - Workshops
- Jacabus Cooper's blacksmith shop and forge became part of the armory (see Jacabus Cooper).
- John Bailey, silversmith and sword maker, operated a silversmith and sword shop at Fishkill (1778-1784) near the armory. He probably sold swords to officers stationed at the depot (see John Bailey).
- Samuel Loudon, official state printer (paper money) and owner of the *New York Packet* newspaper, moved to Fishkill during the British occupation of New York City (1776-1783).
- The New York State Conventions of state representatives were held here during the occupation of New York City.
- The Society of the Cincinnati was founded at Fishkill (1783).
- Baron Von Steuben had his headquarters at Fishkill.

U.S. New London, Virginia, Arsenal

- Located south of Lynchburg near Falmouth, VA, close to the Rappahonnock forge.
- In operation from 1782-1796.
- Made cannon; repaired and made arms.
- Military supervisors: Capt. Thomas Wylie (Artillery Artificers Company), Superintendent Joseph Perkins.

Thomas Carothers	AA	1782
William Farrow	AA	1782
William Francis	AA	1782
John Miles	Sword Maker	
(See John Miles)		

- Made two distinct styles of horseman's saber (approximately 100 of each made):
    - Style one had a plain crossguard; style two had a half-wagon-wheel guard
    - Both had a reverse P knucklebow, bird's-head pommel, and curved flat blade with clipped point
    - Both had a wood grip, covered with leather, wound with two strands of twisted brass wire
    - Both had an iron scabbard with a large outside-mounted mouthpiece and frog stud
        (the scabbards made later at the Virginia Manufactory were of the same style)

The arsenal closed in 1796. The armorers, equipment, and machinery were moved to the New Harpers Ferry, VA, Arsenal.

U.S. Philadelphia, Pennsylvania, Armory

- Established by the Second Continental Congress in Philadelphia (1775); closed in 1821.
- Originally a private armory called the Water Street Armory.
- Sometimes called the Continental Armory.
- Made cannon and gun powder.
- Infantry and naval pikes and spontoons were made (1777-1778).
- It also was a depot and staging facility (cavalry sabers made by Louis Prahl and others were stored here).
- When the British captured Philadelphia and occupied it from September 26, 1777, to June 18, 1778, the armory equipment as well as the military superintendants and many of the workmen moved to other armories at Carlisle and Lebanon, PA. Many returned in 1778 and 1779.
- Five hundred pikes were in the inventory in 1821.
- Military staff in 1777:
    - Col. Benjamin Flowers—commander of armory
    - Capt. Alexander Dow—commander of a corps of artillery artificers
    - Capt. James Gibson—commander of a corps of artillery artificers
    - Capt. Valantine Hoffman—commander of a corps of artillery artificers
    - Capt. Nathaniel Irish—commander of a corps of artillery artificers
    - Capt. John Jordon—commander of a corps of artillery artificers
    - Capt. Theophilus Parke—commander of a corps of artillery artificers
    - Capt. David Pancoast—commander of a corps of artillery artificers
    - Capt. Jesse Rowe—commander of a corps of artillery artificers
    - Capt. Thomas Wylie—commander of a corps of artillery artificers
    - Maj. Charles Lukens—commander of a corps of artillery artificers
    - Capt. Robert Towers—commissary of military stores
- Josiah Wood delivered 1,000 naval pikes to Captain Towers in 1776 (see Josiah Wood).
- Captain Towers delivered 60 boarding pikes to Capt. William Brown of the floating battery *Putnam* in 1776.
- Captain Towers purchased 180 cutlasses (sabers) in 1775 from the following sword makers or dealers:

John Chaloner	10
Isaac Cox	24
Captain Furnam	19
Samuel Howell	11
Elizabeth Miller	52
John Phillips	3
Joseph Sims	7
Francis Tillgham (Tillingham)	5
James Wallace	49

- In early 1777, Gen. George Washington requested that Col. Benjamin Flowers (commander, U.S. Armory, Philadelphia) design and make a new weapon called a lance-pike. It was to be hinged in the middle for easy carrying. It was to be used by riflemen (Col. Daniel Morgan's riflemen) and some units of the Continental Light Horse. The rifleman's lance-pike was to have carrying straps and a spike on the end to dig into the ground. The rest of the weapon was the same as the one used by mounted light horse units.
- Colonel Flowers delivered 500 lance-pikes to Morgan's riflemen in June and another 500 later.
- Lewis Prahl delivered 1,000 horsemen's sabers to Col. Benjamin Flowers in 1777 (see Lewis Prahl).
- Spontoons were made at the armory in 1778.
- Civilian Staff:
    - David Rittenhouse—superintendent
    - Thomas Butler Jr.—chief armorer and superintendent of arms and accoutrements (1775-September 1777)

William Henry Sr.—superintendent of arms and accoutrements
   after British occupation (June 1778-1783)
James Livingston—quartermaster (1777)
Simon Murry—superintendent of blacksmiths (1779-1783)
Ralph Bunford—superintendent of whitesmiths (1779-1783)
James Byers—superintendent of brass founders (1779-1783)

Artisans working at the armory:

John Adams	AA	1777
John Assmus	AA-B	1779
John Baker	AA	1779-1782
John Baldwin	A	1779
Conrad Bartling	AA	1779
Ernest Battis	AA (filer)	1779
John Beaks Sr.	AA	1779
John Beaks Jr.	AA	1779
Samuel Bedford	AA (filecutter)	1779
Daniel Bittings	AA	1777
Daniel Blakley	AA	1777
Joseph Boehm	AA	1779
Joseph Bowne	AA	1779
John Cahill	AA	1777
Thomas Carothers	AA	1777
William Carr	AA	1777
Martin Carroll	BF-AA	1779
Daniel Carteret	A	1778
Joseph Cartwright	AA	1779
Christopher Cave	A-AA	1779
James Charlton	A	1778
James Clark	A	1776
John Clark	AA	1779
Richard Clark	A-AA	1779
William Clark	A-AA	1779-1783
Jonathan Clay	B-AA	1779
Edward Collins	AA	1777
William Colton	AA (filecutter)	1779
John Conway	AA	1779
George Cook	AA	1779
James Cook	AA	1779
John Cotten	B-AA	1779
Joseph Craig	AA	1779
John Dalton	AA	1777
James Davis	AA	1778
Edward Deille	AA	1777
John Diddy	AA	1777
James Dowdal	AA	1777
Michael Engles	B-BF	1777
Jacob Fetters	B	1777
Felix Fitzpatrick	AA	1779
John Flinn	A-AA	1779
Thomas Follett	B	1779
Patrick Fottrell	A	1779
Patrick Fox	A-B-AA	1779

William Francis	AA-B	1779
Jacob Frey	AA	1779
Robert Fullerton (lead furnace)	AA	1779
William Gardner	AA	1779
Adam Garrick	AA	1777
Thomas Glover	AA (filer)	1779
John Goodman Sr.	AA (filer)	1779
Michael Goodman	BF-AA	1777
John Grant (gun powder laboratory)	AA	1779
James Haggerty	B-AA	1778
James Hannah (gun powder laboratory)	AA	1779
Reuben Harriot	AA	1779
John Hartmann (gun powder laboratory)	AA	1779
George Hass	B-AA	1779
Henry Havick (gun powder laboratory)	AA	1779
Fincher Hellings	AA (filer)	1779
Jacob Hiney	AA	1779
George Howard	AA	1779
Thomas Hubb	B-AA	1778
Thomas Huggins	A	1779
John Hunter	A	1779
Philip Iler	B-AA	1778-1779
Henry Jaffel (gun powder laboratory)	AA	1779
Josiah Jenkins	AA	1777
Rene Joissard	AA	1779-1782
James Kelly	AA	1779
Patrick Kelly	AA	1779
Andrew Lachler	A-AA	1779
Christopher Lane	B-AA	1786
David Lard	B-AA	1778
Thomas Lawrence	A-AA	1779
Peter Lessley	A-AA	1779
Alexander McCook	A-AA	1779
William McCowing	AA	1780
James McGill	AA	1779
John McGinley	B-AA	1779
Barney McKinney	A-AA	1779
William McKinney	AA	1779
Hugh McSwain	A	1779
David Martin	A	1778
John Meggs	A-AA	1779
Francis Miller	AA	1777
John Miller	AA	1779
Simon Mitchell (Lead Furnace)	AA	1779
Abraham Motanye	AA	1779
Harry Musgrave	AA	1779
Isaac Nicholls	BF-AA	1779

Thomas Olivier	AA	1779
Thomas Page	AA	1779
William Page	B-AA	1779
Joseph Palmer	A	1778
Samuel Parker	AA-BF	1779
Robert Patterson		1814
John Pendleton	AA (filecutter)	1779
William Peters	AA	1779
John Robbins	AA	1779
Isaac Roberts	AA	1779
Christopher Roth	AA	1777
John Rowe	AA	1779
Abraham Schek	AA (filer)	1779
George Shaw	A-AA	1779
David Sheldrake	AA	1779
William Sheppard	AA	1779
Joseph Simcock	A-AA	1779
John Smalt	AA	1779
James Smith	AA	1779
Stephen Smith	AA	1778-1779
Charles Southart	AA	1779
Samuel Starn	A-AA	1779
Caspar Steel (Stahl)	AA	1779
James Steel (Stahl)	AA	1777
Martin Step	AA	1779
Jacob Stoner	AA	1779
James Sullivan	AA	1777
Joseph Teague	AA	1779
Roger Teague	AA	1779
Richard Thomas	BF	1777
John Thompson	BF	1779
Richard Trested	A	1779
Daniel Trump	A-AA	1779
Glode Uhroe	A-AA	1779
Abraham Umstead	AA	1777
John Wagg	BF	1777
Hierophimus Warner	BF	1779
Patrick Wenn	AA	1777
Frederick Wharton	AA	1779
Francis Wigstead	AA	1777
John Wilson	A	1778
George Yearhouse	AA	1777

U.S. Rock Island, Illinois, Armory

- In operation from 1843-1993.
- Made 1,039 rawhide- and leather-covered wooden scabbards for the M1906 experimental cavalry sword. Delivered to the Ames Manufacturing Co. on December 31, 1906.
- Made some scabbards for the M1913 cavalry saber (1913).
- Made some M1913 cavalry practice swords (1913).
- Made 10 experimental cavalry sabers, Model M-2 (1931).

U.S. Schuylkill, Pennsylvania, Arsenal

- Located in Philadelphia on Gray's Ferry Road on the Schuylkill River.
- Privately owned (1775-1799).
- Purchased by the U.S. government (1799).
- Military storekeeper George Engles (Ingles) (1803-1805).
- Inspector and master armorer George Flegal (1812-1823).
- A report by the secretary of war shows the following edged weapons inventory fit for service (1805):
    33 halberds
    15 officer swords
    208 grenadier's swords
    36 scimitar blades
    5 brass-mounted horsemen's sabers
    3,775 iron-mounted horsemen's sabers
- The 3,775 iron-mounted horsemen's sabers included some from two U.S. contracts for cavalry sabers stored at the arsenal:
    1798 Starr contract (2,000)
    1799 Buel & Greenleaf contract (1,000)
- Edged weapons unfit for service (1805):
    81 grenadier swords
    66 cavalry lances
    1,300 cutlasses (probably naval)
    28 tomahawks
    264 cavalry lance heads
    95 sergeant's swords
- On October 1807, 1,400 hussar-hilt cavalry sabers were on hand.
- By order of Tench Coxe (purveyor of public supplies), all cavalry sword blades on hand were to be hilted with iron hussar-type hilts and scabbarded (1807).
- The arsenal purchased 98 cavalry saber blades from Landsmann, Dietrick & Co., New York, NY (imported from Solingen, Germany in 1808).
- William Strong of Philadelphia was contracted to hilt the blades and make scabbards in 1808 (iron-edged leather scabbard). All of Strong's sabers were rejected by inspector Samuel Alexander, and he reported the problem to Tench Coxe. Coxe ordered Strong to replace them with swords with brass hilts having blades equal to the 1807 Rose contract (probably for a lt. artillery unit).
- The arsenal received 500 cavalry saber blades from the U.S. Springfield, MA, Armory in 1812. Nathan Starr of Middletown, CT, was contracted to hilt the blades and make scabbards. The swords would have a reverse P hilt and an iron-mounted leather scabbard.

U.S. Springfield, Massachusetts, Armory

- Started as a military post on the Mill River (1777).
- Became a military magazine for ammunition storage (1782).
- Permanent building erected (1794).
- It had water-operated grinding and boring mills with trip hammers.
- Became an armory (1794).
- Started arms production (1795).
- Master armorers: Robert Orr (1795-1805); Erskine S. Allin (1847-1878).
- Armory superintendants:
    David Ames   1794-1802
    Joseph Morgan   1802-1805
    Benjamin Prescott   1805-1813
    Harry Lechler   1813-1815
    Lt. Col. Roswell Lee   1815-1833
    Lt. Col. George Talcott   1833

Maj. John Robb	1833-1841
Maj. J.W. Ripley	1841-1854
Col. James S. Whitney	1854-1860

- Tench Coxe (purveyor of public supplies) ordered all cavalry saber blades on hand in all armories to be hilted with iron hussar hilts (1807).
- Three sample cavalry sabers were fabricated for Secretary of War Dearborn (1808).
- The armory sent 500 cavalry blades to the Philadelphia Armory (1812).
- Started sword production (1868).
- Made a national historic site with museum (1974).

Springfield Armory Sword Production (by year)

1868
36 cadet swords (West Point)

1873
1,499 M1860 staff and field officer swords
2 M1860 staff and field officer swords (general's swords)
1 sample M1872 cavalry officer sword
1 sample M1872 artillery officer sword
1,674 M1860 staff and field officer sword scabbards
1,564 M1860 staff and field officer sword cases
71 M1860 staff and field officer sword blades
20 M1860 staff and field officer sword mountings

1874
4 M1860 staff and field officer sword blades
25 cadet swords

1875
2 M1860 staff and field officer general's swords
3 sample M1872 cavalry officer swords

1876
20 M1860 staff and field officer sword scabbards
115 M1860 staff and field officer sword cases
17 M1860 staff and field officer sword blades
28 cadet swords
102 M1872 cavalry sabers
100 M1872 cavalry officer sabers

1877
Refurbished and/or repaired 10,567 assorted M1860 cavalry sabers

1878
30 M1860 staff and field officer swords

1879
200 M1860 staff and field officer swords

1880
5 M1860 staff and field officer swords
14 cadet swords
103 M1872 cavalry officer sabers

1881
100 M1872 cavalry officer sabers

1882
50 cadet swords

1883
51 M1872 lt. artillery officer swords
100 M1860 staff and field officer swords

1884
250 M1860 staff and field officer swords
1 M1872 cavalry saber

1885
500 M1860 staff and field officer swords
1 M1860 staff and field officer general's sword

1886
2 M1860 staff and field officer general's swords
154 M1872 cavalry officer swords
50 M1872 lt. artillery officer swords

1887
100 M1872 cavalry officer swords

1888
3 M1860 staff and field officer general's swords

1889
325 M1860 staff and field officer swords
50 M1872 lt. artillery officer swords

1890
175 M1860 staff and field officer swords
2 M1860 staff and field officer general's swords

1891
1 M1860 staff and field officer general's sword
500 M1872 cavalry officer swords
150 M1872 lt. artillery officer swords

1892
1,000 M1860 staff and field officer swords

1893
3 M1860 staff and field officer general's swords
50 cadet swords

1895
1 M1860 staff and field officer general's sword

1900
200 M1872 lt. artillery officer swords
301 M1872 cavalry officer swords
500 M1860 staff and field officer swords
2 M1860 staff and field officer general's swords

1902
6 M1902 sabers for all officers (special general's saber)
200 M1872 lt. artillery officer sabers
300 M1872 cavalry officer sabers
550 M1902 sabers for all officers

1903
100 M1891 cavalry practice swords
1,555 M1902 sabers for all officers

1904
2,245 M1902 sabers for all officers

1905
377 M1902 sabers for all officers

1906
157 30-inch blade experimental cavalry swords
11 experimental cavalry swords with 28-inch blades
4 experimental cavalry sword scabbards
1 experimental cavalry sword (variation)
1 experimental cavalry sword (variation)

1908
240 M1902 sabers for all officers

1909
200 M1902 sabers for all officers

1910
34 M1902 sabers for all officers
3 experimental cavalry officer sabers

1911
79 experimental cavalry sabers

1912
90 experimental cavalry sabers

1913
2 sample M1913 cavalry swords
3 sample M1913 cavalry sword guards
100 M1902 sabers for all officers

1914
100 M1902 sabers for all officers
50 cadet swords
24,799 M1913 cavalry swords
1915
223 M1913 cavalry officer swords
5,292 M1913 cavalry swords
250 M1913 cavalry non-comm. swords

1916
1,000 M1913 cavalry non-comm. swords
279 M1915 cavalry practice swords (variation)

1918
5,000 M1913 cavalry swords
50 M1915 cavalry practice swords (variation)

1923
14 M1916 cavalry practice swords
75 M1915 cavalry practice swords (variation)

1924
62 M1916 cavalry practice swords

1925
1 experimental cavalry sword, model T-1

1928
1 experimental cavalry sword, model T-2

CHAPTER 2

State Armories and Arsenals Fabricating Swords and Edged Weapons

Fredericksburg Manufactory

- Fredericksburg, VA (1775-1781).
- Called Virginia State Gun Factory.
- Military Supervisors: Col. Fielding Lewis, Maj. Charles Dick (Deike).
- Fabricated muskets and bayonets.
- Had a grinding mill and ammunition magazine.
- Partially dismantled when the British Tarleton's Dragoons began raiding near Fredericksburg (May-June 1781).
- The manufactory was closed and all the equipment and machinery sent to the Point of Fork Arsenal (1783).

Pennsylvania State Gun Factory

- Cherry St., Mulburry Ward, Philadelphia (1776-1779).
- Made muskets and bayonets.
- British occupied Philadelphia from September 28, 1777, to June 18, 1778.
- Factory moved to French Creek, PA, near Valley Forge, Chester Co. (1776-1778).
- Factory moved to Hummelstown, PA (1777-1778).
- Civilian supervisors at Philadelphia and French Creek:
    Superintendent: Benjamin Rittenhouse
    Chief Armorer and Manager: Peter DeHaven
    Assistant Chief Armorer and Manager: Hugh DeHaven
- (See Peter & Hugh DeHaven)
- (See Benjamin Rittenhouse)
- Military supervisors at Philadelphia: Major Meridith, Captain Wilcocks, Captain Peters.

- Armorer at Philadelphia: Joseph DeHaven
- Superintendent at Hummelstown: Capt. Frederick Hummel (1777).
- Lewis Prahl sold brass gun parts to the factory at Hummselstown (see Lewis Prahl).
- Lawrence Birnie set up forges, furnace, and mills at Hummelstown.
- Philadelphia factory closed; tools and equipment sold by George Henry (1779).
- Military supervisors at French Creek: Captain Badly, Colonel Dewes.
- Armorers at French Creek:
    William Atkinson
    Conrad Bartling
    Lawrence Birnie
    Archibald Curry
    Joseph Delavan
    John Eastburn
    William Faries
    John Hamberger (powder factory operator)
    William Hayden Sr.
    Isaac Johns
    William Lane
    John Pugh
    Conrad Switsor
    John Weaver
    Frederick Wharton

Pennsylvania State Gunlock Factory

- Allentown, PA (1777-1778).
- Made muskets and bayonets.
- Temporarily established when the British occupied Philadelphia in 1777 and the Pennsylvania State Gun Factory was taken.
- Superintendant: James Walsh.
- Armorers: Ebenezer Cowell, Andrew Shorer, Richard Wells.
- Repaired over 800 guns and bayonets.

Point of Fork, Virginia, State Arsenal

- Point of Fork, VA (1781-1802).
- Located at the confluence of the James and Rivanna Rivers.
- Made muskets, bayonets, and military clothing.
- Was a storage facility and did arms repair.
- The arsenal was raided and partially destroyed by the British, led by Colonel Simco (June 1781).
- The machinery, equipment, and tools from the Fredericksburg Manufactory were sent here (1783).
- The arsenal stored 3,000 French arms bought by the state of Virginia (1786).
- The arsenal was closed and the equipment and machinery were sent to the new Virginia Manufactory in Richmond (1802).

The Virginia Manufactory

- Richmond, Virginia (1801-1900).
- Superintendents:
    John Clark   1801-1809
    John Staples   1809-1821
- Master Armorer:
    George Williamson Jr.   1801-1821

- Assistant Master Armorers:
    - Daniel Atherton — 1802-1809
    - George Edgington — 1810-1813
    - Abraham Davis — 1813
    - Matthew Woodson — 1814-1821
- Clerks:
    - George Dabney — 1802-1817
    - Thomas Vannerson — 1802-1817
    - George Prosser — 1802-1807
    - Stephen Woodson — 1807-1821

- In 1800, Colonel Robert Gamble sent three horsemen's saber samples to Virginia Governor Monroe.
- Governor Monroe authorized John Clark (manufactory superintendant) to advertise for horsemen saber samples.
- Three sword makers—John Goodman, William Rose, and John Miles Sr.—responded.
- A Virginia contract for 1,000 horsemen's sabers was made with John Miles Sr. (1801).
- The equipment and machinery from the Point of Fork Arsenal were sent here (1802).
- Sword production started at the manufactory in 1804; discontinued in 1821.
- Manufactory was restored by the state of Virginia; the Tredegar Iron Works made and installed the arms machinery, etc. (1860).
- Manufactory taken over by the Confederacy (1861).
- Manufactory destroyed when Richmond burned (1865).
- The west building was restored (1866).
- Virginia public guard headquarters was at the manufactory (1866-1869).
- Became an historical site open to public (1869-1894).
- Torn down (1900).

Virginia Manufactory Sword Production

Saber Type	Date Made	# Made	Scabbard Type
1st Model Variation Cavalry	1804	56	leather and iron
1st Model Cavalry	1805-1806	approx. 1,551	iron
2nd Model Cavalry	1806-1808	approx. 2,659	iron
3rd Model Cavalry	1808-1821	approx. 4,003	iron
Light Artillery	1808-1821	2,040	leather

Some light artillery sabers were fitted with cut-off cavalry blades.

- The hilts had wood "balled" grips and were covered with leather and wound with one thick strand or two thin twisted strands of brass wire (the Confederacy later rewired some with one thick strand of iron wire).
- The iron scabbards had two wood liners with a large slide over mouthpiece (frog stud attached). Styled after the New London Arsenal scabbards.
- The third saber model had japanned scabbards and were made with two hilt sizes.
- All blades were made with imported German steel.

Virginia Manufactory Cavalry Saber Alterations

Year	Quantity	Who Altered	Work done
1814	4,000	Virginia Manufactory	Blades and scabbards shortened
1845	674	Virginia Manufactory	Blades and scabbards shortened
1859	1,000	James T. Ames	Blades shortened and tapered; new tapered scabbards made
1860	500	Virginia Manufactory	Blades shortened and tapered; new tapered scabbards made
1861	1,968	Confederacy Richmond Arsenal	Blades shortened and tapered; new tapered scabbards made

Many of the Confederate scabbards were iron with brass mounts.

Total Made   8,269
Total Altered   8,042
Total Unaltered 227

Federal Period (1795-1815) Sword Makers Who Worked at the Virginia Manufactory

Maker	Year	Work Done
James Bent (Canton, MA)	1809	finished muskets
Samuel Leonard (Canton, MA)	1805-1807	bored and ground musket barrels; forged and tempered artillery sword blades
Henry Deringer Jr. (Philadelphia, PA)	1807-1808	made musket parts and stocked muskets
Daniel Henkels (Philadelphia, PA)	1805-1808	ground, polished, and hilted swords; supplied grindstones
Abraham Nippes (Philadelphia, PA)	1803-1807	made sword hilts and supplied grindstones

Maker	Year	Work Done
James Ritchie (Philadelphia, PA)	1808-1809	ground cavalry sword scabbards
Leonard Ritchie (Philadelphia, PA)	1808-1809	ground cavalry sword scabbards; supplied grindstones
James Winner	1803-1807 and 1814	made sword hilts, blades, and scabbards; made first 56 cavalry sabers (first model variation in 1804); "Winner Me Fecit" found on back of some second model cavalry sabers.

CHAPTER 3
U.S. Sword Makers

EZEKIAL ADAMS WEBSTER, NH 1860-1868
Made belt knives and belt axes.
(Cutler)

JOSEPH ALBOT PHILADELPHIA, PA 1755-1765
Made tomahawks and scalping knives.
(Cutler)

SAMUEL ALEXANDER PHILADELPHIA, PA 1773-1793
WILTBERGER (CHRISTIAN) &
  ALEXANDER (SAMUEL) PHILADELPHIA, PA 1793-1795
SIMMONS (ANTHONY) &
  ALEXANDER (SAMUEL) PHILADELPHIA, PA 1795-1804
SAMUEL ALEXANDER PHILADELPHIA, PA 1804-1830
- U.S. arms inspector at the U.S. Philadelphia Armory (1808-1830).
- Inspected swords made by William Strong (1808).
- John Meer engraved blades for Samuel Alexander.
- Made a sword presented to General Winfield Scott by the State of Virginia (1816).
- (See Christian Wiltberger and Anthony Simmons, Silversmith listing)
- (See John Meer)
- (Goldsmith, Silversmith, Swordsmith)

C. (CYRUS) B. (BALLARD) ALLEN SPRINGFIELD, MA 1811-1830
ALLEN (C.B.) & BARBER (SAMUEL) SPRINGFIELD, MA 1830-1835

ALLEN (C.B.) & BALL (CHARLES)	SPRINGFIELD, MA	1835-1837
ALLEN (C.B.) & FALES (JAMES JR.)	SPRINGFIELD, MA	1837-1840

Maker of George Elgin's cutlass-pistol and John W. Cochren's 7-shot revolver.
C.B. Allen died (1840).
(Cutler, Gunsmith)

HENRY ALLEN   NEW YORK, NY   1812-1848
34 Maiden Lane
NEW YORK, NY   1848-1862
44 Forsyth Street

(Gunsmith)

JACOB ALLEN   NEW YORK, NY   1773-1783
34 Maiden Lane

Probably bought brass gun and sword mountings from brass founder John Taylor (next shop down).
(Gunsmith, Sword Maker)

OLIVER ALLEN   NORWICH, CT   1790-1816
Probably made cavalry sabers for War of 1812.

SPRINGFIELD, MA   1816-1818

Arms inspector at the U.S. Springfield Armory. Inspected some N. Starr M1818 cavalry sabers.

NORWICH, CT   1818-1850

Patented a whaling bomb lance in 1846.
(Gun Maker, Sword Maker, Lance Maker)

WILLIAM ALLEN   NEW YORK, NY   1754-1776
NEW YORK, NY   1776-1795
Fishkill Street

Served in the Revolutionary War.

NEW YORK, NY   1795-1812
38 Maiden Lane
NEW YORK, NY   1812-D1822
108 Maiden Lane

(Gunsmith)

WILLIAM ALLEN   RICHMOND, VA   1816
Worked at Virginia Manufactory as a gunsmith.
(Gunsmith)

JOHN ALLISON   PITTSBURGH, PA   1810-1830
PHILADELPHIA, PA   1830-1836

(Cutler, Whitesmith, Pewterer, Edged Tool Maker)

FREDERICK ALTMAN   COWANSHANNOCK TOWNSHIP, PA   1833-D1855
Armstrong County

(Blacksmith, Gunsmith, Knife Maker, Edged Tools)

JONATHAN ALTMAN   KISKIMINETAS, PA   B1798, 1808-D1882
(Gunsmith, Blacksmith)

PETER ALTMAN (Gunsmith, Blacksmith)	**HEMPFIELD TOWNSHIP, PA** Westmoreland County	1780-1790
AMEDEE ALVISET (Cutler)	**NEW YORK, NY**	1840-1856
JACOB AMBACHER Made hunting knives. (Knife Maker, Gun Maker)	**SANDUSKI, OH** Eric County	1870-1890

THE AMERICAN MASONIC AGENCY
(See D.B. Howell)

THE AMES FAMILY OF MASSACHUSETTS

JOHN AMES Father of David and Oliver. (Gunsmith)	**BRIDGEWATER, MA**	1738-D1803
DAVID AMES Son of John. Served in Capt. Reuben Dow's company of Minutemen during the Revolutionary War. First superintendent of the U.S. Springfield Armory (1794-1802). Made shovels, edged tools, and guns. (Gunsmith, Edged Tools)	**BRIDGEWATER, MA** **SPRINGFIELD, MA**	1760-1783 1783-D1847
OLIVER AMES Son of John. Inspector at the U.S. Springfield Armory. Made shovels during the Civil War.	**BRIDGEWATER, MA** **SPRINGFIELD, MA** **BRIDGEWATER, MA**	1780-1794 1794-1802 1802-1870
OLIVER AMES & SONS Called Ames Shovel & Tool Co. President: Hobart Ames (1923) Treasurer: Oliver W. Wink (1923) (Gunsmith, Edged Tools)	**BOSTON, MA** 90 Ames Building	1870-1925
OAKES AMES	**CHIPOPEE TOWNSHIP, MA**	B1804, 1824-D1873
OAKES ANGIER AMES Son of Oakes.	**CHIPOPEE TOWNSHIP, MA**	1830-1870
OLIVER AMES Son of Oakes. Made bayonets. (Cutler)	**CHIPOPEE TOWNSHIP, MA**	1830-1870

THE AMES FAMILY OF SWORD MAKERS

NATHAN PEABODY AMES SR.   Bc.1772-D1832

NATHAN PEABODY AMES JR.   B1803-D1847

JAMES TYLER AMES   B1810-D1883

- Nathan P. Ames Sr. born around Newburyport, MA (c. 1772).
- He moved to the Pentucket Falls industrial section (on the Merrimac River) in Chelmsford, MA. He served his apprenticeship as a blacksmith in Chelmsford (1787).
- He set up his own blacksmith shop, specializing in edged tools and millwork, in Chelmsford, MA (1791).
- Bought a two-acre site from Moses Tyler at Massic Falls (on the Concord River) in Chelmsford, MA (1797). He set up an iron forge with a trip hammer and did mill repairs.
- Ames temporarily moved to Dedham, MA, and worked at a nail factory after a fire destroyed his forge at Chelmsford (1810-1811).
- Nathan P. Ames Jr. joined his father at his forge (1821).
- Nathan P. Ames Sr. retired because of poor health (1829).
- Nathan Jr. took over the business with James Tyler Ames now in the company.
- The Ames family moved to Chicopee Falls, MA (near Springfield), on the Chicopee River and rented space at the Edmund Dwight textile mill (1829). The Dwight mill was known as the Chicopee Mfg. Co.
- Ames did mill repairs and made mill tools and edged tools (bits, reamers, etc.).
- Sword and cutlery production was started.

Ames Employees, 1831

Edwin Burt
Ambrose Cotten
Nathan Fitz
James K. Fletcher (forged and tempered sword blades, blade grinder)
Joseph L. Keith
Madison Kendall (forged and tempered sword blades, blade grinder)
W.J. Lawrence
Abner Mosman (iron and brass founder)
Silas A. Mosman Jr. (son of Abner), (blade etcher and grinder)
Melzar H. Mosman (son of Silas), (sculptor; later cast bronze statues for Ames, and eventually became superintendent of the Ames bronze molding and finishing department)
John Rand (blade polisher)
Belknap Sargent
Moses B. Sargent
John O. Mead (silver plater)

- Nathan P. Ames Sr. died (1832).
- Nathan P. Ames Jr. purchased the new process of welding cast steel from Daniel Pettibone (1834).
- The Ames Mfg. Co. was formed by Nathan P. Ames Jr. and James Tyler Ames (1834).
- Stockholders included James K. Mills, Ignatius Sargent, and Edmund Dwight.
- Nathan Jr. was general manager and James T. was superintendent of manufacturing.
- Nathan Jr. and James T. moved out of Edmund Dwight's mill and bought land lower down on the Chicopee River 1 1/2 miles west of Chicopee Falls (later called Cabotville Works) in 1834.
- Built new shop facilities and a sword factory (1834).
- Started a leather shop making belts, artillery harnesses, and military accoutrements (1834).

- Introduced the electroplating process into the United States (1834).
- Started construction on a new and sophisticated brass foundry.
- The Chicopee River provided the water power to run the trip hammers and machinery.
- The brass foundry was finished and Ames began casting cannon (1835-1869).
- The community that grew up around the Ames factory became Cabotville. Swords were now marked "Cabotville, MA".
- The Ames Mfg. Co. displayed swords at the Philadelphia Franklin Institute Exhibition and the New York American Institute Exhibition (1835).
- The Ames Mfg. Co. hired Lt. Daniel Tyler (former U.S. government supervisor of inspectors) as a sales representative (1836).
- The Ames Mfg. Co. introduced electroplated silver-hilted swords (1838).
- Made six presentation swords for the state of Virginia (1840).
- The U.S. government commissioned Nathan P. Ames Jr. to tour leading European armories and report on their methods of production (1840).
- The Ames Mfg. Co. purchased the Chicopee Falls Co., Chicopee Falls, MA (1841). Nathan P. Ames Jr. was already a stockholder. The company made saws, pistols, and carbines. It had a large iron forge and foundry. It was reincorporated as the Massachusetts Ames Co. (1850).
- The Ames Mfg. Co. purchased the property of the Springfield Canal Co., Cabotville, MA (1845). An iron foundry was built.
- Foreman: Edson Bonney
- Founder: S.B. Lanckton
- Nathan P. Ames Jr. retired (1846).
- Nathan P. Ames Jr. died and James T. Ames took over the company (1847).
- Cabotville, MA, lost its charter and was incorporated into the town of Chicopee, MA (1848). Swords were now marked "Chicopee, MA".
- Started making gun-makers tools and the Uriah A. Boyden turbine water wheel (1849).
- The Ames Mfg. Co. displayed swords at the Quincy Massachusetts Fair (1850) and swords and gun-stocking equipment at the London, England Crystal Palace Exhibition (1851).
- Started producing bronze artwork and bronze statues (department superintendent: Melzar H. Mosman). Brought several workmen over from Europe. Made such items as the U.S. Senate chamber bronze doors and many statues, including those of Washington, Franklin, and Lincoln (1853).
- The company sold gun-stocking equipment to the British government (1854).
- James T. Ames went to Europe as an agent of the U.S. government to examine gun barrel rolling machinery. He bought some for the Harpers Ferry, VA, and Springfield, MA, Armories (1858).
- Albert G. Woodworth (James T. Ames' son-in-law) started working as an apprentice at Ames Mfg. Co. (1858).
- Ames altered (shortened and tapered blades and made new scabbards) 1,000 Virginia Manufactory cavalry sabers (1859). The swords were stored at the Lexington, VA, Arsenal.
- The Ames Mfg. Co. had a large number of swords contracts with the U.S. government during the Civil War (1861-1865).
- (See Edged Weapons Production)
- The company imported 5,000 German cavalry sabers and sold them to the U.S. government (1862). G.A.&E. Scheidt (NY) was the sword importer (1,000 on January 27; 2,116 on June 26; 1,884 on March 19).
- The Ames Mfg. Co. displayed presentation swords at the New York Fair (1864).
- Ames completed an iron fence for the Springfield U.S. Armory (1865). It was made with posts in the style of halberds with iron provided by the government in the form of old iron cannons.
- Emerson Gaylord became president of the Ames Mfg. Co. and started fraternal sword production (1867).
- The Ames Mfg. Co. sold 100,000 cavalry sabers to the French government for the Franco-Prussian War (1870-1871).
- Emerson Gaylord left the Ames Mfg. Co. (1874).
- James T. Ames retired and Albert C. Woodworth succeeded him as president and general manager (1874).
- Ames sold 236,000 cavalry sabers to the Turkish government and 26 Lowell machine guns to the Russian government for the Russo-Turkish War (1877-1878).

- The Ames Mfg. Co. had 600 employees (1880).
- The Ames Mfg. Co. iron foundry was producing more than 15,000 pounds of castings a day (1880).
- The Ames Mfg. Co. bought The Gaylord Mfg. Co. sword factory, Chicopee, MA (1881).
- The Ames Sword Co. was made a separate division of the Ames Mfg. Co. (1881). The division was moved into the old Gaylord sword factory.

Ames Sword Company Presidents

A.C. Woodworth	1881-1888
J.T. Coolidge	1889
John D. Bryant	1890-1911
A.L. Howard	1912-1921
Charles A. Buckley	1922-1925
Thomas H. Boeshaar	1926-1933

- The Ames Sword Co. had a Boston, MA, branch (1881-1928) on 61 State Street (1881-1922). Harry Jarvis was employed as an engraver. Location changed to 45 Bromfield (1923-1928). It was listed as a regalia manufacturer in the Boston directory.
- The Ames Sword Co. had a Chicago, IL, branch (1881-1893) on 148-154 Monroe Street (manager: J.W. Woodworth).
- The Ames Mfg. Co. issued a tool catalog showing planes, lathes, drill presses, and gun-stocking machinery (1882).
- Advertised in the Chicago city directory as a maker of secret society goods and swords (1891). Issued catalog #51 (supplies for Masonic Lodges) in 1891.
- The Ames Sword Co. issued many catalogs. A special 150-page sword catalog containing over 400 patterns of U.S. regulation and society swords was sent out to Ames authorized dealers once a year. It was first issued on September 25, 1883 and ran through 1925.

The Ames Sword Company Catalog Military Sword Listings (1883)

c. 1834 Officer of the U.S. Revenue Marine Service
c. 1890 Officer of the U.S. Revenue Marine Service
M1860 Cavalry Trooper
M1860 Cavalry Officer
M1860 Cavalry Officer (Presentation)
M1872 Cavalry Trooper (Nonregulation)
M1872 Cavalry Officer
M1840 Lt. Artillery Trooper
M1840 Lt. Artillery Officer
M1840 Lt. Artillery Officer (Presentation)
M1872 Lt. Artillery—Trooper (Nonregulation)
M1872 Lt. Artillery—Officer (Nonregulation)
M1872 Lt. Artillery—Officer (Presentation, Nonregulation)
M1840 Foot Officer
M1850 Foot Officer
M1850 Staff and Field
M1860 Staff and Field-Line Officer
M1860 Staff and Field-General Officer
M1860 Staff and Field (Presentation)

M1852 Naval Officer
M1852 Naval Officer (Presentation)
M1860 Naval Cutlass-Enlisted
M1860 Naval Cutlass-Officer
M1840 Medical Staff Officer
M1840 Paymaster Officer
M1840 Non-Comm.
M1872 Non-Comm.
M1840 Musician's
M1832 Foot Artillery (Enlisted)
M1875 Marine Corps Officer
West Point Cadet

- James Tyler Ames died (1883).
- The Ames Sword Co. was called the Ames Sword Mfg. Co. for two years only (1887-1888).
- The Ames Mfg. Co. went out of business (1889).
- Frank Henderson of Kalamazoo, MI, bought the Chicago branch of the Ames Sword Co. (1893). Became Henderson-Ames (see Henderson-Ames).
- The Ames Sword Company was bought by the M.C. Lilley Co. (1925). It was listed as Ames Sword Co. until 1928. All tools and machinery were moved to the Lilley Plant in Columbus, OH (1925-1931). Only a repair service for uniforms and swords was maintained at Chicopee, MA.
- M.C. Lilley changed its name to The Lilley Co. (1925).
- The Lilley Co. changed its name to Lilley-Ames (1931).
- The Ames Sword Company buildings in Chicoppee, MA, were put up for sale (1934).
- The Ames Sword Company buildings in Chicoppee, MA, were torn down, except the main office building (1935). The main building still stands.
- The Lilley-Ames Co. fraternal and military stock, equipment, machinery, and tools were bought by the C.E. Ward Co. (1951).
- (See M.C. Lilley)
- (See Frank Henderson)
- (See Ward & Stilson)

List of the Ames Co. Authorized Sword Dealers

Bailey & Co.	Philadelphia, PA
H.E. Baldwin	New Orleans, LA
James Conning	Mobile, AL
Glaze & Radcliffe	Columbia, SC
Gregg & Hayden	Charleston, SC
William Horstmann & Sons (1843-1848)	Philadelphia, PA
Horstmann Son & Drucker	New York, NY
Jones, Lowe & Ball	Boston, MA
Rose Lipp	Boston, MA
Charles Naylor	Philadelphia, PA
A.W. Pollard	Boston, MA
Raymold & Whitlock	New York, NY
W.H. Richardson	Richmond, VA
D.C. Roundy	Chicago, IL
Roundy Regalia Co.	Chicago, IL
W.H. Smith	Augusta, GA
William H. Smith	New York, NY

Young, Smith & Co. New York, NY
Alfred Wells & Co. Boston, MA

Ames Edged Weapons Production

Enlisted Men's Swords # Made

M1840 Non-Comm. Sword 38,262
M1840 Musician's Sword 17,550
1841 Naval Cutlass (1842-1845) 6,600
M1860 Naval Cutlass some in 1862; 300 in 1864
Revenue Marine Cutlass (1862) 12
M1832 Foot Artillery Sword 16,200
M1840 Lt. Artillery Saber 19,902
M1833 Cavalry Saber (1834-1839) 6,100
M1840 Cavalry Saber (1845-1858) 21,700
M1860 Cavalry Saber (1858-1865) 91,500
M1906 Cavalry Saber (1906) 18,961
M1906 Experimental Cavalry Saber 1,039
M1906 Extra Cavalry Saber Scabbards 3,000
M1840 Cavalry Saber Scabbards (1864) 1,000
M1860 Cavalry Saber Scabbards (1864) 5,000

Knives

M1874 Sergeant's Entrenching Knife
M1861 Rifleman's Knife
C1849 Mounted Rifleman's Knife 1,000
Presentation Knives

Officer's Swords

Ames made a large number of special order officer and presentation swords, many with silver-mounted hilts. The company made more than 125 presentation swords during the Mexican War alone.
M1832 Medical Staff Officer Swords
M1840 Medical Staff Officer Swords
M1832 Pay Department Officer Swords
M1840 Pay Department Officer Swords
M1835 Revenue Cutters Service Officer Swords
M1870 Revenue Cutters Service Officer Swords
M1840 Lt. Artillery Officer Swords
M1872 Lt. Artillery Officer Swords
M1833 Cavalry Officer Swords
M1840 Cavalry Officer Swords
M1860 Cavalry Officer Swords
M1850 Foot (Infantry) Officer Swords
M1832 General and Staff Officer Swords
M1850 Staff and Field Officer Swords
M1860 Staff and Field Officer Swords
M1902 Saber for all Officers Swords
Virginia Military Institute Cadet Officer Swords
U.S. Military Academy Cadet Officer Swords

M1840 Naval Officer Swords
M1852 Naval Officer Swords
Marine Corp. Officer Swords
M1862 Naval Cutlass Officer Swords
M1839 Topographical Engineer Officer Swords
M1840 Topographical Engineer Officer Swords
c. 1900 U.S. Marine Hospital Service Officer Swords
Saber for Mounted Officers of Infantry

Bayonets

M1847 Sappers, Miners, and Artillery Masketoon Bayonet
M1841 Mississippi Rifle Yataghan Saber Bayonet
M1861 Dahlgren Short Navy Bayonet
M1860 Sharps Navy Rifle Sword Bayonet
M1863 Spencer Navy Rifle Bayonet
M1870 Remington Rolling Block Navy Rifle Bayonet
M1873 Winchester Repeating Rifle Bayonet
Peabody Martini Rifle Saber Bayonets (200,000 made for Providence Tool Co. in 1875)
Jenks Navy Rifle Bayonet
Jenks Navy Carbine Bayonet

Ames State and Local Militia Sword Production

Militia Non-Comm. Officer Sword
Militia Infantry, Artillery, and Cavalry Officer Swords for the following militia units:
    Barstow Zouaves
    Georgia Dragoons
    Irish Jasper Greens
    Cincinnati Massachusetts Militia
    Montgomery True Blues
    Nashua Artillery (Short Sword) (M1832)
    Portsmouth Artillery (New Hampshire)
    3rd Rhode Island Cavalry
    69th Reg. New York State Militia
    4th Reg. New York State Militia
    Massachusetts Volunteer Militia

Ames Special Sword Sales

Made swords for over 60 society or fraternal organizations.
Made swords for the Jefferson Guard unit at the 1904 St. Louis (Louisiana Purchase) Exposition.
State of Texas purchases in 1846:
    280 M1833 Dragoon Sabers with copper scabbards
    18 M1833 Officer Dragoon Sabers
    40 M1832 Foot Artillery Swords
The Glaze & Radcliff Co., Columbia, SC, purchased two presentation swords for Colonel Gladden and Major Butler (heroes of the Mexican War).

Some South Carolina militia officers purchased some M1833 dragoon officer sabers with a palmetto tree engraved on the scabbard.

The "Georgia Hussars" of Savannah, GA, bought some M1833 dragoon officer sabers with hilts of solid silver.

Ames Company Products Other Than Swords

Cartridges, rifle shot, shells, canister shot
Jenks navy rifles
Jenks navy carbines
M1843 navy pistols
Lowell battery machine guns
Protector palm pistols
Bronze church bells
Bronze statuary
Bronze padlocks
Bronze cannons
Bronze howitzer, mortars, and projectiles
Gun-making machinery
Gun-stocking machinery
Axes, hatchets, and tomahawks
Carpenter's compasses
Powder flasks (M1843)
Mess kits
Belt buckles and plates (military, society, police)
Ice skates
Commemorative bronze plaques
Scales
Tableware
Silverware
Uniforms
Horseshoes
Bicycles and Overman tricycles
Hammers
Edges tools, including bits and reamers
Machine tools—lathes, planes, drill presses
Machinist tools
Die-sinking machines
Martin's brick-making machines
Cotton mill machinery
Elridge sewing machines
Iron fencing
Horse-hitching bars
Boyden's turbine water wheels
Boyden's saw sets
Milling machines
Mill shafts, pulleys, gears, and pumps
Pulp machines
Slotting and boring machines
Regalia (including jewelry, pins, ornaments, and badges)
Sword cases (leather and cloth)

Key holders
Door clappers and bells
Typewriters
Knives, daggers, and dirks
Elgin cutlass pistol blades
Gold, silver, and nickel plating
Engraving and die sinking
Brass, bronze, and iron castings

JAMES ANDERSON　　　　　　　　　　　　GLOUCESTER, VA　　　　　B1740-1760
　　　　　　　　　　　　　　　　　　　　　　　WILLIAMSBURG, VA　　　　1760-1780

- Established a blacksmith shop with forge and bellows on the corner of Francis and Cross Streets.
- Began repairing arms.
- Anderson was appointed public armorer (1766-1780).
- Agreed to hire out his shop for gunsmithing work to the Commonwealth of Virginia (1777).
- He was paid for gunsmithing tools by the state and allowed to obtain five apprentices.
- Gunsmiths: James Sharpley, Samuel Campbell.
- Anderson expanded his shop (1779).
- Work performed:
    Gun repair
    Blacksmithing
    Surgical instrument repair
    Made nails
    Made cannon carriage mounts
    Iron work on ships
    Made axes and tomahawks
    Made musket ramrods
    Probably made horsemen's swords
    Made muskets after 1780

- Anderson was made captain of the local company of artificers (1780). The company included 12 gunsmiths, 6 gun-stockers, 24 blacksmiths, and other craftsmen.
- The capital of Virginia was changed to Richmond and Anderson's company was ordered there with all tools and equipment (1780).

　　　　　　　　　　　　　　　　　　　　　　　RICHMOND, VA　　　　　　1780-1781

- Governor Thomas Jefferson ordered eight gunsmiths and one blacksmith be hired for Anderson's shops.
- The British destroyed Anderson's shops (1781).
- Anderson moved back to Williamsburg.

　　　　　　　　　　　　　　　　　　　　　　　WILLIAMSBURG, VA　　　　1781-D1798

(Blacksmith, Gunsmith, Cutler)

JAMES ANDERSON　　　　　　　　　　　　NEW YORK, NY　　　　　　1770-1792
FOSBROOK (WILLIAM), SMITH (THOMAS)
　& ANDERSON (JAMES)　　　　　　　　　NEW YORK, NY　　　　　　1793-1794
JAMES ANDERSON　　　　　　　　　　　　NEW YORK, NY　　　　　　1795-1800
　　　　　　　　　　　　　　　　　　　　　　　65 Cherry Street

Adv. horsemen's swords, hangers, cutlasses, foils, guns, and pistols in the *New York Daily Advertiser* (1798).

(See Williams Fosbrook & Thomas Smith)
(Blacksmith, Gunsmith, Swordsmith)

EDWARD ANNELY   NEW YORK, NY   1730-1770
Maiden Lane

Adv. gun and pistols and engraving (1748-1760).
EDWARD & THOMAS ANNELY   TRENTON, NJ   1770-1797
Armorers to Colony of New Jersey.
(Gunsmith, Cutler, Bayonet Maker)

JOHN ANNELY   NEW YORK, NY   1720-1750
Maiden Lane

(Gunsmith)

THOMAS ANNELY   PHILADELPHIA, PA   1760-1770
EDWARD & THOMAS ANNELY   TRENTON, NJ   1770-1797
THOMAS ANNELY   PHILADELPHIA, PA   1797-1800
U.S. inspector of arms at the U.S. Philadelphia
  Arsenal (1797).
Pennsylvania contract for pistols (1797-1798).
(Gunsmith, Cutler, Bayonet Maker)

FRANCIS AREIS   PHILADELPHIA, PA   1810-1836
Adv. swords, pistols, guns, and gunlocks (1831).
(Gun Maker, Sword Maker, Arms Repair)

GEORGE ARMITAGE   SHEFFIELD, ENGLAND   1775-1795
                                       PHILADELPHIA, PA   1795-D1836

William Pinchin Jr. apprenticed to
  Armitage (1818-1826).
Armitage willed his stock and
  tools to William Pinchin Jr.
(See William Pinchin)
(Silversmith, Silver Plater,
  Military Ornamenter, Sword Hiltor)

ALLEN ARMSTRONG   PHILADELPHIA, PA   1805-1830
(Gunsmith, Silversmith,
  Iron Monger, Hardware, Cutler)

ARMSTRONG, GREENWOOD & ATKINSON
                                         DETROIT, MI   1920

(Regalia)

FRANK S. ARMSTRONG & CO.   CHICAGO, IL   1890-1894
Partner: G. Bray
Adv. society and military supplies, uniforms,
  swords, flags, costumes, and badges (1894).
Bray left to form the Detroit Regalia Co.
  with George D. Adams (1894).
(See Detroit Regalia Co.)
(Regalia, Society Swords)

ARMSTRONG REGALIA CO.	DETROIT, MI	1894-1905

President: Jesse E. Sexton
Vice-President: Frank S. Armstrong
(Regalia, Society Swords)

THOMAS H. ARMSTRONG	DETROIT, MI	1830-1850
T. (THOMAS) H. ARMSTRONG	DETROIT, MI	1850-1853
ARMSTRONG (THOMAS) JONES & CO.	DETROIT, MI	1853-1854
T. (THOMAS) H. ARMSTRONG & CO.	DETROIT, MI	1854-1870

Partner and son: Edwin A. Armstrong (1867-1870).

E. (EDWIN) A. ARMSTRONG & CO.	DETROIT, MI	1870-1894

Thomas H. Armstrong ran the regalia department.
Henderson-Ames bought the Detroit Factory (1894)
  and Armstrong moved to Chicago.

E. (EDWIN) A. ARMSTRONG MFG. CO.	CHICAGO, IL	1894-1915

Manager: J.P. Doyle (1915).
Made M1872 U.S. cavalry officer sabers and
  M1902 sabers for all officers.
Edwin A. Armstrong died (1915).
Adv. secret society and military uniforms, paraphenalia,
  costumes, equipment, banners, flags, and badges.
(Hatter, Military Goods, Regalia, Uniforms,
  Costumes, and Society Swords)

WILLIAM ASHBURN	LONDON, ENGLAND	B1745-1773
	PHILADELPHIA, PA	1773-1774
	WILLIAMSBURG, VA	1774-1780

(Cutler, Edged Tools, Razor and Knife Maker)

JOHN ASHMORE	PHILADELPHIA, PA	1839-1849

(Cutler)

JACOB ASHFIELD	PHILADELPHIA, PA	1775-1783

Partner: John Pollard.
Committee of Safety musket and bayonet maker.
Repaired arms for Pennsylvania militia infantry
  companies commanded by Captain Harmer,
Captain Jones, and Captain LeMar.
(Gunsmith)

WILTON ATKINSON	LANCASTER, PA	1745-1785
	BALTIMORE, MD	1785-D1790
ANNA MARIE ATKINSON	BALTIMORE, MD	1790-1820

Wilton's wife.
(Cutler, Silversmith, Clock Maker)

RALPH ATMAR JR.	CHARLESTON, SC	1780-1797
ATMAR (RALPH JR.) & MONK (JAMES)		
	CHARLESTON, SC	1797-1799
RALPH ATMAR JR.	CHARLESTON, SC	1799-1805

(Cutler, Blacksmith, Gunsmith, Silversmith, Goldsmith)

CORNELIUS ATHERTON	CAMBRIDGE, MA	B1740-1755
	BOSTON, MA	1755-1772

Built a gun factory for Samuel Adams (1769-1772).

	AFTON, NY	1772-1777

Committee of Safety musket and bayonet maker.

	PLYMOUTH, PA	1777-1786
	TAYLORVILLE, PA	1786-1806
	SOUTH BRAINBRIDGE, NY	1806-D1809

(Gunsmith, Rifle and Pistol Maker)

During the Revolutionary War, the individual states formed "Committees of Safety" to organize the defense of the state, including the purchase of arms for their militias. They were sometimes known as "Councils of Safety."

CORNELIUS AUSTIN TRENTON, NJ 1775-1783
Armorer to the Colony of New Jersey (1775).
Committee of Safety musket and
  bayonet maker (1776-1778).
(Gunsmith, Cutler)

EBENEZER AUSTIN	CHARLESTON, MA	B1733-1760
	HARTFORD, CT	1760-1785
	NEW YORK, NY	1785-1795
	BOSTON, MA	1795-D1818

(Silversmith)

ISAAC AUSTIN PHILADELPHIA, PA 1765-D1801
(Silversmith, Clock Maker, Watch Maker)

JAMES AUSTIN CHARLESTON, MA B1750-1780
(Silversmith)

JOHN AUSTIN	PHILADELPHIA, PA	B1757, 1775-1810
	CHARLESTON, MA	1810-D1825

(Silversmith)

NATHANIEL AUSTIN CHARLESTON, MA B1734, 1774-D1878
(Silversmith)

STEPHEN AUSTIN PHILADELPHIA, PA 1775-1795
(Gunsmith, Shot Maker)

THOMAS AUSTIN CHARLESTON, MA 1760-1783
Armorer to the Colony of Massachusetts (1775).
Committee of Safety musket and bayonet maker (1776).
(Cutler, Gunsmith)

L.W. BABBITT	CLEVELAND, OH	1832-1838
	BURLINGTON, IA	1838-1844

Made belt knives.
(Gunsmith, Cutler)

WILLIAM BACON Made belt knives. (Cutler)	NEW YORK, NY	1825-1845
RICHARD BACKHOUSE Owner and operator of the Durham Iron Works. Sold out to George Taylor (1774). (See George Taylor) (Iron Forger, Cutler)	DURHAM TOWNSHIP, PA Bucks County	1727-1774
EMMOR BAILEY (BAYLEY) Apprenticeship. (Silversmith, Clock Maker)	BRANDYWINE, PA Chester County PHILADELPHIA, PA SALEM, NJ LONDON GROVE TOWNSHIP, PA Chester County ARUNDEL CO., PA SHORTCREEK, OH Belmont County WARREN CO., OH	B1763-1780 1780-1788 1788-1790 1790-1805 1805-1814 1814-1815 1815-1820
JOEL BAILEY (BAYLEY) (Silversmith, Gunsmith, Cutler, Clock Maker, Survey Equipment Maker)	BRANDYWINE, PA Chester County	1740-D1797
JOHN BAILEY (BAYLEY) (Goldsmith, Silversmith, Clock Maker, Watch Maker)	PHILADELPHIA, PA LONDON, ENGLAND PHILADELPHIA, PA NEW CASTLE, DE	1740-1754 1754-1757 1757-1797 1797-D1806
JOHN TROWBRIDGE BAILEY Bailey & Kitchen (See Dealer Listings)		
JOHN BAILEY (BAYLEY) Served his apprenticeship in Sheffield, England. **JOHN BAILEY & JAMES YOULE** Bailey's wife made leather scabbards. Shop damaged during the first year of the Revolutionary War. (See James Youle) **JOHN BAILEY**	YORKSHIRE, ENGLAND SHEFFIELD, ENGLAND NEW YORK, NY VERPLANCKS POINT, NY Westchester County FREDERICKSBURG, NY Dutchess County FISHKILL, NY	B1736-1750 1750-1755 1755-1775 1776 1776-1778 1778-1784

- Set up shop at his farm (located near the U.S. Continental Army depot and armory) at Fishkill, NY (bought 400 acres in 1768).
- Used cattle hides for sword scabbards.
- Set up a forge, blacksmith shop, and cutlery shop.
- Did general cutlery work and repaired knives and swords.
- Imported blades from the Weyersburg family, Solingen, Germany. The swords had a running wolf and the name "Andrea Farrara" marked on the blades.
- Made lion-head pommel swords (many with silver hilts) for Revolutionary War officers (could make 24 swords a week).
- Made hunting swords.
- Made a sword for George Washington.
- Sold the farm (1784).

	NEW YORK, NY	1784-1794
JOHN BAILEY & G. HEDDERLY	NEW YORK, NY	1794-1798
JOHN BAILEY	NEW YORK, NY	1798-D1815

(Cutler, Silversmith, Sword Maker, Clock Maker, Surgical Instrument Maker)

JAMES BAILEY   NEW YORK, NY   1815-1830
Son of John.

SILAS NEWTON BAILEY (BAYLEY)   UNIONTOWN, PA   1780-1829
Fayette County

WALKER (HARDESTY) & BAILEY (ELLIS & WILLIAM)   UNIONTOWN, PA   1829-1834
Fayette County

Ellis and William were sons of Silas Newton Bailey.

ELLIS & WILLIAM BAILEY   UNIONTOWN, PA   1834-1835
Fayette County

(Silversmith, Goldsmith, Clock Maker, Jeweler)

SIMEON A. BAILEY (BAYLEY)   BRANDYWINE, PA   1785
Chester County

(Silversmith)

SIMEON BAILEY (BAYLEY)	NEW YORK, NY	1788-1791
SIMEON & ALEXANDER BAILEY	NEW YORK, NY	1791-1792
SIMEON & JOHN BAILEY	NEW YORK, NY	1792-1794
SIMEON BAILEY	NEW YORK, NY	1794-D1799
MRS. SIMEON BAILEY	NEW YORK, NY	1799-1800

(Silversmith, Goldsmith, Jewelers, Brass Founders, Military Equipment)

SIMEON C. BAILEY (BAYLEY)   PHILADELPHIA, PA   1774-1794
(Watch Maker, Silversmith)

WILLIAM BAILEY SR. (BAYLEY)   PHILADELPHIA, PA   1820-1850

WILLIAM BAILEY JR.   PHILADELPHIA, PA   1820-1850
(Silversmith, Goldsmith, Clock Maker)

GEORGE BAKER (Gunsmith)	GEORGES TOWNSHIP, PA Fayette County	1766-D1821
J. (JACOB) S. BAKER Bid on U.S. Navy cutlass contract (1817). Made cutlasses (1817). (Musket Maker, Sword Maker)	PHILADELPHIA, PA	1796-1860
JAMES BAKER Factory manager at Wickham Co. (1830-1834). (Musket Maker)	MILL CREEK, PA PHILADELPHIA, PA	1820-1830 1830-1840
JOHN BAKER (JOHAN) Immigrated to Norristown, PA (1765). Committee of Safety musket and bayonet maker (1776). Artillery artificer at the U.S. Armory. (Gunsmith)	SOLINGEN, GERMANY NORRISTOWN, PA Montgomery County PHILADELPHIA, PA	B1730-1765 1765-1779 1779-1782
MELCHOIR BAKER	HAYDENTOWN, GEORGES TOWNSHIP, PA Fayette County	1761-1781
MELCHOIR BAKER & ALBERT GALLATIN • Owned a gun factory. • Gallatin furnished capital. • Pennsylvania contract for 2,000 muskets (1799). • Made broadswords also. • Employed 100 men.	NICHOLSON TOWNSHIP, PA Fayette County	1781-1801
MELCHOIR BAKER Pennsylvania contract for muskets (1804). (Musket Maker, Sword Maker, Gun Maker)	HAYDENTOWN, GEORGES TOWNSHIP, PA Fayette County CLARKSVILLE, VA	1801-1804 1804-1810
NICHOLAS BAKER (Gunsmith)	GEORGES TOWNSHIP, PA Fayette County	1779-1805
ELIHU BALDWIN Committee of Safety musket and bayonet maker (1776). (Gunsmith)	BRANFORD, CT	1775-1783

JACOB BALDWIN Committee of Safety musket and bayonet maker (1775-1776). Armorer at the U.S. Philadelphia Armory (1779). (Gunsmith)	**WEST CHESTER, PA**	1775-1779
JOHN BALDWIN (Tinsmith)	**EAST CALN, PA** Chester County	1768
PETER BAMMEL (See Pierre Barrell)		
P.C. BANDLE	**CINCINNATI, OH**	1850-1865
JACOB C. BANDLE Son of P.C. Bandle. (Cutler, Gun Maker)	**CINCINNATI, OH**	1865-1902
HENRY BANKS (See James Hunter)		
JOHN BANKS (Gunsmith, Cutler)	**CONCORD TOWNSHIP, PA** Chester County	1775-1783
URI BANKS Committee of Safety contract for 50 gunlocks. Superintendant at the Rappahonnock Forge. (See James Hunter) (Gun Maker)	**PHILADELPHIA, PA** **STAFFORD CO., VA**	1760-1775 1775-1782
JOHN BARLOW Public armorer. (Armorer)	**POINT OF FORK, VA**	1786-1790
CHRISTOPHER BARNES (Cutler)	**PHILADELPHIA, PA**	1860-1865
DAVID BARNES Made iron sword hilts at the Virginia Manufactory. (Swordsmith, Gunsmith)	**RICHMOND, VA**	1805-1821
JOSEPH BARNES (Gunsmith)	**RICHMOND, VA**	B1796-1848
CROMEL BARNEY Made naval boarding pikes for the U.S. Navy (1797). (Pikemaker)	**PHILADELPHIA, PA**	1775-1810
PIERRE BARRELL Changed name to Peter Bammell. Made officer's swords. (Bladesmith, Swordsmith)	**PARIS, FRANCE** **PHILADELPHIA, PA**	B1799-1820 1820-1836

SAMUEL (DEACON) BARRETT CONCORD, NH B1726, 1750-D1801
Son of Thomas.
Committee of Safety musket and bayonet maker (1775).
(Gunsmith)

THOMAS BARRETT CONCORD, NH B1702, 1734-D1779
Committee of Safety musket
 and bayonet maker (1775).
(Gunsmith)

ISAAC BARTON CLONELL, IRELAND 1690-1714
 PHILADELPHIA, PA 1714-1720
(Cutler)

JAMES BARTON CHESTER, PA 1750-1769
 Chester County
(Blacksmith, Whitesmith)

WILLIAM BARTON CUMBERLAND
 TOWNSHIP, PA 1797-1810
 Green County
(Coppersmith)

NATHANIEL BEAN PHILADELPHIA, PA 1777
Swordsmith for Lewis Prahl.
(See Lewis Prahl)
(Sword Maker)

LUTZ & BEALL (HORATIO) WASHINGTON, D.C. 1854-1862
HORATIO BEALL WASHINGTON, D.C. 1862-1866
(Saddler, Military Goods, Regalia)

WILLIAM BEATTY NETHER, PROVIDENCE
 TOWNSHIP, PA 1813-1834
 Chester County

Partner and son: John C. Beatty.
(Cutler, Edged Tool Maker)

BEAVER FALLS CUTLERY CO. BEAVER FALLS, PA 1867-1887
Partners: Dr. C. G. Hussay, Gen. Thomas M.
Howe, James M. Brown.
(Cutler)

CHRISTIAN HENRY BECK BETHLEHEM, PA B1754-D1843
(Gunsmith)

CHRISTIAN BECK PHILADELPHIA, PA 1767
(Gunsmith)

GIDEON BECK LANCASTER CO., PA 1770-1790
(Gunsmith)

JOHN BECK LANCASTER CO., PA 1760-1780
(Gunsmith)

JOHN PHILIP BECK	LEBANANON, PA Dauphin County	B1751, 1770-D1821

Committee of Safety musket
  and bayonet maker (1776-1777).
(Gunsmith)

JOHN VALENTINE BECK	GERMANY BETHLEHEM, PA	B1731-1761 1761-1791

(Gunsmith, Silversmith, Pewterer, Tinner)

LOUIS BECK	PHILADELPHIA, PA	1860-1865

(Cutlery Maker)

S. BECK	PHILADELPHIA, PA	1775-1783

Made horsemen's sabers.
(Gunsmith, Sword Maker)

THOMAS BECK	PHILADELPHIA, PA TRENTON, NJ	1760-1780 1780-1790

(Silversmith, Goldsmith, Cutler)

CHARLES FREDERICK BECKEL	BETHLEHEM, PA Northampton County	B1802, 1815-D1880

Apprenticed to silversmith
  John S. Krause (1815-1820)
Apprentice: Henry David Bishop.
(Silversmith, Clock Maker, Iron Founder, Cutler)

ELIAS BECKLEY SR.	BERLIN, CT	B1735, 1755-D1818

(Gunsmith)

ELIAS BECKLEY JR.	BERLIN, CT	1816-D1828

(Gunsmith)

SAMUEL BECKLEY	BERLIN, CT	1790-1815

Subcontracter for sword blades (M1813 cavalry
  sabers) for Nathan Starr (1813).
(Gunsmith, Blade Maker)

WILLIAM BEEMAN	BOSTON, MA	1775-1783

Committee of Safety musket and
  bayonet maker (1775-1776).
(Gunsmith, Pistol Maker)

BELLVILLE (W.S.) & POWERS (R.B.)	NEW LONDON, OH	1888-1890

Sold out to Clemmons (W.E.) & Curtis (S.O.)
in 1890.
(Regalia)

JOHN JACOB BENDOR	WESTPHALIA, GERMANY PHILADELPHIA, PA ALLEGHENY TOWNSHIP, PA Cambria County	B1740-1797 1797-1802 1802-D1829

(Cutler, Brass Founder, Gunsmith, Lock Maker)

BENICIA ARSENAL	BENICIA, CA	1845-1865

Made naval boarding pikes and 214 lances (1865).

JAMES BENT	CANTON, MA	1788-1808
	RICHMOND, VA	1809

Artificer and polisher of muskets at the
  Virginia Manufactory.

	CANTON, MA	1809-1812, D1847

Worked for Dunbar & Leonard, Canton, MA (1813-1816).
Probably made balled-hilt cavalry sabers
  for the War of 1812.
(See Dunbar & Leonard)
(Sword Maker, Gunsmith)

ABRAHAM BERLIN	EASTON, PA	1735-1810
	Northampton County	

Made flintlock muskets, barrels, and bayonets.
Served in the Pennsylvania
  militia cavalry (1776-1782).
(Blacksmith, Gunsmith)

ISAAC BERLIN	EASTON, PA	B1753-1793
	Northampton County	

Son of Abraham.
Served in the Pennsylvania
  militia cavalry (1776-1782).

	ABBOTTSTOWN, PA	1793-1806
	Adams County	
	EASTON, PA	1806-1810
	Northampton County	

Bought land from his father.

	LEHIGH TOWNSHIP, PA	1810-D1830
	Northampton County	

Made cavalry officer swords, muskets, and bayonets.
(Blacksmith, Gunsmith, Sword Maker)

A. BEYRY	AKRON, OH	1855-1865
	Summit County	

Made hunting knives.
(Gun Maker, Knife Maker)

CHARLES ETHAN BILLINGS	WETHERFIELD, VT	B1835-1855
	HARTFORD, CT	1855-1862

Tool maker for Samuel Colt.

	ILLION, NY	1862-1865

Tool maker for E. Remington Sr.

	HARTFORD, CT	1865-1868

Patented a pistol-sword (1868).

	ALMERT, CT	1868-1869

President of Roper Repeating Rifle.
**BILLINGS (CHARLES ETHAN) & SPENCER
  (CHRISTOPHER M.)**   HARTFORD, CT   1869-1876
(Sword-Pistol Maker, Gun Maker, Gun Tool Maker)

HENRY BINGHAM	**PHILADELPHIA, PA**	**1775-1783**

Committee of Safety musket and bayonet maker (1775).
(Gunsmith)

JAMES BINGHAM	**PHILADELPHIA, PA**	**1800-1850**

(Silversmith, Goldsmith, Clock Maker)

THOMAS T. BINGHAM	**PHILADELPHIA, PA**	**1780-1799**
BINGHAM (THOMAS) & BREARLEY (JAMES)		
	PHILADELPHIA, PA	**1800**
THOMAS T. BINGHAM	**PHILADELPHIA, PA**	**1800-1825**

(Silversmith, Watch Maker,
  Clock Maker, Military Ornaments)

MARK BIRD	**BIRDSBORO, PA**	**1775-1790**

Committee of Safety musket
 and bayonet maker (1776).
(Gunsmith)

CHARLES BIRD & CO.	**PHILADELPHIA, PA**	**1790-1812**

Partner: Mark Bird
(Gunsmith)

BIRD BROS	**PHILADELPHIA, PA**	**1812-1820**

Partners: Mark Bird, Charles Bird.
(Gunsmiths)

JAMES BIRD	**WILLIAMSBURG, VA**	**1720-1770**

Armorer at the public magazine (1740-1758).
Apprentice: Goldsberry Hackett (1762-1770).

BIRD (JAMES) & HACKETT (GOLDSBERRY)	**NORFOLK, VA**	**1771-1774**

Adv. making and repairing guns and pistols,
 and making, repairing, and mounting swords
 and cutlery (1774).

GOLDSBERRY HACKETT	**NORFOLK, VA**	**1775-1776**
	WILLIAMSBURG, VA	**1777-1779**

(Blacksmith, Gunsmith, Sword Maker, Cutler)

LAWRENCE BIRNIE	**DUBLIN, IRELAND**	**1755-1770**

Son of William Birnie.

	PHILADELPHIA, PA	**1770-1777**

Apprenticed under William Birnie (1770-1774).
Operated a watch and clock shop (1774-1777).

	HUMMELSTOWN, PA	**1777-1779**

Worked at the Pennsylvania Gunlock Factory.

	PHILADELPHIA, PA	**1779-1790**

Sold guns, jewelry, and cutlery.
(Jeweler, Cutler, Gunsmith, Clock Maker)

WILLIAM BIRNIE	**DUBLIN, IRELAND**	**1730-1770**
	PHILADELPHIA, PA	**1770-1776**

(Goldsmith, Silversmith,
  Clock Maker, Watch Maker)

CHARLES BLAIR
(See Morrill, Mosman, & Blair)

DAVID BLAISDEL SR. (Gun Maker)	AMESBURY, MA	1730-D1756
DAVID BLAISDEL JR. Did arms repair for the Committee of Safety (1775). (Gun Maker)	CAMBRIDGE, MA	1775-1783
JONATHAN BLAISDEL Armorer to Colony of Massachusetts (1775). Committee of Safety musket and bayonet maker (1775). (Gun Maker)	AMESBURY, MA	1775-1783
TOM BLAKE Made gunlocks and belt knives (1815-1830).	CUMBERLAND CO., TN	1815-1830
C.J. BLITTERSDORF (Knife Maker, Cutler)	PHILADELPHIA, PA 143 No. 4th Street	1780-1849
WILLIAM BLANCHARD (See Soloman Stone) (Cutler, Scythe Maker)	BEAVER CO., PA	1820-1830
TIMOTHY BLOODWORTH Committee of Safety musket and bayonet maker (1776). (Gunsmith)	FAYETTEVILLE, NC	1775-1783
STEPHEN BOARMAN (Cutler, Silversmith)	PARKERSBURG, VA Wood County	1860-1861
JOHN BOEHLER (Cutler, Clock Maker)	GRUENBERG, MORAVIA SAVANNAH, GA PHILADELPHIA, PA	B1719-1736 1736-1740 1740-D1785
ROBERT BOLTON (BOULTON) Armorer to the Colony of Georgia. (Gunsmith, Cutler)	SAVANNAH, GA	1760-1775
JOHN BONNEATHEAU Cleaned and polished swords and made scabbards. (Cutler)	PROVINCE OF SOUTH CAROLINA	1745
E. BOONE (Rifle Maker)	OLEY VALLEY, PA	1800-1820
MOSES BOONE Blacksmith and artillery artificer at the U.S. Philadelphia Armory. (Blacksmith)	CARLISLE, PA Cumberland County PHILADELPHIA, PA	1759-1779 1779-1782

SAMUEL BOONE Nephew of Daniel Boone.	ROMAN CO., NC	1750-1768
	BERKS CO., PA	1768-1777
	FREDERICK, MD	1777-1778
Manager of the Maryland State Gunlock Factory. **SAMUEL BOONE & NICHOLAS WHITE** Bought the Maryland State Gunlock Factory. (Rifle Maker, Musket Maker, and Bayonet Maker)	FREDERICK, MD	1778-1783
SQUIRE BOONE	ROMAN CO., NC	1780-1790
	HARVARDSBURY, KY	1790-1800
Brother of Daniel Boone. (Rifle Maker, Cutler)		
THOMAS BOONE Cousin of Daniel Boone. (Rifle Maker)	BERKS CO., PA	1768-1790
AUGUSTINE BORDEAUX (BORDER) (Rifle Maker, Silversmith)	PHILADELPHIA, PA	1779-1799
DANIEL B. BORDEAUX (BORDER) Son of William. (Silversmith, Clock Maker, Watch Maker)	PHILADELPHIA, PA	B1820, 1840-D1891
WILLIAM BORDEAUX (BORDER) (Cutler, Gunsmith)	PHILADELPHIA, PA	B1800, 1820-D1881
BOSTON NAVY YARD Made naval pikes and boarding axes for War of 1812. Made 90 boarding pikes for refitting of the frigate *Constitution* (1930).	BOSTON, MA	1799-1930
JOHN BOURNS (Cutler, Iron Founder, Cannon Maker, Gunsmith)	ANTRIM, TOWNSHIP, PA Franklin County	1775-D1802
R. BOWEN (See William Stackpole)		
JAMES BOYD (Cutler)	CENTRE CO., PA	1780-1801
PARK BOYD (Brass Founder, Whitesmith)	PHILADELPHIA, PA	1770-1820
ROBERT BOYD	NEW WINDSOR, NY Vistor County	1760-1776
ROBERT BOYD & HENRY WATKEYS Committee of Safety musket and bayonet maker (1776). (Gunsmith)	NEW WINDSOR, NY Vistor County	1776-1783

SAMUEL BOYD	LANCASTER, PA	1770-1794
BOYD (SAMUEL) & TURNER (THOMAS)	LANCASTER, PA	1794-1801

(Blacksmith, Gunsmith)

GEORGE FREDERICK BOYER   PHILADELPHIA, PA   1775-1783
(Cutler)

DAVID BRADY JR.   MT. JOY, PA   1848-1882
Son of David Brady Sr.   Lancaster County
(Cutler)

DAVID BRADY SR.   MT. JOY, PA   1829-1860
    Lancaster County
BRADY EDGED TOOL WORKS   MT. JOY, PA   1860-1885
    Lancaster County

WILLIAM BRADY   MT. JOY, PA   1848-1868
Son of David Brady Sr.   Lancaster County
WILLIAM BRADY & SONS   MT. JOY, PA   1869-1875
(Cutler, Edged Tool Maker, Knife Maker)   Lancaster County

ISRAEL BRADY   MT. JOY, PA   1848-1868
    Lancaster County

Son of David Brady Sr.
(Cutler)

CHRISTOPHER BRAUN   PHILADELPHIA, PA   1860-1865
(Cutler)

JAMES BREARLEY (BREARLY)   PHILADELPHIA, PA   1780-1800
BINGHAM (THOMAS) & BREARLEY (JAMES)   PHILADELPHIA, PA   1800
JAMES BREARLEY   PHILADELPHIA, PA   1800-1825
(See Thomas Bingham)
(Silversmith, Clock Maker,
  Military Ornaments, Cutler)

CHRISTOPHER BREIDENHART   PHILADELPHIA, PA   1775-1783
Committee of Safety musket and bayonet maker.
(Gunsmith, Rifle Maker)

JOHN BRISTOW   BRISTOL, ENGLAND   1865-1885
    CHESTER COUNTY, PA   1885-D1894

(Cutler)

JAMES BROCK   NEW YORK, NY   1780-1790
(Cutler, Gunsmith)

JOHN BROCK   NEW YORK, NY   1830-1850
(Silversmith)

CHAUNCEY BROCKWAY   BROCKWAY, PA   B1821-1840
    SOUTH CARLESTON, NH   1840-1844
    BELLOWS FALLS, VT   1844-1866

BROCKWAY (CHAUNCEY) & SON (NORMAN S.) (Rifle Maker)	BELLOWS FALLS, VT	1866-D1900
NORMAN S. BROCKWAY Son of Chauncey.	SOUTH CHARLESTON, NH	B1841-1844
	BELLOWS FALLS, VT	1844-1861
Rifle maker at U.S. Springfield, MA, Armory.	SPRINGFIELD, MA	1861-1864
Rifle maker for Norwich Arms.	NORWICH, CT	1864-1865
Revolver Maker for Smith & Wesson.	SPRINGFIELD, MA	1865-1866
BROCKWAY (CHAUNCEY) & SON (NORMAN S.)	BELLOWS FALLS, VT	1866-1900
NORMAN S. BROCKWAY Made fraternal swords.	MIDDLETOWN, CT	1900-1905
(Rifle Maker, Revolver Maker, Sword Maker)	WEST BROOKFIELD, MA	1905-D1906
BENJAMIN FRANKLIN BROOKS	UTICA, NY	1810-1828
BLACKWOOD (WILLIAM) & BROOKS (BENJAMIN FRANKLIN)	UTICA, NY	1810-1828
BROOKS (BENJAMIN FRANKLIN) & GRISWALD (JOAB)	UTICA, NY	1832-1840
BROOKS (BENJAMIN FRANKLIN) & VAN VOORHIS	UTICA, NY	1840-1845
B.F. (BENJAMIN FRANKLIN) BROOKS & SON (CHARLES V.)	UTICA, NY	1845-1860
(Silversmith, Goldsmith, Military and Fancy Goods Store)		
CHAPLIN C. BROOKS C. (Chaplin) Brooks Arms & Tool Co. Made rifles, shotguns, edged tools, bayonets, and belt knives. (Gunsmith, Cutler, Edged Tools)	EAST WILTON, ME	1880-1905
CHARLES V. BROOKS	UTICA, NY	1830-1845
B.F. (BENJAMIN FRANKLIN) BROOKS & SON (CHARLES V.) (Silversmith, Goldsmith)	UTICA, NY	1845-1860
FRANCIS BROOKS Adv. as a gunsmith and pistol maker at one shop and a cutler and jeweler at another shop (1791). (Gunsmith, Silversmith, Goldsmith, Pistol Maker, Jeweler, Cutler)	PHILADELPHIA, PA	1770-1795
J. (JAMES), J. (JOHN) & N. (NATHAN) BROOKS U.S. contract for 400 M1818 muskets and bayonets (1808). (Gunsmith)	PHILADELPHIA, PA	1800-1815

JOHN BROOKS (Rifle Maker)	LANCASTER, PA HAMSBURG, PA	1800-1807 1807-1820
NICHOLAS BROOKS Adv. silverware and sword hangers (1775). (Silversmith, Cutler)	PHILADELPHIA, PA	1775-1783
SAMUEL BROOKS **BROOKS (SAMUEL) & WARROCK (WILLIAM)**	PHILADELPHIA, PA	1785-1794
SAMUEL BROOKS (Silversmith)	NORFOLK, VA RICHMOND, VA	1795-1803 1803-1820
THOMAS BROOKS (Silversmith, Brass Founder, Clock Maker)	CARLISLE, VA Cumberland County	1785-1802
ISAAC BROOME State of Pennsylvania contract for 100 cavalry lances for the 6th Pennsylvania Cavalry—Colonel Rush's Regiment of Lancers (1861). (Lance Maker, Cutler)	PHILADELPHIA, PA	1825-1865
WILLIAM BROOME SR. **BROOME (WILLIAM) & CLEMENT (JAMES W.)**	PHILADELPHIA, PA PHILADELPHIA, PA	1825-1835 1835-1837
WILLIAM BROOME (Silversmith)	PHILADELPHIA, PA	1837-1850
WILLIAM BROOME JR. (Silversmith)	PHILADELPHIA, PA	1825-1835
ELIJAH (ELISHA) BROWN U.S. contract for 1,000 muskets (1799). Worked at Virginia Manufactory welding musket barrels (1811-1814). Bid on U.S. naval boarding axe and naval pike contracts (1816-1817). (Musket Maker, Edged Weapon Maker)	PROVIDENCE, RI RICHMOND, VA	1780-1804 1804-D1849
J.M. BROWN Made tomahawks. (Cutler)	GREEN BAY, WI	1820-1840
JAMES BROWN	NEWTOWN TOWNSHIP, PA Cumberland County	1785-1812
BROWN (JAMES), BARKER (ABNER) & **BUTLER (JAMES R)** (Cutler, Blacksmith, Knife Maker, Edged Tools)	PITTSBURGH, PA	1812-1816
JOHN BROWN Lewis Prahl bought John Brown's shop (1800). (Gunsmith)	PHILADELPHIA, PA	1769-1800

JOSEPH BROWN (Gunsmith)	PHILADELPHIA, PA Mulberry Ward	1775-1783
MATTHEW BROWN (Silversmith)	EAST PENNSBORO TOWNSHIP, PA Cumberland County	1750-1760
WILLIAM BROWN Swordsmith for Lewis Prahl. (See Lewis Prahl) (Sword Maker)	PHILADELPHIA, PA	1777
WILLIAM H. BROWN Adv. knives and cutlery (1838-1841). (Gun Maker, Pistol Maker, Cutler, Edged Tools, Hardware)	PITTSBURGH, PA	1830-1847
CHARLES OLIVER BRUFF	CHARLESTON, MD Talbot County ELIZABETH TOWN, NJ NEW YORK, NY Maiden Lane	B1731-1760 1760-1765 1765-1776
Adv. swords for the militia (1775). Adv. swords (small swords) for gentlemen (1775). Made silver-mounted cut and thrust swords, hunting swords, broad swords, and small swords. (Sword Maker, Silversmith)	CHARLESTON, MA Talbot County NOVA SCOTIA	1776-1783 1783-D1787
JAMES BRUFF Son of Charles Bruff. (Sword Maker, Silversmith)	TABOT CO., MD ELIZABETH TOWN, NY NEW YORK CITY, NY	1748-1760 1760-1765 1765-D1780
JOSEPH BRUFF SR.	EASTON, MD PHILADELPHIA, PA	B1730-1765 1765-1785
JOSEPH BRUFF JR. (Goldsmith, Silversmith, Watch Maker, Clock Maker, Jeweler)	EASTON, MD CHESTERTOWN, MD	1705-1800 1800-1803
JOHN BRY Swordsmith for Lewis Prahl. (Sword Maker)	PHILADELPHIA, PA	1777
JACOB BUCHANAN (BUCKHAM) Adv. guns and cutlery (1794 and 1796). (Gunsmith, Blacksmith, Cutler)	NEW YORK, NY CHARLESTON, SC SAVANNAH, GA CHARLESTON, SC	1780-1794 1794-1797 1797-1810 1810-D1814

ABEL BUELL (BUEL)	NEW HAVEN, CT	B1742-1765
BUELL (ABEL) & CHITTENDEN (EBENEZER)	NEW HAVEN, CT	1765
ABEL BUELL	NEW HAVEN, CT	1765-1783
BUELL (ABEL) & MIX (THOMAS)	NEW HAVEN, CT	1783
ABEL BUELL	NEW HAVEN, CT	1783-1799
BUELL (ABEL) & GREENLEAF (DAVID JR.)	HARTFORD, CT	1799

U.S. contract for 1,000 cavalry swords with belts, consigned to U.S. Philadelphia Armory. Inspected by Nobel Orr.

ABEL BUELL   HARTFORD, CT   1799-D1825

Adv. solid silver, silver-plated, silver-washed, gilt-, iron-, or brass-hilted swords and dirks (1799).
Adv. brass or steel pikes, horsemen's swords, and army and navy officer swords and hangers.
(See Thomas Mix and Ebenezer Chittenden-Silversmith Listing)
(See David Greenleaf Jr.)
(Sword Maker, Pike Maker, Silversmith, Engraver)

D.H. BUELL   HARTFORD, CT   1763-1825
(Silversmith)

ELISHA BUELL   HEBRON, CT   1775-1797
    MARLBOROUGH, CT   1797-1835
(Gunsmith)

ENOS BUELL   MARLBOROUGH, CT   1825-1850
Son of Elisha.
U.S. contracts for M1765 and M1808 muskets and bayonets.
(Gunsmith)

JOHN BUELL   NEW HAVEN, CT   B1744-1760-D1783
(Silversmith)

SAMUEL BUELL   MIDDLETOWN, CT   B1742-1780
    HARTFORD, CT   B1780-D1819
(Silversmith)

PETER BURNET   REDSTONE TOWNSHIP, PA   1790-1806
Fayette County
(Cutler)

WILLIAM BURNETT   GREEN BAY, WI   1820-1830
Made tomahawks.
(Cutler)

JOHN BUTLER   LANCASTER, PA   1775-1783
Committee of Safety musket and bayonet maker (1775-1776).
(Gunsmith)

RICHARD BUTLER	LANCASTER, PA	1745-1759
	CARLISLE, PA	1759-1772
	PITTSBURGH, PA	1765-1770

Son of Thomas Sr.
(Gunsmith)

THOMAS BUTLER SR.	LANCASTER, PA	B1720-1759
	CARLISLE, PA	1759-D1791
	Cumberland County	

Made tomahawks.
(Cutler)

THOMAS BUTLER JR.	LANCASTER, PA	1752-1759
	CASLISLE, PA	1759-1772
	PHILADELPHIA, PA	1772-1778

Son of Thomas Butler Sr.
Chief armorer at the
 U.S. Philadelphia Armory (1777-1778).
Succeeded by William Henry Sr.
(Gunsmith)

WILLIAM BUTLER	LANCASTER, PA	1746-1759

Son of Thomas Sr.

	CARLISLE, PA	1759-1765
	PITTSBURGH, PA	1765-1770

(Gunsmith)

PETER BUTZ	LONG SWAMP TOWNSHIP, PA	B1775-1815
	Berks County	

(Gunsmith, Blacksmith, Cutler)

FREDERICK BYERS SR.	ANTRIM TOWNSHIP, PA	B1731, 1751-D1801
	Cumberland County	

(Gunsmith)

FREDERICK BYERS JR.	ANTRIM TOWNSHIP, PA	1789-1809
	Cumberland County	

(Gunsmith)

GEORGE FREDERICK BYERS	PHILADELPHIA, PA	1868-1886
	Upper Delaware Ward	

(Cutler, Edged Weapons)

JAMES BYERS	PHILADELPHIA, PA	1757-1783

Superintendant of the brass foundry at the U.S.
 Philadelphia Armory.
(Whitesmith, Gunsmith,
 Brass Founder, Cannon Maker)

NICHOLAS BYER	LEBANON, PA	1800-1842

(Gunsmith)

P.S. CANU Adv. as watch maker and pistol, sword, and gun repair (1807). (Watch Maker, Whitesmith, Blacksmith)	WILMINGTON, NC	1806-1807
WILLIAM CAMPBELL Gunsmith to Virginia and Maryland Committees of Safety. (Armorer, Cutler, Blacksmith, Gunsmith)	FREDERICK CO., VA ANNAPOLIS, MD HAMPSHIRE CO., VA	1766-1780 1780-1781 1781-D1799
CHRISTIAN CANE Swordsmith for Lewis Prahl. (See Lewis Prahl) (Swordsmith)	PHILADELPHIA, PA	1777
BENJAMIN CARGILL Committee of Safety musket and bayonet maker. Partners: Nathan Frink, Elisha Child. (See Nathan Frink & Elisha Child) (Gunsmith)	GOSHEN, CT	1760-1800
ROBERT CARR (Cutler, Brass Founder)	PHILADELPHIA, PA	1779-1799
WILLIAM CARR Artillery artificer at the U.S. Philadelphia Armory. Armorer at the U.S. Lebanon Armory. (Armorer)	PHILADELPHIA, PA LEBANON, PA	1777 1777-1781
DANIEL CARRELL **JOHN & DANIEL CARRELL** **DANIEL CARRELL** (Cutler, Goldsmith, Silversmith, Clock Maker, Iron Monger, Jeweler, Fowling Pieces)	PHILADELPHIA, PA PHILADELPHIA, PA PHILADELPHIA, PA CHARLESTON, SC PHILADELPHIA, PA	1760-1780 1781-1784 1785-1790 1791-1803 1804-1816
GEORGE CARRELL (Gunsmith)	NORTHAMPTON CO., PA	1820-1835
LAWRENCE CARRELL (Gunsmith)	PHILADELPHIA, PA	1783-1790
JOHN CARRELL (CARREL, CARROLL) **JOHN & DANIEL CARRELL** **JOHN CARRELL** Adv. silver-mounted swords (1787). Adv. cutlery, saddlery, and clocks (1791). (Cutler, Goldsmith, Silversmith, Clock Maker, Iron Monger, Jeweler, Fowling Pieces)	PHILADELPHIA, PA PHILADELPHIA, PA PHILADELPHIA, PA	1760-1780 1781-1784 1785-1796

JOSEPH CARRELL (Silversmith)	**PHILADELPHIA, PA**	**1710-1718**
MARTIN CARRELL Artillery artificer at the U.S. Philadelphia Armory.	**PHILADELPHIA, PA**	**1779**
ADAM CARRUTH U.S. contract for 8,500 bayonets (1816, 1821, and 1823). Took over Elias Earle contract. (Gun and bayonet maker)	**GREENVILLE, SC**	**1809-1823**
JOHN M. CARTER Sword blade and scabbard engraver. Made silver-mounted hilt for a Virginia Manufactory presentation sword. (Silversmith, Engraver)	**RICHMOND, VA**	**1790-1811**
JOSEPH CARTER Forged bayonets at the Virginia Manufactory. (Gunsmith)	**RICHMOND, VA**	**1803**
ROSWELL CARTER Made iron sword hilts at the Virginia Manufactory. (Hiltmaker)	**RICHMOND, VA**	**1808**
TEBULAND CARTER Made iron sword hilts at the Virginia Manufactory. (Hiltmaker)	**RICHMOND, VA**	**1808**
JOHN CARTWRIGHT Made dental and occulist instruments, saddlers, tinners and glass-blower's tools, bowie knives, hunting knives, and dirks. Sold imported guns, rifles, and pistols. (Cutler, Knife Maker, Edged Tools)	**LONDON, ENGLAND** **PITTSBURG, PA**	**B1810-1830** **1830-D1858**
JOSEPH CARTWRIGHT Artillery artificer at the U.S. Philadelphia Armory.	**PHILADELPHIA, PA**	**1777**
WILLIAM CARTWRIGHT Son of John Cartwright. **CARTWRIGHT (WILLIAM) & YOUNG** (Cutters)	**PITTSBURGH, PA** **PITTSBURGH, PA**	**B1830-1858** **1858-1860**
ANDREW CASEBEER **CARLING & CASEBEER (ANDREW)** **ANDREW CASEBEER** (Blacksmith, Iron Founder, Cutler)	**BEDFORD, PA** **BORO, PA** **BORO, PA**	**1747-1767** **1767-1771** **1771-1782**
CARVER (WILLIAM) & HALL (THOMAS) (Blacksmith, Whitesmith, Gunsmith, Cutler)	**ALEXANDRIA, VA**	**1795-1797**

CHRISTOPHER CAVE Armorer at the U.S. Philadelphia Armory (1778-1783). (See U.S. Philadelphia Armory)	PHILADELPHIA, PA	1776-1783
JOSEPH CAVE Son of Thomas Cave.	WEST GOSHEN TOWNSHIP, PA CHESTER CO., PA WESTCHESTER CO., PA MARSHALL TOWN, WEST BRADFORD TOWNSHIP, PA Chester County WESTCHESTER CO., PA PHILADELPHIA, PA	1795-1820 1820 1820-1824 1824-1826 1826-1836 1836-D1841
(Silversmith)		
THOMAS CAVE (Silversmith)	CHESTER CO., PA	1779-1809
JOHN CHALONER Sold 10 cutlasses (sabers) to Captain Robert Towers, Commissary of Military Stores, Philadelphia Armory (1775). (Sword Maker)	PHILADELPHIA, PA	1775-1783
BENJAMIN CHANDLEE SR.	KILMORE, IRELAND Kildare County PHILADELPHIA, PA NOTTINGHAM TOWNSHIP, PA Chester County WILMINGTON, DE	B1685-1702 1702-1712 1712-1740 1740-D1745
Apprenticed to Abel Cottey (1702-1707). (See Abel Cottey) (Cutler, Silversmith, Goldsmith, Clock Maker, Surgical Instrument Maker)		
BENJAMIN CHANDLEE JR. Apprentice: Isaac Jackson (1755-1763). (Cutler, Silversmith, Goldsmith, Clock Maker, Surgical Instrument Maker)	NOTTINGHAM TOWNSHIP, PA Chester County	B1723, 1741-D1791
ELLIS CHANDLEE Son of Benjamin Jr. (Silversmith)	NOTTINGHAM TOWNSHIP, PA Chester County	B1755, 1791-D1815
GOLDSMITH CHANDLEE SR. Son of Benjamin Jr.	NOTTINGHAM TOWNSHIP, PA Chester County	B1751-1775

	WINCHESTER, VA	1775-D1821
GOLDSMITH CHANDLEE JR.	WINCHESTER, VA	1775-1814
	BALTIMORE, MD	1814-1818
HOLLOWAY (ROBERT) & CHANDLEE (GOLDSMITH)	BALTIMORE, MD	1818-1823
GOLDSMITH CHANDLEE JR. (Silversmith)	CLEVELAND, OH	1829-1830
ISAAC CHANDLEE Son of Benjamin Jr. (Silversmith)		B1760, 1791-D1813
JOHN CHANDLEE Son of Benjamin Jr.	NOTTINGHAM TOWNSHIP, PA Chester County	B1757-1795
	WILMINGTON, DE	1795-D1813
(Silversmith)		
WILLIAM CHANDLEE (Silversmith)	READINGS, PA Berks County	1750-1770
STEPHEN CHANDLER Committee of Safety musket and bayonet maker (1776).	HARTFORD, CT	1775-1810
HEMSTEAD (E.) & CHANDLER (STEPHEN) (Silversmith, Gunsmith)	NEW YORK, NY	1810-1825
JAMES CHAPMAN Committee of Safety musket and bayonet maker (1776). (Gunsmith)	BUCKS CO., PA	1770-1785
JOHN CHAPMAN	READINGS, PA Berks County	1775-1783
Committee of Safety musket and bayonet maker. (Gunsmith)		
JOSIAH CHAPMAN Committee of Safety musket and bayonet maker (1776). (Gunsmith)	FREDERICKSTOWN, MD	1775-1783
CLAUDIUS CHAT (Silversmith, Cutler)	PHILADELPHIA, PA	1780-1799
EASTON CHAT (Silversmith, Cutler)	PHILADELPHIA, PA	1773-1793
ROBERT CHAT (Silversmith, Cutler)	PHILADELPHIA, PA	1780-1800

CHEEVER & BURGHARD (Cutler)	ST. LOUIS, MO	1880-1886
ELISHA CHILD Committee of Safety musket and bayonet maker. Partners: Benjamin Cargill, Nathan Frink. (See Benjamin Cargill & Nathan Frink) (Gunsmith)	GOSHEN, CT	1760-1786
CASPAR CHRIST (CRIST) Swordsmith for Lewis Prahl. (See Lewis Prahl) (Sword Maker)	PHILADELPHIA, PA	1777
JOHN JACOB CHRIST (CRIST) THE ELDER Swordsmith for Lewis Prahl. (See Lewis Prahl) (Sword Maker)	PHILADELPHIA, PA CREUGERSTOWN, MD	B1739-1782 1782-D1793
JOHN JACOB CHRIST THE YOUNGER (Coppersmith)	READINGS, PA	1778-1798
LEWIS CHRISTY (Gunsmith)	PHILADELPHIA, PA	1800-1820
MICHAEL CHRISTY (Blacksmith)	MAIDENCREEK TOWNSHIP, PA Berks County	1767-1768
SAMUEL CHRISTY Bayonet maker for Pennsylvania Committee of Safety (1777). (Cutler, Bayonet Maker)	WEST NANTMILL TOWNSHIP, PA Chester County WINDSOR TOWNSHIP, PA York County	1759-1779 1780-1783
WILLIAM T. CHRISTY (Gunsmith)	PHILADELPHIA, PA	1846-1866
JOSIAH CLAPHAM Committee of Safety musket and bayonet maker (1777). (Gunsmith)	WAKEFIELD, YORKSHIRE, ENGLAND POINT OF FORK, VA London County	1710-1739 1739-1783
BENJAMIN CLARK **BENJAMIN & ELLIS CLARK** **BENJAMIN CLARK** (Silversmith, Clock Maker, Watch Maker)	PHILADELPHIA, PA PHILADELPHIA, PA PHILADELPHIA, PA	1790-1811 1811-1840 1840-1851

DANIEL CLARK	PHILADELPHIA, PA Middle Ward	1820-1856

(Gunsmith, Cutler)

EDWARD CLARK	PHILADELPHIA, PA	1795-1815

(Silversmith, Clock Maker, Watch Maker)

ELIAS CLARK	PHILADELPHIA, PA	1800-1808

(Silversmith, Clock Maker, Watch Maker)

EPHRAIM CLARK	PHILADELPHIA, PA	1775-1806
EPHRAIM & CHARLES CLARK	PHILADELPHIA, PA	1806-1812
EPHRAIM CLARK	PHILADELPHIA, PA	1812-D1822

(Silversmith, Clock Maker, Watch Maker)

FRANCIS CLARK	READING, PA Berks County	1775-1783

Committee of Safety musket,
  bayonet, and naval cutlass maker (1776).
(Sword Maker, Gunsmith)

JAMES CLARK	CINCINNATTI, OH	1805-1835

Make belt knives, pistols, and rifles.
(Gunsmith, Cutler)

JAMES CLARK	PHILADELPHIA, PA	1775-1803

Armorer at the U.S. Philadelphia Armory (1776).

	BEDFORD CO., PA	1804-1821

(Armorer, Gunsmith)

JESSE CLARK	PHILADELPHIA, PA	1808-1816

(Silversmith, Clock Maker, Watch Maker)

JOHN CLARK	PHILADELPHIA, PA	1760-1777

Artillery artificer at the U.S. Philadelphia Armory.

	LEBANON, PA	1777-1782

Armorer at the U.S. Lebanon Armory.

	READING, PA Berks County	1783-1810
	SHIPPENBURG, PA	1811-1818

(Armorer, Gunsmith)

PETER CLARK	PHILADELPHIA, PA	1775-1783

Committee of Safety musket
  and bayonet maker (1777).
(Gunsmith)

RICHARD CLARK	PHILADELPHIA, PA	1777

Armorer at the U.S. Philadelphia Armory.

WILLIAM CLARK	PHILADELPHIA, PA	1760-1792

Armorer at the U.S. Philadelphia Armory (1779-1783).
(Gunsmith, Armorer)

WILLIAM T. CLEMENT	GREENFIELD, MA	1816-1844
	SHELBURNE FALLS, MA	1844-1857

Worked for Lamson & Goodnow Mfg. Co.

W. (WILLIAM) T. CLEMENT	NORTHAMPTON, MA	1857-1865

Purchased Bay State Tool Co. (1857).
Cavalry saber maker during the Civil War.

CLEMENT (WILLIAM T.) & NORRIS (SAMUEL)	NORTHAMPTON, MA	1865-1866

Massachusetts contract for 3,000 muskets (1863).

CLEMENT (WILLIAM) & HAWKES MFG. CO.	NORTHAMPTON, MA	1866-1882
CLEMENT CUTLERY CO.	NORTHAMPTON, MA	1882-1956
CLEMENT CO.	NORTHAMPTON, MA	1956-1970

(See Lamson & Goodnow Mfg. Co.)
(Sword Maker, Tool Maker, Pistol Maker, Knife Maker, Gunsmith)

A.W. COATS	PHILADELPHIA, PA	1810-1831
COATS (A.W.) & BOYD (EZEKIEL C.)	PHILADELPHIA, PA	1831-1836

(Silversmith)

ISAAC COATS	PHILADELPHIA, PA	1836-1846

(Silversmith)

JAMES COATS	PHILADELPHIA, PA	1790-1815

Worked for gun and sword maker John Joseph Henry Jr. (1814-1815).
(Gunsmith, Swordsmith)

MOSES COATS (COATES)	EAST CALN, PA	1780-1796
	Chester County	

(Cutler, Edged Weapons Maker)

SANFORD B. COCKE	RICHMOND, VA	B1822-1856

Made guns, rifles, pistols, and cutlery.
(Gunsmith, Cutler)

J.W. COFFMEN	PITTSBURGH, PA	1828-1848

(Cutler, Blacksmith, Edged Tools)

ROBERT COLEMAN	BRICKERSVILLE, PA	1748-1825
	Lancaster County	

Owned and operated the Elizabeth Forge.
Cast cannon and shot for Committee of Safety during the Revolutionary War.
Bought 60 German (Hessian) prisoners of war from Congress (1782 and 1783)
  and made muskets and swords for the Continental Army.
(Iron Master, Iron Forger, Musket and Sword Maker)

JOHN COLER	PHILADELPHIA, PA	1795-1805

U.S. naval contract for 164 naval pikes (1797).
(Pike Maker)

DAVID COLLINS	HARTFORD, CT	1825

Axe maker.
(Edged Tool Maker)

EDWARD COLLINS	PHILADELPHIA, PA	1777

Artillery artificer at the U.S. Philadelphia Armory.

| | LEBANON, PA | 1777-1781 |

Artillery artificer at the U.S. Lebanon Armory.

| **DANIEL W. COLLINS** | SOUTH CANTON, CT | 1800-1826 |

| **SAMUEL W. COLLINS** | SOUTH CANTON, CT | 1800-1826 |
| **COLLINS (SAMUEL W.) & CO.** | SOUTH CANTON, CT | 1826-1966 |

- Partners: Daniel C. Collins, William Wells (died in 1831), John F. Wells (son of William Wells; joined in 1831).
- Samuel and Daniel Collins bought the old Humphrey Grist Mill equipped with a water wheel (1826).
- South Canton became Collinsville, but Collins marked "Hartford, CT" on his products.
- Collins installed his first trip hammer (1828).
- Foreman of the forging shop: B.T. Wingate (1829). He died in 1858.
- Machinist: Elisha K. Root (1831-1853).
- Plant superintendant: Charles Blair (1845-1885).
- (See Charles Blair)
- Collins began as an axe maker but also made plows, machettes, dirks, bowie knives, bayonets, and naval pikes.
- During the Civil War, Collins had offices in New York.
- Collins' major output during the Civil War was sword blades and swords.
- Sold plain and engraved blades.
- The Collins Company was purchased by the Mann Edged Tool Co. (1966).

Collins Civil War Sword Production

- U.S. contracts for 1,000 musician's swords
- U.S. contracts for 648 non-comm. swords
- Made M1850 foot officer swords
- Made M1852 naval officer swords
- Imported M1860 cavalry officer sabers from Solingen, Germany

- Collins sold blades to the following dealers:
    James P. Fitch
    Henry Folsom & Co.
    Gorham & Co.
    Schuyler, Hartley, & Graham
    George W. Simons & Brother
    Tiffany & Co.

- Collins sold swords to the following dealers:
    Benjamin Kittridge
    James P. Fitch
    Miller & Co.
    Schuyler, Hartley, & Graham
    Tiffany & Co.

- Collins made bayonets for the following rifles:
    Navy M1861 Plymouth rifle
    Sharps M1860 rifle
    Sharps-Hamilton M1863 rifle
    Springfield rifles

WILLIAM COLLINS (Silversmith)	BALTIMORE, MD CUMBERLAND CO., PA	1755-1775 1775-1783
ROBERT J. COLVIN Patented a sword-pistol (1862). Patented a pistol-bayonet (1864).	LANCASTER, PA	1861-1865
BENJAMIN COMSTOCK Contract for 160 naval cutlasses to outfit two U.S. frigates.	RHODE ISLAND	1775-1783
JOHN CONEY Made silver-hilted half pikes and silver-hilted small swords. (Gunsmith, Cutler, Silversmith)	BOSTON, MA	B1655, 1675-D1722
PETER CONIN Made tomahawks and scalping knives for the Indian trade. (Edged Weapon Maker)	PHILADELPHIA, PA	1755-1763
CONTINENTAL ARMORY (See U.S. Philadelphia Armory)		
JACOB COOK Adv. repairing and cleaning of swords, pistols, and guns (1798). (Gunsmith, Cutler, Blacksmith)	LANCASTER, PA RICHMOND, VA LANCASTER, PA	1778-1798 1798-1801 1801-1813
JACABUS COOPER Operated a blacksmith shop, which became a part of the U.S. armory and depot at Fishkill during the Revolutionary War. (See U.S. Fishkill Armory) (Armorer)	FISHKILL, NY	1755-1783
EVAN COPE (Cutler, Edged Tool Maker)	WASHINGTON TOWNSHIP, PA Fayette County	1825-1840
HIRAM COPE (Cutler, Edged Tool Maker)	WASHINGTON TOWNSHIP, PA Fayette County	1825-1840
SAMUEL COPE (Cutler, Edged Tool Maker)	WASHINGTON TOWNSHIP, PA Fayette County	1786-1808

NOAH COPLY	**PAXTANG TOWNSHIP, PA** Dauphin County	**1749-1759**

(Blacksmith, Cutler)

ABRAHAM CORK (CORL)	**CHESTER CO., PA**	**B1779, 1803-D1842**

(Silversmith, Gunsmith, Watch Maker, Clock
   Maker, Cutler)

JOHN COTTEN	**PHILADELPHIA, PA**	**1779**

Blacksmith and artillery artificer at the U.S.
   Philadelphia Armory.
(Cutler, Edged Tool Maker, Blacksmith)

RICHARD COTTEN	**FAYETTE CO., PA**	**1784-1815**

(Cutler, Edged Tool Maker)

ROBERT COTTEN	**FAYETTE CO., PA**	**1784-1815**

(Cutler, Edged Tool Maker)

ABEL COUTTY	**TIVERTON,** **DEVONSHIRE, ENGLAND** **PHILADELPHIA, PA**	**B1655-1695** **1695-D1711**

Benjamin Chandlee Sr. apprenticed to Coutty.
(See Benjamin Chandlee Sr.)
(Silversmith, Clock Maker)

JACOB COUTTY	**PHILADELPHIA, PA**	**1661**

(Gunsmith)

SAMUEL COUTTY	**PHILADELPHIA, PA** Dock Ward	**1769-1780**
PERKINS (JOSEPH) & COUTTY (SAMUEL)	**PHILADELPHIA, PA** Dock Ward	**1780-1782**

Repaired arms for Commonwealth of Pennsylvania.
Made flintlock pistols.

SAMUEL COUTTY	**PHILADELPHIA, PA** Dock Ward	**1783-D1795**

(See Joseph Perkins)
(Pistol Maker, Gunsmith)

C. COWAN	**PITTSBURGH, PA**	**1800-1819**

Bought out by Stackpole & Whiting (1816-1819).

R. (RYAR) BOWAN, JR.	**PITTSBURGH, PA**	**1819-1826**

Bought out Stackpole & Whiting (1819).
Made axes, knives, and tomahawks.
Had a slitting and tilt hammer mill.
(See William Stackpole)
(Cutlery Maker)

WILLIAM D. COWAN	**PHILADELPHIA, PA**	**1800-1815**

(Silversmith)

EBENEZER COWELL	**ALLENTOWN, PA** Northampton County	**1755, 1775-1779**

Committee of Safety musket and bayonet
  maker (1775-1777).
Supervisor at Pennsylvania Gunlock Factory
  (1777-1779).

	PHILADELPHIA, PA	**1779-1783**

(Gunsmith)

ROBERT COWELL	**PHILADELPHIA, PA**	**1757-1777**

(Silversmith)

JOHN COWLEY
Cutler to Major Joseph Shipper's Company, 2nd Battalion,
  of the Pennsylvania Regiment of Militia (1757).
(Cutler)

ALBION COX (Silversmith)	**PHILADELPHIA, PA**	**1760-D1795**
ANDREW COX (Blacksmith)	**PHILADELPHIA, PA**	**1760**
CLAUDIUS M. COX	**PHILADELPHIA, PA**	**1790-1820**

Naval pike maker for Daniel Pettibone (1812-1814).
Contract for 200 naval pikes with state of
  Pennsylvania (1814).
(See Daniel Pettibone)
(Cutler, Pikemaker)

ISAAC COX	**PHILADELPHIA, PA**	**1775-1783**

Sold 24 cutlasses (sabers) to Capt. Robert Towers,
  Commissary of Military Stores, Philadelphia Armory (1775).
(Sword Maker)

WILLIAM COX (Pewterer)	**PHILADELPHIA, PA**	**1715-1720**

JOHN COXEY
(See William Rose Jr.)

AARON CRAWFORD
(See Henry Saurbier)

HENRY CROFORD (CRAWFORD)	**IRELAND** **NEW YORK, NY**	**B1791-1820** **1820-1833**

Made belt knives.
(Cutler)

JOHN CRAWFORD	**NEW YORK, NY** **PHILADELPHIA, PA**	**1820-1835** **1835-1850**

(Silversmith)

JOHN S. CRAWFORD
(See Henry Saurbier)

HENRY W. CRESSMAN   PHILADELPHIA, PA   1806-1845
Started as a shoe maker.
Changed to leather military caps during the War of 1812.
Made some scabbards for Ames M1832 foot artillery swords.

JAMES CUNNINGHAM   RICHMOND, VA   1775-1783
Committee of Safety musket
  and bayonet maker (1776).
(Gunsmith)

JOHN CUNNINGHAM   HARTFORD CO., MD   1775-1783
Partner: Isaac Thomas.
Committee of Safety musket
  and bayonet maker (1776).
(Gunsmith)

JESSE CURTIS   WATERBURY, CT   1775-1783
Partner: Thomas Fancher.
Committee of Safety musket
  and bayonet maker (1778-1779).
(Gunsmith)

JOHN CUTLER   BOSTON, MA   1740-1760
Adv. bayonets (1757).
(Gunsmith, Blacksmith)

JOHN A. DAHLGREN   PHILADELPHIA, PA   B1809, 1829-D1870
Invented Dahlgren bayonet.

RICHARD DALHOUSE   BALTIMORE, MD   1775-1783
Committee of Safety musket
  and bayonet maker (1776).
(Gunsmith)

RICHARD DALLAM   HARTFORD CO., MD   1775-1783
Committee of Safety musket and
  bayonet maker (1776).
(Gunsmith)

JOHN DARRAUGH (DARE)   LANCASTER, PA   1760-1776
                                         PHILADELPHIA, PA   1776-1790

Apprenticed to gunsmith
  Joseph Simons (1776-1780).
(See Joseph Simons)
(Silversmith, Gunsmith, Cutler)

BAPTISTE DARTNELL   PHILADELPHIA, PA   1799-1800
(Cutler)

JACOB DAUB   PHILADELPHIA, PA   1775-1783
(Blacksmith, Cutler)

JOHN DAVIDSON Made sword scabbards, slings, cartouche boxes, and sword belts for Pennsylvania Committee of Safety. (Leather Shop)	PHILADELPHIA, PA	1775-1783
JAMES DAVIS Armorer at U.S. Philadelphia Armory.	PHILADELPHIA, PA	1778
MORRIS DAVIS (Blacksmith)	TREDYFFRIN, PA Chester County	1750-1771
THOMAS DAVIS (Cutler, Pewterer)	PHILADELPHIA, PA	1750-1760
JOHN DAWSON (Goldsmith)	PHILADELPHIA, PA	1767
JOHN DAWSON Armorer in Pennsylvania Navy. (Armorer)	PHILADELPHIA, PA	1775-1783
PAUL DAWSON Sword maker for Lewis Prahl. (See Lewis Prahl) (Sword Maker)	PHILADELPHIA, PA	1776-1783
WILLIAM DAWSON (Cutler, Edged Tools, Blacksmith)	PHILADELPHIA, PA North Ward	1749-1783
CHARLES DEGENHARDT	CHICAGO, IL	1838-1861
DEGENHARDT (CHARLES), LOEWE (LUDWIG) & CO. Partner: George Tolle. Made sword bayonets.	CHICAGO, IL	1861-1863
TOLLE (GEORGE) & DEGENHARDT (CHARLES)	CHICAGO, IL	1863-1869
CHARLES DEGENHARDT CO. (Cutler, Surgical Instrument Maker)	CHICAGO, IL	1869-1870
HUGH DEHAVEN Committee of Safety musket and bayonet maker (1775). Assist. Superintendent at Pennsylvania State Gun Factory (1776-1779).	PHILADELPHIA, PA	1755-1779
PETER DEHAVEN SR. Immigrated from France. Set up musket factory.	PHILADELPHIA, PA	1730-1750
PETER DEHAVEN JR. Sold gunlocks to Lewis Prahl (1776). Superintendant at Pennsylvania State Gun Factory (1776-1779).	PHILADELPHIA, PA	1750-1779

DEHAVEN (PETER) & WELLS (RICHARD)	PHILADELPHIA, PA	1779
PETER DEHAVEN	PHILADELPHIA, PA	1779-1780

Appointed Health Officer, Fort of Philadelphia.
(See Lewis Prahl)
(See Pennsylvania State Gun Factory)
(Gunsmith)

ED (EDMUND) DEMOULIN & BROTHER (ULYSSES)
SABASTOPOL, IL   1892-1900

The DeMoulin family immigrated to the United
 States from France (1849) and eventually settled in
 Sabastopol, IL (1892).

	GREENVILLE, IL	1900-1905
DEMOULIN BROS.	GREENVILLE, IL	1905-1991

Partners: Ulysses DeMoulin, Edmund DeMoulin,
 Evastus DeMoulin.
Put out fraternal goods catalogs.
Leslie DeMoulin joined in the 1920s.
William Demoulin, son of Leslie DeMoulin, joined (1938).
Richard DeMoulin, son of William DeMoulin, joined in 1980s.
Made all kinds of fraternal and society regalia and costumes.
Made uniforms of all kinds: military, circus, police, school bands, etc.
(Regalia, Uniforms, Cutlers)

WILLIAM DENT   FAYETTEVILLE, NY   1770-1792

Committee of Safety musket and bayonet maker.
(Gunsmith)

HEINRICH DEINEGER SR.	SOLINGEN, GERMANY	B1756-1769
	PHILADELPHIA, PA	1769-1786

Changed his name to Henry Derringer.

HENRY DERRINGER SR.	EASTON, PA	1786-1806
	PHILADELPHIA, PA	1806-D1833

(Gunsmith)

HENRY DERRINGER JR.   EASTON, PA   B1786-1806
Son of Henry Derringer Sr.

	PHILADELPHIA, PA	1806-1807
	RICHMOND, VA	1807-1808

Worked at the Virginia Manufactory making rifle
 parts and assembling and engraving rifles.
Made patch boxes.

PHILADELPHIA, PA   1808-D1868

- State of Maryland contract for cavalry sabers (1812).
- Adv. swords and cutlasses (1812).
- Bid on U.S. Navy cutlass contract (1816).
- Adv. rifles, guns, pistols, and swords (1831).
- Made Deringer pocket pistols (1841-1860).
- Made 1,000 pairs of pistols (1850).
- Made 500 pairs of pistols (1860).
- Had 15 U.S. government contracts for rifles and muskets.
- Gun makers for Derringer:
    E.G. Owens (1850-1863)
    Henry Slotterbeck (1852-1858)

Frederick Slotterbeck (1852-1858)
Charles Slotterbeck (1852-1858)
(Gunsmith, Sword Maker, Pistol Maker)

PETER JOHANN DERR	SCHAEFFERSTOWN, JEFFERSON TOWNSHIP, PA Berks County	B1793, 1815-D1868

Made knives and edged tools.
(Cutler, Brass Founder, Edged Tool Maker, Blacksmith)

SAMUEL DEWEY	HEBRON, CT	1774-1783

Committee of Safety musket and bayonet maker (1775-1776).
(Gunsmith)

JOHN DEVANE	WILMINGTON, NC New Hanover County	B1757, 1777-D1832

The North Carolina State Gun Factory (1776-1777).
Owners: John Devane, Richard Herring.
Factory destroyed by English (1777).
John Devane was a U.S. Army Captain (1777-1783).

ANTHONY DEVERNAYS	CHARLESTON, SC	1785-1798

(Gunsmith)

FRANCIS (FRANCOIS) DEVERNAYS	CHARLESTON, SC	1775-1777
FRANCIS DEVERNAYS & EMANUEL PINCALL	CHARLESTON, SC	1777-1798

(See Emanuel Pincall)
(Armorer, Gunsmith, Tinners, Cutlers)

GEORGE DEWSNAP	PITTSBURGH, PA	1800-1821
	PITTSBURGH, PA	1821-1824

Employee of John Thornhill (1818-1821).

Made all kinds of standard knives.
Made razors, gunlocks, and firearms,
 as well as currier's and surgeon's knives.
Also gunsmith, saddler, watch maker, and shoe maker.
(See John Thornhill)
(Cutler, Knife Maker, Gunsmith)

MAJ. CHARLES DICK
(See Fredericksburg Manufactory)

WALTER DICK	LONDON, ENGLAND	1754-1774
	CHARLESTON, SC	1774-D1781

(Gunsmith, Cutler, Surgical Instruments)

ANDREW DICKEY	WASHINGTON CO., PA	1796-1800

(Cutler, Edged Tools)

DAVID DICKEY	LONDON, ENGLAND	B1753-1775
	NEW YORK, NY	1775-1778
	MIDDLETOWN TOWNSHIP, PA Cumberland County	1778-1790

| | SALEM TOWNSHIP, PA
Westmoreland County | 1790-D1791 |

(Clock Maker, Gunsmith, Cutler)

MOSES DICKEY   SALEM TOWNSHIP, PA   1790-1810
                                           Westmoreland County

David's brother.
(Clock Maker, Gunsmith, Cutler)

THOMAS DICKEY   HARRISBURG, PA   1790-1810
                                           Dauphin County
                                           WATERFORD,
                                           DONEGAL TOWNSHIP, PA   1810-1814
                                           Lancaster County
                                           MARIELLA, PA   1814-1825
                                           Lancaster County

(Silversmith, Clock Maker)

WILLIAM DICKEY   LOUISBERG, PA   1766-1786
                                           Dauphin County

(Silversmith, Clock Maker)

ANTHONY DIKE   BRIDGEWATER, MA   1775-1783
Committee of Safety musket and bayonet maker (1775-1777).
(Gunsmith)

JAMES G. DILLON   CHAMBERSBURG, PA   1805-1825
                                           BEDFORD, PA   1825-1845

(Silversmith, Gunsmith, Clock Maker, Watch
Maker, Cutler)

ROBERT DINGEE SR.   NEW YORK, NY   1780-1803
DINGEE (ROBERT SR.) & UNDERHILL
                                           NEW YORK, NY   1803-1805
ROBERT DINGEE SR.   NEW YORK, NY   1806-D1843
• Started as saddler and harness maker.
• Branched into military leather caps and accoutrements.
• U.S. contract for 1,000 naval cutlasses with scabbards (1830).
• Originally signed first contract for the M1832 foot artillery sword,
  but N.P. Ames eventually took over the contract.
• Later, he made the scabbards for Ames M1832 foot artillery swords.
(Military Leather Goods, Saddler, Military Insignia and Equipment)

HENRY DISSTON   TEWKEYESBURY, ENGLAND   B1819
• Thomas Disston (Henry's father) and Henry
  moved to Derby Nottingham in 1823 (lace machine
  factory). Thomas taught Henry the mechanical arts
  and how to make lace machines.
• The Disstons emigrated to Philadelphia, PA (1833).
                                           PHILADELPHIA, PA   1833-1842
Thomas Disston died three days after landing
  in Philadelphia.
Henry went to work for saw makers Lindley,
  Johnson, & Whitecraft (1833-1840).

	PHILADELPHIA, PA 21 Bread Street	1840-1843

Saw and tool maker.

	PHILADELPHIA, PA Corner of Second and Arch Streets	1843-1846

Set up a steam-powered saw and tool factory. Made his own factory tools.

	PHILADELPHIA, PA Corner of Third and Arch Streets	1846-1848
	PHILADELPHIA, PA Maiden Street below Front	1848-1851

Had 20 anvils making saws and tools.

	PHILADELPHIA, PA 67 Laurel Street	1851-1864

- Took a trip to Europe (1856) and began to sell his products there (eventually in England, Ireland, Austria, Germany, and Russia).
- Set up a steel-rolling mill (1862).
- During the Civil War, Disston made:
  - Cavalry sabers
  - Guns and bayonets
  - Ammunition
  - Cavalry bits
  - Saws and tools
  - Steel plate for U.S. Navy ships
  - Other metal products

HENRY DISSTON & SONS   PHILADELPHIA, PA   1864-c1900
                             67 and 69 Laurel Street

- Partners and sons: Hamilton Disston, Albert Disston.
- Built a new factory after the old one burned down (1864).
- Eventually his factory complex became a town.
- By 1875, he had 200 anvils working.
- Henry Disston died (1878).
- His sons Hamilton and Albert took over the company.
- The company stock was divided among the 35 family members.

	PHILADELPHIA, PA 6795 State Road	c1900-1963

- During World War I, the Disston Co. designed and made M1917 trench knives. It also made Marine Corps machettes.
- During World War II, when the company was at its height with 12,000 employees, Disston made tanks, tank armor, steel protection for aircraft seats, and heat-treated steel for war materials.
- After the war, the machinery was worn out and sales were poor.
- The Disston family sold the company to the H.K. Porter Co. (1955).
- Porter modernized the company, sold off unprofitable steel mills and lumber yards, and bought new machinery.
- Porter saw the company grow rapidly with the sale of a new cordless grass shear.
- Porter went public (1963).

DISSTON INC.   PHILADELPHIA, PA   1963-1984
                     6795 State Road

Porter sold out to Sandvick Steel Co., Stockholm, Sweden (1974).

U.S. Sword Makers

Disston Inc. became a division of Sandvick Steel.
Sandvick sold Disston to Robert A. Fox (1984).

DISSTON PRECISION INC.	**PHILADELPHIA, PA** 6795 State Road	**1984-1993**

Owner: Robert A. Fox
Make specialty saws.

SAMUEL DORSEY	**ELKRIDGE, MD**	**1775-1783**

Committee of Safety contract for 500 bayonets (1776).

WILLIAM H. DREW	**BUFFALO, NY**	**1850-1860**

(Regalia, Society Swords)

AARON DUBS	**LOWER MILFORD TOWNSHIP, PA** Bucks County	**1810-D1874**

Son of John Dubs.
(Cutler, Blacksmith, Machine Shop, Edged Tools)

DANIEL DUBS	**LOWER MILFORD TOWNSHIP, PA** Bucks County	**1772-1824**

Son of Jacob Dubs.
(Cutler, Blacksmith, Machine Shop, Edged Tools)

JACOB DUBS (DUBBS)	**ZURICH, SWITZERLAND**	**B1710-1732**
	PHILADELPHIA, PA	**1732-1733**
	LOWER MILFORD TOWNSHIP, PA Bucks County	**1733-D1772**

(Cutler, Blacksmith, Machine Shop, Edged Tools)

JOHN DUBS	**LOWER MILFORD TOWNSHIP, PA** Bucks County	**B1788-1844**

Son of Daniel Dubs.
(Cutler, Blacksmith, Machine Shop, Edged Tools)

JAMES DUNBAR	**CANTON, MA**	**B1787-1813**
DUNBAR (JAMES) & LEONARD (SAMUEL)	**CANTON, MA**	**1813-1816**

- Partners: Brother William Dunbar, James Bent.
- U.S. contract for 500 non-comm. swords (April 1813).
- U.S. contract for 1,000 non-comm. swords (August 1813).
- Bid on U.S. government navy cutlass contract (1816).

JAMES DUNBAR	**CANTON, MA**	**1816-D1867**

- (See Samuel Leonard)
- (See James Bent)
- (Sword Maker, Cutler)

WILLIAM DUNWICK	**CHESTER CO., PA**	**1755-1780**

Committee of Safety musket and bayonet maker and arms repair (1775-1776).

(Gunsmith)	**PHILADELPHIA, PA**	**1780-1790**

C.T. EAMES	**MEDWAY, MA**	**1820-1840**

Made spontoons for Medway Mass Militia (1838).

ELIAS EARLE	**CENTREVILLE, SC**	**1800-1820**

U.S. contract for 10,000 bayonets (1815);
 shipped only 1,500.
Contract taken over by Adam Carruth.
(Gunsmith)

ADAM EBERLE	**PITTSBURGH, PA**	**1790-1815**

(Silversmith)

CHARLES EBERLE	**PHILADELPHIA, PA**	**1780-1808**

Arms inspector at the U.S. Philadelphia Armory
 (1807-1808).
Inspected some William Rose 1807 contract cavalry
 sabers.
(Cutler, Gunsmith)

GEORGE EBERLE	**PHILADELPHIA, PA**	**1780-1798**

Son of Henry.

GEORGE & HENRY EBERLE	**PHILADELPHIA, PA**	**1799**
GEORGE EBERLE	**PHILADELPHIA, PA**	**1800-1805**

(Cutler, Gunsmith)

HENRY EBERLE	**ELIZABETHTOWN, PA** Lancaster County	**1745-1783**

Bayonet and knife maker to Pennsylvania
 Committee of Safety (1775-1783).

	PETERSBURG, PA Huntington County	**1783-1799**

Operated Barree Forge.
Partner and son: Jacob Eberle.

GEORGE & HENRY EBERLE	**PHILADELPHIA, PA**	**1799**
HENRY EBERLE	**PHILADELPHIA, PA**	**1800-D1822**

(Cutler, Gunsmith)

JACOB EBERLE	**ELIZABETHTOWN, PA** Lancaster County	**1763-1783**

Son of Henry.

	PETERSBURG, PA Huntington County	**1783-D1861**

Worked with father Henry at Barree Forge (1783-1799).
(Cutler, Gunsmith)

JOHN EBERLE	**ELIZABETHTOWN, PA** Lancaster County	**1760-1780**

Worked for William Henry Sr. (1775-1777).
(Cutler, Gunsmith)

S.E. EBY	**PHILADELPHIA, PA**	**1925-1946**

Made West Point U.S. Military Academy cadet swords.
(Cutler, Sword Maker)

GEORGE ELGIN	**NEW YORK, NY**	**1825-1840**

Patented a cutlass-pistol (1837).
Pistol fabricators: C.B. Allen, Springfield, MA;
  Morrill, Mosman, & Blair, Amherst, MA.
Ames Mfg. Co. made the blades.
(See C.B. Allen)
(See Morrill, Mosman, & Blair)

ANDREW ELLICOTT	**BUCKINGHAM, PA** Bucks County	**B1754, 1765-D1820**

Son of Joseph Ellicott.
(Clock Maker, Surveying Instrument Maker, Cutler)

JOSEPH ELLICOTT	**BUCKINGHAM, PA** Bucks County	**B1732-1766**

Went to England (1767)

	ENGLAND	**1767-1768**
	BALTIMORE, MD	**1769-D1782**

Made 10 horsemen's swords per week for the
  Maryland Committee of Safety (1781-1782).
Built and operated an iron foundry.
Had flour and cotton mills also.
(Clock Maker, Sword Maker, Silversmith, Iron Founder)

MARTIN ELY	**SPRINGFIELD, MA**	**1770-1783**

Committee of Safety musket and bayonet maker (1776).
(Gunsmith)

JAMES E. EMERSON	**BEAVER FALLS, PA**	**1810-1830**
EMERSON (JAMES E.) SMITH & CO.	**BEAVER FALLS, PA**	**1830-1860**

Invented a new knife-making process.

EMERSON (JAMES E.) & SILVER (JOSEPH S.)	**TRENTON, NJ**	**1860-1865**

- Had New York offices (1860-1864).
- Owners of the Keystone Edged Tool Works
  Factory in Philadelphia, PA.
- Owners of the Malleable Iron Works Factory in
  Trenton, NJ (all swords made at Trenton).
- Made plows, axes, edged tools, knives, spades,
  bayonets, U.S. regulation swords, Masonic swords, and regalia.
- Adv. regulation, presentation, and Masonic swords;
  sword belts and hangers; banners; Masonic jewelry;
  regalia; sword cases; and edged tools in the *Army-Navy Journal* (1864).
- Their early 1864 advertisement showed they had an office
  at 447 Broom Street, New York, NY, and their late 1864
  advertisement showed they had agents Schuyler, Hartley, & Graham
  in New York, NY.
- Displayed presenation swords at the New York Fair (1864).
- Sold sword blades to George W. Simons & Brother, Philadelphia, PA.
- (See George W. Simons—Dealer listing)
- (See Schuyler Hartley & Graham—Dealer listing)

(Farm and Edged Tools, Bayonets, U.S. Regulation and Masonic Swords,
  Masonic Regalia, Military Goods)

JOSEPH S. SILVER & CO.	**NEW YORK, NY**	1865-1866

Partner: James E. Emerson.
Still owned the Malleable Iron Works and the Keystone Edged Tool Factory.

JOSEPH S. SILVER JR.	**NEW YORK, NY**	1866-1868

(Farm and Edged Tools, Regalia)

Emerson & Silver Civil War Edged Weapon Production

U.S. contract for 20,000 bayonets of the James E. Emerson patent (1862).
U.S. contracts for 27,060 M1860 cavalry sabers.
U.S. contracts for 3,000 M1840 musician's swords.
U.S. contracts for 12,000 M1840 non-comm. swords.
U.S. contract for M1840 lt. artillery saber in 1863.
Some M1840 lt. artillery sabers used M1860 cavalry sword blades.
Made M1850 foot officers swords.
Made M1850 staff and field officer swords.
Made many presentation swords.
Imported British infantry honeysuckle-hilt officer swords.

THE ENGLES FAMILY
Engle-Ingles-Ingle-Engels-Ingalls

BARNEY ENGLES	**GREENSBORO, PA** Green County	1833-1875

Son of Peter Engles Jr.
(Gunsmith)

CHRISTIAN ENGLES	**GREENSBORO, PA** Green County	1825-1849

Son of Peter Engles Jr.
(Gunsmith)

EZRA ENGLES SR.	**GREENSBORO, PA** Green County	1791-1848

Son of Peter Engles Sr.
(Gunsmith)

EZRA ENGLES JR.	**GREENSBORO, PA** Green County	1815-1838

Son of Ezra Engles Sr.
(Gunsmith)

GEORGE ENGLES	**SOLINGEN, GERMANY**	1775-1796
	PHILADELPHIA, PA	1796-1802
	RICHMOND, VA	1802-1803

Worked at the Virginia Manufactory.

	PHILADELPHIA, PA	1803-1805

Military storekeeper at the U.S. Schuylkill Armory.

	PETERSBURG, VA	1805-1807

(Gunsmith, Whitesmith, Cutler)

JACOB ENGLES	**SOLINGEN, GERMANY**	**1779-1796**
	PHILADELPHIA, PA	**1796-1802**
	RICHMOND, VA	**1802**

Worked at the Virginia Manufactory repairing arms, filing musketlocks, and making tools.
(Gunsmith)

JOHN ENGLES — **MONOCACY, MD** — **1735-1800**
(Gunsmith)

MICHAEL ENGLES — **READINGS, PA** — **1757-1777**
PHILADELPHIA, PA — **1777**

Blacksmith and brass founder at U.S. Philadelphia Armory.

LEBANON, PA — **1777-1781**

Blacksmith and brass founder at U.S. Lebanon Armory.
(Blacksmith, Brass Founder, Cutler)

PETER ENGLES SR. — **MONOCACY, MD** — **1755-1790**
GREENSBORO, PA — **1790-1833**

Son of John Engles.
(Gunsmith)

PETER ENGLES JR. — **MONOCACY, MD** — **1785-1790**
GREENSBORO, PA — **1790-1845**

Son of Peter Engles Sr.
(Gunsmith)

DAVID P. ESTEP — **PITTSBURGH, PA** — **1856-1860**
(Edged Tool Maker, Knife Maker)

E. (EPHRAIM) ESTEP — **LAWRENCEVILLE, PETERS TOWNSHIP, PA** — **1809-1838**
Allegheny County

E. (EPHRAIM) ESTEP & CO. — **LAWRENCEVILLE, PETERS TOWNSHIP, PA** — **1838-1842**
Allegheny County

Partner and son: David P. Estep.
Offices in Pittsburgh, PA.

ESTEP (EPHRAIM) & MORGAN — **PITTSBURGH, PA** — **1842-1844**
E. (EPHRAIM) ESTEP & SONS — **PITTSBURGH, PA** — **1844-1856**

The factory was called "Lawrenceville Works."
Manager: George Cochran.
Partners: David P. Estep Jr., Robert Estep.
Offices in Pittsburgh, PA.
(Edged Tool Makers, Knife Makers)

EPHRAIM ESTEP JR. — **PITTSBURGH, PA** — **1856-1860**
(Edged Tool Maker, Knife Maker)

ROBERT ESTEP — **PITTSBURGH, PA** — **1856-1860**
(Edged Tool Maker, Knife Maker)

THE EVERTS FAMILY
Ebert-Eberts-Ebertz-Everts-Everett

ADAM EVERTZ (Gunsmith)	LEHIGH CO., PA	1810-1822
CHARLES EVERTZ (Silversmith)	LANCASTER, PA	1783-1792
GEORGE EVERTZ (Coppersmith)	UNIONTOWN, PA Fayette County	B1754, 1744-D1827
GEORGE JOHN EVERTZ (Gunsmith)	NORTHAMPTON CO., PA	1800-1807
JAMES EVERTZ (Tinsmith)	UNIONTOWN, PA Fayette County	1824-1844
(JOHANN) JOHN EVERTZ Changed name to Everett.	SOLINGEN, GERMANY	1776-1796
	PHILADELPHIA, PA RICHMOND, VA	1796-1821 1821
Worked at the Virginia Armory hardening and polishing musket parts (1821). (Gunsmith)		
SAMUEL EVERTZ Changed name to Everett.	SOLINGEN, GERMANY	1776-1796
	PHILADELPHIA, PA RICHMOND, VA	1796-1803 1803
Worked at Virginia Manufactory filing and grinding musket mounts and making tools (1803). (Gunsmith)		
BENJAMIN EVANS Son of David Evans. Apprenticed to Benjamin Rittenhouse (1785-1801).	PHILADELPHIA, PA	B1770-1801
(Clock Maker, Surveying Equipment Maker, Silversmith)	CHESTER CO., PA	1801-D1836
DANIEL EVANS Apprentice: William Bowers (1773-1780). Armorer and tomahawk maker to Committee of Safety (1775-1783). (Blacksmith, Whitesmith, Cutler, Armorer)	PHILADELPHIA, PA	1753-1783
DAVID EVANS (Gunsmith, Blacksmith, Goldsmith, Silversmith, Clock Maker)	PHILADELPHIA, PA BALTIMORE, MD	1756-1776 1776-1796

GEORGE EVANS SR. | LONDON, ENGLAND | 1776-1796
| PHILADELPHIA, PA | 1796-D1798
(Edged Weapons, Cutler, Surgical Instrument Maker)

GEORGE EVANS & CO. | PHILADELPHIA, PA | 1885-1905
Made swords and edged weapons.
(Swordsmith)

ISRAEL EVANS | PHILADELPHIA, PA | 1775-1781
(Blacksmith, Cutler)

JOSEPH EVANS | PHILADELPHIA, PA | 1756-1785
Apprenticed to Daniel DuPuy & Son (1772-1779).
(Silversmith, Clock Maker)

JOSHUA EVANS | CHESTER CO., PA | 1766
(Blacksmith)

LEWIS EVANS | PHILADELPHIA, PA | 1766-1786
(Silversmith)

OLIVER EVANS | PHILADELPHIA, PA | 1791-1796
Apprenticed to John Fitch.
(Silversmith, Clock Maker)

PETER EVANS | PHILADELPHIA, PA | 1757-1780
| North Ward
Made edged weapons and bayonets.
(Cutler)

SEPTIMUS EVANS | HILLTOWN, PA | 1795-1810
(Clock Maker) | Bucks County

WILLIAM EVANS | PHILADELPHIA, PA | 1795-1848
(Silversmith, Clock Maker)

THOMAS FANCHER | WATERBURY, CT | 1775-1783
Partner: Jesse Curtis.
Committee of Safety musket and bayonet maker
 (1778-1779).
(Gunsmith)

THOMAS FARR | CHARLESTON, SC | 1775-1783
Made naval pikes for South Carolina Committee
 of Safety during the Revolutionary War.
(Pike Maker)

MARTIN FENSEL | UNION CO., OH | 1820-1826
(Gunsmith)

PETER FENSEL | UNION CO., OH | B1842-1857
Son of Martin Fensel.

| KENTON, OH | 1857-1887
| MARYSVILLE, OH | 1887-D1930

(Gun Maker, Cutler)

JOSEPH FENTON Made belt knives. (Cutler)	FRANKLIN, OH	1840-1865
JOEL FERREE	LANCASTER, PA LEACOCK TOWNSHIP, PA Lancaster County	B1731-1752 1752-D1784
Committee of Safety musket and bayonet maker (1775). (Gunsmith)		
CONRAD FESIG (Blacksmith, Clock Maker)	READINGS, PA Berks County	1760-1815
PETER FESIG Son of Conrad Fesig. (Silversmith, Gunsmith, Cutler)	READINGS, PA Berks County	1780-1790
JACOB FESSLER Committee of Safety contract for 50 bayonets (1781). (Cutler, Silversmith, Clock Maker)	LANCASTER, PA	1775-1783
(JOHANN) JOHN JACOB FESSLER SR.	ZURICH, SWITZERLAND LANCASTER, PA FREDERICK, MD	B1757-1766 1766-1790 1790-D1820
Apprentice: John Meyers. (Cutler, Silversmith, Clock Maker)		
JOHN FESSLER JR. Son of (Johann) John Jacob Fessler Sr. (Cutler, Silversmith, Clock Maker)	FREDERICK, MD	1800-1830
JACOB FETTERS Blacksmith for U.S. Philadelphia Armory.	PHILADELPHIA, PA	1777
WILLIAM FETTERS Arms maker for Lewis Prahl. (See Lewis Prahl)	PHILADELPHIA, PA	1777
PHILIP FINK (Cutler, Knife Maker)	BETHEL TOWNSHIP, PA Lebanon County	1850
JOHN FITCH	EAST WINDSOR, CT EAST HARTFORD, NJ TRENTON, NJ	B1743-1763 1763-1769 1769-1776
Made files and metal buttons. Committee of Safety musket and bayonet maker and arms repair (1776). Gun shop burned down by British troops (1776).		
	WARMINSTER TOWNSHIP, PA Bucks County	1776-1788

Apprentice: Jacabus Scout
(Silversmith)

Rebuilt gun shop.
Made silver-hilted naval officer hangers and dirks.

Apprentice: Oliver Evans.

(Silversmith, Clock Maker, Dirk and Sword
 Maker, Gunsmith, Arms Repair, Mechanic,
 Steamboat Inventor)

	TRENTON, NJ	1788-1791
	PHILADELPHIA, PA	1791-1796
	BARDSTOWN, KY	1796-D1796

GEORGE FLEGAL

Apprentice to gunsmith George Kreps.

Gunsmith at the Virginia Manufactory.

Inspector of arms and master armorer at the
 U.S. Schuylkill Arsenal (1814-1826).
 Inspected some of William Rose's 1812
 non-comm. and cavalry swords.
(Gunsmith, Silversmith, Swordsmith, Armorer)

PHILADELPHIA, PA	1790-1810
HAGERSTOWN, MD	1806-1810
RICHMOND, VA	1810-1812
PHILADELPHIA, PA	1812-1835

MICHAEL FLORES

(Cutler, Edged Tools, Blacksmith)

WURTEMBERG, GERMANY	1720-1740
PHILADELPHIA, PA	1740-1763
LEHIGH CO., PA	1763-D1785

BENJAMIN FLOWERS
(See U.S. Philadelphia Armory)

HENRY FLOWER PHILADELPHIA, PA 1733-1766
Adv. gilding of sword hilts (1755).
(Silversmith, Watch Maker, Clock Maker)

SAMUEL FLOWER DURHAM TOWNSHIP, PA 1756-1790
Berks County

Owned and operated Durham Furnace.
(Iron Founder)

LUDWIG FOHRER PHILADELPHIA, PA 1775-1783
Committee of Safety Musket and bayonet
 maker and arms repair (1775-1776).
(Gunsmith)

ABRAHAM GERRITZE FORBES NEW YORK, NY 1765-1795
(Silversmith)

BENJAMIN G. FORBES NEW YORK, NY 1805-1825
**FORDHAM (MERIT) & FORBES
 (BENJAMIN G.)** NEW YORK, NY 1825-1830
(Silversmith)

COLIN VAN GILDER FORBES C. (COLIN VAN GILDER) & J.W. (JOHN WESLEY) FORBES	NEW YORK, NY	1790-1810
	NEW YORK, NY	1810-1825
COLIN VAN GILDER FORBES (Cutler, Edged Tools, Silversmith, Gunsmith)	NEW YORK, NY	1825-1840
GARRETT FORBES Son of William Garrett Forbes. (Swordhilter, Silversmith)	NEW YORK, NY	B1785, 1800-D1851
GILBERT FORBES Made axes, bayonets, muskets, and rifles. (Cutler, Silversmith, Gunsmith, Edged Tools)	NEW YORK, NY	1750-1776
JOHN WESLEY FORBES C. (COLIN VAN GILDER) FORBES & J.W. (JOHN WESLEY) FORBES	NEW YORK, NY	B1781-1810
	NEW YORK, NY	1810-1825
J.W. (JOHN WESLEY) FORBES	NEW YORK, NY	1825-1840
	WORCHESTER, MA	1840-D1864
Adv. scythes and rifles (1850). (Cutler, Edged Tools, Silversmith, Gunsmith)		
WILLIAM GARRETT FORBES FORBES (WILLIAM. GARRETT) & LOCKWOOD (JAMES)	NEW YORK, NY	B1751-1773
	NEW YORK, NY	1773-1799
WILLIAM GARRETT FORBES (Silversmith, Sword Hiltor)	NEW YORK, NY	1799-1835
GEORGE FORD SR. Son of Peter Ford. (Clock Maker, Surveying Equipment Maker)	LANCASTER, PA	B1773, 1800-D1843
GEORGE FORD JR. (Son of George Ford Sr.) (Silversmith)	LANCASTER, PA	B1811, 1825-D1864
JOHN FORD SR. Son of Peter Ford. Armorer to Commonwealth of Pennsylvania. (Gunsmith, Silversmith)	HARRISBURG, PA Dauphin County	B1780, 1801-D1862
MATTHEW FORD Armorer to the armed boat *Dickinson*. (Armorer)	PHILADELPHIA, PA	1775-1783
PETER FORD	LIVERPOOL, ENGLAND	1750-1770
	YORK CO., PA	1770-1790
(Silversmith, Clock Maker)		
SAMUEL FORD	PHILADELPHIA, PA	1770-1801
	BALTIMORE, MD	1801-1803

Made Colichmarde-bladed small swords.
(Silversmith, Sword Hiltor)

WILLIAM FORD   PHILADELPHIA, PA   1810-1830
(Silversmith)

WALTER FORTUNE   PHILADELPHIA, PA   1795-1816
    PITTSBURGH, PA   1816-1826

(Blacksmith, Whitesmith, Cutler, Edged Tools)

WILLIAM FOSBROOK   NEW YORK, NY   1768-1792
Bought James Potter's stock of horsemen's swords
  and blades when he went out of business (1782).
Adv. Potter's light horse swords (1789).
Adv. light horse sword blades (1792).
FOSBROOK (WILLIAM) SMITH (THOMAS)
  & ANDERSON (JAMES)   NEW YORK, NY   1793-1794
FOSBROOK (WILLIAM) & SMITH (THOMAS)   NEW YORK, NY   1795-1796
(See James Anderson)
(See Thomas Smith)
(Cutler, Surgical Instrument Maker)

ADAM FOULKES
(See John Young)

JOHN FOX   PHILADELPHIA, PA   1748-1775
    READING, PA   1775-1776
    Berks County

Apprentice: Peter Cribs.
Repaired arms for the Philadelphia Committee
  of Safety (1776).
(Cutler, Gunsmith, Blacksmith)

PATRICK FOX   PHILADELPHIA, PA   1779
Armorer at the U.S. Philadelphia Armory.
(See Philadelphia Armory)
(Armorer)

HENRY FOXALL   BALTIMORE, MD   1779-1800
Made 100 boarding pikes for the ship *Adams* (1799).
(Pike Maker)

JOSEPH FRANCKLEBERRY   PHILADELPHIA, PA   1777
Sword maker for Lewis Prahl.
(Swordsmith)

FRATERNAL SUPPLIES INC.
(See C.E. Ward)

JACOB FREY (FRY)   PHILADELPHIA, PA   1777-1779
Swordsmith for Lewis Prahl.
Artillery artificer at the U.S. Philadelphia Armory (1779).
(See Lewis Prahl)
(Swordsmith)

NATHAN FRINK GOSHEN, CT 1775-1783
Committee of Safety musket and bayonet maker.
Partners: Elisha Child, Benjamin Cargill.
(See Elisha Child & Benjamin Cargill)
(Gunsmith)

GIDEON FROST BOSTON, MA 1775-1783
Frost Gun Works.
Employee: Benjamin Guillam.
Committee of Safety musket and bayonet maker.
(Gunsmith)

FULLER REGALIA & COSTUME CO. WORCHESTER, MA 1895-1903
(Regalia, Society Swords, Uniforms, Flags)

ROBERT FULTON LANCASTER, PA 1760-1790
Committee of Safety musket
 and bayonet maker (1779).
(Silversmith, Gunsmith, Watch Maker)

JACOB FUNK MUSKINGUM CO., OH 1790-1816
(Gun Maker, Sword Maker)

CAPT. FURNAM PHILADELPHIA, PA 1775-1783
Sold 19 cutlasses and 7 pair of pistols to
 Capt. Robert Towers, Commissionary of
 Military Stores at the Philadelphia Armory (1775).
(Sword Maker, Pistol Maker)

JACOB GABBOTT
(See Joshua Humphreys)

LUCIAN GABLE RICHMOND, IN 1840-1865
 Wayne County

Patented a sword-pistol (1862).

ALBERT GALLATIN
(See Melchoir Baker)

CHARLES GAMBLE PHILADELPHIA, PA 1845-1860
(Silversmith, Clock Maker)

ROBERT GAMBLE AYR TOWNSHIP, PA 1800-1820
  BEDFORD CO., PA 1820-1825

(Silversmith, Clock Maker)

COL. ROBERT GAMBLE RICHMOND, VA 1780-1810
Sent three sample cavalry sabers to Virginia
 Governor Monroe (1800).
Supplied many iron and steel products to the
 Virginia Manufactory (1802-1806).
(Sword Maker)

THOMAS GAMBLE
(See Boyle & Gamble Confederate listings)

AMOS GARRETT	HARTFORD COUNTY, MD	1775-1783

Committee of Safety musket
 and bayonet maker (1776).
Contract to make 47 bayonets (1776).
Operated a saltpeter factory (1776).
Also did gun repair.
(Gunsmith)

BENJAMIN GARRETT	GOSHEN, PA Chester County	B1771, 1800-D1856

(Silversmith, Clock Maker)

HERMAN GARRETT	BOSTON, MA	1650-1683

Armorer to the Colony of Massachusetts.
(Gunsmith, Swordsmith)

MATTHEW GARRETT	UPPER DARBY TOWNSHIP, PA Chester County	1760-1779

Son of William Garrett.

WILLIAM GARRETT & SON (MATTHEW)	UPPER DARBY TOWNSHIP, PA	1779-1785

(Sword and Blade Maker, Blacksmith)

PHILIP GARRETT	PHILADELPHIA, PA	B1780-1822

Son of Thomas Garrett.

WARD (JOHN) & GARRETT (PHILIP)	PHILADELPHIA, PA	1822-1824
PHILIP GARRETT & SON (THOMAS C.)	PHILADELPHIA, PA	1824-1835
PHILIP GARRETT	PHILADELPHIA, PA	1835-D1851

(See John Ward-Silversmith listings)
(Silversmith, Clock Maker,
 Watch Maker, Machinist)

THOMAS GARRETT	PHILADELPHIA, PA	1760-1790

(Silversmith, Clock Maker)

THOMAS C. GARRETT	PHILADELPHIA, PA	1810-1824

Son of Philip Garrett.

PHILIP GARRETT & SON (THOMAS C.)	PHILADELPHIA, PA	1824-1835
GARRETT (THOMAS C.) & HARTLEY (SAMUEL)	PHILADELPHIA, PA	1835-1837
GARRETT (THOMAS C.) & HAYDOCK (EDEN)	PHILADELPHIA, PA	1837-1840
THOMAS C. GARRETT & CO.	PHILADELPHIA, PA	1840-1850

(See Samuel Hartley)
(See Eden Haydock-Silversmith listings)
(Silversmiths)

WILLIAM GARRETT	UPPER DARBY TOWNSHIP, PA Chester County	1766-1779

Operated a sword blade mill and leather mill.
Sold blades to Lewis Prahl.

WILLIAM GARRETT & SON (MATTHEW)	**UPPER DARBY TOWNSHIP, PA** Chester County	**1779-1785**

(See Lewis Prahl)
(Sword and Blade Maker, Blacksmith)

THOMAS GASKIL	**PHILADELPHIA, PA**	**1755-1783**

Arms maker for Committee of Safety (1776).
(Blacksmith, Iron Founder, Arms Maker)

J. LEONARD GATTERMYER	**BAVARIA, GERMANY**	**1729-1749**
	BETHLEHEM, PA	**1749-1760**

(Cutler, Blacksmith)

EMERSON GAYLORD	**CHICOPEE, MA**	**B1817-1856**

Worked for Ames Mfg. Co. in the leather shop.
Became foreman (1841-1856).
Left Ames and set up his own leather shop (1856).

EMERSON GAYLORD & CO.	**CHICOPEE, MA**	**1856-1863**

Still made leather goods for Ames Mfg. Co.
Made leather military accoutrements for
  the state of Georgia.

GAYLORD (EMERSON) MFG. CO.	**CHICOPEE, MA**	**1863-1881**

- Made bayonets for M1855 muskets; belt plates for Wells Fargo Co. and Tiffany Co.; steel locks and mailboxes; society swords; and M1860 staff and field officer swords.
- Made swords using surplus blades bought from Ames Mfg. Co.
- U.S. contracts for over 200,000 leather products during the Civil War.
- Stockholder in Ames Mfg. Co. (1867-1872).
- President of Ames Mfg. Co. (1872-1874).
- Ames Mfg. Co. bought the Gaylord Mfg. Co. sword factory (1881).
- Emerson Gaylord retired (1881).

GAYLORD (ARTHUR) & CHAPIN (FREDERICK)	**CHICOPEE, MA**	**1881-1886**

Arthur was Emerson's son.

GAYLORD CO.	**CHICOPEE, MA**	**1886-1976**

(Leather Goods, Military and Society Swords,
  Regalia, Brass Founder, Die Sinker, Engraver)

JAMES GEDDY	**WILLIAMSBURG, VA**	**1700-D1743**

Sword hiltor.
(Gunsmith, Silversmith, Brass Founder)

DAVID & WILLIAM GEDDY	**WILLIAMSBURG, VA**	**1738-1751**

Sons of James.
Adv. cutler's work; sword blades polished,
  blued, and hilted; sword scabbards.

WILLIAM GEDDY	**WILLIAMSBURG, VA**	**1751-D1784**

(Brass Founder, Gunsmith, Armorer, Cutler)

JAMES GEDDY	**PETERSBURG, VA**	**B1731-1783**
JAMES GEDDY & SONS	**PETERSBURG, VA**	**1783-1807**

Partners and sons: William Waddill Geddy,
  James Geddy Jr.

James Geddy Sr. died (1807).
(Silversmiths, Sword Hiltors)

J.V. GERLACH	MINERSVILLE, PA Schuykill County	1860-1865

(Cutler)

CEASER GHISELIN (GISLING)	PHILADELPHIA, PA ANNAPOLIS, MD BALTIMORE, MD PHILADELPHIA, PA	B1670-1716 1716-1718 1718-1726 1728-D1733

(Silversmith, Goldsmith)

RICHARD GHISELIN (GISLING)	PHILADELPHIA, PA	1700-1720

Made belt knives, belt axes, and tomahawks.
(Cutler, Edged Weapons)

WILLIAM GHISELIN	PHILADELPHIA, PA	1750-1780

Grandson of Ceaser Ghiselin.
(Silversmith, Goldsmith)

ROBERT GILL	BALTIMORE, MD	1779-1799

Made 200 boarding pikes (100 each) for the
 ships *Maryland* and *Chesapeake* (1799).
(Pike Maker)

WILLIAM GLAZE
(See Confederate listings)

JACOB GMINDER	REUTLINGEN, WURTEMBURG, GERMANY BALTIMORE, MD	B1835-1849 1849-D1898

- Employee: J.H.F. Hahn (1876-1898).
- Made presentation swords.
- Adv. military equipment, military ornaments,
  silver plating, and fine swords for presentation (1863-1864).
- J.A. Limerick bought Gminder's business when he died (1898).
- (See J.A. Limerick)
- (See J.H.F. Hahn)

(Military Goods, Cutlery, Sword Hiltor, Regalia, Society
 Swords, Silversmith, Silver Plater, Military Ornaments)

CHRISTIAN GOBRECHT	PHILADELPHIA, PA	1815-1845

(Silversmith)

DAVID GOBRECHT	LANCASTER, PA HANOVER, PA York County	B1775-1779 1779-1830

(Gunsmith, Silversmith, Cutler, Clock Maker)

JOHN GOLCHER (GOUCHER)	EASTON, PA	1775-1800

Committee of Safety barrel maker (1777).
(Gunsmith)

THOMAS GOLCHER (GOUCHER)	PHILADELPHIA, PA	1758-1774
THOMAS GOLCHER & THEODORE WILEY	PHILADELPHIA, PA	1774-1775

Cutler and bayonet makers.

THOMAS GOLCHER	PHILADELPHIA, PA	1775-1783

Committee of Safety barrel maker (1776).
Made edged tools.
(See Theodore Wiley)
(Cutler, Gunsmith)

JOHN GONTER	LANCASTER, PA	B1760-1790

Gunsmith in Lancaster militia (1777-1783).

	ELIZABETHTOWN, MD	1790-1798
	HAGERSTOWN, MD	1798-1810
	COLUMBIA, PA	1810-1820
	Lancaster County	
	READING, PA	1820-1824
	Berks County	

(Gunsmith)

PETER GONTER SR.	LANCASTER, PA	B1711-D1768

(Cutler, Whitesmith, Blacksmith, Gunsmith)

PETER GONTER JR.	LANCASTER, PA	B1751-D1819

Son of Peter Gonter Sr.
(Cutler, Whitesmith, Blacksmith, Gunsmith)

JOHN GOODMAN SR.	PHILADELPHIA, PA	1758-1805

Armorer and artillery artificer at the U.S.
  Philadelphia Armory (1779).
Sent a cavalry saber sample to the state of
  Virginia (Virginia Manufactory) in 1801.
Listed as a whitesmith in the Philadelphia
  city directory (1798).
(Blacksmith, Whitesmith, Armorer, Sword Maker)

JOHN GOODMAN JR.	PHILADELPHIA, PA	1780-1850

Son of John Goodman Sr.
Helped Jacob Faser set up a gun and sword shop
  in Philadelphia (1850).
Listed as a whitesmith in the Philadelphia
  city directory (1798).

	WASHINGTON, PA	1850-1854
	Washington County	

(See Jacob Faser Confederate listings)
(Silversmith, Whitesmith, Sword Maker)

MICHAEL GOODMAN	PHILADELPHIA, PA	1757-1777

Artillery artificer at the
  U.S. Philadelphia Armory (1777).
(Blacksmith)

NICHOLAS GOODMAN	WESTMORELAND CO., PA	1825-1840

(Gunsmith)

JONATHAN GOODWIN Committee of Safety musket and bayonet maker (1778). (Gunsmith)	LEBANON, CT	1775-1783
EPHRAIM GOOSLEY (Gunsmith, Cutler, Brass Founder, Edged Tools)	YORKTOWN, VA	1728-D1751
CARLOS GOVE	WENTWORTH, NH BOSTON, MA COUNCIL BLUFFS, IA Pottowattamie County ST. JOSEPH, MO COUNCIL BLUFFS, IA Pottowattamie County	B1817-1835 1835-1840 1840-1844 1844-1854 1854-1862
GOVE (CARLOS) & CO. Partners: John P. Lower, George Schoyan.	DENVER, CO	1862-1882
C. (CARLOS) GOVE & SON Partner and son: Albert F. Gove. (Gunsmith, Cutler, Tomahawk Maker)	DENVER, CO	1882-D1900
ALFRED GRAVES (Cutler, Clock Maker, Silversmith)	WILLOW GROVE, PA Montgomery County	1825-1845
WILLIAM GRAY **GRAY (WILLIAM) & CORBY (JOHN)** **WILLIAM GRAY** (Blacksmith, Gunsmith, Cutler)	CHARLESTON, SC CHARLESTON, SC CHARLESTON, SC	B1772-1811 1812-1819 1820-D1823

WILLIAM H. GRAY
Adv. as a maker of military ornament (1856).
Adv. as an epaulette maker (1862).
Made presentation swords with blades from
  Wilhelm Clauberg, Solingen, Germany.
Adv. sword hilting (1863-1865).
Made gas fixtures after the Civil War.
(Silversmith, Silver Plater, Military Ornaments,
  Sword Hiltor)
	PHILADELPHIA, PA	1844-1866

WILLIAM GREAVES & SON Made belt knives and edged tools. (Cutler)	PHILADELPHIA, PA	1845-1865
DAVID GREENLEAF JR. Apprenticed under Thomas Harland.	HARTFORD, CT NORWICH, CT HARTFORD, CT	B1765-1785 1785-1790 1790-1799
BUELL (ABEL) & GREENLEAF (DAVID JR.) U.S. contract for 1,000 cavalry sabers.	HARTFORD, CT	1799
DAVID GREENLEAF JR. Operated a blacksmith shop.	COVENTRY, CT	1799-1805
GREENLEAF (DAVID JR.) & OAKES (FREDERICK) Silversmith and cutlery shop.	HARTFORD, CT	1805-1811

DAVID GREENLEAF JR.	HARTFORD, CT	1811-D1835

Served in cavalry during the War of 1812.
(See Abel Buell)
(See Frederick Oakes—Dealer listings)
(Sword Maker, Clock Maker, Blacksmith, Silversmith)

JOHN GREER	YORK, PA	1775-1791

(Cutler)

RICHARD GRIDLEY	SHARON, MA	B1711, 1730-1772

Operated iron-smelting furnace at Massapoag Pond.

GRIDLEY (RICHARD) & QUINCY (EDMOND)	SHARON, MA	1772-1775

Made iron goods.

RICHARD GRIDLEY	SHARON, MA	1775-D1796

- Made mortars, howitzers, and naval equipment (including cutlasses) during the Revolutionary War.
- He was a lieutenant colonel in the artillery and later became Chief Engineer for the Continental Army (June 1775-August 1776).
- (See Edmond Quincy)

(Sword Maker, Artillery Maker, Military Equipment, Civil and Military Engineer)

JOHN A. GRIFFITHS	LONDON, ENGLAND	1810-1830
	CINCINNATI, OH	1830-1852
GRIFFITHS (JOHN A.) & SIEBERT (HENRY L.)	CINCINNATI, OH	1852-1854

Made Bowie knives, rifles, and shotguns.

JOHN A. GRIFFITHS	CINCINNATI, OH	1854-1866

U.S. contract for 5,000 rifles (1864).
(Gun Maker, Cutler)

MATTHEW GRIMES	PHILADELPHIA, PA	1777

Swordsmith for Lewis Prahl.
(See Lewis Prahl)
(Sword Maker)

JAMES GROVES	PHILADELPHIA, PA	1820-D1851

(Cutler)

GEORGE GRUBB	PHILADELPHIA, PA	1780-1806

(Cutler)

HENRY BROWN GUEST	LONDON, ENGLAND	1757-1777
	PHILADELPHIA, PA	1777-1780

Adv. small swords (1778).
(Jeweler, Silversmith, Clock Maker, Sword Hiltor)

SIRE GUIBERT	NEW YORK, NY	1861-1865

Patented a sword-revolver (1864).
(Gunsmith)

SAMUEL M. GULDING	OLEY TOWNSHIP, PA Berks County	B1697-1718

(Cutler, Blacksmith)

SAMUEL M. GULDING & PETER ENGEL	OLEY TOWNSHIP, PA Berks County	1718-1725

(Cutler, Blacksmith)

WILLIAM GUNN   CHARLESTON, SC   1778-1805
Adv. cutler's trade, including cleaning, grinding,
  and sharpening hunting swords (*cutteaux de chase*)
  and knives. Also repaired and cleaned guns and pistols.

GUNN (WILLIAM) & BEAUCHEE (FRANCIS D.)	CHARLESTON, SC	1805-1807
WILLIAM GUNN	CHARLESTON, SC	1807-D1813

(Cutler, Gunsmith, Blacksmith)

GOLDSBERRY HACKETT
(See James Bird)

DAVIS HAGEN	MOUNT NEBO, MARTIC TOWNSHIP, PA Lancaster County	1830-1850

Son of Henry B. Hagen.

DAVIS HAGEN JR.	MOUNT NEBO, MARTIC TOWNSHIP, PA Lancaster County	1850-1875

Son of Davis Hagen.

DAVID HAGEN	MOUNT NEBO, MARTIC TOWNSHIP, PA Lancaster County	1850

Son of John Hagen Sr.

ELIJAH HAGEN SR.	MOUNT NEBO, MARTIC TOWNSHIP, PA Lancaster County	1830-1850

ELIJAH HAGEN JR.	MOUNT NEBO, MARTIC TOWNSHIP, PA Lancaster County	1850

Son of John Hagen Sr.

JOHN HAGEN SR.	MOUNT NEBO, MARTIC TOWNSHIP, PA	1840-1883

Son of David Hagen.

JOHN HAGEN JR.	MOUNT NEBO, MARTIC TOWNSHIP, PA Lancaster County	1850-1870

JOSHUA HAGEN	MOUNT NEBO, MARTIC TOWNSHIP, PA Lancaster County	1850

Son of John Hagen Sr.
(Cutlers, Axe Makers, Edged Tools, Edged Weapons)

MAJ. P.V. HAGNER
U.S. ordnance officer who purchased a French foot officer sword as a sample for the U.S. M1850 foot officer sword (1848).

ISAAC HAINES SR. (Cutler, Plough Maker)	GOSHEN, PA Chester County	1730-1770
ISAAC HAINES JR. (Cutler, Plough Maker)	GOSHEN, PA Chester County	1750-1770
HALBACH & SONS (Pistol Maker, Cutler)	BALTIMORE, MD	1775-1785
SAMUEL HALL Committee of Safety musket and bayonet maker (1775-1778). (Gunsmith)	EAST HADDAM, CT	1775-1783
CHARLES HAMMOND Made axes, hatchets, hammers, and tomahawks.	BOSTON, MA	B1805-1850
	CHETTENHAM TOWNSHIP, PA Montgomery County	1850-1855
	PHILADELPHIA, PA	1855-1862

C. (CHARLES) HAMMOND & SON — PHILADELPHIA, PA — 1862-1864
- Partner and son: George Hammond.
- Made M1840 cavalry sabers during the Civil War.
- U.S. contract for 5,000 axes and 5,000 hatchets (1864).
- William Beatty & Sons, edged tool makers, worked at the same address as C. Hammond & Son (1862-1864).

(Edged Tool Maker, Sword Maker, Tomahawk Maker)

GEORGE HAMMOND & SONS Called the Hammond Edge Tool Works. (Edged Tools)	PHILADELPHIA, PA	1864-1901
CROSBY HAMMOND (Silversmith)	PHILADELPHIA, PA	1820-1825
PETER HAMMOND (Silversmith)	PHILADELPHIA, PA	1800-1820
SAMUEL HAMMOND (Silversmith)	PITTSBURGH, PA	1820-1839
WILLIAM C. HAMMOND (Gunsmith)	YORK CO., PA	1815-1835

HENRY W. HAROLD
(See Louis Bickel)

CHARLES W. HARRIS	HARTFORD, CT	1732-1755
	PITTSBURGH, PA	1755-1765
(Gunsmith)		

DANIEL HARRIS   PHILADELPHIA, PA   B1746, 1766-D1821
(Gunsmith)

GEORGE HARRIS	PITTSBURGH, PA	1795-1850
	WRIGHTSVILLE, PA	1850-1854
	York County	

Adv. in Riddle's Pittsburgh Directory as a
  sword manufacturer (1815).
(Silversmith, Swordhilter)

HENRY HARRIS	PAXTON TOWNSHIP, PA	1775-1783
	Daupin County	

(Gunsmith)

ISAAC HARRIS   SAVAGETOWN, MD   1772-1783
Committee of Safety musket and bayonet maker
 (1776-1777).
(Gunsmith)

JASON L. HARRIS   PITTSBURGH, PA   1800-1820
(Flintlock Rifle Maker)

JOHN HARRIS   PITTSBURGH, PA   B1727, 1747-D1791
Artillery artificer at U.S. Fort Pitt Armory (1778-1783).

JOHN HARRIS	YORK, PA	1775-1805
	York County	

- Obtained a U.S. contract for 300 blades for boarding pikes from Tench Coxe, purveyor of public supplies (June 1797).
- U.S. contract for 300 M1797 boarding pikes (1797); 100 each for frigates *Constitution*, *Constellation*, and *United States*.
- Made six boarding pikes for frigate *Ganges* (1798).

(Gunsmith, Pike Maker, Cutler)

DR. ROBERT HARRIS	SPRINGFIELD TOWNSHIP, PA	1775-1783
	Chester County	

Gunpowder maker to Committee of Safety (1776).
Built a powder mill (1776).

SAMUEL HARRIS	AUGUSTA TOWNSHIP, PA	1775-1783
	Northumberland County	

Committee of Safety arms repair (1777).
(Gunsmith)

WILLIAM HARRIS	HARRISBURG, PA	B1760-1820
	PLEASANT TOWNSHIP, OH	1820-D1834
	Seneca County	

(Gunsmith)

ISAAC HARROW	TRENTON, NJ	1710-1740

Immigrated from England.
Operated a planing and blade mill.
Made knives and axes.
(Edged Tool Maker, Cutler)

CHARLES HART
(See Charles Blair)

JOHN HART	LANCASTER, PA	1762-1767

(Cutler)

MARTIN HASLE	PARIS, FRANCE	1801-1822
	NEW ORLEANS, LA	1822-1829

(Cutler, Sword Maker, Knife Maker)

G. HEDDERLY
(See John Bailey)

CALEB HEFFEY	ALEXANDRIA, VA	1807-1808

(Gunsmith, Whitesmith, Cutler)

GEORGE HEIGHBERGER		
(HEIBERGER-HEIGHLERGER)	PHILADELPHIA, PA	1760-1790

Made 55 horsemen's swords (1781).
Repaired arms for the Pennsylvania Committee
  of Safety (1781-1785).
(Sword Maker, Gunsmith)

FRANK HENDERSON	KALAMAZOO, MI	1850-1871
HENDERSON (FRANK) & GIDDINGS		
(THERON F.)	KALAMAZOO, MI	1871-1873
FRANK HENDERSON	KALAMAZOO, MI	1873-1893

Put out fraternal goods catalogs.
Henderson bought the Chicago branch of Ames
  Sword Co. (1893).

HENDERSON-AMES	KALAMAZOO, MI	1893-1923
	& CHICAGO, IL	

- Made U.S. regulation swords, including cadet swords.
- Issued many military goods, regalia, and society sword catalogs.
- Bought the Detroit regalia factory of E.A. Armstrong (1894), including sword plant, stock, tools, machinery, furniture, and fixtures.
- Authorized agents: L.C. Bruce (Boston, MA), M.V. Kinsey (Atlanta, GA), E.C. Phillips (Boston, MA).
- M.C. Lilley bought Henderson-Ames (1923).
- (See Ames Sword Co.)
- (See L.C. Bruce—Dealer listings)
- (See M.V. Kinsey—Dealer listings)
- (See E.C. Phillips—Dealer listings)
- (See M.C. Lilley)

(Regalia, Military Goods, Uniforms, Society and Military Swords)

ABASUERES HENDRICKS	WHOREKILL, PA	1640-1675
	NEW AMSTERDAM, LONG ISLAND	1675-D1727

Made silver-hilted swords and infantry pikes.
(Silversmith, Blacksmith, Cutler, Sword Hiltor)

JAMES HENDRICKS	PHILADELPHIA, PA Middle Ward	1746-1800

Edged tools, edged weapons,
 and infantry pike maker.
Apprentice: William Ward (1767-1769).
Adv. cutlery and scales (1766).
(Cutler, Pike Maker)

JOHN HENDRICKS	ALBANY, NY	1835-1840
	PHILADELPHIA, PA	1840-1890

Made belt knives and tomahawks.
(See William Ward)
(Cutler, Silversmith, Edged Weapons)

ANTON HENINGER	NEW HAVEN, CT	1861-1865

Knife and dirk maker.
(Cutler)

DANIEL HENKELS	SOLINGEN, GERMANY	1779-1796
	PHILADELPHIA, PA	1796-1805
	RICHMOND, VA	1805-1806

Worked at the Virginia Manufactory.
Hilted and forged sword blades.

	PHILADELPHIA, PA	1806-1817

- Sword and gun shop.
- First to use steam power in his Philadelphia gun factory.
- Stepson of Daniel Nippes, who married Henkel's mother.
- Had seven employees (1814).
- Had a contract with Winner & Nippes to make 1,700 stands of M1808 muskets (1815).
- Made balled-hilt cavalry sabers for the War of 1812.
- (See Daniel Nippes)
- (See James Winner)

(Sword Maker, Gun Maker)

ABRAHAM HENRY	NAZARETH, PA	B1748-1781
	LANCASTER, PA	1781-D1811

Son of William Henry Sr.
(Gun Maker)

GRANVILLE HENRY	BOULTON, PA	B1835-D1912

Son of James Henry.
Succeeded his father (1894).
(Gun Maker)

JAMES HENRY	PHILADELPHIA, PA	B1809-1836
	BOULTON, PA	1836-D1894

Son of John Joseph Henry Jr.
Succeeded his father (1836).
(Gun Maker)

JOHN HENRY NEE DEVENNY	SCOTLAND	1700-1722

Immigrated to Lancaster, PA (1722).

	LANCASTER, PA	1722-1730
JOHN HENRY	LANCASTER, PA	1733-1773

Son of John Henry Nee DeVenny.
(Gun Maker)

JOHN JOSEPH HENRY SR.	LANCASTER, PA	B1758, 1775-D1811

Son of William Henry Sr.
(Gun Maker)

JOHN JOSEPH HENRY JR.	NAZARETH, PA	B1786-1808
	PHILADELPHIA, PA	1808-D1836
	Northern Liberties	

- Son of William Henry Jr.
- Built a gun factory in Philadelphia called The Boulton Works, making muskets, rifles, pistols, and horsemen's sabers.
- His brother Joseph was partner in the factory.
- Also had a rifle, musket, and barrel factory in Bushkill Township, Northampton County, PA.
- Made files, musket, and rifle locks and mountings.
- In charge of the Committee of Defense of Philadelphia (1812).
- Employees: James Coats, Isaac Vandergrift, Jeremiah Vandergrift.
- Had several U.S. government musket and pistol contracts.
- Had a U.S. contract for up to 3,000 cavalry sabers (1812); inspected by Marine T. Wickham.
- Had a Maryland contract for 1,000 cavalry sabers (1813).
- Son James succeeded him.
- (See James Coats)

(Gun Maker, Pistol Maker, Saber Maker)

JOSEPH HENRY	NAZARETH, PA	1790-1816

Son of William Henry Jr.
Partner with John Joseph Henry Jr.
(Gun Maker)

WILLIAM HENRY SR.	LANCASTER, PA	B1729, 1749-D1786

- Son of John Henry Nee DeVenny.
- Armorer to Braddock's Expedition (1755).
- Committee of Safety musket and bayonet maker (1776-1777).
- Superintendant of arms and accoutrements at the U.S. Philadelphia Armory (1778-1783).

(Armorer, Gun Maker, Iron Monger)

WILLIAM HENRY JR.	LANCASTER, PA	B1757-1778
	NAZARETH, PA	1778-1796
	LANCASTER, PA	1796-D1821

Son of William Henry Sr.
(Gun Maker)

ANDREW HERTZOG   YORK, PA   1775-1783
Committee of Safety repairs (1776).
(Gunsmith)

FREDERICK HERTZOG   GEORGES TOWNSHIP, PA   1790
Fayette County

(Pistol Maker)

JACOB HERTZOG   GEORGES TOWNSHIP, PA   1803-1823
Fayette County

(Blacksmith, Edged Tools, Cutler, Gunsmith)

GEORGE HEWES   FULTON TOWNSHIP, PA   1740-1750
Lancaster County

(Edged Tools, Cutler)

JOSIAH HEWES   PHILADELPHIA, PA   1775-1783
Committee of Safety musket
 and bayonet maker (1776).
(Gunsmith)

ANDREW G. HICKS   CLEVELAND, OH   1835-1865
Made edged tools, belt knives, and riflemen's knives.
(Cutler, Knife Maker)

ABRAHAM HIESTAND   UPPER MILFORD TOWNSHIP, PA   1768-1788
Northampton County

(Cutler)

J. BURLEY HILL   BOSTON, MA   1816
Offered to make 500 to 2,000 boarding pikes
 for navy contract (1816).
(Cutler, Pike Maker)

MEDAD HILLS	DURHAM, CT	B1729-1741
	GOSHEN, CT	1741-1808

Committee of Safety musket and bayonet
 maker (1776-1777).
Edward and Miles Beach were inspectors at
 their factory (1776-1777).
(Musket, Rifle, Pistol, and Bayonet Maker)

GEORGE HINTON   PHILADELPHIA, PA   1767-1790
Made belt knives.
(Cutler)

ANDREW HODGE Committee of Safety cutlass maker (1776). (Sword Maker)	PHILADELPHIA, PA	1775-1783
BATTES HOFFMAN (Cutler, Edged Tools, Blacksmith)	COCALICO TOWNSHIP, PA Lancaster County	1750-D1806
CONRAD HOFFMAN **HOFFMAN (CONRAD) & DAHOOF** (Cutler, Edged Tools, Surgical Instrument Maker)	LANCASTER, PA PITTSBURGH, PA	1790-1810 1810-1812
DANIEL HOFFMAN (Cutler)	LANCASTER, PA	1834-1850
FREDERICK HOFFMAN Made bills, pikes, tomahawks, and facine knives during the Revolutionary War. Had a U.S. boarding axe (poleaxe) contract (1797). Bid on a U.S. Navy boarding axe contract (1806). (Blacksmith, Edged Weapon Maker)	PHILADELPHIA, PA	1750-1820
JAMES M. HOFFMAN (Silversmith)	PHILADELPHIA, PA	1800-1820
JOHN H. HOFFMAN Sword hiltor for F.W. Widmann (1820-1848). (See F.W. Widmann) (Silversmith, Swordhiltor)	PHILADELPHIA, PA	1800-1851
VALENTINE HOFFMAN **CAPT. VALENTINE HOFFMAN** Supervisor at U.S. Philadelphia Armory. Supervisor at U.S. Lebanon Armory. Supervisor of blacksmiths at U.S. Carlisle Armory. (Cutler, Blacksmith, Edged Tools)	COCALICO TOWNSHIP, PA Lancaster County PHILADELPHIA, PA LEBANON, PA CARLISLE, PA	1759-1777 1777 1777-1778 1779
WILLIAM HOFFMAN (Silversmith)	PITTSBURGH, PA	1819-1839
ISAAC HOGLAN Bid on navy boarding axe (poleaxe) contract (1816). (Cutler)	GEORGETOWN, D.C.	1790-1820
HENRY HOLLINGSWORTH Committee of Safety musket and bayonet maker (1776-1777). (Gunsmith)	ELKTON, MD	1756-D1803
J.T. HOLMES (Cutler, Edged Tools)	NEW BRIGHTEN, PA Beaver County	B1827-1860

JOHN HOLMES   **TEMPERANCE VILLAGE, PA**   **1839-1857**
Allegheny County

Called Holmes Axe Factory.
(Cutler, Edged Tools)

JAMES R. HOLMES   **TEMPERANCE VILLAGE, PA**   **1839-1857**
Holmes Axe Factory   Allegheny County
Changed name to Eagle Cutlery Works.

                           PITTSBURGH, PA   **1857-1860**

(Cutler, Edged Tools)

SAMUEL HOLMES   **PHILADELPHIA, PA**   **1775-1783**
Pennsylvania Committee of Safety contract for
   50 cutlasses (sabers) in 1776.
(Cutler, Sword Maker)

THE HOPE FURNACE   **SCITUATE, RI**   **1765-1812**
Founded by the Brown Family (1765).
Stockholders in 1765:
       John Brown
       Joseph Brown
       Moses Brown
       Nicholas Brown
       Stephen Hopkins
       Job Hawkins
       Caleb Arnold
       Israel Wilkinson
- Named after Hope Brown, mother of John, Joseph, Moses, and Nicholas.
- The major product of the furnace was pig iron but also made cooking equipment (pots, pans, kettles, etc.), nails, anchors, and chains.
- From 1775-1812 (Revolutionary War and War of 1812), made swords, cannon shot (offered 11 sizes), and cannon balls.
- Had several Rhode Island Committee of Safety contracts for cannon.
- Made cannon for the Continental Navy and many privateers.
- Had offices in Providence, RI.
- Employees: Amos Atwell (blacksmith, 1776-1783), Ezekiel Hopkins (blacksmith and sword maker, 1765-1783).
- Blacksmiths and stockholders: Rufus Hopkins (1775-1810), Stephen Hopkins (1765-1790), Sylvanus Hopkins (1805-1810).
- The Hope Furnace closed in 1812.
- Abraham Wilkinson bought the blacksmith's tools (1812).

ELISHA HOPKINS   **SCITUATE, RI**   1750-1770
                        COVENTRY, RI   1770-1783

Son of Jeremiah.
(Blacksmith, Gunsmith)

ESEK HOPKINS   **SCITUATE, RI**   B1718-D1802
Brother of Stephen and Jeremiah.
Privateer in Seven Year War (1756-1763).
Brigadier General, commander of the Rhode
   Island troops (1775).
Commander and chief of the Continental Navy
   (1775-1778).

EZEKIAL HOPKINS	SCITUATE, RI	1740-1765

Son of Jabez.
Blacksmith and sword maker at Hope Furnace (1765-1783).
(Blacksmith, Sword Maker).

JABEZ HOPKINS	SCITUATE, RI	1720-1740

Iron master and blacksmith.
(Blacksmith)

JEREMIAH HOPKINS	SCITUATE, RI	1730-1770
	COVENTRY, RI	1770-1783

Brother of Stephen and Esek.
(Blacksmith)

RUFUS HOPKINS	SCITUATE, RI	1755-1812

Stockholder, blacksmith, and furnace manager
  at Hope Furnace (1775-1812).
(Blacksmith)

STEPHEN HOPKINS	SCITUATE, RI	1735-1790

Brother of Jeremiah and Esek.
Stockholder and blacksmith at Hope Furnace
  (1765-1790).
(Blacksmith)

SYLVANUS HOPKINS	SCITUATE, RI	1785-1812

Son of Rufus.
Stockholder and blacksmith at Hope Furnace
  (1805-1812).
(Blacksmith)

DAVID B. HOWELL	NEW YORK, NY	1862-1865
D. (DAVID) B. HOWELL	NEW YORK, NY	1865-1874

Bought William Price & Co. (1868).
Called the American Masonic Agency.
(Society and Presentation Swords, Regalia)

JACOB HOWELL	PHILADELPHIA, PA	1775-1783

Committee of Safety contract for infantry pikes
  and entrenching tools (1776).
(Pike Maker, Armorer, Military Goods Dealer,
  Cutler, Edged Weapons)

JAMES HOWELL	PHILADELPHIA, PA	1780-1800
RICHARDSON (JOSEPH) & HOWELL (JAMES)	PHILADELPHIA, PA	1800-1801
JAMES HOWELL & CO.	PHILADELPHIA, PA	1801-1815

(See Joseph Richardson)
(Silversmith)

SAMUEL HOWELL	PHILADELPHIA, PA	1755-1800

Sold 11 cutlasses to Capt. Robert Towers,
  Commissary of Military Stores, U.S. Philadelphia
  Armory (1775).
(Silversmith, Sword Maker)

WILLIAM T. HOWELL
(See Dealer listings)

JOHN HUBB
(See Silversmith listings)

THOMAS HUBB	**PHILADELPHIA, PA**	1777-1778

Swordsmith for Lewis Prahl (1777).
Blacksmith and artillery artificer at the U.S.
 Philadelphia Armory (1778).
(Sword Maker)

ABRAHAM HUBER	**MANCHESTER TOWNSHIP, PA**	1779-1799

(Gunsmith)   York County

CHRISTIAN HUBER	**REAMSTOWN, PA**	1750-D1789

Lancaster County

(Clock Maker, Silversmith)

GEORGE HUBER SR.	**BETHLEHEM, PA**	1730-D1764

(Blacksmith, Cutler)

GEORGE HUBER JR.	**BETHLEHEM, PA**	B1760, 1780-D1813

(Blacksmith, Cutler)

HENRY HUBER JR.	**PHILADELPHIA, PA**	1845-1876
HUBER TOOL WORKS	**PHILADELPHIA, PA**	1876-1880

Made bowie knives.
(Cutler, Knife Maker, Edged Tools)

HENRY HUBER SR.	**PHILADELPHIA, PA**	1775-1815

Pennsylvania Committee of Safety contract for
 gunpowder.
(Gunsmith, Gunpowder Maker)

JOHN HUBER	**HARRISBURG, PA**	1790-1810

(Clock Maker, Silversmith)

RUDOLPH HUG	**CINCINNATI, OH**	1861-1865

Made sword bayonets, surgical and dental instruments.
(Cutler, Bayonet Maker)

JOSHUA HUMPHREYS	**AUGUSTA CO., VA**	1775-1783

Partners: Joshua Perry, Alexander Simpson, Jacob Gabbott.
Committee of Safety musket and bayonet maker.
(Gunsmith)

EDWARD HUNT	**PHILADELPHIA, PA**	1700-1725

(Silversmith, Goldsmith, Whitesmith, Cutler)

DAVID HUNTER	**BERKLEY CO., VA**	1775-1783

Partner: Peter Light.
Committee of Safety musket and bayonet maker (1776).
Contract for 200 muskets.
(Gunsmith)

HENRY HUNTER	SHEFFIELD, ENGLAND	1815-1850
	NEW BRIGHTON, PA	1850-1860
	Beaver County	

(Cutler)

JAMES & ADAM HUNTER	SCOTLAND	1710-1732
	STAFFORD CO., VA	1732-1775

- Began as merchants.
- Bought a farm.
- Farm superintendent: John Strode.
- Bought an iron forge near Falmouth and established Hunters Iron Works, located on the Rappahonnock River across from the Virginia State Gun Factory at Fredericksburg, VA.
- Made farm tools, edged tools, and anchors.

JAMES HUNTER	STAFFORD CO., VA	1775-1782

Changed name to The Rappahannock Forge (1775).
    Superintendent: Uri Banks (1775-1782).
    Clerk: Henry Banks, son of Uri Banks (1775-1782).
    Foreman: John Strode (1775-1782).
    Arms Foreman: Joseph Perkins (1775-1777).

- Uri Banks recruited skilled workmen in Philadelphia (1776).
- Made muskets, bayonets, carbines, pistols, horsemen's sabers, camp kettles, spades, shovels, and wall guns.
- Virginia contract for 200 stands of muskets (1776).
- Virginia contract for all the muskets (with bayonets and ramrods) that could be made in one year (1776).
- Made horsemen's sabers for the 1st Regiment (under Colonel Bland) and the 3rd Regiment (under Colonel Baylor) of the Virginia Continental Dragoons (1776-1778).
- Hunter was asked to repair muskets damaged at Richmond, VA, during an attack by British Raider Benedict Arnold (1780). He declined because of a lack of armorers.
- Arms production was stopped temporarily because of a lack of skilled armorers (1780).
- After the battle of Guilford Courthouse, VA, Lt. Col. George Washington ordered Maj. Richard Call of the 3rd regiment of Continental Dragoons to send a captured British horsemen's saber (from Tarlton's Light Horse) to Virginia Governor Jefferson, to be forwarded to James Hunter at the Rappahannock Forge (probably a stirrup-hilted light horse saber) as a pattern for a U.S. light horse saber (1781).
- Hunter informed Governor Thomas Jefferson that he would have to stop saber production again unless his sword cutlers and artificers were furloughed (May 1781).
- Hunter told Governor Thomas Jefferson that he was removing and relocating his tools, machinery, and equipment because British Col. Banastre Tarlton's Light Horse cavalry regiment was raiding in the area of Fredericksbrug, VA (June 1787).
- The move was supervised by a General Weedon (retired).
- The tools, machinery, and equipment were returned later, the facility actually enlarged (350 feet long, 4 stories high), and the armorers and workmen recalled.
- Hunter informed the Committee of Safety that he had, in hand, 1,000 horsemen's sabers patterned after Washington's captured British saber (November 1781).
- The Rappahannock Forge closed (1782).
- James Hunter died (1785).
- (See Joseph Perkins)
- (See John Strode)

JOHN HUNTER	PHILADELPHIA, PA	1779

Armorer at U.S. Philadelphia Armory.
(Armorer)

NICHOLAS HUNTER Manager of the Mt. Pleasant Forge.	BERKS CO., PA	1815-1828
HEZEKIAH HUNTINGTON Committee of Safety musket and bayonet maker (1775-1778). Partners: Amasa Palmer, Edward Williams. (Gunsmith)	WINDHAM, CT	1775-1790
PHILLIP HUNTINGTON (Silversmith)	NORWICH, CT	B1770, 1790-D1825
ROSWELL HUNTINGTON (Silversmith)	NORWICH, CT	B1763, 1780-D1836

CALEB HUSE
(See Confederate listings)

SAMUEL HUSE	NEWBURYPORT, MA	1802-1840

- The Huse family ran a brass foundry and iron foundry.
- Cast brass, copper, and iron products for ships.
- Made cooking stoves and hollowware.
- Did foundry work for N.P. Ames Sr. for many years (Ames born in Newburyport also).
- Huse cast the hilts and mounts for the N.P. Ames M1832 foot artillery swords.
- James T. Ames married Huse's daughter Eleanore (1838).

(Brass Founder, Sword Hiltor)

CHRISTIAN ISCH	LANCASTER, PA	1775-1775
ISCH (CHRISTIAN) & REIGERT (PETER) Committee of Safety musket and bayonet maker (1776). (Gunsmith)	LANCASTER, PA	1775-1783
PETER ISCH (Blacksmith)	LANCASTER, PA	1755-1779
EPHRAIM JACKSON (Silversmith)	PHILADELPHIA, PA	1810-1820
GEORGE JACKSON	CHESTER CO., PA	1800-1827
	BALTIMORE, MD	1827-1832
	WILMINGTON, DE	1832-D1836
(Silversmith, Blacksmith, Clock Maker)		
ISAAC JACKSON Apprenticed to Benjamin Chandlee (1755-1763).	CHESTER CO., PA	B1734-1763
	NEW GARDEN TOWNSHIP, PA Chester County	1763-D1807
(Cutler, Silversmith, Blacksmith, Clock Maker, Brass Founder)		
JOHN W. JACKSON	LANCASTER, PA	1825-1845
ZAHM (MICHAEL) & JACKSON (JOHN W.) (Silversmith, Military and Fancy Goods)	LANCASTER, PA	1845-1860

JOSEPH JACKSON	BALTIMORE, MD	1800-1815
	RICHMOND, VA	1815-D1831

(Cutler, Silversmith, Surgical Instruments Maker, Presentation Sword Maker)

RALPH JACKSON   PHILADELPHIA, PA   1700-1720
(Blacksmith, Silversmith)

SAMUEL JACKSON   BALTIMORE, MD   1831-1895
- Son of Joseph Jackson.
- Rehilted a George Washington sword.
- Made presentation swords for Brig. Gen. L. Bennett Riley and Gen. John E. Wood.
- Sold M1852 navy officer swords.
- Adv. swords and military equipment (1892).

(Cutler, Silversmith, Surgical Instrument Maker, Presentation Sword Maker)

THOMAS JACKSON   PHILADELPHIA, PA   1830-1850
(Silversmith)

JAMES JENKINS   PHILADELPHIA, PA   1776-1795
                          Dock Ward

(Gunsmith, Silversmith)

JOHN JENKINS   PHILADELPHIA, PA   B1735, 1750-D1796

Made a presentation sword for Col. John Withy during the Revolutionary War.
(Silversmith, Sword Hiltor)

JOSIAH JENKINS   PHILADELPHIA, PA   1771-1777
Artillery artificer at the U.S. Philadelphia Armory.

                                        LEBANON ARMORY   1777-1781

Artillery artificer at the U.S. Lebanon Armory.
(Blacksmith)

THOMAS JENKINS	LONDON, ENGLAND	1720-1740
	PHILADELPHIA, PA	1740-1760

(Watch Maker, Silversmith)

JOSEPH JENKS SR.   LYNN, MA   1620-1650
Built an iron forge and made scythes, edged tools, and knives.
(Cutler, Edged Tools)

JOSEPH JENKS JR.   PAWTUCKET FALLS, RI   1650-1680
Son of Joseph Jenks Sr.
Built an iron forge with trip hammers, foundry, carpenters shop, and sawmill.
Made axes, knives, edged tools, hammers, anchors, and heavy iron products.
(Cutler, Edged Tools)

SOLOMON JENNINGS	RICHMOND, ME	1752-1754
	FORT HALIFAX, ME	1754-1756

(Armorer)

HENRY JOHNS Committee of Safety contract for infantry pikes (1775). (Pike Maker)	**PHILADELPHIA, PA**	1775-1783
DONNELLY JOHNSON (Cutler)	**BOSTON, MA**	1855-1902
JAMES M. JOHNSON (Silversmith, Clock Maker, Watch Maker)	**UNIONTOWN, PA** Fayette County **WASHINGTON BORO, PA**	1800-1817 1817-1820
RENALDO JOHNSON Made edged weapons for the Indian trade. (Cutler)	**PHILADELPHIA, PA**	1800-1810
SAMUEL JOHNSON Bid on U.S. Navy boarding axe (poleaxe) contract (1816). (Cutler)	**WASHINGTON D.C.**	1800-1820
SETH JOHNSON Committee of Safety musket and bayonet maker (1777). (Gunsmith)	**OLD RUTLAND, MA**	1775-1783
ABRAHAM JONES Made axes and edged tools. (Edged Tool Maker)	**UPPER PROVIDENCE TOWNSHIP, PA** Delaware County	B1820-1850
AQUILLA JONES Apprentice: Henry Scout. (Cutler)	**PHILADELPHIA, PA** Mulberry Ward	1765-1780
AMOS JONES Committee of Safety musket and bayonet maker (1776). (Gunsmith)	**COLCHESTER, CT**	1752-1783
BENJAMIN JONES Made belt knives (Cutler)	**TREDYFFRINE TOWNSHIP, PA** Chester County	1755-1784
CHARLES JONES Blacksmith with Capt. Andrew Graff's Lancaster County militia.	**PHILADELPHIA, PA**	1776-1783

DANIEL JONES PHILADELPHIA, PA 1730-1760
Apprentice to Richard Allen (1745-1750).
(Silversmith)

EDWARD JONES BUTE CO., NC 1775-1783
Committee of Safety musket and bayonet maker.
(Gunsmith)

ELISHA JONES NETHER PROVIDENCE TOWNSHIP, PA 1760-1770
Chester County

(Blacksmith, Cutler)

JAMES JONES PHILADELPHIA, PA 1790-D1815
(Silversmith)

JOHN JONES RADNOR, PA 1769-1779
(Blacksmith, Cutler) Chester County

JOHN JONES PHILADELPHIA, PA 1730-D1768
(Silversmith)

ROBERT JONES PHILADELPHIA, PA 1776-1783
Blacksmith with Capt. Andrew Graff's Lancaster
  County militia.
(Blacksmith)

WILLIAM JONES PHILADELPHIA, PA 1775-1783
Committee of Safety musket and bayonet maker.
(Gunsmith)

CASPER JOST WHITE PLAINS TOWNSHIP, PA 1775-1785
Dauphin County
Committee of Safety musket and bayonet
  maker (1775-1776).

  LEBANON CO., PA 1785-1790
(Gunsmith)

HENRY D. JUSTI PHILADELPHIA, PA 1850-1890
(Dental and Surgical Instruments, Cutlery Maker)

THE JUSTICE FAMILY

ALFRED B. JUSTICE & CO. PHILADELPHIA, PA 1837-1851
149 High Street
Same location as G.M. & G.R. Justice & Co.

A. (ALFRED) B. JUSTICE & CO. PHILADELPHIA, PA 1851-1857
5th and Commerce
Same location as Steinmetz & Justice.
  and Philip S. Justice.

  PHILADELPHIA, PA 1857-1889
  14 North 5th Street
Same location as Philip S. Justice.

Partner: Florance W. Grugan.
(Hardware Manufacturers)

A.R. JUSTICE & CO. PHILADELPHIA, PA 1881-1935
14 North 5th Street

- Same address as Philip S. Justice.
- Adv. as hardware manufacturers and cutlery makers (1885).
- Adv. as silversmiths and silverware makers (1892).
- Adv. plated ware (1895).
- Adv. cut glass (1910).
- Partners: Herbert M. Justice, F. Millwood Justice, C. Arthur Roberts (1892 on).
- Succeeded Philip S. Justice (1887).
- Sold hollowware made by Hicks Silver Co.
- Sold pearl-handled knives by Medford Cutlery Co.
- Sold hollowware and flatware by Riverton Silver Co.

G. (GEORGE) M. & G. (GEORGE) R. JUSTICE CO.
  PHILADELPHIA, PA 1837-1851
  149 High Street

Same location as Alfred B. Justice & Co.
Hardware manufacturers and dealers.

JUSTICE (GEORGE M.), STEINMETZ (WILLIAM) & JUSTICE (GEORGE R.) PHILADELPHIA, PA 1851-1860
5th and Commerce

Same location as A.B. Justice & Co. and
  Philip S. Justice.
William Steinmetz was a gun maker.
Hardware manufacturers
  and dealers and gun makers.

(JUSTICE (GEORGE M. & GEORGE R.) & STEINMETZ PHILADELPHIA, PA 1860-1865
5th and Commerce

Had 10 employees and made 2,500 guns (1860).
Hardware manufacturers
  and dealers and gun makers.

HOWARD R. JUSTICE PHILADELPHIA, PA 1870-1881
14 North 5th Street

Son of Philip S. Justice.
Same location as Philip S. Justice.
Made iron fencing.

PHILIP S. JUSTICE PHILADELPHIA, PA 1837-1851
36 Commerce Street
PHILADELPHIA, PA 1851-1857
5th and Commerce Street

Same location as A.B. Justice & Co. and Justice,
  Steinmetz, & Justice.
Hardware manufacturer
  and dealer and gun importer.

JUSTICE (PHILIP S.) & WILSON (PHILIP) PHILADELPHIA, PA 1857-1859
14 North 5th Street

Same location as A.B. Justice & Co.
Hardware manufacturer and dealer.
Rifle and gun makers and importers.
Wilson was a gunmaker.
After 1859, Wilson was listed as an agent for
  Justice at 432 Chestnut.

P. (PHILIP) S. JUSTICE PHILADELPHIA, PA 1859-1887
  14 North 5th Street

- Hardware manufacturer and dealer.
- Railroad car spring and supplies maker.
- Gunlock, rifle, bayonet, and sword maker during the Civil War.
- Gun and gunlock importer.
- Adv. in the Boyd's Pennsylvania State Business Directory as having been an importer and maker of sporting arms and rifles for almost 20 years (1861).
- Adv. as a railway supplies agent and/or maker in the Philadelphia city directories (1862-1887).
- Succeeded by A.R. Justice & Co.

Philip S. Justice Civil War U.S. Arms Contracts

4,000 rifled muskets	1861
125 rifles and bayonets	1861
174 M1860 cavalry officers sabers	1861
13,685 M1860 cavalry sabers	1861-1862
40 lt. artillery officer sabers	1861
1,050 lt. artillery sabers	1861
400 experimental Enfield-type muskets	1863

Some guns and gunlocks marked "P.S.J. & Co."
Some guns and all swords marked "P.S. Justice"

- Philip S. Justice moved to Sheffield, England (c. 1865). (The Justice family may have originally come from Sheffield.)
- Started P.S. Justice & Co., Cyclops Works in Sheffield.
- The Cyclops Works made railroad car wheels.
- Justice moved to London (c. 1870).
- Took on a partner, J. Howard Mitchell, in his U.S. company (c. 1870).
- The P.S. Justice firm in the United States began to sell steel (c. 1875). It advertised in the "Machinists and Machinery Manufacturers" (iron founders) section of the *United States Hardware and Metal Trades Directory* (1875).
- Philip S. Justice died (1887).

KALAMAZOO REGALIA CO. KALAMAZOO, MI 1927-1933
Reincorporated Henderson-Ames (1933-1949).
W.A. Sougale was the company sales representative (1945).
(Regalia Swords)

PETER KASCHELINE Committee of Safety musket and bayonet maker (1775-1776). (Gunsmith)	**NORTHAMPTON CO., PA**	**1775-1783**
JACOB KEELEY (KEELY)	**EAST VINCENT TOWNSHIP, PA** Chester County	**1740-D1777**
Partners and sons: Mathias Keeley, Sabastion Keeley. Committee of Safety musket and bayonet maker (1775-1777). (Gunsmith)		
PRINCE KEENE Committee of Safety musket barrel and bayonet maker (1776). (Gunsmith)	**PROVIDENCE, RI**	**1775-1783**
PETER KEENER Committee of Safety musket and bayonet maker (1776).	**BALTIMORE, MD**	**1750-1795**
KEENER (PETER) & SON (JOHN) (Gunsmith)	**BALTIMORE, MD**	**1795-1806**
JOHN KEENER	**BALTIMORE, MD**	**B1771-1795**
KEENER (PETER) & SON (JOHN)	**BALTIMORE, MD**	**1795-1806**
JOHN KEENER (Gunsmith)	**BALTIMORE, MD**	**1806-1851**
SAMUEL KEENER Committee of Safety musket and bayonet maker (1776). (Gunsmith)	**BALTIMORE, MD**	**1775-1783**
CHARLES KELLER (Silversmith)	**PHILADELPHIA, PA**	**1820-1840**
ELIAS KELLER	**YARDLEYVILLE, PA** Bucks County	**1861-1865**
KELLER (ELIAS) & BROTHER (Gun Maker)	**HARRISBURG, PA**	**1865-1875**
GEORGE KELLER (Silversmith)	**PHILADELPHIA, PA**	**1825-1845**
JOHN KELLER (KEHLER) U.S. contract for cavalry sabers (1812). "U.S." stamped on blade.	**LANCASTER, PA**	**1780-1820**
	CARLISLE, PA Cumberland County	**1820-1845**
(Gun Maker, Sword Maker)		

JOHN W. KELLER CARLISLE, PA 1845-1870
Cumberland County

Succeeded John Keller.
(Gunsmith)

MICHAEL KELLER YORK CO., PA 1775-1783
Bayonet scabbard maker for Pennsylvania
  militia units.
(Blacksmith)

DAVID KELLY BALTIMORE, MD 1795-1805
Had a U.S. contract for M1797 boarding pikes
  (1797-1799).
(Pike Maker)

DANIEL KENT WEST BLADFORD
 TOWNSHIP, PA 1690-1706
 Chester County

(Cutler)

JOHN KERLIN (KIRLIN-KERLING) BUCKS CO., PA B1753, 1773-1776
Committee of Safety musket and bayonet
  maker (1776).

 WESTMORLAND CO., PA 1776-1786
 AMITY TOWNSHIP, PA 1786-D1801
 Berks County

(Gunsmith)

JOHN KERLIN JR. AMITY TOWNSHIP, PA 1780-1801
 Berks County

Son of John Kerlin.
JOHN JR. & SAMUEL KERLIN BUCKS CO., PA 1801
JOHN KERLIN BUCKS CO., PA 1801-D1826
(Gunsmith)

SAMUEL KERLIN AMITY TOWNSHIP, PA 1780-1801
 Berks County

Son of John Kerlin.
JOHN JR. & SAMUEL KERLIN BUCKS CO., PA 1801
SAMUEL KERLIN BUCKS CO., PA 1801-1820
(Gunsmith)

THOMAS KERLIN PHILADELPHIA, PA 1775-1786
Committee of Safety musket and bayonet
  maker (1777).

 NORTHUMBERLAND CO., PA 1786-1805

(Gunsmith)

ARCHIBALD KERR PHILADELPHIA, PA 1790-1813
U.S. contract for 1,000 cartridge boxes.
(Leather Shop)

JAMES KERR (Cutler, Edged Tools)	STRABANE TOWNSHIP, PA Washington County	1796-1814
JOHN KERR (Cutler, Gunsmith)	CARLISLE, PA Cumberland County	1775-1812
MICHAEL KERR (Gunsmith)	PHILADELPHIA, PA	1788-1800
ADAM KETLER (Blacksmith, Cutler, Edged Tools)	NORRISTOWN, PA	1815-1820
KEYSTONE EDGED TOOLS WORKS (See Emerson & Silver)		
NICHOLAS KIER (Knife Maker)	PITTSBURGH, PA	1840-1860
JACOB KIEWLE	GERMANY EXETER TOWNSHIP, PA Berks County	B1718-1750 1750-1760
(Cutler, Edged Tools Maker)		
BENJAMIN KING U.S. Navy M1797 boarding pike contract (1797-1799). (Pike Maker)	BALTIMORE, MD	1775-1805
DANIEL KING SR. (Coppersmith)	PHILADELPHIA, PA	1767-1800
DANIEL KING JR. (Whitesmith)	PHILADELPHIA, PA	1790-1811
ISAAC KING	PHILADELPHIA, PA CAMDEN, NJ SUMERSET, PA	1790-1815 1815-1818 1818-1825
Adv. guns, pistols, swords, and dirks (1818). (Gunsmith, Swordsmith)		
JOHN KING (Silversmith)	PHILADELPHIA, PA	1800-1820
WILLIAM KING (Silversmith)	PHILADELPHIA, PA	1800-1816
ADAM KINSLEY	CANTON, MA	1767-1789
LEONARD (JONATHAN) & KINSLEY (ADAM) Operated a rolling and slitting mill (bought by Paul Revere in 1799).	CANTON, MA	1789-1798
KINSLEY (ADAM) & PERKINS (JAMES) U.S. contract for 2,000 muskets (1798).	BRIDGEWATER, MA	1799-1801

ADAM KINSLEY	BRIDGEWATER, MA	1801-1807
FRENCH (THOMAS), BLAKE (SAMUEL), & KINSLEY (ADAM)	BRIDGEWATER, MA	1807-1818

Thomas French (B1778-D1862).
U.S. contract for muskets (1808).

LEONARD (CHARLES), KINSLEY (ADAM), & DANA (DANIEL)	CANTON, MA	1816

Charles Leonard (B1798-D1819).
Bid on U.S. Navy cutlass contract (1816).
(See James Perkins)
(See Leonard Family)
(Gun Maker, Sword Maker)

A. KIRCHNER (KUSHNER)	PHILADELPHIA, PA	1830-1850

(Cutler)

JOHN K. KIRCHNER (KUSHNER)	PHILADELPHIA, PA	1850-1865

Succeeded A. Kirchner.
(Cutler)

PETER KIRKWOOD	CHESTERTOWN, MD	1780-1799
	ANNAPOLIS, MD	1799-1801

Made silver-hilted naval dirks.
(Silversmith, Dirk Maker)

WILHELM KIRSCHBAUM	SOLINGEN, GERMANY	1725-1740
	PHILADELPHIA, PA	1740-1745

(Gunsmith, Cutler)

ANDREW KLINEDINST	YORK, PA	1820-1850

(Silversmith, Whitesmith, Gunsmith, Cutler)

JOHN (JOHANN) GODFRIED KNECHT	SOLINGEN, GERMANY	1771-1791
	RICHMOND, VA	1791-1796
	BALTIMORE, MD	1796-1816

Adv. making and grinding of surgical instruments, knives, razors, scissors and sword blades.
(Gunsmith, Blacksmith, Cutler, Blade Maker)

JULIUS KNECHT
(See F.W. Widmann)

RUDOLPH KOCH	FORT MICHILIMACKINAC, MI	1749-1783

Made axes, hatchets, and tomahawks.
(Cutler, Blacksmith)

PETER W. KRAFT
(See Confederate listings)

CHARLES A. KRYTER	WHEELING, WV	1773-1783

(Gun Maker, Cutler)

LAMSON (EBENEZER G. & NATHANIEL), GOODNOW (EBENEZER & ABEL P.) & YALE (B.B.)	WINDSOR, VT	1856-1864

Sold rifle stock-carving machinery to Providence Tool Works (1860).
U.S. contract for 50,000 muskets.

E. (EBENEZER) G. LAMSON & CO.	WINDSOR, VT	1864

U.S. contract for 1,000 Palmer Patent carbines.

WINDSOR MFG.	WINDSOR, VT	1864-1869

President: Ebenezer G. Lamson.
U.S. contract for 1,000 Ball Patent repeating carbines.
(Gunsmith)

EBENEZER G. LAMSON	SHELBURNE FALLS, MA	1820-1842
EBENEZER G. & NATHANIEL LAMSON	SHELBURNE FALLS, MA	1842-1844
LAMSON (EBENEZER G. & NATHANIEL) & GOODNOW (EBENEZER & ABEL F.)	SHELBURNE FALLS, MA	1844-1872

Employee: W.T. Clement.
Made bowie and belt knives and scythes.
Had a branch in New York;
  bought by Herman Boker (1872).
(See W.T. Clement)
(Cutler, Knife Maker, Edged Tool Maker)

J. LAMSON	BENNINGTON, VT	1815-1860

(Gunsmith)

TRUMAN LAMSON	BENNINGTON, VT	1840-1865
LAMSON (TRUMAN) & HUBBARD (COLEMAN S.)	BOSTON, MA	1865-1910

(Gunsmith, Swordsmith, Regalia and Society Swords)

WILLIAM LAMSON	BOSTON, MA	1775-1808

(Gunsmith)

LANDERS, FRARY & CLARK	NEW BRITAIN, CT	1865-1918

U.S. contracts for:
        15,000 military knives (1916)
        15,000 M1913 cavalry swords (1916)
        M1913 cavalry officer swords
        Bayonets
        Bowie knives
Blades marked "L.F. & C."
(Knife and Sword Maker)

PETER (PIERRE) LANDRY	RICHMOND, VA	1806-1808
	NORFOLK, VA	1808-1814
	PETERSBURG, VA	1814-1815
	NORFOLK, VA	1815-1822
	NEW ORLEANS, LA	1822-1823

(Silversmith, Gunsmith, Jeweler, Cutler)

JOEL LANE
(Cutler)

PHILADELPHIA, PA   1860-1865

RICHARD LATHAM
Adv. cutlery business in all its branches (1769).
(Gunsmith, Cutler)

CHARLESTON, SC   1769-D1784

LATOUCHE REGALIA CO.
Rented the space in the Wunderly Tavern
  building vacated by C.E. Ward (1910).
(Regalia)

NEW LONDON, OH   1910-1915

ROBERT B. LAWTON
Patented a pepperbox pistol-sword (1837).
Used an Ames M1832 foot artillery sword blade.
(Gunsmith)

NEWPORT, RI   1833-1840

ADAM LAYER
Swordsmith for Lewis Prahl.
(See Lewis Prahl)
(Sword Maker)

PHILADELPHIA, PA   1777

F. (FELIX) LEFEVRE
(Silversmith)

PHILADELPHIA, PA   1818-1848

ISAAC LEFEVRE

	PARIS, FRANCE	1688-1707
	PHILADELPHIA, PA	1708-1710
	ESOPUS, NY	1710-1712
	PEQUEA VALLEY, LAMPETER TOWNSHIP, PA Lancaster County	1712-1746

(Silversmith, Gunsmith)

JOHN FELIX LEFEVRE

	PARIS, FRANCE	1760-1782
	PHILADELPHIA, PA	1783-1809

**LEFEVRE (JOHN FELIX) & GRANVELLE
  (RENE L. & LOUISA M.)**   PHILADELPHIA, PA   1810-1811
J. (JOHN) F. (FELIX) LEFEVRE   PHILADELPHIA, PA   1812-D1813
U.S. contract for 216 brass-hilted artillery
  non-comm. swords (1812).
(Silversmith, Sword Hiltor, Sword Maker,
  Brass Founder)

PERIN LEFEVRE

	PARIS, FRANCE	1760-1782
	PHILADELPHIA, PA	1783-1796

(Silversmith, Jeweler, Clock Maker)

PHILIP LEFEVRE
Son of Isaac LeFevre.

	ESOPUS, NY	B1710-1712
	PEQUEA VALLEY, LAMPETER TOWN, PA Lancaster County	1712-D1766

(Gunsmith, Silversmith, Edged Tool Maker)

THEODORE LEFEVRE (Silversmith)	PHILADELPHIA, PA	1800-1820
THOMAS LEIPER Erected a blade mill on the Crum River. (Cutler, Edged Tools, Edged Weapons)	DELEWARE CO., PA	1824-1830

THE LEONARD FAMILY

CHARLES LEONARD Son of Jonathan Leonard. Charles Leonard, Adam Kinsley, and Daniel Dana bid on a U.S. Navy cutlass contract (1816).	CANTON, MA	1808-1826
	SANDWICH, MA	1826-1845
ELIPHALET LEONARD Gunsmith to Committee of Safety.	EASTON, MA	B1739, 1759-D1778
JONATHAN (QUAKER) LEONARD Son of Eliphalet Leonard.	EASTON, MA	B1759, 1779-1789
LEONARD (JONATHAN) & KINSLEY (ADAM)	CANTON, MA	1789-1799
Operated a rolling and slitting mill on the Naponset River. Paul Revere bought the mill (1799).		
JONATHAN LEONARD	CANTON, MA SANDWICH, MA	1799-1876 1826-D1845
(See Adam Kinsley) (See Paul Revere—Silversmith listings)		
J. (JONATHAN) W. LEONARD William H. Milner purchased Leonard Co. (1857). (See William H. Milnor) (Presentation Swords, Society Swords, Regalia)	NEW YORK, NY	1845-1857
ROBERT LEONARD Son of Jonathan Leonard. U.S. contract for 5,000 muskets (1808). Partners: Charles Leonard, Jonathan Leonard.	CANTON, MA	1808-1826
	SANDWICH, MA	1826-1845
SAMUEL LEONARD Son of Jonathan Leonard.	CANTON, MA	B1775, 1795-1808
	RICHMOND, VA	1808-1812
Worked at Virginia Manufactory. Forged and tempered artillery sabers. Probably made balled-hilt cavalry sabers for the War of 1812.		
DUNBAR (JAMES) & LEONARD (SAMUEL) Partners: James Bent, William Dunbar. U.S. contract for 1,500 sergent's swords (1813).	CANTON, MA	1812-1816
SAMUEL LEONARD	CANTON, MA	1816-D1854

JOHN LETELIER	**PHILADELPHIA, PA**	1755-1793
	WILMINGTON, DE	1793-1795
	CHESTER CO., PA	1795-1798
	PHILADELPHIA, PA	1798-1803
	WASHINGTON, D.C.	1803-1810

(Silversmith, Clock Maker, Surgical Instrument Maker, Jeweler, Cutler)

CURTIS LEWIS (LEWES)	**EAST CALN, PA** Chester County	B1769-1820
	READING, PA	1820-D1847

(Cutler, Clock Maker, Silversmith)

JOHN I. LEWIS	**PHILADELPHIA, PA**	1820-1837
JOHNSON (WILLIAM E.) & LEWIS (JOHN I.)	**PHILADELPHIA, PA**	1837-1845
JOHN I. LEWIS	**PHILADELPHIA, PA**	1845-1865

(Silversmith, Clock Maker)

THEOPHILUS LEWIS	**PHILADELPHIA, PA**	1775-1796

(Silversmith)

U.S. LEXINGTON ARSENAL **LEXINGTON, VA** 1776-1865
- Authorized by state of Virginia (1776).
- Stored large quantities of Virginia Manufactory (Richmond, VA) arms, muskets, pistols, and cavalry and lt. artillery sabers.
- James T. Ames altered (shortened and tapered blades; made new scabbards) 1,000 Virginia Manufactory cavalry sabers stored at Lexington Arsenal (1859).
- Used as a Confederate ordnance depot during the Civil War.

PETER LIGHT
(See David Hunter)

MITCHELL C. LILLEY **COLUMBUS, OH** B1819-1865
- Served in the Mexican War (1847-1848).
- Bookbinder and publisher.
- Published Masonic and Odd Fellows books.
- Partners: Charles M. Siebert, Christian Siebert.
- Lilley served in the Civil War (1861-1862).

M. (MITCHELL) C. LILLEY & CO. **COLUMBUS, OH** 1865-1882
- President: Mitchell C. Lilley.
- Partners: Charles H. Lindenburg, Henry Lindenberg, John Siebert.
- Started regalia and sword (society, U.S. regulation, and theatrical) production (1865).
- Made M1872 cavalry officer swords.
- Issued many military and society goods catalogs.
- Mitchell C. Lilley died (1882).

THE M.C. LILLEY & CO. **COLUMBUS, OH** 1882-1925
   President: Charles H. Lindenberg.
   Vice President: John Siebert.
   General Manager: Philip Lindenberg.
   Secretary, Treasurer: William Scarlett.

- Had offices in New York.
- Had offices in Boston, MA, at 46 Cornhill.
- Expanded into a complete line of military swords, uniforms, accessories, and equipment.
- Issued many military and society goods catalogs, including a 1919 presentation sword catalog.
- Sold a Masonic manual called *Tactics and Manual for Knights Templars*.
- The manual included:
    - Sword and Bugle Signals
    - Rules for Camps and Competitive Drills
    - Military Orders and Correspondence
    - Ceremonies and Hints for Knightly Courtesies
    - Commandery Working Text
    - Burial and Religious Services
    - Consecration of Banners
    - Grand Encampment Ceremonials
    - School of the Mounted Knight
    - Sword Exercise
    - Manual of the Sword (Mounted) (Dismounted)
    - Parade and Review
    - The Templar Uniform
    - Crosses and Heraldic Cinctures
- The M.C. Lilley & Co. advertisement in the manual offered
    - Military and band uniforms
    - Swords (military, society, and theatrical)
    - Laces, fringes, and cords (imported)
    - Silks and velvets
    - Lodge supples and uniforms for all societies
    - Banners and flags
    - Emblematic pictures (societies)
- The M.C. Lilley & Co. purchased the Henderson-Ames Company (1923).
- The M.C. Lilley & Co. purchased the Ames Sword Company (1925).

THE LILLEY CO.   **COLUMBUS, OH**   **1925-1931**

Issued sword catalogs.
The Ames equipment, tools, machinery, etc. were
 moved from Chicopee, MA, to Columbus, OH (1925-1931).

THE LILLEY-AMES CO.   **COLUMBUS, OH**   **1931-1951**

- Had a U.S. contract for 2,938 M1941 naval cutlasses with scabbards (1941).
- Made a complete line of U.S. regulation swords, including Marine Corps, West Point cadet, and Annapolis cadet swords.
- Issued many military and fraternal goods catalogs.
- The company failed to diversify as regalia sales declined, and C.E. Ward bought Lilley-Ames (1951).
- (Military Goods, Swords, Regalia, Uniforms)

LILLEY AMES CO.   **COLUMBUS, OH**   **1951-1953**

Operated as a badge manufacturer.
(See C.E. Ward)
(See N.P. Ames)

BENJAMIN LINCOHN   **BALTIMORE, MD**   **1775-1805**

U.S. Navy contract for 200 M1797 boarding
 pikes—100 for ship "pickering" and 100 for
 ship "herald" (1797).

JOSEPH LINCOHN
(See U.S. Philadelphia Armory)

COLONEL OLIVER LIPPINCOTT　　　　CHICAGO, IL　　　　1860-1880
- Locations:
    - 195-197 Lake Street　　1860-1875
    - 195 Lake Street　　　　1875-1879
    - 81 Randolph Street　　 1879-1880
- U.S. contract for M1872 cavalry officer swords.
- Made M1860 staff and field officer swords.
- The company burned down in the Chicago fire (1871) but was rebuilt.
- Adv. in the Chicago city directory under government, society, and military goods.

(Military Goods, Regalia, Society Swords)

WILLIAM LITHGOW　　　　THOMASTON, ME　　　1739-1749
　　　　　　　　　　　　　　BRUNSWICK, ME　　　 1740-1754
　　　　　　　　　　　　　　HALIFAX, ME　　　　　 1754

Armorer to the Colony of Maine.
(Armorer)

NICODEMUS LLOYD　　　　PHILADELPHIA, PA　　　1800-1810
Made tomahawks and cutlery.
(Cutler)

W.A. LLOYD　　　　　　　PHILADELPHIA, PA　　　1800-1810
(Silversmith)

JAMES LOCK (LOCKE)　　KEENE, NH　　　　　　B1790-1818
　　　　　　　　　　　　　　WELLSBOROUGH, PA　　1818-D1874
　　　　　　　　　　　　　　Tiogg County

(Gunsmith, Silversmith, Stonecutter, Cutler)

LUDWIG LOEWE
(See Charles Degenhardt)

NICHOLAS LOW　　　　　PHILADELPHIA, PA　　　1775-1783
Made 158 naval cutlasses for the Committee of Safety (1776).
(Blacksmith, Sword Maker)

WILLIAM LOW　　　　　　PHILADELPHIA, PA　　　B1755-1785
Armorer in the Pennsylvania militia.
(Armorer)

WILLIAM LOW　　　　　　OVID, NY　　　　　　　1793-1818
　　　　　　　　　　　　　　Seneca County
- Had a state of New York contract for 250 cavalry sabers, 300 rifles, and 250 pistols (1813).
- The arms were used to outfit a new New York militia cavalry regiment.
- The unit was raised by Governor Daniel Tompkins to defend the Canadian border during the War of 1812.

- Arms marked "S.N.Y."
(Sword Maker, Rifle Maker, Pistol Maker)

DAVID LOWERY Committee of Safety musket and bayonet maker (1777). (Gunlocks, Gunsmith)	WETHERSFIELD, CT	1775-1783
CALEB LOWNES (Silversmith)	PHILADELPHIA, PA	1779-1783
DAVID LOWNES (Silversmith)	PHILADELPHIA, PA	1770-D1810
EDWARD LOWNES	PHILADELPHIA, PA	B1792-1816
LOWNES (JOSEPH & EDWARD) & ERWIN **(HENRY & JOHN)**	PHILADELPHIA, PA	1816-1817
EDWARD LOWNES (See Henry & John Erwin-Silversmith listings) (Silversmith, Goldsmith, Watch Maker)	PHILADELPHIA, PA	1817-D1834
GEORGES LOWNES	SPRINGFIELD, PA Chester County	1760-1790
HUGH LOWNES	SPRINGFIELD, PA Chester County	1760-1790
SLATER LOWNES (Blacksmiths, Cutlers)	SPRINGFIELD, PA Chester County	1760-1790
JOSEPH LOWNES Apprentice: Samuel Williamson (1787-1792).	PHILADELPHIA, PA	B1758-1816
LOWNES (JOSEPH & EDWARD) & ERWIN **(HENRY & JOHN)**	PHILADELPHIA, PA	1816-1817
JOSEPH & JOSIAH H. LOWNES Josiah, Joseph's son, died (1822). (Silversmith, Goldsmith, Watch Maker, Sword Hiltor)	PHILADELPHIA, PA	1817-D1820
JOHN LUDWIG Committee of Safety bayonet maker and arms repair (1776). (Gunsmith, Silversmith, Watch Maker)	PHILADELPHIA, PA	1775-1792
JOSEPH LUMBARD (See Springfield Armory)		
F. LUSIGNANT (Cutler)	FORT WAYNE, IN	1820-1840

PETER LYDICK	PHILADELPHIA, PA	1755-1775
	BALTIMORE, MD	1775-1810

Committee of Safety musket and bayonet maker (1776-1777).
(Gunsmith)

ROBERT MANN SR.	PHILADELPHIA, PA	1775-1783

Swordsmith for Lewis Prahl (1777).
(See Lewis Prahl)
(Sword Maker, Cutler)

JOSEPH MANNING	NEW YORK, NY	1820-1845
	MEDINA, OH	1845-1855

Made belt knives, belt axes, and tomahawks.
(Silversmith, Cutler)

HENRY MANSFIELD	SLATERVILLE, RI	1800-1820
MANSFIELD (HENRY) & LAMB (ESTUS)	SLATERVILLE, RI	1820-1861

Operated a cotton textile factory.
Built a scythe factory in Forestdale, RI (1824).

MANSFIELD (HENRY) & LAMB (ESTUS)	FORESTDALE, RI	1861-1871

- Had seven Civil War U.S. contracts for M1860 cavalry sabers totaling 37,458.
- The first 2,000 had scabbard mounts made of malleable iron, which were rejected by the government but later accepted at a lower price.
- Imported 458 cavalry sabers (80 M1840s; 378 M1860s) from A&F Kirschbaum, Solingen, Germany (1862).
- Also made gun parts.
- After the war, the company went back to its original business of cotton textiles and edged tools.
- G. & W. Slater bought Mansfield & Lamb (1871).

GEORGE F. MANZ	PITTSBURGH, PA	1818-1867
	WHEELING, WV	1868-1869

(Cutler, Gun Maker, Pistolmaker)

BENJAMIN MARKLEY	NEW HANOVER TOWNSHIP, PA Philadelphia County	1760-1785

(Cutler)

JACOB MARKLEY	NORTHUMBERLAND CO., PA	1750

(Cutler)

MARSH & STONE
(See Soloman Stone)

WILLIAM W. (WALKER) MARSTON	NEW YORK, NY	B1872, 1840-D1872

Made a three-barrel knife-pistol
(Cutler)

JAMES MARTIN	THOMASTON, ME	1758-1759

Armorer to the Colony of Maine.

JOHN MARTIN	BALTIMORE, MD	1775-1805

U.S. Navy contract for M1797 boarding pikes (1797-1799).
(Pike Maker)

COLONY OF MARYLAND
Ordered 250 basket-hilted swords with belts from England (1742).

JOSEPH MASSY	EASTON, PA Chester County	1751-1771

(Blacksmith, Cutler)

JOHN MATTHEWS	SHEFFIELD, ENGLAND	B1816-1835
	PITTSBURG, PA	1835-1850

(Cutler, Knife Maker)

WELCOME MATHEWSON	GLOUCESTER, MA	B1778, 1800-1842
	BURRILVILLE, RI	1843-D1877

Made and repaired guns, edged tools, knives, bayonets, swords, spontoons, and knife, bayonet, and sword blades.
(Sword, Blade, Spontoon, Gun, and Pistol Maker; Silversmith, Cutler)

JOHN MAYWEG	PHILADELPHIA, PA	1794-1814
MAYWEG (JOHN) & NIPPES (DANIEL)	PHILADELPHIA, PA	1814-1815

U.S. contract for 2,000 cutlasses (1814).

JOHN MAYWEG	PHILADELPHIA, PA	1815-1829
JOHN & WILLIAM MAYWEG	PHILADELPHIA, PA	1829-1830

(See Daniel Nippes)
(Gun Maker, Sword Maker)

THOMAS MCCARTHY	PITTSBURGH, PA	1830-1840

(Cutler, Surgical Instrument Maker)

DANIEL MCCLINTOCK	LETTERKENNY TOWNSHIP, PA Cumberland County	1770-1781
	GUILFORD TOWNSHIP, PA Cumberland County	1781-1785

Made cavalry sabers, belt knives, and bayonets.

	TEBOYNE TOWNSHIP, PA Cumberland County	1785-1790

(Cutler, Edged Weapon Maker)

HUGH MCCONNELL	SAN FRANCISCO, CA	1850-1865

Made bowie knives and surgical instruments. Bought out Frederick Will (1863).
(See Frederic Will)
(Cutler)

JAMES MCCORMICK	IRELAND	1756-1776

ROBERT MCCORMICK	IRELAND	1756-1776
James and Robert McCormick immigrated to Philadelphia, PA (1776)		
	PHILADELPHIA, PA	1776-1801

Set up a gun factory in the Old Globe Mill (1798).
Superintendent: James Haslett.
U.S. contract for 3,000 muskets and bayonets (1798).
Virginia contract for 4,000 muskets (1799).

MCCORMICK (JAMES & ROBERT) & JOHNSTON (RICHARD)	PHILADELPHIA, PA	1801

Pennsylvania contract for 1,000 muskets (1801).
John Miles Sr. bought the McCormick Globe Mill Factory (1801).
(See John Miles Sr.)
(Gunsmith, Clock Maker)

CHARLES MCDONALD	RICHMOND, IN Wayne County	1861-1865

Made bowie and hunting knives.
(Cutler)

GEORGE MCGUNNEGLE	CUMBERLAND CO., PA	1735, 1756-1787
	PITTSBURGH, PA	1787-D1820

Repaired guns for the Committee of Safety (1776-1783).
Adv. knives, tomahawks, and sword grinding in the *Pittsburgh Gazette* (1787).
(Gunsmith, Blacksmith, Whitesmith, Iron Founder, Brass Founder)

WILLIAM MCKNIGHT	PITTSBURGH, PA	1795-1803
MCKNIGHT (WILLIAM) & MCLURG (JOSEPH SR., JOSEPH JR. & ALEXANDER)	PITTSBURGH, PA	1803-1815
Had an air furnace and cannon factory.		
WILLIAM MCKNIGHT	PITTSBURGH, PA	1815-1820

Adv. in the Pittsburgh business directory as a sword and edged tool maker (1815).
(Edged Tools, Sword Maker, Cannon Maker, Coppersmith, Tinsmith)

WILLIAM MCLAWS	SCOTLAND	1770-1790
	PHILADELPHIA, PA	1790-1803

Naturalized (1796).
Sold solid-brass-hilted, eagle-head-pommel officer short sabers.
(Cutler, Saddler, Harness Maker)

JAMES MCNAUGHT	LONDON, ENGLAND	1800-1816
BOLTON (J.) & MCNAUGHT (JAMES)	RICHMOND, VA	1816-1817
JAMES MCNAUGHT	RICHMOND, VA	1817-D1825

Adv. pistols, guns, dirks, and officer's hangers (1820).
Also made rifles, dirk pistols, and crossbows.
(Gun, Dirk, and Sword Maker)

WILLIAM MEADOWS	ENGLAND	B1731-1776
	PHILADELPHIA, PA	1776-1783

(Silversmith, Sword Hiltor)

SAMUEL MEALS	MENALLEN TOWNSHIP, PA	1830-1860
	Adams County	

(Cutler, Knife Maker)

JOHN W. (WILLIAM) MEER	BIRMINGHAM, ENGLAND	1774-1790
	PHILADELPHIA, PA	1790-D1834

- Exhibited at the Columbian Exposition in Philadelphia (1795).
- Naturalized (1798).
- Engraved blades for presentation swords made by Joseph and William Rose Sr. for naval heros of the War of 1812.
- Used a lacquer-etching engraving system.
- Engraved blades for Thomas Fletcher and Samuel Alexander.
- Decorated Masonic aprons.
- Keeper of weights and measures for city of Philadelphia (1814-1818).
- Painter on enamel and engraver on stone.

(Artist and Sword Engraver, Japanner)

M. MELCHER	BALTIMORE, MD	1775-1805

U.S. Navy contract for M1797 boarding pikes (1797-1799).
(Pike Maker)

HENRY MELLINGER	LANCASTER CO., PA	1850-1883

(Knife Maker, Edged Tool Maker, Cutler)

WILLIAM MELLINGER	LANCASTER CO., PA	1765-1785

(Cutler)

GEORGE MENG (MING)	PHILADELPHIA, PA	1790-1800

(Cutler)

WOLERE MENG (MING)	PHILADELPHIA, PA	1765-1783

Armorer to the Colony of Pennsylvania.
Committee of Safety bayonet scabbard (leather) maker (1776).
Also made bayonet belts and cartouche boxes.
(Leather Shop, Armorer)

BENJAMIN MEREDITH	BALTIMORE, MD	1800-1817

(Blacksmith, Whitesmith, Gunsmith, Cutler)

JOHN MESSERSMITH	BALTIMORE, MD	1750-1776
	LANCASTER, PA	1776-1816

Partner: Jacob Messersmith.
Committee of Safety musket and bayonet maker (1776).
(Gunsmith)

SAMUEL MESSERSMITH	BALTIMORE, MD	B1732, 1752-D1803

Committee of Safety arms maker and arms
  repair (1776).
(Gunsmith)

JOHN MILES SR.	LONDON, ENGLAND	B1752-1790
	PHILADELPHIA, PA	1790-1792
	NEW LONDON, VA	1792-1797

Worked at U.S. New London Arsenal.

	PHILADELPHIA, PA	1797-1800

- Set up a musket and pistol factory.
- Adv. small arms (1798).
- Pennsylvania contract for 2,000 musket (1798).
- U.S. contract for 400 muskets (1798).

	PHILADELPHIA, PA Globe Mill	1801-D1818

- Bought the Robert McCormick Gun Factory
  at the Old Globe Mill (1801).
- Pennsylvania contract for 2,000 muskets (1801).
- Sent two cavalry saber samples to the state of Virginia (inspected
  at the Virginia Manufactory) (1801).
- Virginia contract for 1,000 cavalry sabers (hussar hilt) (1801).
- Some marked "1st regiment-Virginia Cavalry Dinwidde."
- Some marked "4th regiment-Virginia Cavalry Essex."
- Virginia contract for 3,025 muskets and 250 pair of pistols (1801).

(Sword and Musket Maker)

JOHN MILES JR.	LONDON, ENGLAND	B1777-1790

Son of John Sr.

	PHILADELPHIA, PA	1790-1808
	BORDERTOWN, NJ	1808-D1852

U.S. contract for 9,200 muskets (1808).
(Musket Maker)

MILITARY SUPPLY CO. (MILSCO)		1941-1945

Made M1941 Klewang-type (open hilt) naval cutlass
  used by World War II shore parties and non-comms.
  as a ceremonial sword.
Some issued to an engineers battalion in Inchon,
  North Korea, during the Korean War.

THE MILLARD FAMILY

CHARLES MILLARD	DELEWARE CO., NY	B1771-1814
AMASA MILLARD	DELEWARE CO., NY	c.1775-1814
NATHANIEL MILLARD	DELEWARE CO., NY	c.1775-1814

The three Millard brothers moved to Sauquoit
  in the Sauquoit Valley, Paris Township, NY (1814).

CHARLES AND AMASA MILLARD	SAUQUOIT, PARIS TOWNSHIP, NY	1814-1840

- Charles and Amasa Millard set up a scythe-
  manufacturing business in the machine shop
  of the Quaker Co. wool-weaving mill (1814-1816).
- They installed trip hammers at the machine shop.

- They then opened another scythe shop at the nearby Willowvale, NY, machine shop owned by Amos and Oliver Rogers.
- Made cotton- and wool-weaving machinery at Willowvale.

DAVID J. MILLARD DELEWARE CO., NY B1804-1814

Moved to Sauquoit with his father Charles and uncles Amasa and Nathaniel (1814).

SAUQUOIT,
PARIS TOWNSHIP, NY 1814-1840

- Worked in the Millard brothers' scythe shops.
- Educated himself and became a district schoolmaster.
- Elected town clerk (1835).
- Became superintendant of the Farmers Factory (cotton weaving mill) in South Sauqoit in 1835 (founded by Ephraim Davis in 1812).
- Married Clarissa Mosher (1835).
- David J. Millard's father, Charles, died (1837).
- Millard moved to the village of Paris Furnace near Utica, NY, and opened his own farm implement factory (1840).

PARIS FURNACE,
PARIS TOWNSHIP, NY 1840-1849
Oneida County

- Called the Paris Furnace Company.
- Millard purchased the Bowles (Nathan H.) and Beach (Daniel) farm implement factory (1840). (Bowles and Beach had succeeded Ephraim Davis and Nathan H. Bowles in 1834. They bought the shovel factory—opened in 1814—of Elijah Cobb and Nathan Robinson in 1818.)
- Millard's brother Sterling A. Millard (B1811-D1883) worked at the factory, becoming supervisor (1852-1853).
- Factory superintendant: Cornelius J. Knickerbocker.
- Millard expanded rapidly, erecting new shops, storehouses, and workmen residences (tenements).
- Built a road from the factory to his residence.
- Bought additional property at the site of the old Paris Furnace (erected in 1792 by Isaac Paris) on the Sauqoit Creek.
- A hoe factory was built on the property.
- Made hayforks, hoes, scythes, plow points, and other farm implements.
- His business grew rapidly as he set up agents for his products across the country.
- Millard became one of the largest manufacturers of farm implements in the United States and one of its first millionaires.
- He purchased the old Scollard Tavern and Inn from Horace Luce, remodeled it, and made it his new residence (eventually 35 rooms). The inn was originally ordered built as a government post house by the British Colonial Governor Sir William Johnson in 1775. Mr. Scollard bought it in 1800 and turned it into a tavern and inn. Horace Luce bought it around 1820. The house was later used as a station in the Underground Railroad.
- The name of the village of Paris Furnace was officially changed to Clayville in honor of Henry Clay (1849). The name had been changed locally at Millard's suggestion at a Whig meeting (1844).

CLAYVILLE,
PARIS TOWNSHIP, NY 1849-D1875
Oneida County

- Called the Paris Furnance Company.
- Sterling Millard left to set up his own farm implement factory further up on the Sauqoit Creek on Crooked Hill Road (1854).
- Seeing the need for swords in the coming Civil War, Millard went to Solingen, Germany (c. 1860), and brought back German swordsmith George (Georg) Scheuch.
- Scheuch was a member of the famous Scheuch family of swordsmiths, hiltors, goldsmiths, and jewelers who lived in Munich and Dresden in the late sixteenth and early seventeenth centuries.

Anton Scheuch	Munich and Dresden	1582-1610
Isreal Scheuch	Munich and Dresden	1580-1606
George Scheuch	Dresden	1613-1630

- George Scheuch showed Millard how to fabricate cavalry swords.
- Millard then obtained a U.S. government contract for 10,000 M1860 cavalry sabers (1861).
- Charles E. Wilson (C.E.W.) of Clayville inspected many of the sabers.
- George Scheuch later married D.J. Millard's daughter and eventually lived, with his family, in Millard's mansion. Millard also made M1860 staff and field officer swords.
- He sold sword blades to Tiffany & Co. of New York, NY.
- Millard retired because of ill health (1865).
- He and his wife Clarissa then began to live at his son-in-law's (Samuel J. Look) house.
- Look had married Millard's daughter Sarah Jane Millard.
- Samuel J. Look (B1829) was secretary-treasurer of Millard's company from 1869 to 1875 and probably earlier.
- David J. Millard died (1875).
- Benjamin F. Avery of Louisville, KY, purchased the company, to make his own hoes and hayforks (1875).
- Samuel J. Look and his wife Sarah Jane then moved to Louisville to work at Avery's factory.

STERLING A. MILLARD **DELAWARE CO., NY** B1811-1814
He moved with his father Charles and brother David J. Millard to Sauquoit, NY (1814).

SAUQUOIT,
PARIS TOWNSHIP, NY 1814-1840

Worked in the Millard brothers' scythe shops.
Moved with his brother David J. Millard to Paris Furnace, NY (1840).

PARIS FURNACE,
PARIS TOWNSHIP, NY 1840-1849
Oneida County

Worked at the Paris Furnace Co.
Sterling's son Charles S. Millard born (1842).
Sterling's son George A. Millard born (1847).
The name of village of Paris Furnace changed to Clayville (1849).

CLAYVILLE,
PARIS TOWNSHIP, NY 1849-1854

Continued to work with his brother at the Paris Furnace Company.
Eventually become factory supervisor (1852-1853).
Left to set up his own farm implement factory further up the Sauqoit Creek (1854).

S. (STERLING) A. MILLARD & CO.	CLAYVILLE, PARIS TOWNSHIP, NY	1854-D1883

- Sterling's son William J. Millard born (1857).
- His other son Charles S. Millard became a partner after he left the 117th Ohio Infantry because of poor health (1864).
- Sterling A. Millard died (1883).

(Farm Implements)

CHARLES S. MILLARD	PARIS FURNACE, PARIS TOWNSHIP, NY	B1842-1849

Son of Sterling A. Millard.
The name of the Village of Paris Furnace was changed to Clayville (1849).

	CLAYVILLE, PARIS TOWNSHIP, NY	1849-1864

Probably worked at his father's farm implement factory (started in 1854).
Served in the Civil War (1862-1864), becoming a first lieutenant and adjutant of the 117th Ohio Infantry.
He resigned because of ill health (1864).

S. (STERLING) A. MILLARD & CO.	CLAYVILLE, PARIS TOWNSHIP, NY	1864-1883

Partner: Charles S. Millard.

ELIZABETH MILLER	BOSTON, MA	1775-1783

Sold 52 cutlasses to Capt. Robert Towers, Commissary of Military Stores, U.S. Philadelphia Armory (1775).
(See U.S. Philadelphia Armory)
(Sword Maker, Cutler)

FRANCIS MILLER	PHILADELPHIA, PA	1777

Armorer and artillery artificer at the U.S. Philadelphia Armory.

	LEBANON, PA	1778-1781

Armorer at the U.S. Lebanon Armory.
(See Armory listings)
(Blacksmith)

GEORGE MILLER	PHILADELPHIA, PA	1780-D1806

(Silversmith, Clock Maker)

JOHN MILLER	PHILADELPHIA, PA	1779

Artillery artificer at the U.S. Philadelphia Armory.
(Blacksmith)

JOHN L. MILLER	PHILADELPHIA, PA	1860-1865

(Cutler)

NATHAN MILLER	EAST GREENWICH, RI	B1755, 1775-D1804

Revolutionary War bayonet maker.
(Cutler)

PETER MILLER (Silvermsith, Clock Maker)	**PHILADELPHIA, PA**	**1772, 1790-D1855**
SAMUEL MILLER Adv. swords, hangers, cutlasses, pistols, and firelocks (1742). Bought out John Pim (1730). (Gunsmith, Sword Maker, Cutler)	**BOSTON, MA**	**1725-1745**
WILLIAM MILLER **WARD (JOHN) & MILLER (WILLIAM)** **WILLIAM MILLER** (Silversmith, Clock Maker)	**PHILADELPHIA, PA** **PHILADELPHIA PA** **PHILADELPHIA, PA**	**1812-1822** **1822-1824** **1824-1847**
WILLIAM H. MILNER William Price bought Milner (1858). (See William Price) (Presentation and Society Swords, Regalia)	**NEW YORK, NY**	**1857-1858**
NATHANIEL MITCHELL Son of Samuel. (Blacksmith, Cutler)	**UNIONTOWN, GERMAN TOWNSHIP, PA**	**1814-1850**
RICHARD MITCHELL (Cutler)	**MIDDLETOWN TOWNSHIP, PA** Bucks County	**1775-1783**
SAMUEL MITCHELL Operated a blade mill with tilt hammer. (Cutler, Edged Tools)	**UNIONTOWN, GERMAN TOWNSHIP, PA**	**1790-D1821**
E.E. MITCHENER (Regalia, Society Swords)	**SHELTONVILLE, GA**	**1855-1860**
JOHN LEWIS MOISSON Adv. as a gunsmith with a cutlery business in all its branches (1812). (Gunsmith, Cutler)	**PARIS, FRANCE** **CHARLESTON, SC**	**1800-1807** **1807-D1830**
FREDERICK MOLLER (Regalia, Society Swords)	**NEW YORK, NY**	**1840-1845**
EDWARD MORGAN (Gunsmith)	**MONTGOMERY CO., PA**	**1775-1783**
GEORGE MORGAN (Gunsmith)	**PHILADELPHIA, PA**	**1756-1776**
GIDEON MORGAN **MORGAN (GIDEON) & HART (FERDINAND)**	**PITTSBURGH, PA** **PITTSBURGH, PA**	**1800-1818** **1818-1820**

GIDEON MORGAN (Silversmith, Watch Maker)	PITTSBURGH, PA	1820-1825
JOHN MORGAN (Blacksmith, Cutler)	KENNETT, PA Chester County	1750-1766
JOHN MORGAN **HOOKER (WILLIAM) & MORGAN (JOHN)** **JOHN MORGAN** (Silversmith)	PHILADELPHIA, PA PHILADELPHIA, PA PHILADELPHIA, PA	1798-1813 1813-1814 1814-1831
JOSEPH MORGAN	MORRISTOWN, NY PHILADELPHIA, PA SPRINGFIELD, MA	1759-1796 1796-1800 1800-1805

Arms inspector at the U.S. Springfield Arsenal.
Superintendant at the U.S. Springfield Arsenal
 (1802-1805).
(Cutler, Whitesmith, Gunsmith, Pistolmaker,
 Brassfounder)

THOMAS MORGAN Apprenticed to Benjamin Rittenhouse (1765-1770).	WORCHESTER, MA	1750-1770
	BALTIMORE, MD PHILADELPHIA, PA	1771-1778 1779-1795

Apprentice: Robert Leslie.
(See Benjamin Rittenhouse)
(Silversmith, Clock Maker)

HENRY A. MORRILL	EAST AMHERST, MA	1815-1836
CHARLES BLAIR	EAST AMHERST, MA	1816-1836
MORRILL (HENRY A.), MOSMAN (SILAS A. JR.) & BLAIR (CHARLES)	EAST AMHERST, MA	1836-1838

Made George Elgin's cutlass pistols, bowie
 knife-pistols (Ames Mfg. Co. made the blades),
 and regular pistols.

MORRILL (HENRY H.) & BLAIR (CHARLES)	EAST AMHERST, MA	1838-1839
CHARLES BLAIR	COLLINSVILLE, CT	1839-1885

- Superintendant at Collins & Co. (1839-1845).
- Collins was a cutler and edged weapons maker.
- Had a separate contract for 1,000 pikes
  with John Brown (1857).
- Made 12 samples (1857).
- Made 954 pikes (1858).
- Blair made the handles and cross guards;
  Charles Hart of Collinsville made the blades
  (a New Haven company made the ferrules).
- Blair made patented axe bits (1869).
- (See Silas A. Mosman)
- (See Collins & Co.)
- (See Charles Hart)

(Pike Maker, Pistol Maker, Cutler, Edged Tools)

BENJAMIN MORRIS (Silversmith, Clock Maker)	HILLTOWN, PA Bucks County	1760-1783
ENOS MORRIS Son of Benjamin. (Silversmith, Clock Maker)	HILLTOWN, PA Bucks County	1770-1783
JOHN MORRIS (Silvermsith)	PHILADELPHIA, PA	1815-1840
JOHN MORRIS (Gunsmith)	PHILADELPHIA, PA Southwark Township	1768-1783
SAMUEL MORRIS Committee of Safety naval cutlass maker (1776). (Sword Maker)	PHILADELPHIA, PA	1775-1783
MURDOCK MORRISON (See Confederate listings)		
ABRAHAM MORROW Committee of Safety musket and bayonet maker and arms repair (1777). U.S. rifle contract (1791).	PHILADELPHIA, PA	1775-1806
MORROW (ABRAHAM) & BERNARD (B.) (Gunsmith, Silversmith)	PHILADELPHIA, PA	1806-1808
ABNER MOSMAN Worked for Ames Mfg. Co. (1831-1836). (See Ames Family)	CABOTVILLE, MA	1790-1836
DEXTER F. MOSMAN U.S. arms inspector (1862-1863). Inspected some M1840 lt. artillery sabers made by C. Roby, Chelmsford, MA (1863).	SPRINGFIELD, MA	1862-1863
MELZAR H. MOSMAN Son of Silas. Cast bronze statues for the Ames Mfg. Co.	CABOTVILLE, MA	1875-1895
SILAS A. MOSMAN JR. Son of Abner. Worked for Ames Mfg. Co. (1831-1836).	CABOTVILLE, MA	1811-1836
MORRILL (HENRY A.), MOSMAN (SILAS A. JR.) & BLAIR (CHARLES)	EAST AMHERST, MA	1836-1838
SILAS A. MOSMAN JR. Went back to work for the Ames Mfg. Co. as a grinder, etcher, and founder. (See Henry A. Morrill) (Cutler, Pistolmaker, Etcher, Founder)	CABOTVILE, MA	1838-1870

NICHOLAS MUNSHORE (Blacksmith, Cutler)	COVENTRY, PA Chester County	1769
AMOS MUNSON (Silversmith)	NEW HAVEN, CT	B1753, 1770-D1785
THEOPHILUS MUNSON Infantry pike maker and armorer to the Colony of Connecticut (1711). (Armorer, Pike Maker)	NEW HAVEN, CT	B1675, 1700-D1747
JAMES MURRAY Made razors and knives. (Cutler)	YORK, PA	1780-1805
SHELDON NASH Made belt knives. (Cutler, Silversmith)	CINCINNATI, OH	1850-1863
ALEXANDER NELSON Committee of Safety contract for 600 muskets and bayonets (1777).	PHILADELPHIA, PA	1775-1819
CANBY (CHARLES) & NELSON (ALEXANDER)	WESTCHESTER, PA Chester County	1819
ALEXANDER NELSON (Gunsmith, Silversmith, Watch Maker)	CHESTER CO., PA	1820
FRANCIS NELSON (Gunsmith)	PHILADELPHIA, PA	1775-1783
WILLIAM NEVIN Partners: Anthony Pinkney, Charles White. Committee of Safety contract for 1,000 naval pikes; Charles White made the shafts (1776). (Pike Maker)	ANNAPOLIS, MD	1775-1783
MOSES NEWTON Committee of Safety musket, bayonet, and lock maker (1776). (Gunsmith)	HARTFORD, CT	1775-1783
NEW YORK NAVAL YARD (N.Y.N.Y.) • Made naval boarding axes and pikes for the War of 1812. • Auctioned off 585 boarding pikes (1827). • Accepted delivery of 1,000 naval cutlasses from Robert Dingee of New York (1830). • (See Robert Dingee) • Sent 300 pikes to Flag Officer Foote in New Orleans (1862).	NEW YORK, NY	

STATE OF NEW YORK
The state of New York at convention in New York on September 4, 1776, set up a committee of 12 men to obtain 4,000 cavalry lances (800 to be made in each of the five counties).
Stephan Ward, William Miller, and Thaddeus Crane were appointed in Westchester County.

JOHN NICHOLSON SR.	PHILADELPHIA, PA	1754-D1799

- Made 60 muskets and bayonets for the Committee of Safety (1775-1776).
- Adv. muskets, pistols, blunderbusses, and cutlasses (1781).
- Repaired arms for the Committee of Safety (1791-1792).
- Pennsylvania contracts for rifles and pistols (1797).
- U.S. inspector at the Philadelphia Armory (1797-1790).

(Sword Maker, Gun Maker)

R.B. NICHOLSON	PHILADELPHIA, PA	1799-1810

Son of John Nicholson Sr.
Succeeded John Sr.

JOHN NICHOLSON JR.	PHILADELPHIA, PA	1799-1810

Son of John Nicholson Sr.
Arms inspector at the U.S. Philadelphia Armory (1799-1807).
(Sword Maker, Gun Maker)

THE NIPPES FAMILY

ABRAHAM NIPPES	SOLINGEN, GERMANY	1777-1796
	PHILADEPHIA, PA	1796-1803
	RICHMOND, VA	1803-1807

Worked as a sword hiltor at the Virginia Manufactory.

	PHILADELPHIA, PA	1807-1856

Lived at 262 St. John Street in 1813.
Employee: John Hine (barrel maker).
Finished James Winner's U.S. contract for 500 cavalry sabers (1811).
Adv. as a gunsmith at 111 Dillwyn in the McElroy Philadelphia Directory (1842).
(Gun Maker, Sword Maker)

ALBERT S. NIPPES	MILLCREEK, PA	1830-1860

Son of Daniel Nippes.
(Gun Maker)

DANIEL NIPPES	SOLINGEN, GERMANY	1777-1796
	PHILADELPHIA, PA	1796-1808

WINNER (JAMES) & NIPPES (DANIEL) & CO.	PHILADELPHIA, PA	1808

U.S. contract for 9,000 M1808 muskets.

WINNER (JAMES), NIPPES (DANIEL) & STEINMAN (JOHN)	PHILADELPHIA, PA	1808-1810

Made 500 M1808 muskets for 1808 contract.

DANIEL NIPPES	PHILADELPHIA, PA	1810-1814

U.S. contract for 1,000 cavalry sabers (1810).
Lived at 262 St. John Street (1813).

MAYWEG (JOHN) & NIPPES (DANIEL)	PHILADELPHIA, PA	1814-1815

U.S. contract for 2,000 cutlasses.

DANIEL NIPPES	MILL CREEK, PA	1815-1848

Established Nippes Gun Factory at Mill Creek, PA.
Called Rose Glen Mill.
Had three U.S. contracts for muskets.
Had one U.S. contract for rifles.

	MERION TOWNSHIP, PA Montgomery County	1848-1850

(See James Winner)
(See Mayweg & Nippes)
(Gun Maker, Sword Maker)

CHARLES NIPPES	PHILADELPHIA, PA	1800-1825

Lived at 262 St. John Street (1823).
(Gun Maker)

J.A. NIPPES	PHILADELPHIA, PA	1800-1816

(Gun Maker)

WILLIAM NIPPES	SOLINGEN, GERMANY	1777-1796
	PHILADELPHIA, PA	1796-1836

Lived at 262 St. John Street (1813).
(Gun Maker, Sword Maker)

MARTIN NITSCHMANN	MORAVIA	1729-1749
	BETHLEHEM, PA	1749-1760

(Cutler)

ANTHONY NOBLE	MARTINSBURG, VA	1775-1783

Partner: Adam Stephen.
Committee of Safety musket
  and bayonet maker (1777).
(Gunsmith)

BENJAMIN NOLL	CRUMRU TOWNSHIP, PA Berks County	1840-1850

Made edged weapons.
(Gunsmith, Cutler)

HENRY NOLL	YORK, WASHINGTON TOWNSHIP, PA Franklin County	B1791, 1821-D1855

Son of John Jr.
(Gunsmith, Cutler)

JOHN NOLL SR. (Flintlock Maker, Silversmith)	LANCASTER CO., PA	B1725, 1745-D1805
JOHN NOLL JR.	LANCASTER CO., PA	B1747-1788
	YORK, WASHINGTON TOWNSHIP, PA Franklin County	1788-D1824

Made silver-mounted officer short sabers with mahogany grips and eagle-head pommels.
(Flintlock Maker, Swordsmith, Silversmith)

PETER NOLL	CRUMRU TOWNSHIP, PA Berks County	1840-1850

Made edged weapons.
(Gunsmith, Cutler)

NORTH WAYNE TOOL CO.	NORTH WAYNE, MA	1835-1968

Sword maker during the Civil War.
(Tool Maker, Sword Maker, Machete Maker)

WILLIAM OPY	PHILADELPHIA, PA	1755-1763

Made tomahawks and scalping knives for the Indian trade.
(Cutler)

JAMES ORMSBEE	BALTIMORE, MD	1775-1805

U.S. Navy contract for M1797 boarding pikes (1797-1799).
(Cutler)

HUGH ORR	LOCHINWINIOCH, RENFREWSHIRE, SCOTLAND	B1717-1737
	BRIDGEWATER, MA	1737-D1798

Manufactured 500 stands of muskets (1748).
Made scythes and bayonets.
(Gunsmith, Cutler, Edged Tool Maker)

ROBERT ORR Son of Hugh Orr.	BRIDGEWATER, MA	1755-1795
	SPRINGFIELD, MA	1795-1808

Arms inspector and master armorer at the U.S. Springfield Arsenal.
(Armorer)

LOT OSBORN	WATERBURY, CT	1775-1783

Committee of Safety musket and bayonet maker (1776-1779).
(Gunsmith)

ROBERT OWINGS (Cutler)	ADAMS CO., PA	1790-1820

JOHN PAGE Committee of Safety musket and bayonet maker (1775). (Gunsmith)	PRESTON, CT	1768-1783
AMASA PALMER Partner: Hezekiah Huntington. Committee of Safety musket and bayonet maker (1775-1778). (Gunsmith)	WINDHAM, CT	1775-1783
JOSEPH PALMER Apprentice to Samuel Wigfall (1773-1778). Armorer at U.S. Philadelphia Armory (1778-1783). (Cutler, Knife Maker)	PHILADELPHIA, PA	1753-1783
THOMAS & THEODORE PALMER Committee of Safety musket and bayonet makers (1776). (Gunsmith)	PHILADELPHIA, PA	1770-1785
JOHN PARKER Committee of Safety musket and bayonet maker (1776). (Silversmith, Gunsmith)	BALTIMORE, MD	B1750-1783
RICHARD PARKER (Silversmith)	PHILADELPHIA, PA	1770-1785
SAMUEL PARKER Committee of Safety musket and bayonet maker (1776). Made brass gun parts. Artillery artificer and brass founder at the U.S. Philadelphia Armory (1779). (Gunsmith, Brass Founder)	PHILADELPHIA, PA	1775-1790
WILL PARKER (Cutler, Edged Tools)	BELFORD, ENGLAND PHILADELPHIA, PA	B1751-1773 1773-1783
WILLIAM PARKER (Silversmith, Goldsmith)	PHILADELPHIA, PA PROVIDENCE, RI LEWES, DE Sussex County	1750-1770 1770-1777 1778
JOSEPH PARKINSON Partners and brothers: Thomas Parkinson, William Parkinson. Made muskets, tomahawks, and scalping knives for the Virginia Committee of Safety. (Gunsmith, Cutler)	YOGOGANIA CO., VA	1776-1783

JOHN PARSON Immigrated to Pittsburg, PA (1818). (Cutler)	DUBLIN, IRELAND PITTSBURGH, PA	1800-1818 1818-1837
JOHN PARRY SR. (Silversmith)	PHILADELPHIA, PA	1795-1825
JOHN PARRY JR. Successor to David Rittenhouse (1796). (See David Rittenhouse) (Silversmith)	PHILADELPHIA, PA	B1773, 1796-D1835
ROWLAND PARRY **PARRY (ROWLAND) & MUSGRAVE (JAMES)** (Silversmith)	PHILADELPHIA, PA PHILADELPHIA, PA	1775-1793 1793-1796
THOMAS PARRY **PARRY (THOMAS) & SMITH (THOMAS)** **THOMAS PARRY** (Silversmith, Jeweler, Regalia, Military Ornaments, Cutler)	PHILADELPHIA, PA PHILADELPHIA, PA PHILADELPHIA, PA CAMDEN, NJ	1845-1874 1874-1879 1879-1913 1913-1925

STEPHEN PASCHALL
Made a sample infantry pike for Dr. Benjamin
  Franklin, President of the Pennsylvania Committee
  of Safety (1775).
Apprentice: John Riley Jr. (1771-1775).
(Pike Maker, Cutler, Pewterer)
	PHILADELPHIA, PA	1750-1783

THOMAS PASCHALL (Cutler, Pewterer)	BRISTOL, ENGLAND PHILADELPHIA, PA	1660-1681 1681-1718
WILLIAM PASCHALL (Silversmith, Pewterer)	PHILADELPHIA, PA	1670-D1696
HIRAM PEABODY (See Confederate Maker listing)		
JOSEPH PEARSON (Cutler, Blacksmith)	LOWER DARBY TOWNSHIP, PA Chester County	1767-1769
THOMAS PEARSON Made tomahawks for the Indian trade. (Cutler, Blacksmith, Edged Tools)	LONDON, ENGLAND PHILADELPHIA, PA	1657-1677 1677-1680
ABIEL PEASE Made very distinctive officer small swords and horsemen's sabers. (Clock Maker, Sword Maker)	ENFIELD, CT	B1761, 1780-D1828

DANIEL PEASE Made belt axes and knives. (Cutler)	BLUE HILL, NY	1860-1869
ANDREW J. PEAVEY Patented two knife-pistols (1865-1866). (Gunsmith)	SOUTH MONTVILLE, ME	1864-1876
DANIEL PECK	PHILADELPHIA, PA RICHMOND, VA PETERSBURG, VA	1775-1795 1795-1797 1797-1808
Adv. cleaning, polishing, and repairing of firearms; swords, sidearms, edged weapons, and surgical instruments (1802-1808). (Blacksmith, Gunsmith, Whitesmith, Cutler)	RALEIGH, NC	1808-1828
ROBERT PEEBLE Committee of Safety musket and bayonet maker (1776). (Gunsmith)	CUMBERLAND CO., PA	1775-1783
PENSACOLA NAVY YARD (N.Y.P.) Had 500 naval pikes in stock (1820).	PENSACOLA, FL	1820
CHRISTOPHER PERFECT Committee of Safety musket and bayonet maker (1776). (Gunsmith)	LOUNDON CO., VA	1755-D1791
HENRY H. PERKINS Arms inspector at U.S. Philadelphia Armory (1808-1818). Inspected N. Starr M1813 cavalry sabers, M1812 improved cavalry sabers, and M1813 non-comm. swords. (See Nathan Starr) (Gunsmith)	PHILADELPHIA, PA	1790-1818
JACOB PERKINS	NEWBURYPORT, MA PHILADELPHIA, PA	B1766-1815 1815-D1849
Arms inspector at U.S. Philadelphia Armory (1821). (Gunsmith, Silversmith)		
JAMES PERKINS **KINSLEY (ADAM) & PERKINS (JAMES)** U.S. contract for 2,000 muskets (1798). **JAMES PERKINS** (See Adam Kinsley) (Gun Maker)	BRIDGEWATER, MA BRIDGEWATER, MA BRIDGEWATER, MA	1778-1798 1798-1801 1801-1810
JOSEPH PERKINS	LONDON, ENGLAND PHILADELPHIA, PA FALMOUTH, VA	1737-1774 1774-1775 1775-1777
Foreman at James Hunter's Rappahonnock forge.		

	PHILADELPHIA, PA Dock Ward	1777-1780
Operated a gun shop. **PERKINS (JOSEPH) & COUTTY (SAMUEL)**	PHILADELPHIA, PA Dock Ward	1780-1783
Adv. guns, pistols, and ship's muskets (1781). **JOSEPH PERKINS**	PHILADELPHIA, PA	1783-1792
Repaired arms for the Commonwealth of Pennsylvania.		
	NEW LONDON, VA	1792-1796
Superintendent of the U.S. New London Armory.		
	HARPERS FERRY, VA	1796-1798
First master armorer at the U.S. Harpers Ferry Arsenal.		
	PHILADELPHIA, PA	1798-1799
Arms inspector at the U.S. Philadelphia Armory.	PHILADELPHIA, PA	1799-1803
Operated a gun shop. (See James Hunter) (See Samuel Coutty) (Musket Maker, Pistol Maker, Sword Maker)		
LUKE PERKINS (Gunsmith)	BRIDGEWATER, MA	1790-1810
REUBEN PERKINS	SUSQUEHANNA, PA GREEN CO., PA WASHINGTON TOWNSHIP, PA Belmont County	1755-1775 1775-1783 1783-1805
(Gunsmith)		
THOMAS PERKINS	PHILADELPHIA, PA PITTSBURGH, PA	1785-1805 1805-1825
THOMAS PERKINS & CO. (Goldsmith, Silversmith, Clock Maker, Watch Maker, Iron Forger, Jeweler, Cutler)	PITTSBURGH, PA	1825-1850
WILLIAM PERKINS Made axes, edged weapons, and edged tools. (Cutler, Blacksmith)	PHILADELPHIA, PA	1775-1790
JOSHUA PERRY (See Joshua Hmphreys)		
J. (JULIUS) R. PETTIS & CO.	TROY, NY	1865-1880
WILLIAM R. PETTIS (Regalia, Uniforms)	TROY, NY	1880-1885
DANIEL PETTIBONE	WISTONBURY, CT MIDDLEBURY FALLS, CT	B1770-1798 1798-1804

- Daniel Pettibone, Ezekial Chapman, and Josiah Nichols' worked in Jonathan Nichols Jr.'s gun factory.

- Nichols had a U.S. contract for muskets (1798).
- Pettibone, Chapman, and Nichols patented a cast-steel process (1802).
- Pettibone showed the process to sword maker Nathan Starr (1804).

ALBANY, NY	1804-1808
PHILADELPHIA, PA	1808-1836

- Arms inspector for the U.S. Philadelphia Armory (1808-1809).
- Inspected Rose 1807 cavalry sabers.
- Possible U.S contract for cavalry sabers (1810)— a saber marked "Pettibone Cast Steel, U.S." is known.
- Made naval pikes for the state of Massachusetts (1812-1814).
- Employee: Claudius M. Cox, pike maker (1812-1814).
- Made pistols, belt knives, and axes.
- Patented a lead-shot machine (1813).
- Invented a process for welding cast steel to iron, used for making tools, swords, bayonets, lance heads, and pike heads (1813).
- The U.S. Ordnance Department bought a license to use the process in 1813 and again in 1817.
- Patented a barrel-boring machine (1814).
- Bid on the U.S. Navy boarding pike contract (1816).
- Sold a license to use process of welding cast steel to iron to James T. Ames (1834).

(Cutler, Sword Maker, Pike Maker, Inventor, Gunsmith)

JAMES H. PETTIBONE CINCINNATI, OH 1846-1866
  CINCINNATI, OH 1866-1871

Employee and successor to John Boner.
(Military Fancy and Society Goods, Swords)

PETTIBONE (JAMES H.) MFG. CO. CINCINNATI, OH 1871-1900

- Sold M1840 Pay Department and medical officer's swords.
- Sold M1872 cavalry officer's swords.
- Bought out Thomas J. Mustin's military stocks (1873).
- Published a Masonic manual called *Tactics and Manual for Knights Templars* (1886 and 1888).
- James H. Pettibone died (1889).

THE PETTIBONE BROS. MFG. CO. CINCINNATI, OH 1900-1976

- President: L.H. Brooks.
- Secretary: A.V. Fuhrman.
- Vice President and General Manager: James Pettibone (son of James H. Pettibone).
- In 1903, The Pettibone Mfg. Co. adv. in its letterhead as makers of:
    Military goods
    Uniforms for all organizations
    Swords (regulation and fraternal)
    Regalia and lodge supplies for all secret societies
    Fraternal art and books
    Importers of gold and silver trimmings
- Issued many military, society, and fraternal goods catalogs.
- Sold M1840 cavalry sabers, M1840 medical and pay department officer swords, M1860 staff and field officer swords, M1850 foot officer swords, and M1902 saber for all officers.
- (See John Boner-Dealer listings)

- (See Thomas D. Mustin-Dealer listings)
(Military Goods, Uniforms, Regalia, U.S. Regulation
   Swords, Fraternal Goods and Swords)

JOHN PHILLIPS PHILADELPHIA, PA 1775-1783
Sold three cutlasses to Capt. Robert Towers,
   Commissary of Military Stores at the
   U.S. Philadelphia Armory (1775).
(Cutler, Silversmith, Sword Maker)

JOHN W. PHILLIPS PHILADELPHIA, PA 1830-1850
(Silversmith)

JAMES PHIPS PEMEQUID, ME B1615, 1638-1643
 WOOLWICH, MA 1643-D1654
Armorer to the Colonies of Maine and Massachusetts.
(Armorer)

ISAAC PIERCE BERLIN, CT 1813
Made blades for Nathan Starr M1813 cavalry saber contract.
(See Nathan Starr)

PIKE 1775-1783
Name found on Revolutionary War naval cutlasses.

EDWARD PILKINTON CHESTER CO., PA 1765-1775
(Whitesmith, Blacksmith, Cutler)

THOMAS PILKINTON CHESTER CO., PA 1765-1776
(Whitesmith, Blacksmith, Cutler)

JOHN PIM BOSTON, MA 1705-1730
Adv. hunting guns, pistols, carbines,
   and brass- and iron-hilted swords (1720).
Bought out by Samuel Miller (1730).
(See Samuel Miller)
(Gunsmith, Sword Maker)

EMANUEL PINCALL CHARLESTON, SC 1775-1777
FRANCIS DEVERNAY & EMANUEL PINCALL CHARLESTON, SC 1777-1798
Adv. arms repair and sword parts (1777).
EMANUEL PINCALL CHARLESTON, SC 1798-1800
(See Francis Devernay)
(Gunsmith, Armorer, Cutler, Arms Repair, Tinner)

GUILLAUME PINCHINAT PARIS, FRANCE 1760-1776
 PHILADELPHIA, PA 1776-1783
Changed name to William Pinchin.
Went back to Paris, France (1783-1784).

WILLIAM PINCHIN PHILADELPHIA, PA 1784-1810
(Silversmith, Silver Plater, Military Ornamentor)

WILLIAM PINCHIN JR.	PHILADELPHIA, PA	1803-D1862

- Son of Guillaume Pinchinat.
- Apprentice to George Armitage (1818-1826).
- Succeeded George Armitage, who died in 1826.
- Horstmann Bros. & Co. bought Pinchin's tools and equipment (1862).
- (See George Armitage)
- (Silversmith, Silver Plater, Military Ornamentor, Military Goods, Sword Hiltor)

ANTHONY PINKNEY
(See William Nevin)

WILLIAM PINTARD	PHILADELPHIA, PA	1780-1800

(Cutler)

PITTSBURGH CUTLERY CO.	PITTSBURGH, PA	1861-1866

Owner: William N. Ogden.
(Cutler)

FAYETTE R. PLUMB	ST. LOUIS, MO	1900-1975

Had a U.S. contract for M1917 bolo knives.
(Cutler, Knife Maker)

GEORGE PLUMLEY	PHILADELPHIA, PA	1725-1750

(Cutler)

JOHN POLLARD
(See Jacob Ashfield)

SETH POMEROY	NORTHAMPTON, MA	B1703, 1730-D1777

Became a general in the Revolutionary War.
Made officer's swords for himself and other officers.
Member of Pomeroy gun-making family.
(Gunsmith, Sword Maker)

JAMES POTTER	NEW YORK, NY Maiden Lane	1755-1786

- Made very distinctive horsemen's sabers (officer and enlisted men) during the Revolutionary War.
- Made a sword for Maj. Benjamin Talmadge of the 2nd Continental Dragoons.
- Adv. for filers and forgers to help make swords (1777).
- Went out of business and went to England (1782).
- William Fosbrook bought James Potter's stock of swords and blades (1782).
- (See William Fosbrook)

(Sword Maker)

WILLIAM LUKENS POTTS	PHILADELPHIA, PA	B1771-1798
Apprentice to Benjamin Rittenhouse (1796-1798).		
	PITTSTOWN, NJ	1798-1801
	ALEXANDRIA TOWNSHIP, NJ Hunterdon County **NOCKAMIXON**	1801-1807

| | TOWNSHIP, PA
Bucks County | 1807-1816 |
| | PHILADELPHIA, PA | 1816-D1854 |

(Silversmith, Gunsmith, Clock Maker,
 Surveying Instrument Maker, Iron Monger, Cutler)

JAMES POUPARD　　　　　　　　LONDON, ENGLAND　　1750-1772
　　　　　　　　　　　　　　　　　PHILADELPHIA, PA　　1772-1815

(Silversmith, Goldsmith, Engraver, Jeweler,
 Clock Maker, Sword Hiltor)

LEWIS PRAHL　　　　　　　　　**BLOCKLEY TOWNSHIP, PA**
　　　　　　　　　　　　　　　　 Philadelphia County　　c. 1750-1784

- Prahl operated a blade mill, brass foundry, and musket factory.
- Committee of Safety contract for 1,000 spontoons and pikes (1775).
- Committee of Safety contract for 1,000 horsemen's sabers (1777). The sabers were delivered (24 a week) to Col. Benjamin Flowers, commander of the U.S. Philadelphia Armory.
- Committee of Safety contract for 108 horsemen's sabers (1781).
- Committee of Safety contract for 23 bayonets (1781).

　　　　　　　　　　　　　　　　 PHILADELPHIA, PA　　1784-D1809

- Made very distinctive solid-brass-hilted, eagle-head pommel horsemen's sabers for local militia units, including the 2nd Troop, Philadelphia City Cavalry.
- Made solid-brass-hilted, lion-head pommel horsemen's sabers.
- These distinctive swords were typical of the Philadelphia area in the late 1700s and early 1800s.
- Made silver-mounted hussar-hilted officer's short sabers.
- Prahl bought blades from William Garrett, Upper Derby Township, Chester County, PA, and William Rose, Blockley Township, Philadelphia County, PA.
- Sold blades to Christian Wiltberger.
- (See William Garrett)
- (See William Rose)
- (See Christian Wiltberger-Silversmith listings)

(Silversmith)

Lewis Prahl's Philadelphia Addresses

Blacksmith	West Marlborough Street (Northern Liberties)	1784-1791
Blacksmith	13 Wood Street	1791-1792
Whitesmith	16 Knuckle Street	1792-1793

Gunsmith	3rd Street at East Delaware and 465 North 2nd Street (at East Delaware Street)	1793-1795
Whitesmith and Cutler	465 North 2nd Street (at East Delaware Street)	1795-1809

- Prahl bought John Brown's goldsmith shop (1800).
- It is possible that Prahl sold his Blockley Township property and buildings to William Rose when he moved to Philadelphia (1784). They certainly knew each other and were both blacksmiths and cutlers living in Blockley Township, which was just outside of Philadelphia. Rose was born in 1754 and Prahl was born in the early 1750s.
- Lewis Prahl armorers at Blockley Township (1777):
    Nathaniel Bean (Swordsmith)
    William Brown (Swordsmith)
    Jon Bry (Arms maker)
    Christian Cane (Swordsmith)
    Casper Christ (Swordsmith)
    Jacob Christ (Swordsmith)
    Paul Dawson (Swordsmith)
    Joseph Fankleberry (Swordsmith)
    William Fetter (Arms maker)
    Jacob Frey (Fry) (Swordsmith)
    Matthew Grimes (Swordsmith)
    Alexander Greentree (Arms maker)
    Thomas Hubb (Swordsmith)
    Adam Layer (Swordsmith)
    Robert Mann Sr. (Swordsmith)
    Thomas Quigsall (Swordsmith)
    Lewis Smith (Swordsmith)
    Stephen Smith (Swordsmith)
    George Strebey (Swordsmith)
    Patrick Vaughn (Swordsmith)
    Conrad Waltner (Swordsmith)
- Prahl requested the Pennsylvania Committee of Safety to exempt John Bry, William Fetter, Alexander Greentree, and Stephen Smith from military service (1776). They were needed to complete his arms contracts.
- Committee of Safety contract for 150 stands of muskets (1775). Used as samples to be given to other musket makers. Sabastion Keely got one (1775).
- The Committee of Safety delivered 100 pounds of brass to Prahl (1776).
- The Committee of Safety ordered and sent to Prahl a number of musket locks from Peter DeHaven of the Pennsylania State Gun Factory (1776).
- Made brass musket mountings and delivered them to the Pennsylvania State Gun Factory (1777).
- Ordered gun-making supplies from Tench Coxe (1790).

(Cutler, Sword Maker, Blade Maker, Gunsmith, Blacksmith, Silversmith, Whitesmith, Brass Founder)

LEWIS PRAHL JR.   **PHILADELPHIA, PA**   **1780-D1814**
Son of Lewis Prahl.
Armorer at Fort Mifflin.
(Gunsmith)

SAMUEL PRAHL	**PHILADELPHIA, PA**	**1780-1820**

Son of Lewis Prahl Sr.
(Gunsmith)

MICHAEL PRICE	**SAN FRANCISCO, CA**	**1859-D1888**

(Cutler, Knife Maker)

VIRGIL PRICE	**NEW YORK, NY**	**1838-1858**
WILLIAM PRICE CO.	**NEW YORK, NY**	**1858-1868**

Partner: Virgil Price
Virgil Price patented a sword hanger (1864). It was manufactured by Emerson & Silver.

VIRGIL PRICE	**NEW YORK, NY**	**1868-1875**

Had a design patent for the sword hilt and scabbard of the Independent Order of Odd Fellows (1873).
(See Emerson & Silver)

WILLIAM PRICE	**NEW YORK, NY**	**1838-1858**

Purchased William H. Milnor Co. (1858).

WILLIAM PRICE CO.	**NEW YORK, NY**	**1858-1860**

Partner and brother Virgil Price.
D.B.Howell purchased William Price Co. (1868).
(See D.B. Howell)
(Presentation Swords, Masonic Swords and Regalia)

JOHN PRINGLE	**PHILADELPHIA, PA**	**1755-1790**

Committee of Safety contract for 48 muskets and bayonets and 12 cutlasses (1775-1776).
Partner: William York.

	CAMBRIA CO., PA	**1790-1840**

(Sword Maker, Gunsmith)

PROVIDENCE TOOL CO.	**PROVIDENCE, RI**	**1846-1885**

- President: Richard Borden.
- Offices in New York and London in 1860s.
- Frederick Howe hired as tool and machinery designer and fabricator (1860).
- Machinist: James A. Crocker.
- General Manager and Sales Manager: John B. (Brighton) Anthony (1860-1885).
- Anthony moved company into military armaments.
- Rifle stock-carving machines bought from Lamson, Goodnow, & Yale (1860).
- U.S. contract for 82,000 rifled muskets (1861-1864).
- U.S. contract for 1,000 M1860 cavalry sabers (1861).
- U.S. contract for 5,000 M1860 cavalry sabers (1862).
- U.S. contract for 4,434 (originally rejected) cavalry sabers (1863).
- Made musket barrels for Ames Keaq Co., Manchester, NH (1862).
- Adv. Peabody's breech-loading muskets, carbines, and sporting rifles in the *Army-Navy Journal* (1866-1867).
- Bought surplus M1861 rifled musket parts from the U.S. Springfield Armory (1869), which were repaired, assembled, and sold to state militias.

- Made over 70,000 bayonets (three types)
- Turkish contract for 600,000 Peabody-Martini rifled muskets (1873-1875).
- Other products made:
  - Tools
  - Hardware (chains, hinges, axes)
  - Ships chandlery
  - Sewing machines (Singer, Keats, Household, Brandt)
- The Providence Tool Company went bankrupt (1883).
- The Providence Tool Company became the Rhode Island Tool Co. (1885-1917).

THOMAS QUIGALL	PHILADELPHIA, PA	1777

Swordsmith for Lewis Prahl.
(See Lewis Prahl)
(Sword Maker)

EDMOND QUINCY
(See Richard Gridley)

EDWARD RANDOLPH
(See Joseph Richardson Jr.)

RAPPANHONNOCK FORGE
(See James Hunter)

ROBERT READ	CHARLESTOWN, MD Kent County	1775-1783

Committee of Safety musket and bayonet maker (1776-1777).
(Gunsmith)

WILLIAM READ	CHARLESTOWN, MD Kent County	1775-1799

Committee of Safety musket and bayonet maker (1775-1776).

	BALTIMORE, MD	1799-1807

(Gunsmith)

DAVID REDDICK	BALTIMORE, MD ANNVILLE, PA	1756-1783 1783-1800

Committee of Safety musket and bayonet maker (1776).
(Gunsmith)

THE REICHE FAMILY OF PENNSYLVANIA
<u>Reicke-Reich-Ritchie-Richie-Rickey</u>

GEORGE REICHE	PHILADELPHIA, PA	1765, 1785-D1811

(Silversmith, Gunsmith, Clock Maker)

HENRY REICHE	PHILADELPHIA, PA	1810-1814

(Gunsmith)

JOHN REICHE (Coppersmith)	WEST NEWTON, PA Westmoreland County	1780-1797
JOHN REICHE (Silversmith)	PHILADELPHIA, PA	1786-1808
JOHN FREDERICK REICHE (Silversmith, Goldsmith)	GERMANY PHILADELPHIA, PA	1774-1794 1794-1810
LEONARD & JAMES REICHE (RICKEY) Ground cavalry sword scabbards at the Virginia Manufactory. Probably made balled-hilt cavalry sabers for the War of 1812. Made militia artillery non-comm. swords with William Rose blades (c. 1812).	PHILADELPHIA, PA RICHMOND, VA PHILADELPHIA, PA	1790-1808 1808-1809 1809-1812
AUGUSTUS VICTOR REINEMAN SR. (Cutler, Gunsmith, Silversmith, Watch Maker, Clock Maker)	SOLINGEN, GERMANY ST. THOMAS, PA Franklin County CHAMBERSBURG, PA	B1812-1832 1832-1834 1834-D1898
AUGUSTUS VICTOR REINEMAN JR. (Cutler, Gunsmith, Silversmith, Watch Maker, Clock Maker)	CHAMBERSBURG, PA	B1847, 1867-D1907
PHILIP JACOB REIZENBACH (Cutler)	NEW YORK, NY BETHLEHEM, PA	1750-1770 1770-1775
WILLIAM M. RICE (Regalia, Masonic Swords)	NEW YORK, NY	1858-1865
WILLIAM RICH Armorer to Colony of Maine.	SACO, ME	1741-1743
FRANCIS RICHARDSON SR. (Silversmith, Goldsmith, Brassfounder, Clock Maker)	NEW YORK, NY PHILADELPHIA, PA	D1687-1717 1717-D1729
FRANCIS RICHARDSON JR. Son of Francis Richardson Sr. (Silversmith, Goldsmith, Brassfounder, Clock Maker)	NEW YORK, NY PHILADELPHIA, PA	B1706-1717 1717-D1782

JAMES RICHARDSON (Cutler)	**PHILADELPHIA, PA**	**1775-1783**
JOHN RICHARDSON	**PHILADELPHIA, PA**	**1790-1819**
RICHARDSON (JOHN) & DELLEKER (SAMUEL) (Silversmith, Clock Maker)	**PHILADELPHIA, PA**	**1819-1822**
J. (JOHN) G. RICHARDSON Patented a sword-blade rolling machine (1873). Eliphalet Remington & Sons Company bought a 50-percent interest. (Cutler, Machinist)	**PHILADELPHIA, PA**	**1855-1877**
JOSEPH RICHARDSON SR. Son of Francis Richardson Sr. (Silversmith, Goldsmith, Brass Founder, Clock Maker)	**NEW YORK, NY** **PHILADELPHIA, PA**	**B1711-1717** **1717, 1725-D1770**
JOSEPH RICHARDSON JR. Son of Joseph Richardson Sr.	**PHILADELPHIA, PA**	**B1752-1777**
JOSEPH & NATHANIEL RICHARDSON	**PHILADELPHIA, PA**	**1777-1790**
JOSEPH RICHARDSON JR. Employee: James Smithers, engraver (1795-1802).	**PHILADELPHIA, PA**	**1790-1800**
RICHARDSON (JOSEPH JR.) & HOWELL (JAMES)	**PHILADELPHIA, PA**	**1800-1801**
JOSEPH RICHARDSON JR. Apprentice: Edward Randolph (1801-1806). Adv. presentation swords and knives of the highest quality during the War of 1812. (See James Howell) (Cutler, Knife Maker, Sword Maker, Clock Maker, Silversmith)	**PHILADELPHIA, PA**	**1801-D1831**
NATHANIEL RICHARDSON Son of Joseph Richardson Sr.	**PHILADELPHIA, PA**	**B1754-1777**
JOSEPH & NATHANIEL RICHARDSON	**PHILADELPHIA, PA**	**1777-1790**
NATHANIEL RICHARDSON (Cutler, Knife Maker, Sword Maker, Clock Maker, Silversmith)	**PHILADELPHIA, PA**	**1790-D1827**
THOMAS RICHARDSON (Silversmith, Clock Maker)	**PHILADELPHIA, PA**	**1861-1865**
RIDGEWAY (ALLEN) & RUFE (JOHN) Made bayonets for Jenks muskets during the Civil War. (Cutler, Bayonet Maker, Farm Forks)	**GERMANTOWN, PA**	**1856-1866**
RITCHIE & RICKEY (See Reiche Family)		

BENJAMIN RITTENHOUSE	NORRISTOWN, PA	B1740-1765
	WORCESTER TOWNSHIP, PA	1765-1770
Apprentice: Morgan Thomas.		
	PHILADELPHIA, PA	1770-1776
Apprentice: Peter Ribletin.		
	PHILADELPHIA, PA	1776-1777
Manager of the Pennsylvania Gun Factory.		
	PHILADELPHIA, PA	1777-1798
Apprentice: Williams Lukens Potts.		
(See Penn Gun Factory)		
(Silversmith, Gunsmith, Clock Maker, Surveying Instrument Maker)		

DAVID RITTENHOUSE — NORRISTOWN, PA — B1732-1776
Brother of Benjamin Rittenhouse.
Apprentices: David Shoemaker, Thomas Parker (1770-1771).

PHILADELPHIA, PA — 1776-1777

Superintendant of the U.S. Philadelphia Armory (1776-1777)

PHILADELPHIA, PA — 1777-D1796

Succeeded by John J. Parry.
(See Philadelphia Armory)

GEORGE ROBERTS — PHILADELPHIA, PA — 1780-1800
(Cutler)

ISAAC ROBERTS — PHILADELPHIA, PA — 1779
Artillery artificer at the U.S. Philadelphia Armory.
(Armorer)

JOSEPH ROBERTS — PHILADELPHIA, PA — 1775-1783
Armorer to the armed boat *Hancock*.
(Armorer)

CHRISTOPHER ROBY — DUNSTABLE, MA — B1814-1834
— NASHUA, NH — 1834-1840

Moved to Nashua and worked for the Lowell & Nashua Railroad (c. 1834), eventually becoming a superintendent.

ROBY (CHRISTOPHER) SAWYER (FREDERICK T.) & CO. — WEST CHELMSFORD, MA — 1840-1846
West Chelmsford was part of the town of Chelmsford.
Partner: Joseph Bowers.
(Merchants, Storekeepers)

ROBY (CHRISTOPHER) SAWYER (FREDERICK T.) & CO. — WEST CHELMSFORD, MA — 1846-1853
- Partner: Joseph Farwell.
- On September 28, 1846, Sawyer bought the old Farwell Scythe Factory building, land, and three of the four residences from Lincohn Drake. Drake had just bought the properties from the Farwell brothers, sons of Deacon John Farwell, who built the factory in 1820 and retired in 1844. The Farwell brothers removed the machinery to a new factory in Fitchburg, MA. Joseph Farwell stayed in West Chelmsford as a partner with Roby and Sawyer.

- On September 30, 1846, Sawyer sold the property to Roby.
- On December 15, 1846, Roby sold one-half interest back to Sawyer.
- On April 28, 1847, Roby bought the one-half interest back, including 203 Main (his future residence). Roby, Sawyer, and Farwell refitted the factory with new machinery.
- They produced a large amount of Grain-Cradle scythes.
- The scythe factory was located at 190 Main Street, near School Street, next to a waterway called Stoney Brook (providing water power for machinery) running from the Merrimac River.
- The factory was destroyed by fire (1851) but rebuilt.
- Frederick T. Sawyer retired (1853).
- Roby formed a new company called C. Roby & Co.

C. (CHRISTOPHER) ROBY & CO. **WEST CHELMSFORD, MA** **1853-1867**
- Partner: George Stark.
- Made scythes, machettes, and belt knives.
- Built a new finishing shop and a storehouse (1860-1861).
- Roby converted his factory to sword production (1861).
- During the Civil War, Roby made a complete line of regulation swords and had many U.S. contracts.
- Advertised swords in the *Army-Navy Journal* (1864).
- Added two new workshops (1864)
- Roby authorized agents: Joseph Raynes & Co., Blodget & Brown, Amos Sanford & Co.
- C. Roby & Co. went bankrupt (1867) but began again as Roby Mfg. Co.

Roby Civil War Sword Production

Sold 410 cavalry sabers on an open purchase to the U.S. government (1861)
U.S. contracts for 32,200 M1860 cavalry sabers (1863-1865)
    (7,000 delivered after the war)
U.S. contract for 3,500 M1840 musician's swords (1863-1865)
U.S. contract for 12,500 M1840 non-comm. swords (1863-1865)
U.S. contract for lt. artillery sabers (1864)
U.S. contract for 1,000 leather scabbards for M1840 non-comm. swords (1866)

Also made:
    M1840 medical officer swords
    M1840 paymaster officer swords
    M1860 cavalry officer swords
    M1850 foot officer swords
    M1860 staff and field officer swords
    M1852 naval officer swords
    Chaplain officer swords
    Sword belts and sashes
    Eagle-pommel bowie knives

ROBY (CHRISTOPHER) MFG. CO. **WEST CHELMSFORD, MA** **1867-1875**
Made Masonic swords and regalia; militia officer swords; and edged tools, scythes, and knives.
Hiscox File Co. bought Roby Mfg. Co. (1875).
Hiscox in business until at least 1894.

CHRISTOPHER ROBY   WEST CHELMSFORD, MA   1875-D1897

- Roby was postmaster (1852-1886).
- Roby was an active Mason and a farmer in his later years (after 1875).
- Roby was commander of the Spaulding Light Cavalry of Chelmsford, MA (1864-1877).
- On August 30, 1864, Roby officially formed The Spaulding Light Cavalry, Troop F, Independent Division of Militia of Massachusetts (I.D.M.).
- On October 17, 1864, it was officially redesignated as Company F of Cavalry of the Massachusetts Voluntary Militia (M.V.M.) (1864-1907).
    - Commander: Christopher Roby (Captain).
    - First Lieutenant: Edgar L. Parkhurst.
    - Second Lieutenant: Warren C. Humblett.
- It had 98 total members, many from Roby's sword factory.

(U.S. Regulation Swords, Masonic Swords, Scythes and Edged Tools, Machettes, Knives)

Employees at Christopher Roby's sword factory who also were members of his Spaulding Light Cavalry Troop

Name	Role
Charles L. Barton	Machinist
Elijah D. Bearse	Brass Moulder
Joseph Bickford	Sword Maker
W.H. Brown	Sword Gilder
J.R. Bunker	Sword Maker
Jonas C. Butterfield	Sword Maker
John N. Campbels	Machinist
Eugene W.S. Dutton	Machinist
George E. Durant	Blacksmith
Luther B. Eaton	Machinist
Frank Furlong	Sword Maker
Arthur S. Holt	Sword Maker
G.W. Hunt	Sword Maker
Edward Hyde	Machinist
George Lawrence	Sword Maker
L.M. Lawrence	Sword Maker
Jonas B. Longley	Sword Maker
Samuel Naylor	Sword Maker
John L. Parker	Machinist
S.J. Parker	Sword Maker
Alfred G. Parkhurst	Sword Maker
A.W. Parkhurst	Sword Maker
J.A. Parkhurst	Sword Maker
W.A. Parkhurst	Sword Maker
Fred J. Ripley	Machinist
John Shanly	Machinist
Frank W. Spaulding	Sword Maker
Lewis C. Young	Sword Maker

WILLIAM RODE (ROD) (Watch Maker, Silversmith, Cutler)	PHILADELPHIA, PA	1775-1798
THOMAS RODE (ROD) Sickle and knife maker. Sword Maker for War of 1812. (Edged Tools, Knife Maker, Sword Maker)	PITTSBURGH, PA	1800-1815
WILLIAM ROGERS (Cutler)	HANOVER TOWNSHIP, PA Lancaster County	1775-1783
JOHN A. ROHR (Armor Maker, Watch Maker, Silversmith)	PHILADELPHIA, PA	1790-1815
JOHN FREDERICK ROHR (Cutler, Gunsmith, Edged Tool Maker)	PHILADELPHIA, PA	1750-1775

THE ROSE FAMILY OF CUTLERS

The Rose family was probably related to the Rose family of cutlers of Sheffield, England.

	Born	Died
William Rose	1754	1810
Joseph Rose Sr.	1778	1819
Son of William Rose		
Benjamin F. Rose	c.1785	?
Son of William Rose		
William Rose Sr.	1783	1854
William Rose Jr.	1810	1883
Son of William Rose Sr.		
Joseph Rose Jr.	1823	1881
Son of William Rose Sr. by second marriage		
Rudolph F. Rose	1826	c.1895
Son of William Rose Sr. by second marriage		
John W. Rose	1828	c.1895
Son of William Rose Sr. by second marriage		

WILLIAM ROSE
Was in the 8th Co., 7th Batallion, of the
  Philadelphia Militia (1777).
Made bayonets for the Pennsylvania Committee
  of Safety (1780).
	PHILADELPHIA, PA	B1754-1782

	BLOCKLEY TOWNSHIP, PA Philadelphia County	1782-c.1800

- Built a blacksmith shop on a one-acre site,
  `bounded on the west by Mill Creek (1784).
- He may have bought the property and buildings
  of Louis Prahl of Blockley Township when Prahl
  moved to Philadelphia (1784).

- Had a blacksmith shop, saw mill, tilt mill with trip hammers, and blade mill by 1798.
- Made saddlers, farrier's tools, and other edged tools.
- Sword blades gradually became Rose's major output.
- The Rose's sold blades to:
    - Louis Prahl (Sword Maker)
    - James Reiche (Sword Maker)
    - Leonard Reiche (Sword Maker)
    - Standish Barry (Silversmith)
    - William Ball Jr. (Silversmith)
    - Liberty Brown (Silversmith)
    - Fletcher & Gardiner (Silversmith)
    - Jacob Kucher (Silversmith)
    - Harvey Lewis (Silversmith)
    - General James Wolf (Silversmith)

WILLIAM ROSE & SONS BLOCKLEY TOWNSHIP, PA c. 1800-1810
- Partners: William Rose and his sons Joseph, Benjamin F., and William Sr.
- Had a U.S. contract for 2,000 iron-mounted cavalry sabers (1807).
- Made many iron-hilted cavalry sabers for state militias.
- Had several U.S. contracts for M1797 naval cutlasses (probably during the War of 1812).
- Made many officer swords, some with eagle-head pommels, and bayonets.
- William Rose died (1810).
- There were 225 sword blades in his inventory when he died.

WILLIAM ROSE & SONS BLOCKLEY TOWNSHIP, PA 1810-1825
- Partners: William Rose Sr. and brothers Joseph Rose and Benjamin F. Rose.
- Made 72 presentation swords ordered by Congress for naval heros of the War of 1812.
- John W. Meer Sr. engraved the blades.
- William Rose Sr. sent an iron-mounted cavalry saber sample to Tench Coxe, Purveyor of Public Supplies (1811).
- Rose made many officer swords for state militias (infantry, artillery, and cavalry).
- Had U.S. contracts for 500 iron-mounted cavalry sabers and 1,000 artillery non-comm. swords (1812).
- Joseph Rose had a separate U.S. contract for 1,000 artillery non-comm. swords (1812) (also used by marine non-comms.).
- The Roses bought additional property in Blockley Township (1815).
- The Roses opened a cutlery shop in Hamilton Village (next to the new property) in c. 1817-1825.
- Beside swords and sword blades, the Roses made surgical instruments, scissors, saddlers, farrier's tools, and edged tools.
- Joseph Rose died (1819).
- Benjamin F. Rose died (c. 1825).

WILLIAM ROSE (SR.) & WILLIAM ROSE (JR.) BLOCKLEY TOWNSHIP, PA 1825-1840
Blockley Township became West Philadelphia (1840).

WEST PHILADELPHIA, PA 1840-1849

WILLIAM ROSE (SR.) & SON	**WEST PHILADELPHIA, PA**	**1849-1854**

- Partner and son: William Rose Jr.
- William Rose Sr. had three sons by a second marriage (1820) who also worked in the Rose shop: Joseph Rose Jr., Rudolph F. Rose, John W. Rose.
- Employees: John Coxey (cutler), George Ezeey (cutler).
- William Rose Sr. died (1854).

WILLIAM ROSE (JR.) & BROS.	**PHILADELPHIA, PA**	**1854-1890**

- Partners and brothers: William Rose Jr. (D1883), Joseph Rose Jr. (D1881), Rudolph F. Rose, John W. Rose.
- Showed presentation swords at the New York Fair (1864).
- Also made edged tools, including trowels and round knives.
- Was not listed in the cutler section of McElroy's Philadelphia Directory after 1861, probably because they began to specialize in tools.

WILLIAM ROSE & BROS.	**SHARON HILL, PA**	**1890-1944**

- Partners: Rudolph F. Rose (died c. 1895), John W. Rose (died c. 1895).
- Made tools for bricklayers, tile setters, plasterers, and stone masons.
- Issued tool catalogs.
- The company was purchased by O.B. Goodwin (c. 1895).
- Goodwin's son, George K. Goodwin, took over the company (1908).

W. ROSE INC.	**SHARON HILL, PA**	**1944-1993**

George K. Goodwin ran the company until he died (1967).
Goodwin's daughter took over and ran the company until she retired (1989).
Edward B. King and his sons (former employees) bought the company (1989).

CONRAD ROSE	**NEW YORK, NY**	**1850-1855**

(Blacksmith)

J. ROSE & SON	**NEW YORK, NY**	**1800-1860**

Made tomahawks for the Indian trade (1806).
(Cutler)

JOSEPH ROSE JR.	**NEW YORK, NY**	**1850-1854**

Son of William Rose Sr. (second marriage).
(Gunsmith)

PETER ROSE	**NEW YORK, NY**	**1845-1850**

(Surgical Instrument Maker)

WILLIAM H. ROSE	**NEW YORK, NY**	**1850-1855**

(Blacksmith)

ELIJAH ROSS	BROWNSVILLE, PA	B1786-1804
	ZANESVILLE, OH	1804-D1864
	Muskingam County	

Arms maker for War of 1812.
Partners and sons: Alexander C. Ross, George Ross, James Ross.
(Rifle, Pistol, and Sword Maker)

MARK ROUNDS	SEARBORO, ME	1681-1684
	NEWCASTLE, ME	1684-1699
	SACO, ME	1699-1715
	FALMOUTH, ME	1715-1730

Armorer to Colony of Maine.
(Armorer)

JAMES ROWLAND & CO.	PHILADELPHIA, PA	1861-1865
(Iron Maker)

MAXWELL ROWLAND	PHILADELPHIA, PA	1860-1865
(Edged Tool Maker)

SLEIGH ROWLAND	ALLEGHENCY CITY, PA	B1800-1847
	PITTSBURGH, PA	1847-1850
	NEW BRIGHTON, PA	1850-1855
	Beaver County	

(Cutler)

WILLIAM ROWLAND	PHILADELPHIA, PA	1775-1783
(Saw Maker, Sword Maker)

WILLIAM C. ROWLAND	PHILADELPHIA, PA	1875-1920

Made society swords.
Sold M1902 saber for all officers.
(Military Goods, U.S. Regulation and Society Swords)

HAMILTON RUDDICK	BOSTON, MA	1861-1868

Made staff and field officer swords, naval cutlasses, M1852 naval officer swords, and cavalry sabers.
(Machinist, Sword Maker)

JOHN RUSSELL	DEERFIELD, MA	1832-1836

Partner and brother: Francis Russell.
Green River Works on Green River.
Made chisels.

JOHN RUSSELL MFG. CO.	GREENFIELD, MA	1836-1867
	TURNER FALLS, MA	1867-1872
JOHN RUSSELL CUTLER CO.	TURNER FALLS, MA	1873

(Jeweler, Silversmith, Bowie Knife Maker)

THOMAS RUTTER	GERMANTOWN, PA	1700-D1729

Established the Pool Forge, the first iron forge in Pennsylvania.
Probably made edged weapons.
(Blacksmith, Iron Forger)

HARRY SAFFORD	MARIETTA, OH	1780-1790
	ZANESVILLE, OH	1790-1815

Made swords and belt knives.
(Cutler, Sword Maker, Knife Maker)

DANIEL H. SALLADE (SOLLIDAY)	SUMNEYTOWN, PA	1820-1824
	EVANSBURG, PA	1824-1830
	Montgomery County	
	PHILADELPHIA, PA	1830-1850

(Silversmith, Watch Maker, Clock Maker,
 Brass Founder, Sword Hiltor)

JOHN SALLADE (SOLLIDAY)	SUMNEYTOWN, PA	1770-1810

(Silversmith, Watch Maker, Clock Maker,
 Brass Founder, Sword Hiltor)

SAMUEL SAMPSON	LONDON, ENGLAND	B1796-1820
	NEW YORK, NY	1820-1826

(Cutler)

HENRY SAUERBIER	NEWARK, NJ	1830-1851
CRAWFORD (AARON), BROWN, &		
SAUERBIER (HENRY)	NEWARK, NJ	1851-1852
(Edged Tool Maker)		
HENRY SAUERBIER	NEWARK, NJ	1853-1855

Had office in New York, NY.

HENRY SAUERBIER & CO.	NEWARK, NJ	1856-1874

- U.S. contract for 100 M1850 foot officer swords (1861).
- Made M1840 (variation) cavalry swords, M1840 (variation) cavalry officer sabers, Civil War nonregulation officer swords, M1850 foot officer swords, and M1860 staff and field officer swords.
- Made very unusual presentation swords with picture, soldier-head, and precious stone pommels.
- Sold swords to Shannon, Miller, & Crane; Schuyler, Hartley, & Graham; and other retailers.
- Sold sword blades to many silversmiths.
- Henry Sauerbier died (1874).

(Edged Tool Maker, Sword Maker, Blade Maker, Cutler)

H. (HENRY) SAUERBIER'S SON		1874-1887
PETER SCHICKER	LANCASTER, PA	1730-1750

(Cutler)

CHARLES SCHILLING	PHILADELPHIA, PA	1860-1920

Made scabbards for M1902 saber for all officers.
(Scabbard Maker)

CONRAD SCHRECKENGOST	SWITZERLAND	1780-1800
	BERKS COUNTY, PA	1800-1801
	VALLEY TOWNSHIP, PA	1801-D1839
	Armstrong County	

Made tomahawks and lances.
(Gunsmith, Edged Weapon Maker)

(JOHN) LEONARD SCHREIBER   CINCINNATI, OH   1845-1875
Adv. swords (1864).
Made sword bayonets marked "Bahn Frei"
  during the Civil War.
Made surgical instruments and cutlery.
(Sword Maker, Bayonet Maker, Surgical
  Instrument Maker, Cutler)

GEORGE SCHREINER   PITTSBURGH, PA   1800-1820
(Cutler)

COLONEL GEORGE L. SCHUYLER
U.S. government purchasing agent in Europe.
Purchased 21,850 French M1822 lt. cavalry sabers,
  Montmorency pattern (1861).

NATHAN SCOTHORN SR.   PITTSBURGH, PA   1750-1815
(Tinsmith, Coppersmith)

NATHAN SCOTHORN JR.   PITTSBURGH, PA   1770-1800
(Silversmith, Goldsmith, Clock Maker, Watch
  Maker, Brass Founder, Sword Hiltor)

JACOBUS SCOUT   WARMINSTER TOWNSHIP, PA   B1736, 1755-D1829
                           Bucks County

Armorer with Continental Army in Trenton,
  NJ, during the Revolutionary War (1775-1783).
Apprenticed to John Fitch (1783-1788).
Became a silversmith (1788-1829).
(See John Fitch)
(Armorer, Rifle Maker, Silversmith)

DANIEL SEARLES   ANNE ARUNDEL CO., MD   B1782-1802
                      FORT HAMILTON, OH   1802-1806
                      Butler County

Adv. as a gunsmith and whitesmith (1806).

                      CINCINNATI, OH   1806-1809

Adv. as a gun, pistol, sword, and dirk maker
  (1808).

                      JEFFERSONVILLE,   1809-1816
                      INDIANA TERRITORY

Son Charles L. Searles born (1811).
Daniel served in the 6th Regiment of the
  Indiana militia, becoming a captain during
  the War of 1812.

                      JEFFERSON, IN   1816-1817

Indiana became a state in 1816.
DANIEL SEARLES & DAVID J. TAYLOR   JEFFERSON, IN   1817-1818
DANIEL SEARLES   BATON ROUGE, LA   1818-D1860
- Searles adv. rifles, pistols, and a bowie
  knife in the 1840 *Baton Rouge Gazette*.

- Made several bowie knives for Col. James Bowie's brother, Rezin Pleasant Bowie (1830).
- Bowie gave some of them to his friends as gifts.
- Searles also made an eagle-head pommel knife for Col. James Bowie. The knife later became the property of Bowie's friend, Jaun N. Sequin.
- Sequin left the Alamo on Bowie's horse on Feb. 29, 1836. He also administered Bowie's estate after he was killed at the Alamo.
- Rees Fitzpatrick (famous sword maker, silversmith, and goldsmith) did work for Searles in Baton Rouge.
- Searles lived behind Rees Fitzpatrick's house on St. Philip Street near America Street.
- Gunsmith Sylvester Hyatt did work for Searles.
- Hyatt purchased Searles' tools (1860).
- Silversmith C. Moore, located in Rees Fitzpatrick's shop from 1838 on, did work for Searles.
- (Gunsmith, Knife Maker, Dirk Maker, Sword Maker)

BENJAMIN SEBASTION   HOST, TULPEHOOKEN TOWNSHIP, PA   B1828, 1880-D1886
Berks County

Son of William Sebastion.
(Cutler, Edged Tool Maker, Blacksmith, Brass Founder)

EDWARD SEBASTION   HOST, TULPEHOOKEN TOWNSHIP, PA   1831-1880
Berks County

Son of William Sebastion.
(Cutler, Edged Tool Maker, Blacksmith, Brass Founder)

SEBASTION BROS.   1880-1886
Edward and Benjamin.

WILLIAM SEBASTION   HOST, TULPEHOOKEN TOWNSHIP, PA   1810-1880
Berks County

(Cutler, Edged Tool Maker, Blacksmith, Brass Founder)

WILLIAM SHANNON   HARRISBURG, VA   B1745-1805
PHILADELPHIA, PA   1805-1807
STANTON, VA   1807-1808

W. (WILLIAM) & H. (HUGH) SHANNON   PHILADELPHIA, PA   1808-1816
U.S. contract for M1808 muskets and bayonets (1812).
PHILADELPHIA, PA   1816-D1823

(Cutler, Gunsmith)

EDWARD G. SHAW   PHILADELPHIA, PA   1825-1835
(Silversmith)

JAMES SHAW   PHILADELPHIA, PA   1835-1845
(Silversmith)

JOSHUA SHAW	LINCOLNSHIRE, ENGLAND	B1777-1814
	BORDERTOWN, NJ	1814-1817
	PHILADELPHIA, PA	1817-1859
	BURLINGTON, NJ	1859-D1860

Invented percussion cap.
(Artist, Inventor)

LEMUEL SHAW — PHILADELPHIA, PA — 1790-1812
Made squaw axes for the Indian trade.
(Edged Weapon Maker)

W.H. SHAW — DETROIT, MI — 1861-1865
U.S. contract for 800 cavalry lances made for
 Colonel Arthur Rankins.
Regiment of Lancers, 1st Michigan Cavalry (1862).
(Lancemaker)

SAMUEL SHEBLE — PHILADELPHIA, PA — 1820-1840
S. (SAMUEL) & J.A. SHEBLE — PHILADELPHIA, PA — 1840-1860
194 and 206 North 2nd

Hardware makers.
**SHEBLE (SAMUEL) LAWSON, & FISHER
 (JOHN M.)** — PHILADELPHIA, PA — 1860-1861
3 North 5th (office)

Factory location: Frankford, PA.
John M. Fisher was a mathematical, engineering,
 surgical, and naval instrument maker.
Adv. in the Philadelphia Directory (1848)
(Hardware, Cutlery, and Instrument Makers)
SHEBLE (SAMUEL) & FISHER (JOHN M.) — PHILADELPHIA, PA — 1861-1870
3 North 5th (office)

Factory location: Frankford, PA.
Farm implement (hay and manure forks), sword,
 and cutlery makers during the Civil War.
U.S. contract for 203 lt. artillery sabers (1861).
U.S. contract for 1,000 non-comm. swords (1862).
Made M1840 and M1860 cavalry sabers (variation),
 M1850 foot officers swords, and M1860 naval cutlasses.
SAMUEL SHEBLE — PHILADELPHIA, PA — 1870-1889
3 North 5th

Partner and son: William Y. Sheble.
Made farm implements.
**SHEBLE (SAMUEL & WILLIAM Y.) &
 KLEMM (JOHN)** — PHILADELPHIA, PA — 1889-1895
3 North 5th

Farm fork makers.

JEREMIAH SHEFFIELD — SOUTH KINGSTON, RI — 1775-1783
Committee of Safety musket and bayonet
 maker (1775-1776).
(Gunsmith)

HENRY SHEIRLEY (SCHIVELY) — PHILADELPHIA, PA — 1770-1800
(Cutler, Bowie Knife Maker)

JOHN SHELL (Cutler, Edged Weapons)	PHILADELPHIA, PA Northern Liberties	1775-1783
JOHN SHERTZ (Cutler)	LANCASTER, PA	1857-1865

JACOB SHOUGH   PHILADELPHIA, PA   1800-1814

Arms inspector at U.S. Philadelphia Armory
  (1808-1811).
Inspected some Rose cavalry sabers (c. 1807).
Inspected James Winner cavalry sabers (c. 1810).
(See James Winner)
(Gunsmith)

HENRY SHULER   MIFFLIN CO., PA   B1751, 1771-D1820
(Blacksmith, Cutler)

JOSEPH S. SILVER
(See James E. Emerson)

JOSEPH SIMONS (SIMMONS)   LANCASTER, PA   1760-1794

Committee of Safety musket and bayonet
  maker (1776).
Apprentice: John Darraugh (1776-1780).
(See John Darraugh)
(Gunsmith)

JOSEPH SIMS   PHILADELPHIA, PA   1775-1783

Sold seven cutlasses to Capt. Robert Towers,
  Commissary of Military Stores, U.S. Philadelphia
  Armory (1775).
(Cutler, Sword Maker)

ALEXANDER SIMPSON
(See Joshua Humphreys)

HENRY H. SINKLER	PHILADELPHIA, PA	1840-1868
SINKLER (HENRY H.) & WALL	PHILADELPHIA, PA	1868-1872
SINKLER (HENRY H.) & CLENELL **(WILLIAM H.)**	PHILADELPHIA, PA	1872-1878

Made insignia die blocks for Horstman Bros.
  & Co.
(Military Ornaments, Machinists, Iron
  Forger, Brass Founder, Military Goods,
  Metal Worker)

STEPHEN SISNEY   REDSTONE TOWNSHIP, PA   1800-1812
                                                   Fayette County

(Cutler)

JEREMIAH SLITERMAN
Armorer to colony of Georgia (1766-1768).

WILLIAM SMEETON BALTIMORE, MD 1775-1805
U.S. Navy contract for M1797 boarding pikes
  (1797-1799).
Also made rammers.
(Pike Maker)

JAMES SMITH PHILADELPHIA, PA 1779
Artillery artificer at the U.S. Philadelphia Armory.
(Armorer)

JOHNSTON SMITH
(See John Young Sr.)

JOSHUA SMITH CHARLESTOWN, PA 1749-1769
 Chester County

(Cutler)

LEONARD SMITH PIKELAND, PA 1749-1769
 Chester County

(Cutler, Blacksmith)

LEWIS SMITH PHILADELPHIA, PA 1775-1783
Swordsmith for Lewis Prahl (1777).
(See Lewis Prahl)
(Sword Maker)

STEPHEN SMITH PHILADELPHIA, PA 1775-1783
Swordsmith for Lewis Prahl (1777).
Artillery artificer at the U.S. Philadelphia
  Armory (1778-1779).
(Sword Maker, Blacksmith)

THOMAS SMITH LONDON, ENGLAND 1770-1792
FOSBROOK (WILLIAM), SMITH (THOMAS)
  & ANDERSON (JAMES) NEW YORK, NY 1793-1794
FOSBROOK (WILLIAM) & SMITH (THOMAS) NEW YORK, NY 1795-1796
THOMAS SMITH NEW YORK, NY 1797-D1803
Gun and cutlery shop. 21 Front Street
Made and repaired swords, dirks, and bayonets.
(See William Fosbrook)
(See James Anderson)
(Sword Maker, Gunsmith, Cutler)

WILLIAM SMITH PHILADELPHIA, PA 1775-1783
Armorer on Pennsylvania Navy armed boat
  Congress (1776).
(Armorer)

JAMES SMITHERS
(See Joseph Richardson)

CHAUNCEY SNELL	AUBURN, NY	B1825-1834
	CORNING, NY	1834-D1870

Invented the Snell bayonet.
(Gunsmith)

ELIJAH SNELL	AUBURN, NY	1795-D1834

(Gunsmith)

JEREMIAH SNOW SR.	NORTHAMPTON, MA	B1735-1760
	SPRINGFIELD, MA	1760-1783

Served briefly in Revolutionary War.
Made brass-hilted horsemen's sabers using imported blades (many with triple fullers) during the Revolutionary War.
Made brass-hilted officer short sabers.

	WORCHESTER, MA	1783
	SPRINGFIELD, MA	1783-1790

(Silversmith, Goldsmith, Jeweler, Brass Founder, Sword Maker)

JEREMIAH SNOW JR.	SPRINGFIELD, MA	B1764-1783
Son of Jeremiah Snow Sr.		
	AMHERST, MA	1783-1809
	WILLIAMSBURG, MA	1809-1825

(Silversmith, Goldsmith, Jeweler, Brass Founder, Sword Maker)

RALPH SNOW	SPRINGFIELD, MA	B1766-1771
Son of Jeremiah Snow Sr.		
	WILLIAMSBURG, MA	1821-1830
	TRAY, NY	1830-D1839

(Silversmith, Goldsmith, Jeweler, Brass Founder, Sword Maker)

E. (EDWIN) F. SNYDER	PHILADELPHIA, PA	1839-1859

(Cutler)

HENRY SNYDER	LYNN TOWNSHIP, PA	1775-1783
	Lancaster County	

(Gunsmith)

JACOB SNYDER (SNIDER)	PHILADELPHIA, PA	1750-1769
	Northern Liberties	

(Blacksmith, Cutler)

JOHN SNYDER	TREDYFFRINE TOWNSHIP, PA	1800-1820
	Chester County	

Made belt axes and knives.
(Cutler)

TOBIAS SNYDER	HOLIDAYSBURG,	
	LIBERTYTOWN, PA	1840-1850
	Bedford County	

Brother of Jacob Snyder Sr.
(Gunsmith)

GEORGE SPIER	LOWER DARBY TOWNSHIP, PA Chester County	1751-1771

(Blacksmith, Cutler)

HENRY SPITZER SR.	RICHMOND, VA NEW MARKET, VA	B1731-1783 1783-1795

Partner and son: Henry Spitzer Jr.
Committee of Safety musket and bayonet maker (1776).
(Gunsmith)

WILLIAM STACKPOLE	PITTSBURGH, PA WHITING, PA	1790-1816 1816-1819

Bought out cutlery maker C. Cowan (1816).
Succeeded by R. Bowen (1819).
Made axes, knives, and tomahawks.
Had a slitting mill with tilt hammers.
(See C. Cowan)

PETER STANDLEY
(See Samuel Wheeler)

THE STARR FAMILY

	Born	Died
Joseph Starr	c. 1735	c. 1800
Nathan S. Starr Sr. Son of Joseph Starr	1755	1821
Nathan S. Starr Jr. Son of Nathan S. Starr Sr.	1784	1852
Elihu William Nathan Starr Son of Nathan S. Starr Jr.	1812	1891
Ebenezer Townsend Starr Son of Nathan S. Starr Jr.	1816	c. 1885

NATHAN S. STARR SR.	MIDDLETOWN, CT	B1755-1798

- Apprenticed to a European-born sword maker (1769).
- Appointed armorer to Col. Francis Sage's Regiment of Connecticut Militia (1776).
- Armorer to State of Connecticut (1777).
- Made scythes, nails, iron hardware, cart tires, sleighs, plane blades, farm implements, and household cutlery.
- Did general blacksmithing for many years.
- Starr Scythes were sold by Andrew Johnson (1789).
- Starr sold guns and grindstones.

NATHAN STARR & CO.	MIDDLETOWN, CT	1798-1799

- Partners: Nathan S. Starr Sr., Francis Sage.
- Had the first U.S. contract for horsemen's sabers (2,000) (1798). Sabers stored at the Schuylkill Arsenal, PA.

- Sage and his son Wilbert did the grinding and polishing of the blades.

STARR (NATHAN S. SR.), SAGE (FRANCIS) & WARNER (WILLIAM) EAST HADON, CT 1799-1800

A separate company making scythes, axes, and fire engines.

NATHAN S. STARR SR. MIDDLETOWN, CT 1799-1812

- Nathan S. Starr Jr. began working in his father's shop at 14 years old (1798).
- Made boarding pikes and cutlasses for the U.S. Navy.
- Starr inspected navy pistols made by Simeon North, Berlin, CT (1808).
- Made 50 M1797 cutlasses for the 24-gun sloop *Connecticut*, built in Middletown, CT, in 1799.

NATHAN S. STARR (SR.) & SON MIDDLETOWN, CT 1812-1837

- Partner: Nathan S. Starr Jr. (joined the company after working in New York for a short time).
- The Starrs built a sword factory on Staddle Hill on the West River (1813).
- The factory had seven water wheels driving trip hammers, grindstones, polishing wheels, lathes, drills, and bellows.
- The factory was near the pistol factory of Simeon North and the rifle factory of Robert Johnson.
- Employed 84 workers during the War of 1812 but by 1820 had only 20 workers.
- Had many U.S. sword, rifle, and musket contracts.
- Bought barrels from Isaac Holliester & Co., Litchfield, CT, and Hezekiah Scoville, Haddam, CT.
- Polished rods for Simeon North pistols.
- Nathan S. Starr Sr. died (1821).
- Nathan S. Starr Jr. discontinued most sword production to concentrate on firearms (c. 1828).

N. (NATHAN S. JR.) STARR & SON MIDDLETOWN, CT 1837-1845

Partner and son: Elihu William Nathan Starr.
Had one U.S. rifle contract.

NATHAN S. STARR JR. MIDDLETOWN, CT 1845-D1852

ELIHU WILLIAM NATHAN STARR MIDDLETOWN, CT 1845-D1891

STARR ARMS CO. NEW YORK, NY 1845-1867

- President: Ebenezer Townsend Starr (1845-1865).
- President: H.H. Wolcott (1865-1867).
- Offices located in New York, NY; armories at Yonkers, NY, Morrisania, NY, and Binghamton, NY.
- U.S. contracts for Starr revolvers and Starr breech-loading rifles during the Civil War.
- Sold army, navy, and marine officer swords.
- Also sold pistols made by Colt, Sharps, Smith & Wesson, Deringer, Elliot, and Moore.
- Its early 1864 adv. in the *Army-Navy Journal* shows them selling swords and military goods for army, navy, and Marine Corps officers.
- Its late 1864 adv. shows only rifles and pistols at the Yonkers, NY, armory.
- Issued a gun catalog (1864).

- Made and sold Wolcott carbines and Starr rifles.
- Had eight firearm patents (1858-1865).

EBENEZER T. STARR   YONKERS, NY   1867-c. 1885

Had three firearm patents (1874, 1876, 1882).
(Gunsmith)

WILLIAM O. STARR & WILLIAM S. STARR   NEW YORK, NY   1867-1880
(Gunsmith)

SAMUEL R. STARR   NEW YORK, NY   1880-1886
(Gunsmith)

Starr Edged Weapon Production

1798-1828	Made many iron-hilted cavalry sabers for state militias.
1811	Sent one sample brass-mounted and two sample iron-mounted cavalry sabers to Tench Coxe, Purveyor of Public Supplies (contract of 1812).
1812	Mounted 500 cavalry saber blades for the U.S. Springfield Armory.
1812-1814	Sold swords to B&J Cooper, New York, during War of 1812.
1813	At the request of Callender Irvine, Commissary General of Purchases, made some brass-mounted officer swords to be stocked at the U.S. Philadelphia Armory.
1815	Sent one sample navy cutlass and one sample boarding pike to Commodore John Rodgers, president of the Board of Navy Commissioners (contract of 1816).
1815	Subcontracts for M1813 cavalry saber contract: Ira Crowfoot — Scabbard finishing Clark Bradley — Punch and turn pommel nuts Alfred David — Polish blades and scabbards; buff guards John Rodgers — Punch caps, guards, and loops Isaac Pierce — Made blades Samuel Beckley — Made blades
1816	Subcontract for M1816 naval cutlass contract: John Rodgers — Made hilts and attached them to blades
1817	U.S. contract for 5,000 musket bayonets
1817	U.S. contract for 5,000 musket ramrods; subcontractor Clark Bradley tempered rods
1817	Started to make fake Damascus blades, called Columbian Damask (surface etched)
1817	Sent one sample non-comm. sword and one cavalry saber to the U.S. Commissary General of Purchases Callender Irvine (contract of 1818)

1817	Made sword presented by the state of Connecticut to Commodore Isaac Hull of the U.S. frigate *Constitution*
1819	Subcontracts for M1818 non-comm. sword contract: Benjamin Smith — Grinded blade guards and caps Orestes Winston — Forged blades Clark Bradley — Tempered and hilted blades Ira Crowford — Fitted out, finished, and jappaned scabbards
1819	Subcontracts for M1818 cavalry saber contract: Clark Bradley — Hilted blades Samuel Taylor — Polished blades, caps, guards, and ferrules
1820	Made presentation swords for Col. Richard M. Johnson and Col. Decius Wadsworth
1822	Made presentation swords for Gen. Andrew Jackson and Gen. Edmund P. Gaines (ordered by state of Tennessee)
1829	Made nine pattern swords for Col. George Bomford, U.S. Ordnance Department (swords for non-comm. officers and musicians of artillery and infantry) The M1832 foot artillery sword was eventually adopted, however. It was designed by Marine T. Wickham and patterned after the French M1816 sword (N.P. Ames made M1832 swords)
1831	Made some militia lt. artillery sabers for the Philadelphia City Troop

Starr U.S. Sword Contracts

Date	Type	Amount	Inspectors
1798	Cavalry saber	2,000	Decius Wadsworth
1799	M1797 cutlasses for sloop *Connecticut*	50	
1808	M1797 boarding pike	2,000	Joseph Hull Henry H. Perkins
1808	Naval cutlass	2,000	Joseph Hull
1812	Cavalry saber	1,000	Charles Williams
1812	Improved cavalry saber	4,050	Henry H. Perkins
1813	Cavalry saber	9,650	Oliver Allen Luther Sage Henry H. Perkins
1813	Officers cavalry saber	31	
1813	Non-comm. sword	2,000	Marine T. Wickham Charles Williams Henry H. Perkins
1816	Naval cutlass	1,000	Thomas H. Stevens
1816	M1797 boarding pike	1,000	Henry H. Perkins
1818	Cavalry saber (Some sold to South Carolina militia units)	10,600	Luther Sage John Newbury Joseph Weatherhead

1818	Non-comm. sword	4,000	Luther Sage
1826	Naval cutlass	2,000	Elishu Tobey

1798-1828: The Starr Family also made some special-order officer swords, some with eagle-head pommels, for state militias.

1798-1829: Starr also sold blades to silversmiths and hiltors.

Starr Firearm Production

1823	U.S. contract for 4,000 M1817 rifles
1828	U.S. contract for 5,000 M1816 muskets
1840	U.S. contract for 6,000 M1817 rifles
1861-1865	U.S. contracts for 47,952 Starr Patent revolvers
1861-1865	U.S. contracts for 20,601 Starr Patent breech-loading rifles
1864	Made Starr four-shot rimfire pistols
1865	Made Starr rimfire carbines
1866	Ebenezer T. Starr and James H. Merrill invented a revolving carbine (tested and rejected by the U.S. government)

CASPER STEEL (STAHL)   PHILADELPHIA, PA   1779
Artillery artificer at U.S. Philadelphia Armory.
(Blacksmith)

JAMES STEEL (STAHL)   PHILADELPHIA, PA   1777
Artillery artificer at the U.S. Philadelphia Armory.
                                                          LEBANON, PA   1778-1781
Armorer at the U.S. Lebanon Armory.
(See Armory listings)

JOHN STEEL (STAHL)   BOSTON, MA   1750-1790
Armorer to the Massachusetts Bay Colony (1774)
Committee of Safety musket and bayonet maker (1775).
(Gunsmith)

JOHN GEORGE STEEL (STAHL)   WURTENBURG, GERMANY   B1800-1834
                                                                      BALTIMORE, MD   1834-1837
                                                                      QUEMAHONING
                                                                      TOWNSHIP, PA   1837-1870
                                                                      Somerset County

(Cutler, Edged Tools)

PETER STEEL (STAHL)   CHESTER CO., PA   1765-1769
(Cutler, Blacksmith)

FREDERICK STEINMAN   PHILADELPHIA, PA   1825-1860
Son of John Steinman.
JUSTICE (PHILLIP S.) & STEINMAN
 (FREDERICK)   PHILADELPHIA, PA   1860
FREDERICK STEINMAN   PHILADELPHIA, PA   1861-1865
(See Philip S. Justice)
(Gunsmith)

JOHN STEINMAN	PHILADELPHIA, PA	1770-1803
	RICHMOND, VA	1804

Worked at the Virginia Manufactory as a lock maker.

	PHILADELPHIA, PA	1805-1807
WINNER (JAMES), NIPPES (DANIEL) & STEINMAN (JOHN)	PHILADELPHIA, PA	1808-1811

Produced 500 M1808 muskets.
Marked "W.N.S."

JOHN STEINMAN	PHILADELPHIA, PA	1812-1845

(See James Winner and Daniel Nippes)
(Gunsmith)

ADAM STEPHEN
(See Anthony Noble)

JOHN STEPHENS & CO.	PHILADELPHIA, PA	1775-1783

Committee of Safety musket and bayonet maker (1777).
(Gunsmith)

ROBERT STERRY
Armorer for Col. Christopher Harris' Rhode Island Regiment (1755-1763).

GEORGE STEWART	PHILADELPHIA, PA	1824-1850
	LEWISTOWN, PA	1850-1857
	NORWICH, CT	1857-1860

(Silversmith, Cutler, Gunsmith)

HENRY STILES	READING, PA	1775-1783
	Berks County	

(Silversmith, Sword Hiltor)

JOHN STILES	MIDDLETOWN, PA	B1788-1809

(Gunsmith)

JOSEPH STILES	MIDDLETOWN, PA	1775-1783

Committee of Safety gun repair.
(Gunsmith)

EDMUND R. STILSON	NEW LONDON, OH	1875-1895

- Son of Frederick H. Stilson.
- E.R. Stilson married Clyde Eugene Ward's sister Edith Rose Ward (1893).
- Stilson bought Clemmon's half interest in the regalia company of Ward (Clyde Eugene) and Clemmons (William E.) (1895). The company was valued at $500.
- Edmund R. Stilson had a son, Ward K. Stilson (1896).

WARD (CLYDE EUGENE) & STILSON (EDMUND R.)	NEW LONDON, OH	1895-1905

They expanded the business considerably, eventually building a factory (1903).

Stilson bought out Ward's half interest in the company for $50,000 (1905).
Ward than started his own regalia business called C.E. Ward Co.

WARD-STILSON CO.   **NEW LONDON, OH**   1905-1910
- Owner: Edmund R. Stilson.
- Stilson's regalia business thrived, and he issued many regalia catalogs, which included swords.
- The Ward-Stilson Co. opened a separate business office on the second and third floors of the Wunderly Tavern building on Motter Street (1906).
- Started making Masonic robes and paraphernalia (1908).
- Stilson expanded again and rented part of the first floor and the second floor of the Gettle Building on South Main Street (1908).
- C.E. Ward Co. bought out the Ward-Stilson Co. (1910).
- Stilson decided to move to Anderson, IN (150 miles away), and set up another regalia factory (Ward-Stilson Co. of Anderson, IN).
- Stilson was able to convince some of his old employees to join him in Indiana.

WARD-STILSON CO.   **ANDERSON, IN**   1910-1953
- Owner: Edmund R. Stilson.
- Issued many regalia catalogs.
- In the 1920s, as society and Masonic memberships declined and with many companies already manufacturing regalia, business began to slip.
- Unlike C.E. Ward, Stilson did not diversify into other areas early enough. He began to make women's dresses, but the company still had financial problems.
- Edmund R. Stilson died (1934). His son Ward K. Stilson succeeded him.
- During World War II, Stilson made gas masks at his factory at 2501 Fairview Street.
- The C.E. Ward Co. of New London, OH, bought the Ward-Stilson Co. and closed the factory (1953).
- (See Clyde Eugene Ward)

SOLOMAN STONE   **ST. UGIR TOWNSHIP, PA**   1800-1823
Alleghengy County

MARCH & STONE (SOLOMAN)   **BEAVER FALLS, BEAVERY CO., PA**   1823-1824

Succeeded by William Blanchard (1824-1836).
(Edged Tools, Cutler)

GEORGE STREBEY   **PHILADELPHIA, PA**   1777
Swordsmith for Lewis Prahl.
(See Lewis Prahl)
(Swordsmith)

JOHN STRODE   **STRAFFORD CO., VA**   1760-1781
Superintendant at James and Adam Hunter's farm near Falmouth, VA.
Forge foreman at Hunters Iron Works and Rappahonnock Forge (1775-1781).

| | CULPEPPER CO., VA | 1781-1802 |

Submitted bids on musket fabrication to the state of Virginia (1796-1797).
State of Virginia arms inspector (1801-1802).
(See James Hunter)
(Gun Maker, Pistol Maker, Sword Maker)

MATTHEW STRONG PHILADELPHIA, PA 1789-1810
22-24 Sassafras Street

A relative of William Strong.
(Sword Maker, Silversmith)

WILLIAM STRONG PHILADELPHIA, PA 1789-1810
22-24 Sassafras Street

- Made hussar-hilted cavalry sabers for state militias.
- Mounted 98 cavalry saber blades for the U.S. Schuylkill Arsenal (1808).
- Samuel Alexander rejected all of the sabers.
- Tench Coxe, U.S. Purveyor of the Public Supplies, required Strong to replace the sabers with new ones, having brass hilts and blades equal to the Rose 1807 contract (probably for an artillery unit).
- (See U.S. Schuylkill Arsenal)
- (Silversmith, Sword Maker)

JACOB SYLVIUS LAMPETER TOWNSHIP, PA 1800-1820
Lancaster County

(Cutler)

BENJAMIN TAYLOR UPPER MACKFIELD TOWNSHIP, PA 1740-1752
Bucks County

(Blacksmith, Cutler)

GEORGE TAYLOR DURHAM TOWNSHIP, PA 1775-1784
Bucks County

Purchased the Durham Iron Works from Richard Backhouse (1776).
(Gunsmith)

JOHN TAYLOR PHILADELPHIA, PA 1775-1790
Committee of Safety musket and bayonet maker (1775-1777).

CHARLESTON, SC 1790-1795

(Gunsmith)

JOSEPH TAYLOR NOTTINGHAM TOWNSHIP, PA 1820-1827
Washington County

(Cutler)

SAMUEL TAYLOR PHILADELPHIA, PA 1795-1800
(Silversmith, Clock Maker)

WILLIAM TAYLOR (Goldsmith, Silversmith)	PHILADELPHIA, PA	1770-1850
GEORGE TEFF Committee of Safety musket and bayonet maker (1775-1776). (Gunsmith)	SOUTH KINGSTON, RI	1775-1783
J. (JACOB) TEUFEL (Surgical Instruments Maker, Sword Maker)	PHILADELPHIA, PA	1850-1860

STATE OF TEXAS
- William Bryan and Edward Hall of New Orleans shipped 924 bowie knives to Texas on the schooner *Caroline* and 150 cavalry sabers on the schooner *Tamaulipos* (1836).
- The Texas General Consul authorized the purchase of 200 sergeant's swords, 1,000 bowie knives, and 1,000 tomahawks (1837).
- The Texas Ordnance Department purchased from the Ames Mfg. Co. 280 M1833 dragoon sabers, 40 M1832 foot artillery swords, and 18 M1833 dragoon officer sabers (1840).

BENJAMIN THOMAS	HINGHAM, MA MIDDLETOWN, CT	1740-1810 1810-1820
Bid on U.S. Navy boarding axe (poleaxe) contract (1816). (Gunsmith)		
ISAAC THOMAS Partner: John Cunningham. Committee of Safety musket and bayonet maker (1776). (Gunsmith)	HARTFORD CO., MD	1774-1783
THOMAS THOMPSON (Hatter, Sword Canes)	WASHINGTON CO., PA	1777-D1827
JOHN THORNHILL	SHEFFIELD, ENGLAND PITTSBURG, PA	1798-1818 1818-1824
Employee: George Dewsnap (1818-1821). Made belt knives. (See George Dewsnap) (Cutler)		

<u>**TIFFANY & CO.**</u>

CHARLES LEWIS TIFFANY Helped father run a country store.	CONNECTICUT	B1812-1837
TIFFANY (CHARLES LEWIS) & YOUNG (JOHN B.)	NEW YORK, NY 259 Broadway	1837-1841
Agent in Paris: Gideon F.T. Reed. (Silversmiths)		

TIFFANY (CHARLES LEWIS), YOUNG (JOHN B) & ELLIS (JABEZ LEWIS)	NEW YORK, NY 259, 260, 271 Broadway	1841-1848
TIFFANY & CO.	NEW YORK, NY 550 and 552 Broadway	1848-1870
	NEW YORK, NY Union Square	1870-1905
	NEW YORK, NY 5th Ave. and 37th St.	1905-1940
	NEW YORK, NY 5th Ave. and 57th St.	1940-1993

(Silversmiths, Jewelers)

Tiffany European Offices

TIFFANY (CHARLES LEWIS), REED (GIDEON F.T.) & CO.	PARIS, FRANCE 79 Rue Richelieu	1850-1868
TIFFANY & CO.	PARIS, FRANCE	1868
TIFFANY & CO.	LONDON, ENGLAND	1868

- Tiffany contracted with the New York silversmith John Chandler Moore to make hollowware (1851).
- His son, Edward C. Moore, then became manager of Silver Products Manufacturing for Tiffany (designed many of the pieces).
- Tiffany bought John C. Moore Co. (1868).
- John C. Moore died (1891).
- Tiffany employees: John William Orr, wood engraver, designer (1845-1887); John Quincy Adams Ward, sculptor and designer (1830-1910); Paulding Farnham, sculptor and designer (1889-1920).

Tiffany's Civil War Blade and Sword Purchases

Bought sword belt plates from Gaylord Mfg. Co.
Bought blades from D.J. Millard.
Bought blades from Collins & Co.
Bought blades from Ames Mfg. Co.
Imported blades from France, England, and Germany.
Imported Damascus steel blades from Solingen, Germany.
Imported blades from Schnitzer & Kirschbaum, Solingen, Germany.
Imported M1850 staff and field swords and blades from Paul D. Lunesehloss, Solingen, Germany.
Imported M1850 foot officer swords.

- Tiffany bought the building at 552 Broadway and set up his military store (1861).
- Made many one-of-a-kind silver-mounted presentation swords, especially during the Civil War.

- Many of the Civil War swords were designed by Edward C. Moore (John's son).
- Continued to make presentation swords until after World War I.
- Made presentation swords for Schuyler, Hartley & Graham.
- Issued presentation sword catalogs (1854-1868). They indicated that blades were imported from England and Germany (Solingen). The illustrations were done by wood engraver John William Orr (B1815-D1887).
- Displayed swords at the New York Fair (1864).
- Adv. in the *Army-Navy Journal* (1863-1866) as a depot of general equipment (everything for the soldier or officer), including camp furniture, foreign and domestic arms, and uniforms.
- Adv. in Frank Leslie's *New York Weekly* (1862). They adv. rich staff and dress army and navy swords, blades of English manufacture, blades of Solingen on the Rhine, and blades of Collins of Hartford.
- Sold French and English rifles, German and French swords, U.S. regulation swords, army and navy swords, army shoes, caps, badges, medals, ambulances, uniforms, gold epaulettes, cap ornaments, gold braid, buckles, powder, and grenades.
- Tiffany was an agent for Derringer pistols.
- (See D.J. Millard)
- (See Collins & Co.)

(Silversmiths, Jewelers, Cutlery, Presentation Swords, Rifles and Pistols)

Tiffany's Civil War Arms Contracts

U.S. contracts for 12,454 imported cavalry sabers (1861-1863), including the following:
Iron-hilted M1840-style sabers from Paul D. Luneschloss (PDL), Solingen, Germany (stopped fuller).
Iron-hilted British M1821 sabers from Robert Mole & Son (R.M. & S.B.), Birmingham, England (unstopped fuller).
Iron-hilted British M1821-style sabers from Schnitzler & Kirschbaum (S & K), Solingen, Germany.
U.S. contract for 6,815 imported non-comm. swords (1861-1862).
U.S. contract for 145 short artillery swords (1861-1862).
U.S. contract for 10 pioneer swords with sawback blades (1861).
U.S. contract for Enfield rifles.
U.S. contract for Leflaucheau carbines.
U.S. contract for Leflaucheau revolvers.
Tiffany & Co. sold all its military stocks to Shannon, Miller, & Co. (1866) but continued to sell presentation revolvers and presentation swords until the early 1900s.
Advertised presentation revolvers and swords in the Tiffany Bluebook Catalog (1890-1909).
(See Shannon, Miller, & Crane)

FRANCIS TILLGHAM PHILADELPHIA, PA 1775-1783
Sold five cutlasses and seven pair of pistols to Capt. Robert Towers, Commissary of Military Stores, U.S. Philadelphia Armory (1775).
(Cutler, Sword Maker, Gunsmith)

CHRISTOPHER TILMAN PHILADELPHIA, PA 1782-1785
(Cutler)

JOHN TODD NEW ORLEANS, LA 1830-1840
Made a knife for Col. James Bowie.
(Knife Maker)

MILES TODD (Gunsmith, Cutler, Whitesmith, Blacksmith)	RICHMOND, VA	1800-D1817
GEORGE TOLLE (See Charles Degenhardt) (Gunsmith)		
CAPT. ROBERT TOWERS (See U.S. Philadelphia Armory)		
BENJAMIN TOWN Partner: John Willis. Committee of Safety musket and bayonet maker (1775). (Gunsmith)	PHILADELPHIA, PA	1775-1783
JOHN TREAT Armorer for Colony of Maine. (Armorer)	THOMASTON, ME	1745-1759
JOSHUA TREAT Son of John Treat. Armorer for Colony of Maine. (Armorer)	THOMASTON, ME FORT POWNAL, ME	1759-1770 1770-1774
JAMES TRISTIN (TUSTIN) Made axes, knives, and tomahawks. Repaired guns. (Whitesmith, Gunsmith, Machinist, Edged Tools, Cutler)	SOHO, ENGLAND PITTSBURG, PA	B1774-1811 1811-1850
BALTZER TROUT (Blacksmith, Gunsmith, Cutler)	CARBONDALE TOWNSHIP, PA Berks County	1775-1783
EVAN TRUMAN (Edged Tools, Knife Maker, Axe Maker)	PHILADELPHIA, PA	1775-1785
JAMES TUSTIN (See James Tristin)		
NATHAN B. TYLER **TYLER (NATHAN B.) RIFLEWORKS** (Rifle, Shotgun, Pistol and Knife Maker)	VIENNA, OH VIENNA, OH WARREN, OH Trumbull County	B1828-1857 1857-1891 1891-1896
UNITED STATES ARMS CO. **UNITED STATES ARMS & CUTLERY CO.** (Pistol Maker, Knife Maker)	BROOKLYN, NY ROCHESTER, NY	1873-1878 1878-1886

UNITED STATES SMALL ARMS CO. Made knife-pistol.	CHICAGO, IL	1900
JOHN (JOHANNES) UNSELL Committee of Safety musket and bayonet maker (1776-1777). (Gunsmith)	HAGERSTOWN, MD FREDERICK, MD	1750-1766 1766-1783
ABNER UPDEGRAFF Made scalping knives and axes. (Cutler, Edged Tool Maker)	PITTSBURGH, PA	1800-1841
JACOB UPDEGRAFF (Gunsmith)	SCHULYKILL CO., PA	1800-1810
WILLIAM UPDEGRAFF Made axes and knives. (Cutler, Edged Tool Maker)	PITTSBURGH, PA	1834-1872
JOHN VANDERGRIFT Committee of Safety musket and bayonet maker (1775-1776). (Gunsmith)	BUCKS CO., PA	1775-1783
PATRICK VAUGHN Swordsmith for Lewis Prahl. (See Lewis Prahl) (Sword Maker)	PHILADELPHIA, PA	1777
C. VARDIS Made bayonets during the Revolutionary War.	PHILADELPHIA, PA	1775-1783
FRANCIS VOITIER Armorer to Colony of Louisiana. (Sword Maker, Gun Maker)	PARIS, FRANCE NEW ORLEANS, LA	1700-1720 1720-1725
LEON VOITIER (See Confederate listings)		
JAMES WALLACE Sold 49 cutlasses to Capt. Robert Towers, Commissary of Military Stores, U.S. Philadelphia Armory (1775). (See U.S. Philadelphia Armory) (Cutler, Sword Maker)	PHILADELPHIA, PA	1775-1783
JOHN WALLACE **WALLACE (JOHN) & BEGGS** **JOHN WALLACE** **WALLACE (JOHN) & WILSON (JAMES)** (Silversmith, Clock Maker, Watch Maker)	PITTSBURGH, PA PITTSBURGH, PA PITTSBURGH, PA PITTSBURGH, PA	1800-1829 1829-1830 1830-1841 1841-1842

NATHANIEL WALLACE	LONDON GROVE, PA Chester County	1749-1769

(Cutler, Blacksmith)

JOHN WALKER	PIKELAND, PA Chester County	1746-1766

(Cutler, Blacksmith)

SIMON WALKER U.S. Navy contracts for M1797 boarding pikes and M1797 cutlasses (1797-1799). (Sword and Pike Maker)	BALTIMORE, MD	1775-1805

CONRAD WALTNER Swordsmith for Lewis Prahl. (See Lewis Prahl) (Sword Maker)	PHILADELPHIA, PA	1777

CLYDE EUGENE WARD Clyde Eugene Ward and his father Jacob Ward (truck farmer) moved to New London, OH (1882) (west of Akron). Clyde's mother, Ellen (Nellie) Ward, had passed away (1877).	SULLIVAN TOWNSHIP, OH	B1873-1882
	NEW LONDON, OH	1882-1891

- Ward became a clerk at Elders Grocery Store (1886).
- Began operating a grocery business for Riley Brundage on the second floor of the Brundage furniture store on East Main Street (1889-1892).
- Bought one-half interest (S.O. Curtis' interest) in the regalia company of Clemmons (William E.) and Curtis (S.O.) for $138 (1891).
- Clemmons and Curtis had been making badges and collars and selling books and forms to members of the Junior Order of the Order of United American Mechanics (J.O.U.A.M.).
- Clemmons and Curtis had bought the business (1890) from Bellville (William S.) and Powers (R.B.), who started it (1888).

WARD (CLYDE EUGENE) & CLEMMONS (WILLIAM E.)	NEW LONDON, OH	1891-1895

- Ward acquired an order for 600 cloth collars with bullion-cloth-covered trim from the Independent Order of Odd Fellows (bullion cloth is made with gold or silver thread).
- A friend and executive from The M.C. Lilley Co. of Columbus, OH (probably Philip Lindenberg, general manager, or John Siebert, vice president), told him what bullion cloth was and where to find it. He then sent a Lilley Company employee to show Ward how to use it.
- Ward bought the grocery business he was managing for Riley Brundage for $300 (1892).
- Rented the Riley Brundage building and started his own furniture store. He added a confectionary shop and cigar stand.
- Married Daisy Estelle White (1895).

- Edmund R. Stilson (Ward's brother-in-law, having married Ward's sister Edith Rose Ward in 1893) bought out William E. Clemmon's half interest in the regalia business (1895). The company was now valued at $500.

WARD (CLYDE EUGENE) & STILSON (EDMUND R.)   NEW LONDON, OH   1895-1905

- Expanded into J.U.O.A.M. robes, emblems, and rosettes.
- Many of the cloth collars, badges, emblems, rosettes, and robes they were now making were fabricated at the Ward and Stilson homes by Daisy Ward and Edith Rose Stilson.
- They started using the second floor of the Brundage building Ward was renting as their regalia shop.
- Two women operating two tredle (foot-operated) sewing machines worked in the new regalia shop.
- As their business grew, they rented a local specialty shop (1898) and used a dynamo to run their new electric sewing machine.
- Ward's son, Sterling Wentworth Ward, born (1898).
- Ward & Stilson built a two-story regalia factory (1903).
- Ward then sold his furniture business in the Brundage building to H.S. Stratton.
- G. (Guy) B. Swanger married Ward's other sister, Anna Marguette Ward (1904).
- Ward sold his half interest in Ward & Stilson to E.R. Stilson for $50,000 (1905).
- Stilson maintained the factory and changed the name to the Ward-Stilson Co.
- Ward than formed his own company, C.E. Ward Co.
- (See Edmund R. Stilson)

C. (CLYDE) E. (EUGENE) WARD CO.   NEW LONDON, OH   1905-1984

- President: Clyde Eugene Ward.
- Vice President: Jacob Ward (Clyde's father).
- Partners:
    - Anna Marguette Swanger (sister)
    - Fred Bigelow
    - George Prosser
    - Ernest Hubler
    - Clarence Hubler
- The Hublers were related to Jacob's wife Ellen (Hubler) Ward.
- Ward built his own regalia factory (two stories with basement) at the corner of James and Williams Streets (1905).
- The factory included a business office, stockroom, shipping room, cutting room, scenery studio, sewing room, and workshop.
- A second line of sewing machines was quickly installed as business increased.
- Ward used the Kilmer Wood Factory to make its wooden products.
- The C.E. Ward Co. expanded its regalia products to include swords (not made by Ward), banners, bugles, horns, harps, jewelry, scenery, magic lanterns, coal oil lamps, and electric arc lights. He was also selling choir and academic robes, band uniforms, and society costumes and robes.

- Ward sold his products all over the United States and Canada and had seven traveling salesmen. His business exceeded $250,000 in 1909.
- Bought out the Ward-Stilson Co. owned by Edmund R. Stilson, including the factory, built in 1903, and Stilson's Wunderly Tavern offices, in 1910.
- The C.E. Ward Company rented and remodeled part of the first floor and all of the second and third floors of the St. James Hotel at South Railroad Street and Railroad Avenue (1910). It then vacated the Wunderly building location.
- The Latouche Regalia Company then rented the Wunderly Tavern Building space.
- Ward built an 11,000-square-foot factory with a 78-foot frontage on Williams Street (1910).
- The Curtiss and Elder Co. became Ward's wooden product manufacturer (1911).
- Ward bought a seven-passenger Stanley Streamer automobile (1911).
- Opened his own wooden product factory on North Main Street (1913).
- Started a new company called The New London Mfg. Co. making raincoats, autocoats, and rubberized products (1914).
- Remodeled the old Ward-Stilson Co. factory that he bought in 1910 for use by the new company.
    President: C.E. Ward.
    Manager: C.E. Ebert.
    Secretary: George Prowley.
    Treasurer: Fred Bigelow.
    Trustee: Guy B. Swanger.
- They sold some of their products to local merchants like A. White and D. Barnes.
- The C.E. Ward Co. was selling regalia and costumes to the following societies (1914).

C.E. WARD CATALOGS
#18 Furniture (All Societies)
#19 Improved Order of Red Men (I.O.R.M.)
#20 Encampment-Independent Order of Odd Fellows (I.O.O.F.)
#21 Masonic-Royal Arch (M.R.A.)
#22 Order of Eastern Star
#23 Brotherhood of American Yoeman
#24 Pythian Sisters
#25 Junior Order of the Order of United American Mechanics (JR. O.U.A.M.)
#26 Degree of Pocahontas
#27 Loyal Order of Moose
#28 Knights of Pythias (K.P.)
#29 Independent Order of Odd Fellows (I.O.O.F.)
#30 Masonic Blue Lodge (M.B.L.)
#31 Rebekah

- The C.E. Ward Company adopted a yellow business envelope with Clyde Eugene Ward's picture on the upper left hand corner.
- Jacob Ward died (1918).
- Sterling Wentworth Ward (Clyde's son) joined the company (1921) after finishing his education at Ohio State University. He became vice president.
- Sterling married Dolores Buck (1930) and they had a son, Sterling Wentworth Ward Jr.
- C.E. Ward had another son, Rodney Eugene Ward (B1913-D1968), who joined the navy and was an ensign (1940).
- The Ward Company erected a brass foundry, making brass regalia and sword mounts (1924).
- Ward rented the rest of the first floor of the St. James Hotel (1924).
- Erected a new factory.(42 feet x 84 feet, 2 stories) at 80 South Railroad Street (1924).
- Began making his own swords (1927).
- Clyde Eugene Ward died (1943).
- His son Sterling took over the business.

- Sterling Wentworth Ward died (1946).
- The C.E. Ward Co. bought the Lilley-Ames Co. of Columbus, OH (1951). Many of the Lilley-Ames employees moved from Columbus to New London, OH (80 miles).
- The C.E. Ward Co. bought the Ward-Stilson Co. (E.R. Stilson, president) of Anderson, IN (1953). The factory was then closed.
- The C.E. Ward Co. put out a large catalog, #541 (1954). It included the following products:
    - Military swords
    - Presentation swords
    - Fraternal swords
    - Lodge robes and supplies
    - Lodge room furniture
    - Fraternal uniforms
    - School band uniforms
    - Flags and banners
    - College caps, gowns, and hoods
    - High school caps and gowns
    - Church choir and clergy vestments
    - Church confirmation gowns
    - Church alter hangings
    - Church brass products
- The C.E. Ward Co. issued many regalia, society goods, and sword catalogs.
- The C.E. Ward Co. was purchased by the Crowell, Collier, & MacMillan Co. (1968). C.C.M. kept the Ward name.
- The C.E. Ward Co. was purchased from C.C.M. by Oak Hall Cap & Gown Co. (1980).
- Keith V. Bailey was hired as manager (1981).
- The C.E. Ward regalia and sword operations were set up as a separate company—The C.E. Ward Fraternal Supply Co. (1984).

C.E. WARD FRATERNAL SUPPLY CO.   **NEW LONDON, OH**   **1984-1987**
- Manager: Keith V. Bailey.
- Began to reproduce Civil War swords. Forty different styles were made.
- Used some of the original Ames Mfg. Co. hilt molds.
- Used the Lilley-Ames Co. name (owned by C.E. Ward) in its advertising copy.
- Keith V. Bailey bought the C.E. Ward Fraternal Supply Co. (1987).

FRATERNAL SUPPLIES INC.   **NEW LONDON, OH**   **1987-1993**
- Owner: Keith V. Bailey.
- Bailey rechartered and incorporated the Ames Sword Co. and Lilley-Ames Co. names, which he uses in his advertising and on his catalogs.
- Bailey's company makes:
    - R.O.T.C. swords
    - Society swords (Knights of Columbus, etc.)
    - Civil War reproduction swords
    - Decorative swords
    - Special-order swords (one presented to Gen. Norman Schwarzkopf)
- All sword parts are made at the factory.
- Sword blade grinding and polishing are also done there.
- Maintains a complete foundry.
- Plating and engraving are done by factory experts.
- Fraternal Supplies Inc. is one of the few sword manufacturers still operating in the United States.

WILLIAM WARD	PHILADELPHIA, PA	1751-1771

Ward worked for James Hendricks (1767-1769).
(See James Hendricks)
(Cutler)

AXEL WARFIELD	FREDERICKTOWN, MD	1775-1783

Committee of Safety musket and bayonet
  maker (1777).
(Gunsmith)

THOMAS WASHBORN	RICHMOND, ME	1740-1742

Armorer for the Colony of Maine.

WASHINGTON NAVY YARD (NYW)		1799-1993

Made War of 1812 boarding axes and spiked-head
  boarding pikes (inspected by Joseph Tarbell).
Made approximately 3,000 M1917 naval cutlasses (1917).

THE WATERS FAMILY

ANDRUS WATERS	B1752-D1778
ASA WATERS SR.	B1742-D1814
Brother of Andrus Waters.	
ELIJAH WATERS	B1768-D1814
Son of Asa Waters Sr.	
ASA WATERS JR.	B1769-D1840
Son of Asa Waters Sr.	
ASA HOLMAN WATERS	B1808-D1889
Son of Asa Waters Jr.	

ANDRUS WATERS & ASA WATERS SR.	SUTTON, MA	1776-1778

Opened a gun shop on Singletary Creek.
Gunsmiths to Committee of Safety.
Andrus Waters died (1778).

ASA WATERS SR., ASA WATERS JR., **ELIJAH WATERS**	SUTTON, MA	1779-1812

Built an armory on Blackstone River.
Installed gun and bayonet machinery (1797).

A. WATERS & CO.	MILLBURY, MA	1812-1814

Partners: Asa Waters Sr., Asa Waters Jr., Elijah Waters.
Asa Waters Sr. and Elijah Waters died (1814).

A. WATERS & SON	MILLBURY, MA	1814-1840

Partners: Asa Waters Jr., Asa Holman Waters.
U.S. contract for 1,000 bayonets (1818).
Made axes and shovels.
Asa Waters Jr. died (1840).

A. (ASA) H. (HOLMAN) WATERS & CO.	MILLBURY, MA	1840-1887

- Employee and later partner: Benjamin Flagg.
- Flagg bought gun and bayonet-making
  machine and opened his own business.
- U.S. contract for cutlasses for the Fresh Water Navy (1862).
- Made M1862 revenue cutters swords.
- Asa Holman Waters died (1887).

- (See B. Flagg & Co.-Confederate listings)
- (Gunsmith, Cutler, Sword Maker)

HENRY WATKEYS   NEW WINDSOR, NY   1772-1776
Ulster County

ROBERT BOYD & HENRY WATKEYS   NEW WINDSOR, NY   1776-1783
Ulster County

(See Robert Boyd)
(Gunsmith, musket and bayonet maker)

EMMOR TRESO WEAVER   CHESTER CO., PA   B1786-1808
PHILADELPHIA, PA   1808-D1860

- Locations:
    - 17 Elfreth Alley   1808-1820
    - 20 N. 4th Street   1820-1825
    - 1 Loxely Court   1820-1825
    - 73 N. 3rd Street   1825-1829
    - 11 N. 4th Street   1829 (sword factory)
- Started as a gold and silver watchcase maker.
- Later became a general silversmith and jeweler.
- Opened a sword factory.
- Became a sword and blade maker, gilder, and hiltor.
- Imported and mounted blades from Schnitzler (Phillip Jakob) & Kirschbaum (Wilhelm B.S.) and other Solingen, Germany, makers.
- Mounted blades imported from Birmingham, England.
- Made infantry officer swords with spooned-knuckle bows.
- Made cavalry officer swords and staff and field officer swords.
- Consulted with Benjamin Franklin on lightning rod points.
- Made Masonic jewelry.

(Watch Maker, Silversmith, Goldsmith, Jeweler, Sword Maker)

JOSHUA WEAVER   WEST CHESTER, PA   B1753, 1775-D1827
(Silversmith)

JOHN WEINRICH   HEIDELBERG TOWNSHIP, PA   1760-1770
Berks County

(Cutler, Gunsmith)

JOHN, GEORGE & JEDEDIAH WEISS
(See Silversmith listings)

RICHARD WELLS   PHILADELPHIA, PA   1756-1779
Armorer at Pennsylvania State Gunlock
Factory (1776-1779).

DEHAVEN (PETER) & WELLS (RICHARD)   PHILADELPHIA, PA   1779-1780
(See Peter Dehaven)
(Gunsmith)

J.S. WELLS   RICHMOND, VA   1775-1783
Committee of Safety musket and bayonet
maker and arms repair (1776).
(Gunsmith)

WILLIAM WELLS
(See Collins & Co.)

HENRY WETZEL	**KREAMER, PA** Snyder County	B1799, 1820-D1879

Made scythes and sickles.
(Cutler, Edged Tools)

THOMAS WHEAT	**WASHINGTON, DC**	1815-1820

Made axes and tomahawks.
(Cutler)

LEICESTER WHEELER	**PHILADELPHIA, PA**	1790-1812

Worked at the Virginia Manufactory making sword mountings (1812).
(Swordsmith)

SAMUEL WHEELER	**PHILADELPHIA, PA** North Ward	B1744, 1765-1790

- Adv. knives, razors, surgical instruments, and blades (1772).
- U.S. contract (1775) for 100 boarding pikes (10 per boat x 10 boats).
- Also made scythes, sickles, and edged tools.
- Made repairs, along with Theodore Wiley, on the Boring Mill & Cannon Foundry at the U.S. Philadelphia Armory (1776).
- Made anchor chains for U.S. warships (1777).
- Apprentices:
    Godfrey Hanible (1771-1772).
    Joseph Wood (1772-1775).
    Peter Standley (1772-1782).
    Charles Jennings (1771).
- (See Theodore Wiley)

(Cutler, Edged Tools, Surgical Instruments, Pike Maker, Blade Maker)

ISRIEL WHELAN	**PHILADELPHIA, PA**	1795-1805

U.S. contract for spontoons (1801).
(Cutler, Polearm Maker)

WILLIAM WHETCROFT	**CORK, IRELAND**	B1735-1755
	ANNAPOLIS, MD	1755-1774
WHETCROFT (WILLIAM) & HIGGINSON (SAMUEL)	**ANNAPOLIS, MD**	1774-1775

(Goldsmiths, Silversmiths)

WHETCROFT (WILLIAM) & MCFADON	**ANAPOLIS, MD**	1775-1777

Built an iron foundry.
Committee of Safety musket and bayonet maker (1775-1781).

WILLIAM WHETCROFT	**ELK RIDGE, MD**	1777-1783

Operated the Patapsco Slitting Mills.

	ANNAPOLIS, MD	1783-D1799

(Silversmith, Goldsmith, Gunsmith)

RUGGLES WHITING
(See William Stackpole)
(Cutler)

AMOS WHITTEMORE	BOSTON, MA	1755-1797

Committee of Safety musket, bayonet, and
 rifle maker (1775).
(Silversmith, Gunsmith)

EDWARD WHITTEMORE	BOSTON, MA	1750-D1772

(Silversmith)

JAMES W. WICKHAM	PHILADELPHIA, PA	1790-1836

Partner in Wickham & Co. (1818-1836).
(Gunsmith)

MARINE T. (TYLER) WICKHAM	PHILADELPHIA, PA	B1780-1799

Son of Thomas Wickham.

	EMMITSBURG, MD	1799-1802

Apprenticed to John Armstrong.

WICKHAM (MARINE T.) & MATHEWS	FREDERICK, MD	1802-1804
MARINE T. WICKHAM	HARPERS FERRY, MD	1804-1811

Master armorer at the U.S. Harpers Ferry Arsenal.

	PHILADELPHIA, PA	1811-1817

Arms inspector and later chief inspector at the
 U.S. Schuylkill Arsenal (1811-1816).
Inspected the U.S. horsemen's saber contract
 made by John Joseph Henry (1812).
Inspected 200 of the U.S. M1813 non-comm.
 sword contract made by N. Starr.

WICKHAM & CO.	PHILADELPHIA, PA	1817-D1834

- Partners: Marine T. Wickham, James W.
   Wickham, William W. Wickham.
- Factory Manager: James Baker (1830-1834).
- Adv. muskets, pistols, sabers, swords, dirks,
   and foils in the Philadelphia city directory (1819).
- Operated a gun factory in Philadelphia.
- U.S. contract for 5,000 M1821 muskets (1823).
- Additional U.S. contract for 1,000 M1821 muskets (1823).
- Made navy muskets (1826).
- Marine T. Wickham designed the prototype for the
   M1832 foot artillery sword using the French M1816 sword
   as a pattern.
- Inspected arms at the John Joseph Henry Jr. gun factory
   (Boulton Works) in Philadelphia (1829-1834).
- Marine T. Wickham died (1834).

(Gunsmith, Military Goods, Guns and Swords, Hardware, Importer)

THOMAS WICKHAM	PHILADELPHIA, PA	1755-1798

Pennsylvania and New Jersey Committee of
 Safety gunsmith (1775-1776).
(Gunsmith)

WILLIAM W. WICKHAM	PHILADELPHIA, PA	1790-1834

Chief armorer at U.S. Schuylkill Arsenal
  (1814-1817).
Partner in Wickham & Co. (1818-1834).
(Gunsmith)

FREDERICK WILLIAM (WILHELM)		
WIDMANN	BREMEN, GERMANY	B1795-1816
F. (FREDERICK) W. (WILLIAM) WIDMANN	PHILADELPHIA, PA	1816-D1848

- Opened a shop at 98 North 3rd Street (near William H. Horstmann) as a military ornamentor, die sinker, and metal worker (1818).
- Eventually, Widmann made swords (many for William H. Horstmann).
- Imported and mounted blades from Schnitzler & Kirschbaum and Gebruder Weyersberg of Solingen, Germany.
- Sold swords to A. Young & Son of Columbia, SC.
- Bought silver for sword hilts from William H. Horstmann.
- Used electro-galvanic gilding and gold plating.

Widmann Sword Production

M1834 revenue cutter swords
M1840 foot officer swords
M1840 medical officer swords
Militia artillery officer swords with eagle-head pommel
Marine Corps officer swords
Navy officer swords
Hunting swords
Small swords
Solid-brass-hilt eagle-head sabers
Naval dirks

- Widmann sword factory workmen:
    Apprentice and artisan: Jacob Faser (1827-1848).
    Sword maker: Julius Knecke.
    Sword maker: Lewis Loemmel.
    Silversmith: John H. Hoffman (1846-1848).
- Widmann adv. as an ornamental sword manufacturer and sword mounter in *U.S. Military* magazine (1840-1842) and *Citizens Soldier* Magazine (1843-1844).
- F.W. Widmann died (1848).
- Bequeathed his sword pattern design books to Jacob Faser.
- The William H. Horstmann Co. bought the stock and equipment for $200 (1848).
- Julius Knecke and Jacob Faser went to work for Horstmann and helped start his sword shop (1849).
- Horstmann continued to make swords in the Widmann style.
- (See William H. Horstman-Dealer listings)
- (See A. Young & Son-Dealer listings)
- (See Jacob Faser-Confederate listings)

- (See John H. Hoffman)

(Silversmith, Ornamental Sword Mounter, Die Sinker, Military Ornamentor, Armorer, Metal Worker)

SAMUEL WIGFALL	PHILADELPHIA, PA Middle Ward	1750-1785

- Contract with Committee of Safety for 200 gunlocks (1775).
- Partner: Maremaduke Blackwood
- Apprentice: Joseph Palmer (1773-1778).
- Made belt knives.

(Cutler, Gunsmith, Knifemaker)

THEODORE WILEY (WYLIE)	PHILADELPHIA, PA	1755-1774
THOMAS GOLCHER & THEODORE WILEY	PHILADELPHIA, PA	1774-1775

Cutlers and bayonet makers.

THEODORE WILEY	PHILADELPHIA, PA	1775-1808

- Armorer to Committee of Safety (1775-1776).
- Repaired muskets and edged weapons.
- U.S. contract for bayonets (1797).
- Along with Samuel Wheeler, made repairs on the boring mill and cannon foundry at the U.S. Philadelphia Armory (1776).

(Gunsmith, Armorer, Cutler, Swordsmith, Bayonet Maker)

THOMAS WILEY (WYLIE)	PITTSBURGH, PA	1759-1777
CAPTAIN THOMAS WILEY	PHILADELPHIA, PA	1777

Supervisor at the U.S. Philadelphia Armory.

	LEBANON, PA	1777-1782

Supervisor at the U.S. Lebanon Armory.

	NEW LONDON, VA	1782-1783

Supervisor at the U.S. New London Arsenal.

THOMAS WILEY	PITTSBURGH, PA	1783-1795

Adv. for an apprentice to learn the blacksmith, whitesmith, and cutlery business (1789).
(See Armory listings)
(Blacksmith, Whitesmith, Cutler)

FREDERICK A. WILL	SAN FRANCISCO, CA	1850-1860
WILL (FREDERICK A.) & KESMODEL (FRANK)	SAN FRANCISCO, CA	1860-1863

Bought Hugh McConnell Company (1863).

WILL (FREDERICK A.) & FINCK (JULIUS)	SAN FRANCISCO, CA	1863-1934

(Cutler, Knifemaker, Surgical Instrument Maker)

EDWARD WILLIAMS
(See Hezekiah Huntington)

JOHN WILLIS
(See Benjamin Town)

PHILIP WILSON	PHILADELPHIA, PA	1835-1857
JUSTICE (PHILIP S.) & WILSON (PHILIP)	PHILADELPHIA, PA	1857-1858
PHILIP WILSON & CO.	PHILADELPHIA, PA	1858-1870

Agent for Philip S. Justice Company swords.
Made and imported pistols, rifles, and shotguns.
(See Philip S. Justice)
(Gun and Pistol Maker, Military and Sporting
  Equipment Maker and Importer)

WILLIAM WING	PHILADELPHIA, PA	1775-1805

U.S. Navy contract for M1797 boarding
 pikes (1797-1799).
U.S. Navy contract for pistols.
(Pistol and Pike Maker)

JAMES WINNER	PHILADELPHIA, PA	1790-1803
	RICHMOND, VA	1803-1807

Armorer at the Virginia Manufactory.
Forged musket parts.
Made sword hilts and scabbards.

WINNER (JAMES), NIPPES (DANIEL), & CO.	PHILADELPHIA, PA	1807-1808
WINNER (JAMES), NIPPES (DANIEL),		
** & STEINMAN (JOHN)**	PHILADELPHIA, PA	1808-1811
JAMES WINNER	PHILADELPHIA, PA	1811-1815
	RICHMOND, VA	1815-1824

Armorer at the Virginia Manufactory.
(Gunsmith, Sword Maker)

James Winner's Production while at the Virginia Manufactory

Forged sword blades and hilts
Assembled complete swords
Made iron scabbards
Made 56 First Model (variation) Virginia Manufactory cavalry sabers (1804)
Made some Second Model cavalry sabers marked "J. Winner Fecit"

James Winner's Production while in Philadelphia, PA

Made dragoon officer swords
Had sent a sample cavalry saber to Tench Coxe, Purveyor of Public Supplies (1809)
U.S. contract for 500 cavalry sabers (1810) (inspected by Marine Wickam); only 109 were made (22 passed inspection)
Abraham Nippes finished the contract (1811)
Winner (James) Nippes (Daniel) & Co. had a U.S. contract for 7,000 M1808 muskets (1808)
Made 500 muskets (part of 1808 contract) in 1808-1811
Winner & Nippes contracted with Daniel Henkels for 1,700 muskets (completed 1808 contract) in 1815
Winner bid on the U.S. Navy cutlass contract (1816)

ORESTES WINSTON	MIDDLETOWN, CT	1800-1825

Forged blades (as a subcontractor to N. Starr)
 for non-comm. swords (contract of 1818).
(See N. Starr)
(Blacksmith, Blademaker)

ELISHA WINTERS | CHESTERTOWN, MD | 1775-1783
Committee of Safety musket and bayonet
  maker (1775-1778).
(Gunsmith)

MICHAEL WITHERS | LANCASTER, PA | B1733, 1775-D1821
Committee of Safety musket and bayonet
  maker (1775).
(Gunsmith)

FRANZ WOLF | COLUMBUS, OH | 1834-1852
Made hunting knives, bowie knives, and
  surgical instruments.
(Knife Maker, Surgical Instrument Maker)

JACOB WOOD | MOUNT BETHAL, PA | 1775-1783
  Northampton County

(Gunsmith)

JOHN WOOD JR. | ROXBURY, MA | 1755-1800
Committee of Safety musket and bayonet
  maker (1775-1776).
 | BOSTON, MA | 1800-1801

(Gunsmith)

JOSIAH WOOD | NORRINGTON TOWNSHIP, PA
  Philadelphia County | 1775-1783

- Committee of Safety musket and bayonet maker (1775-1777).
- Committee of Safety contract for 1,000 naval pikes (100-150 per month) (1776).
- Delivered to Captain Towers at the U.S. Philadelphia Armory.
- Committee of Safety contract for naval cutlasses (1776).
- Made very distinctive horsemen's sabers.

(Gunsmith, Pike Maker, Sword Maker, Edged Tools)

JOSEPH WOOD | PHILADELPHIA, PA | 1750-1775
Apprenticed to Samuel Wheeler (1772-1775).
(Cutler, Edged Tool Maker)

ROBERT WOOD | PHILADELPHIA, PA | 1775-1783
(Blacksmith)

W.A. WOODRUFF | CINCINNATI, OH | 1840-1850
Made tomahawks.
(Cutler)

ACHOR WORLEY | REDSTONE TOWNSHIP, PA | 1775-1783
  Fayette County

(Edged Tool Maker)

DAVID WORLEY JR. | DONEGAL TOWNSHIP, PA | 1820-1850
  Washington County

(Gunsmith)

FRANCIS WORLEY (Blacksmith, Cutler)	YORK, PA	1775-1783
GEORGE WORLEY (Silversmith)	YORK, PA	1790-1805
THOMAS WORLEY Partners: Henry and Philip Sheetz. Committee of Safety rifle maker.	MECHLENBURG, VA	1775-1776
Listed as blacksmith and cutler. (Blacksmith, Gunsmith, Cutler)	WASHINGTON CO., MD	1776-D1807
JOHN YAGER Pennsylvania Committee of Safety naval pike maker (1812). (Cutler, Pike Maker)	PHILADELPHIA, PA	1800-1812
BENJAMIN YARD Committee of Safety musket and bayonet maker (1776-1777). (Gunsmith)	TRENTON, NY	1775-1783
WILLIAM YORK (See John Pringle)		
HENRY YOST Committee of Safety musket and bayonet maker (1775-1776). (Gunsmith)	GEORGETOWN, MD	1775-1783
JOHN YOST Committee of Safety musket and bayonet maker (1775-1782). (Rifles, Gunsmith)	GEORGETOWN, MD	B1743-1795
JAMES YOULE Apprenticed as cutler in Sheffield.	SHEFFIELD, ENGLAND	1715-1735
	NEW YORK, NY	1735-1755
JAMES YOULE & JOHN BAILEY	NEW YORK, NY	1755-1775
JAMES YOULE Adv. silver-mounted eagle-, lion-, and dog-head pommel swords, guns, pistols, and razors (1787-1788). (See John Bailey) (Cutler, Sword Hiltor, Silversmith, Gun and Pistol Maker)	NEW YORK, NY	1775-1794
YOUNG & SON (See Dealer listings)		
HENRY YOUNG (Musket Maker)	EASTON, PA Northampton County	1774-1786
JOHN YOUNG SR.	EASTON, PA Northampton County	1755-1805

- Brother of Henry Young.
- Partners: Johnston Smith, Adam Foulkes.
- Contract with the Continental Congress for 1,000 muskets and bayonets (1775).
- Pennsylvania Committee of Safety contract for 130 rifles (1776).
- Made officer swords.
- Engraved his own sword blades.
- Engraved guns for his brother Henry.

(Gunsmith, Sword Maker, Engraver, Cutler)

JOHN YOUNG Armorer to Colony of Maryland. (Armorer)	ANNAPOLIS, MD	1728-1740
NATHANIEL M. YOUNG Made belt knives and tomahawks. (Edged Weapon Maker)	FAIRFIELD CO., OH	1803-1813
WILLIAM W. YOUNG (Cutler, Edged Tools, Surgical Instrument Maker, Gun Dealer)	PHILADELPHIA, PA	1861-1865

THE ZAHM FAMILY

EDWARD ZAHM Son of Mathias.	LANCASTER, PA	1827-1840
EDWARD & HENRY L. ZAHM (Gunsmith, Silversmith, Clock Maker)	LANCASTER, PA	1845-1880
GOTTFRIED ZAHM (Gunsmith, Silversmith, Clock Maker)	LANCASTER, PA	1770-1825
GOTTFRIED M. ZAHM Son of Mathias. (Gunsmith, Silversmith, Clock Maker)	LANCASTER, PA	B1817, 1835-D1895
HENRY L. ZAHM Son of Mathias.	LANCASTER, PA	1831-1845
EDWARD & HENRY L. ZAHM (Gunsmith, Silversmith, Clock Maker)	LANCASTER, PA	1845-1880
MATHIAS ZAHM (Gunsmith, Silversmith, Clock Maker)	LANCASTER, PA	1795-1840
MICHAEL ZAHM Son of Gottfried.	LANCASTER, PA	B1811-1845
ZAHM (MICHAEL) & JACKSON (JOHN W.) (See John W. Jackson) (Silversmith, Military and Fancy Store)	LANCASTER, PA	1845-1860
JESSE SHENTAN ZANE (Silversmith, Brass Founder, Iron Monger, Cutler)	WILMINGTON, DE PHILADELPHIA, PA	1794-1812 1812-1815

CHAPTER 4

European Sword Makers and Dealers Who Exported to Union Dealers during the Civil War

LOCATION/MAKER	BLADE MARKING
Solingen, Germany	
J.E. Bleckman	Bow
Henrich Boker	
Carl Brock Jr.	
William Clauberg	Standing knight
Clemen & Jung	Shield with Z
Carl Joseph Falkenberg	
A. & E. Holler	A & EH
Wilhelm Hoppe	Beehive
E. & F. Horster	E & FH
F. Horster Jr.	
C. Jurman	
C.R. Kirschbaum	
W.R. Kirschbaum	Knight's head
Paul D. Luneschloss	P.D.L.
Maas & Schoverling	
Friedrick Plucker Jr.	Rabbit head
A. & A. Schnitzler	
Schnitzler (Phillip Jakob) & Kirschbaum (Wilhelm B.S.)	S & K
Wilhelm Walsheid	
Isaac Wester & Co.	W & C
Gebruder Weyersberg	King's head
England	
Hawkes & Co. (London)	
Robert Mole & Son (Birmingham)	R.M.S.B.

CHAPTER 5

U.S. Sword Dealers

B.B. ABRAHAMS & CO.	PHILADELPHIA, PA	1900-1920

Sold M1902 saber for all officers.
(Military Goods)

ADARE & FISHER	PHILADELPHIA, PA	1860-1865

(Military Goods)

WILLIAM ADDIS	CINCINNATI, OH	1853-1855

(Regalia and Society Swords)

FREDERICK ALFORD
(See A.W. Pollard)

HENRY V. (VINCENT) ALLIEN	NEW YORK, NY	1830-1851

Partner in Horstmann Brothers & Co. (1850-1851).

HORSTMANN BROTHERS & ALLIEN (HENRY V.)	NEW YORK, NY	1851-1870

Partner and son: Laurent A. Allien.

HENRY V. ALLIEN	NEW YORK, NY	1870-1876
HENRY V. ALLIEN & CO.	NEW YORK, NY	1876-1948

- Had factory in Lyons, France.
- Made M1872 cavalry officer swords.
- Made M1902 saber for all officers.
- Sold military equipment to the 77th New York National Guard.
- Henry V. Allien died (1889).
- (See William H. Horstmann)

(Silk Importer, Trim and Fringe, Military Goods, Cutler, Regalia, U.S. Regulation and Society Swords)

AMERICAN MILITARY SUPPLY CORPORATION   NEW YORK, NY   1872-1892
(Academy Swords)

JAMES APPLETON
(See J.A. Merrill)

JAMES ARMIGER
(See Canfield & Brother)

ARMY-NAVY COOP
(See H.F. Loudan)

ARMY-NAVY EMPORIUM
(See Herman Fersenheim)

ARMY & NAVY STORE
(See Alexander Sloan)

ARMY & NAVY STORE CO. INC.   NEW YORK, NY   1900-1920
Issued military catalogs.
Sold M1902 saber for all officers.
(Military Goods)

ASSOCIATED MILITARY STORES   CHICAGO, IL   1917-1925
320 W. Jackson Blvd.

Had branches at Leavenworth, KS, and Camp Lewis, WA.
Issued a military catalog of regulation equipment for U.S. Army officers.
Sold M1902 sabers for all officers.

JOSIAH & AUGUSTUS BACHELDERS
(See Samuel Davis)

BAILEY & ESSER   MILWAUKEE, WI   1875
Sold M1872 cavalry officer sabers.
(Military Goods)

JOHN C.W. BAILEY   CHICAGO, IL   1866-1880
164 Clark Street

(Regalia Dealer and Publisher)

JOSEPH TROWBRIDGE BAILEY SR.   PHILADELPHIA, PA   1806-1832
BAILEY (J.T. SR.) & KITCHEN (ANDREW B.)   PHILADELPHIA, PA   1832-1846

Andrew B. Kitchen died (1846).
BAILEY & CO.   PHILADELPHIA, PA   1846-1854
Partners:
    J.T. Bailey Sr.
    J.T. Bailey Jr.

F.W. Bailey
Jeremiah Robbins
Used paste enamel on many hilts.
George B. Sharpe was an engraver and hiltor.
Joseph Trowbridge Bailey Sr. died (1854).

JOSEPH T. BAILEY (JR.) & CO.   PHILADELPHIA, PA   1854-1878
Made medical officer swords.
Displayed presentation swords at the New
   York Fair (1864).
Made swords presented to Generals Francis P. Blair,
   George A. McCall, and D.B. Birney.
Imported blades from W. Clauberg, Solingen,
   Germany.

BAILEY (J.T. JR.), BANKS (GEORGE W.) &
BIDDLE (SAMUEL)   PHILADELPHIA, PA   1878-1894
George B. Sharpe still employed as blade
   engraver and hiltor.

BAILEY, BANKS & BIDDLE CO.   PHILADELPHIA, PA   1894-1993
(See George B. Sharpe)
(See Samuel Biddle-Silversmith listings)
(See George W. Banks)
(Jeweler, Silversmith, Sword Hiltor, Presentation
   Swords, Military Goods Publisher)

ANSON BAKER   NEW YORK, NY   1820-1853
ANSON BAKER & SONS   NEW YORK, NY   1853-1860
Partners: Charles Baker, Alfred Baker, Anson Baker Jr.
Anson Baker Sr. died (1860).
(Silversmith, Silver Plater, Hardware, Military
   Goods, Swords, Guns)

JOHN A. BAKER   NEW YORK, NY   1815-1846
JOHN A. BAKER CO.   NEW YORK, NY   1847-1863
Issued military catalogs.
John A. Baker died (1862).
Widow Laura S. Baker took over.
BAKER (LAURA S.) &
MCKENNEY (JAMES H. SR.)   NEW YORK, NY   1864-1883
McKenney was a former employee.
Adv. military goods and swords in the
   Army-Navy Journal (1864-1870).
Sold M1872 cavalry officer sabers and M1860
   staff and field officer swords.

J. (JAMES) H. MCKENNEY & CO.   NEW YORK, NY   1883-1888
Partners: James H. McKenney Jr., James A. Ridabock.
Salesman: Howard Waldo.
Sold M1860 staff and field officer swords.

JAMES A. RIDABOCK & CO.   1888-1966
- Successor to J.H. McKenney.
- Issued military catalogs.
- James A. Ridabock died (1899).
- Widow Francis Ridabock and son Henry G.
   Ridabock took over the company.

- Sold M1860 staff and field officer swords.
- The Cleary Uniform Co. bought out Ridabock (1966).

(Saddler, Hatter, Military Goods, Swords, Uniforms, Regalia)

F. (FRANCIS) B. BALDWIN   NEW YORK, NY   1860-1864
Military clothing dealer.
Sold out to Joshua M. Varian (1864).
(See J.M. Varian & Sons)

HORACE E. BALDWIN   NEWARK, NJ   1816-1842
BALDWIN (HORACE E.) & CO.   NEWARK, NJ   1842-1870
Partners: Isaac Baldwin, Elihu Bliss.
Had a branch in New Orleans.
(See Elihu Bliss-Silversmith listing)
(Jeweler, Silversmith, Watches, Military Goods, Swords)

H. (HORACE) E. BALDWIN & CO.   NEW ORLEANS, LA   1844-1852
Branch of Baldwin & Co. of Newark, NJ.
Ames Mfg. Co. authorized agent.
Sold silver-hilted swords to Clark Rackett & Co.,
  Augusta, GA.
(Jeweler, Silversmith, Watches, Military Goods, Swords)

ISAAC BALDWIN   NEWARK, NJ   1800-1817
TAYLOR (JOHN) & BALDWIN (ISAAC)   NEWARK, NJ   1817-1842
(Jeweler, Silversmith, Watches, Military Goods,
  Swords)
(See John Taylor-Silversmith listing)
BALDWIN (HORACE E.) & CO.   NEWARK, NJ   1842-1870
Partners: Isaac Baldwin, Elihu Bliss.

JABEZ L. BALDWIN   BOSTON, MA   B1777-1813
BALDWIN (JABEZ) & JONES (JOHN B.)   BOSTON, MA   1813-D1819
(See John B. Jones)
(Silversmith, Military Goods)

J. (JESSE) H. BALDWIN   NEW YORK, NY   1861-1863
                                                    63 Maiden Lane

Partners: Francis B. Johnson, Jesse Baldwin.

                                               NEW YORK, NY   1864
                                               58 Maiden Lane
                                               NEW YORK, NY   1864-1865
                                               84 Maiden Lane

(Hardware, Military Goods)

O.S. BALDWIN   WILMINGTON, NC   1845-1865
Adv. uniforms, military goods, pistols, and
  swords (1861).

                                                   NEW YORK, NY   1865-1875

(Clothier, Military Goods, Swords, Pistols)

HENRY BALL
BALL, BLACK, & CO.
(See Silversmith listings)

S.S. BALL
(See John B. Jones)

GEORGE W. BANKS	**PHILADELPHIA, PA**	**1829-1878**

Partner in J.E. Caldwell Co. (1849-1878).
(See Bailey, Banks, & Biddle)

BAILEY (J.T.), BANKS (GEORGE W.) & **BIDDLE (SAMUEL)**	**PHILADELPHIA, PA**	**1878-1894**

JOSEPH BANKS	**PHILADELPHIA, PA**	**1800-1820**

(Silversmith, Clock Maker)

THE BANNERMAN FAMILY

FRANCIS BANNERMAN V	**DUNDEE, SCOTLAND**	**1830-1854**
FRANCIS BANNERMAN VI	**DUNDEE, SCOTLAND**	**1851-1854**

Son of Francis Bannerman V.
The Bannerman family immigrated to Brooklyn, NY (1854).

FRANCIS BANNERMAN V	**BROOKLYN, NY**	**1854-1865**

Opened a retail store, selling a variety of goods,
  including government surplus.
Had a store and warehouse near the Brooklyn
  Navy Yard (1858-1867).
Served in the Civil War and was disabled.
To supplement the family income, his son Francis
  Bannerman VI began dragging the Hudson River
  for saleable scrap during the Civil War.

FRANCIS BANNERMAN & SON	**BROOKLYN, NY**	**1865-1893**

- Partners: Francis Bannerman V, Francis Bannerman VI.
- After the war, the Bannermans expanded the scrap business and bought heavily at U.S. Navy auctions at the Brooklyn Navy Yard.
- Opened a store and warehouse at 14 Atlantic Avenue, where they started to sell ships, chandlery, and army-navy surplus (1867-1887).
- Bought huge amounts of Union and Confederate war surplus over the years.
- Opened a store and warehouse at 43 Atlantic Avenue (c. 1875-1881). Francis Bannerman VI ran the store.
- Opened a military store and warehouse at 1114 Butler Street (1881-1905).
- The first catalog was issued from 1114 Butler Street (1884).
- David Bryce Bannerman (son of Francis VI) eventually handled catalog sales.
- A military store and warehouse was opened at 118 Broad Street in New York (c. 1890-1895). Catalogs were issued from there.
- A military store and warehouse was opened at 27 Front Street in New York (c. 1895-1897).
- A military store and warehouse was opened at 579 Broadway in New York (1897-1905). Catalogs were issued from there.
- The Bannermans purchased approximately 90 percent of the Spanish-American War surplus (1898).
- Three large warehouses were leased on the Brooklyn waterfront to store the military goods.
- Much military surplus was also purchased from England, France, and Germany over the years.

FRANCIS BANNERMAN & SONS   **BROOKLYN, NY**   **1893-1905**
- Partners: Francis Bannerman VI (B1851-D1918), Francis Bannerman VII (son of Francis Bannerman VI; B1873-D1945), David Bryce Bannerman (son of Francis Bannerman VI; B1875-D1957).
- Francis Bannerman VI purchased Pollepel Island in the Hudson River, 50 miles upstream from New York and within the borders of Fishkill, NY (1900).
- Many warehouses, magazines, shops, and armories, as well as the family residence, were built there, all in the style of a Scottish castle.
- Superintendents at Pollepel Island: Jim Small, Charlie Kovak, Frank Crawford (1922-1959).
- Bannerman attempted to sell large amounts of military equipment to the Japanese War Department for the Russo-Japanese War (1904).

FRANCIS BANNERMAN & SONS   **NEW YORK, NY**   **1905-1918**
- Bannerman purchased a large building at 501 Broadway (1905).
- An adjacent building at 499 Broadway was purchased later that year.
- This location then became the headquarters of the company until 1959.
- It had a retail store, warehouse, and military museum.
- Francis Bannerman VI died (1918).

FRANCIS BANNERMAN SONS   **NEW YORK, NY**   **1918-1958**
- Charles J. Scott became general manager in charge of the 501 Broadway location (1918-1959).
- Also had offices in Brussels, Belgium.
- Francis Bannerman VII died (1945).
- Charles S. Bannerman (David's son) became a partner (1945).
- The first annual catalog was issued from 501 Broadway (1905). The last catalog was issued in 1955.
- Revised price lists and mailings continued.
- A reference catalog (hundredth anniversary) was issued (1965).
- David B. Bannerman died (1957).
- Charles S. Bannerman became president (1957).

FRANCIS BANNERMAN SONS INC.   **NEW YORK, NY**   **1958-1959**
President: Charles S. Bannerman.

FRANCIS BANNERMAN SONS INC.   **BLUE POINT, NY**   **1959-1973**
- The 501 Broadway location was closed.
- A retail store and large mail-order warehouse was opened at Blue Point, NY, on the bay at the foot of Corey Avenue on Merrick Road.
- President: Charles S. Bannerman.
- James F. Hogan (who joined the company in 1946 after Francis Bannerman VII died in 1945) became vice-president and general manager (1959).
- The military stocks at Pollepel Island were gradually sold off (1959-1966).
- Some antiques were donated to the Smithsonian Institution and the West Point Military Academy Museum.
- Pollepel Island was sold to the New York Taconic State Park Commission (1967).

- Charles S. Bannerman retired and James F. Hogan bought his company stock (1968).
- The Pollepel Island Arsenal buildings were destroyed in a fire (1969). The outside walls, turrets, and battlements still remain.

FRANCIS BANNERMAN SON INC.   BELLPORT, NY   1973-1993
- Owner: James F. Hogan.
- Over the years, a substantial percentage of Bannerman's sales were made to war departments, military organizations, and military units (U.S. and overseas).
- Large quantities of military goods were sold to other dealers and department stores.
- Fraternal societies and cadet corps bought large amounts.
- Wild West shows, carnivals, and circuses bought from Bannerman.
- Of course, thousands of military collectors bought from Bannerman's many catalogs, especially in the later years.
- Much U.S. war surplus (broken or damaged) was melted down and sold for scrap metal.
- Cannons and firearms were also repaired, refurbished, and sold.
- No other military goods dealer in the United States has had such an impact on collectors of antique military goods.

CHARLES BARNUM   NEW YORK, NY   1861-1865
(Clothier, Military Uniforms)

S.O. BARNUM   BUFFALO, NY   1880-1905
Sold M1860 staff and field officer swords.
(Military Goods, Swords)

ERASTUS BARTON
(See Silversmith listings)

EDWARD D. BEACH   NEW YORK, NY   1861-1865
                              12 Maiden Lane
(Jeweler, Silversmith)

MILES BEACH   HARTFORD, CT   1743-1777
                          GOSHEN, CT   1777-1778

Miles and Edmond Beach were arms inspectors at the Hill Gun Factory.

                                      HARTFORD, CT   1778-1785
BEACH (MILES) & SANFORD (ISAAC)   HARTFORD, CT   1785-1790
BEACH (MILES) & WARD (JAMES)   HARTFORD, CT   1790-1797
MILES BEACH   HARTFORD, CT   1797-1828

Adv. swords and hangers (1799).
(See James Ward)
(See Isaac Sanford-Silversmith listings)
(Jeweler, Silversmith, Clock Maker, Brass Founder, Sword Hiltor)

SAMUEL BECK   NEW YORK, NY   1885-1895
(Military Goods)

WILLIAM BECK   CINCINNATI, OH   1850-1872

WILLIAM BECK & SON (Regalia, Military Goods)	CINCINNATI, OH	1872-1895
JOSEPH T. BELL (Saddler, Military Goods)	NEW YORK, NY	1830-1855
N.O. BENJAMIN (Military Goods)	NEW YORK, NY	1861-1865
STEPHEN & ASA RHODES	BOSTON, MA	1823-1849
BENT (CHARLES SR.) & BUSH (FRANCIS SR.)	BOSTON, MA	1849-1932

- Succeeded Rhodes Co.
- Charles Bent Sr. died (1853).
- Charles Bent Jr. and Francis Bush Jr. took over the company.
- Adv. as a military depot selling military goods and swords in the *Army-Navy Journal* (1864-1870).
- Sold M1840 medical officer swords, M1860 staff and field officer swords, and M1902 sabers for all officers.

(Hatters, Military Goods, Hardware, Regalia, Swords)

BENZIGER BROTHERS (Regalia)	CINCINNATI, OH	1875
L. BERNSTEIN Sold M1852 naval officer swords. (Military Goods)	BROOKLYN, NY	1900-1920
BETTS (FREDERICK B.), NICHOLS (BARAK J.) & CO.	NEW YORK, NY 129 Maiden Lane	1854-1867

Offices in New Orleans, LA, Augusta, GA,
  Newark, NJ, and Charleston, SC.
(Saddlers, Military Goods)

LOUIS BICKEL	AKRON, OH	1863-1883
BICKEL (LOUIS) & HAROLD (HENRY W.)	AKRON, OH	1884-1887
LOUIS BICKEL	AKRON, OH	1888-1892

(See Henry W. Harold)
(Gunsmith, Cutlery)

BIGELOW & SMITH
(See Normand Smith)

JOHN, JAMES, & THOMAS T. BINGHAM
(See Maker listings)

W.P. BINGHAM (Regalia)	INDIANAPOLIS, IN	1865-1870

BISHOP & CO.
(See J.D. Wolfe)

HENRY H. BISHOP (Gunsmith, Cutler)	BOSTON, MA	1800-1857
HENRY W. BISHOP Son of Henry H. Bishop. (Gunsmith, Cutler)	BOSTON, MA	1820-1860
WILLIAM BISHOP SR.	BOSTON, MA	1808-1860
WILLIAM BISHOP JR. Son of William Bishop Sr. (Gunsmith, Cutler)	BOSTON, MA	1830-1848
B.M. BLACK & CO. (Military Outfitter)	PHILADELPHIA, PA	1861-1865
JAMES BLACK Apprentice to Michael Brother (1773-1780).	PHILADELPHIA, PA	1758-1780
Made bowie knives. (Silversmith, Cutler)	PHILADELPHIA, PA	1780-1825
JOHN BLACK	PHILADELPHIA, PA	1795-1810
MCMULLEN (JOHN) & BLACK (JOHN)	PHILADELPHIA, PA	1812-1850
JOHN S. BLACK Son of John Black. (See John McMullen-Silversmith listings) (Silversmith, Watch Maker)	PHILADELPHIA, PA	1835-1860
CALVIN T. BLAKE Employee at Boyd & Co. (1858-1859).	SAN FRANCISCO, CA	1838-1859
CALVIN T. BLAKE & CO. Adv. military goods and swords (1863). (Hatters, Military Goods, Swords)	SAN FRANCISCO, CA	1860-1870
HENRY T. BLODGET	NEW YORK, NY	1830-1850
BLODGET (HENRY T.), **CLARKE & BROWN (CLARK S.)** Branch in Boston	NEW YORK, NY	1850-1858
BLODGET (HENRY T.), **BROWN (CLARK S.) & CO.** Agents for the C. Roby Co. Went bankrupt (1868).	NEW YORK, NY	1858-1868
HENRY T. BLODGET (See C. Roby Co.) (Military Equipment, Regulation and Masonic Swords)	NEW YORK, NY	1868-1870
ORISON BLUNT (See W.J. Syms & Brother)		
WILLIAM BLYNN Employee of William Platt & Co. (1845-1850).	COLUMBUS, OH	B1830-1850
BLYNN (WILLIAM) & BALDWIN (THOMAS)	COLUMBUS, OH	1850-1860

WILLIAM BLYNN	**COLUMBUS, OH**	1860-D1866

(Silversmith, Jeweler, Watch Maker, Military Goods)

HERMANN BOECKER   **REMSCHEID, GERMANY**   1800-1837

Immigrated to New York, NY (1837) and changed name to Herman Boker.

H. (HERMAN) BOKER & CO.   **NEW YORK, NY**   1837-1970

- Imported knives, edged tools, cutlery, and swords from his brother Heinrich (Henry) Boecker, Remscheid and Solingen, Germany.
- Imported swords from other German makers, including Maas & Shoverling, Solingen, Germany, during the Civil War.
- Boker Civil War U.S. arms contracts (all imported):
  - 45,533 cavalry sabers
  - 1,646 lt. artillery sabers
  - 569 non-comm. swords
  - 289 cavalry officer swords
  - 122 foot officer swords
  - 33 staff and field officer swords
  - 10,000 muskets
- Bought the New York office and branch of the Lamson & Goodnow (1872).
- Got permission to use the chestnut tree logo of the Heinrich Boker Co., Solingen, Germany (early 1900s).
- John Boker Sr. and Jr. of the Boker Co. began knife and tool production in a Maplewood, NJ, factory (early 1900s).
- The Boker family sold out to Wiss & Sons, Newark, NJ (c. 1960).
- The Wiss Company sold out to Cooper Industries, Newark, NJ (c. 1970).
- The Heinrich Boker Gmbl. Company of Solingen, Germany, established a branch office in Golden, CO, called Boker U.S.A. (1986).

BOKER U.S.A. INC.   **GOLDEN, CO**   1986-1993

GEORGE BOETTHER
(See George Evans)

HENRY BOGUE	**BALTIMORE, MD**	1836-1856
HENRY BOGUE &		
HENRY W. HARRINGTON	**BALTIMORE, MD**	1856-1866
HENRY BOGUE & SON (ROBERT H.)	**BALTIMORE, MD**	1866-1884

(Military Tailor, Military Goods)

LOUIS T. BOLAND SR.	**COLUMBIA, SC**	1820-1840
	ALBANY, NY	1840-1848
L. (LOUIS) T. BOLAND	**NEW YORK, NY**	1848-1883

Partner: Louis T. Boland Jr. (died 1883).
Louis T. Boland Sr. died (1876).
(Silversmith, Silver Plater, Sword Hiltor, Military Ornaments)

S.B. BOND & CO.	**NEW YORK, NY**	1875

Sold M1872 cavalry officer swords
(Military Goods)

JOHN BONER	**CINCINNATI, OH**	**B1827-1871**

Employee and successor to
  Peter Smith Co. (toys) (1847-1857).
James Pettibone was an employee
  of and successor to Boner (1872).
(Regalia, Society Swords,
  Military and Fancy Goods)

BOSTON REGALIA CO.
(See Samuel P. Leighton)

CHARLES A. BOSTWICK & CO.	**NEW HAVEN, CT**	**1840-1852**

Partners: Charles A. Bostwick Jr.,
  Charles G. Bostwick.

GEORGE M. BOSTWICK	**NEW HAVEN, CT**	**1852-1855**
BOSTWICK (GEORGE M.) &		
TROWBRIDGE (HENRY)	**NEW HAVEN, CT**	**1855-1870**
L. BOSTWICK	**NEW HAVEN, CT**	**1860-1870**
JOHN A. BOSTWICK	**NEW HAVEN, CT**	**1870-1879**

(Saddler, Leather Goods, Military Goods)

E. (ELIAS) R. BOWEN	**CHICAGO, IL**	**1859-1870**

Located at 20 South Clark Street (corner of
  Lake Street), P.O. Box 846.
Adv. regulation and presentation swords, military
  goods, revolvers, Henry repeating rifles and all other
  cartridge rifles and carbines, and regalia in the
  Army-Navy Journal (1863-1864).
(Military Goods, Guns, Swords, Regalia)

JAMES BOWN	**ENGLAND**	**B1823-1833**

Immigrated to Canada, then New York, NY (1833).

	NEW YORK, NY	**1833-1843**
	PITTSBURGH, PA	**1843-1848**
BOWN (JAMES) & TETLEY (ABRAM)	**PITTSBURGH, PA**	**1848-1862**

Partner and son: John Tetley.
The company was called Enterprise Gun Works.
Agent for Colt revolvers.
Manufactured general cutlery and hunting and
  pocket knives.

JAMES BOWN	**PITTSBURGH, PA**	**1862-1875**

Bought out John and Abram Tetley.

JAMES BOWN & SON (WILLIAM H.)	**PITTSBURGH, PA**	**1875-1880**
JAMES BOWN & SONS		
(EDWIN S., JAMES W., AND WILLIAM H.)	**PITTSBURGH, PA**	**1880-1883**

James Bown died (1901).

BROWN (W.S.) & HIRTH (AUGUST)	**PITTSBURGH, PA**	**1883-1889**
W.S. BROWN	**PITTSBURGH, PA**	**1889-1894**

Bought Enterprise Gun Works.
(Gun Maker, Bayonet Maker, Knife Maker, Cutler,

Hardware, Surgical and Dental Instruments,
Gun and Pistol Importer)

JOHN BOYLAN   NEW YORK, NY   1863-1904
Adv. military clothing for officers of the National
  Guard and military goods in the *Army-Navy Journal* (1869).
(Tailor, Uniforms, Military Goods)

BRANTLEY'S UNIFORM & REGALIA HOUSE   CHICAGO, IL   1875
Sold M1872 cavalry officer swords.
(Regalia)

EDWARD BRAY   NEW YORK, NY   1830-1850
BRAY (EDWARD) & REDFIELD   NEW YORK, NY   1850-1860
    15 Maiden Lane
MERWIN (JOSEPH) & BRAY (EDWARD)   NEW YORK, NY   1860-1868
    267 Broadway

(Silversmith, Military Goods, Gun Maker)

C.G. BRAXMAR CO.   NEW YORK, NY   1875
    10 Maiden Lane

(Regalia)

PAUL BREMOND   PHILADELPHIA, PA   1830-1847
Partner: John Bremond.
BREMOND (PAUL & JOHN) &
  FLORENCE (THOMAS B.)   PHILADELPHIA, PA   1847-1849

THOMAS BREMOND   PHILADELPHIA, PA   1849-1858
(Military Goods, Hatter, Regalia)

BRIDGEPORT GUN IMPLEMENT CO.   BRIDGEPORT, CT   1890
Made belt knives.
(Gun Maker, Knife Maker)

H. (HENRY) S. (SANDS) BROOKS   NEW YORK, NY   1800-1827
Partner and brother: David Brooks.
H.S. Brooks died (1827).
HENRY BROOKS & SON   NEW YORK, NY   1828-1832
Partner and son: Daniel H. Brooks.
HENRY BROOKS & CO.   NEW YORK, NY   1833
H. (HENRY) & D. (DANIEL) H. BROOKS   NEW YORK, NY   1833-1849
BROOKS BROTHERS   NEW YORK, NY   1850-1945
Partners: Henry, Elisha, Edward S., and Daniel H. Brooks.
Adv. army, navy, and state militia uniforms in the
  Army-Navy Journal (1869).
(Clothier, Uniforms, Military Goods, Regalia)

SETH E. BROWN   CONCORD, NH   B1821, 1843-D1884
Bought out by Moses M. Chick (1849).
(Silversmith, Jeweler, Watch Maker, Military Goods)

BROWNING (WILLIAM C. &
  JAMES H.), KING (HENRY) & CO.   NEW YORK, NY   1855-1918

Had branches in Chicago, IL, and Boston, MA.
(Clothier, Uniforms, Regalia)

L.C. BRUCE	**BOSTON, MA**	**1915-1917**
Authorized dealer for Henderson-Ames.		
	WORCESTER, MA	**1917-1919**

(See Henderson Ames-Maker listings)
(Military and Fraternal Swords, Regalia)

BUHL HAT MAKING CO.	**DETROIT, MI**	**1837-1845**
F. (FREDERICK) &		
C. (CHRISTIAN) BUHL & CO.	**DETROIT, MI**	**1846-1850**
F. (FREDERICK) BUHL & CO.	**DETROIT, MI**	**1851-1870**
F. (FREDERICK) BUHL, NEWLAND & CO.	**DETROIT, MI**	**1871-1875**
WALTER BUHL & CO.	**DETROIT, MI**	**1876-1882**

(Hatters, Regalia, Military Goods)

S. (SAMUEL) C. BUNTING SR.	**PHILADELPHIA, PA**	**1822-1861**
S. (SAMUEL) C. BUNTING JR.	**PHILADELPHIA, PA**	**1861-1865**

Sold cavalry sabers.
(Merchant, Hardware Dealer, Military Goods, Guns and Swords)

BURGER & BAUMGARD	**NEW YORK, NY**	**1910-1920**

Sold M1902 sabers for all officers.
(Military Goods)

GEORGE BURRELL (BURRILL)	**NEW YORK, NY**	**1810-1835**
BURRELL (GEORGE) & BEEBE (JOHN O.)	**NEW YORK, NY**	**1836**
GEORGE BURRELL	**NEW YORK, NY**	**1837-1840**
C. (CHARLES) A. BURRELL	**ROCHESTER, NY**	**1840-1908**

(Silversmith, Gunsmith, Cutler)

EDWIN D. BURT & CO.	**WASHINGTON, DC**	**1861-1865**

Partners: John W. Burt, Elisha Dix, M.A. Moor.
Adv. military goods and swords for sale (1864-1865).
(Military Goods, Swords)

JOHN A. BUSH	**PEORIA, IL**	**1862-1865**

Partner: Charles H. Deane.
(See Charles H. Deane)
(Regalia Swords, Military Goods)

HARVEY RAYMOND CABERAY	**NEW YORK, NY**	**1830-1847**
SHERWOOD & WHATLEY	**CHICAGO, IL**	**1847-1854**
Employee: Harvey R. Caberay.		
CARTER (OTIS G.) & CABEREY (HARVEY R.)	**CHICAGO, IL**	**1855-1859**
H. (HARVEY) R. CABERAY	**CHICAGO, IL**	**1860-D1907**
	60 State Street	

- Adv. as manufacturers and dealers in military and naval goods of the finest quality, including presentation swords, in the *Army-Navy Journal* (1864).
- Authorized agent of C.C. Carber.
- (See Sherwood & Whatley)

(Jeweler, Silversmith, Military Goods, Presentation Swords, Regalia)

CADY & OHMSTEAD JEWELRY CO.	KANSAS CITY, MO	1914-1918

Sold M1902 saber for all officers.
(Military Goods)

JOHN D. (DAY) CALDWELL	CINCINNATI, OH	B1816, 1865-D1902

Imported swords from
  William Clauberg, Solingen, Germany.
Had a branch in Philadelphia, PA.
(Military Goods, Regalia)

CANFIELD (IRA C.) & BROTHER (WILLIAM B.) & CO.	BALTIMORE, MD	1834-1880

- Partners: Thomas Welch, Joseph B. Meredith, James Arminger.
- Adv. a full stock of presentation and regulation swords, camp equipment, military goods, and pistols in the *Army-Navy Journal* (1863-1864).
- Bought out Hugh Gelston Jewelry Co. (1834).
- (See Joseph B. Meredith-Silversmith listing)

(Silversmith, Military and Fancy Goods, Swords, Cutlery, Pistols)

WILLIAM CARRINGTON	NEW YORK, NY	1760-1784
CARRINGTON (WILLIAM) & THOMAS (THOMAS)	NEW YORK, NY	1784-1790
W. (WILLIAM) CARRINGTON & CO.	CHARLESTON, SC	1790-1820
JAMES EYLAND & CO.	CHARLESTON, SC	1820-1832

Partners: William Carrington, W.G. Chance.
(Jeweler, Silversmith, Military Goods)

CHANDLER (STEPHEN) & DARROW (EDMUND)	NEW YORK, NY	1843-1870

Also called Masonic Publishing & Mfg. Co.
Had a branch in Atlanta, GA.
(Masonic Supplies, Regalia, Silversmiths)

CHAPLIN & IHLING
(See Ihling Brothers)

SIMON G. CHEEVER	BOSTON, MA	1817-1840

Partner in Sheldon (John) & Co. (1837-1840).

SHELDON (JOHN) & CHEEVER (SIMON G.)	BOSTON, MA	1840-1846
CHEEVER (SIMON G.) & MCBURNEY (CHARLES)	BOSTON, MA	1847-1848
S. (SIMON) G. CHEEVER	BOSTON, MA	1849-1866
S. (SIMON) G. CHEEVER & CO.	BOSTON, MA	1867-1870

(Saddler, Leather Goods, Military Goods)

JACOB D. CHEVALIER	NEW YORK, NY	1822-1838
JOHN D. CHEVALIER	NEW YORK, NY	1838-1862
JOHN D. CHEVALIER & SONS	NEW YORK, NY	1862-1868

(Cutler, Bowie Knives, Surgical Instruments)

CHICAGO GUN & CUTLERY CO.	CHICAGO, IL	1884-1895

(Cutler)

CHICAGO UNIFORM & CAP CO. (Regalia)	CHICAGO, IL	1875
MOSES CHICK Bought out Seth E. Brown (1849). (Watch Maker, Military Goods, Fancy Goods)	CONCORD, NH	1830-1860
CINCINNATI REGALIA CO. George W. Morris was a company representative (1902). Put out fraternal goods catalogs. (Regalia, Jeweler)	CINCINNATI, OH	1900-1920
CITY CLOTHING STORE (See O.S. Baldwin)		
HENRY G. CLAGSTONE Adv. presentation swords and military goods (1864). (Military Goods, Presentation Swords)	PHILADELPHIA, PA	1860-1864

CLARK, RACKETT & CO.
Partners: Francis C. Clark, Horace Clark,
  George Rackett.
Sold a presentation sword for Captain Josiah Tatnall
  (naval hero of Mexican War) that was purchased
  by the state of Georgia.
Sword made by H.E. Baldwin & Co., New Orleans, LA.
(Silversmith, Military Goods Dealer)
	AUGUSTA, GA	1840-1852

CLARK & ROGERS (Military Goods)	NEW ORLEANS, LA	1810-1815
JAMES C. COLLINS (Military Surplus Goods)	PHILADELPHIA, PA	1861-1900
PELEG COLLINS	PROVIDENCE, RI CINCINNATI, OH	B1799-1824 1825-1828
COLLINS (PELEG) & SHIPP (SAMUEL)	CINCINNATI, OH	1829-1835
PELEG COLLINS	CINCINNATI, OH	1836-1842
HAZAN (NATHAN L.) & COLLINS (PELEG)	CINCINNATI, OH	1843-1847
PELEG COLLINS (See Samuel Shipp) (See Nathan L. Hazen) (Military Goods)	CINCINNATI, OH	1848-1850
E. (ELIAS) COMBS & CO. Adv. swords and dirks (1855). (Regalia, Masonic Equipment, Swords)	NEW YORK, NY	1844-1858
CONTINENTAL CLOTHING CO. (Clothier, Military Goods and Uniforms)	BOSTON, MA	1860-1865

HENRY PROUSE COOPER	**LIVERPOOL, ENGLAND**	**1849-1869**
HENRY P. COOPER	**NEW YORK, NY**	**1870-1882**

Adv. as a merchant tailor selling army, navy, and masonic uniforms in the *Army-Navy Journal* (1870-1880).

H. (HENRY) P. COOPER — **NEW YORK, NY** — **1883-1890**
(Tailor, Military Uniforms)

BENJAMIN COOPER	**NEW YORK, NY**	**1790-1813**
JEREMIAH COOPER	**NEW YORK, NY**	**1790-1813**
B. (BENJAMIN) & J. (JEREMIAH) COOPER	**NEW YORK, NY** 7 Maiden Lane	**1814-1840**

Bought swords from Nathan Starr.

HENRY T. COOPER	**NEW YORK, NY**	**1841-1851**
H. (HENRY) T. COOPER & A. (ALBERT) COOPER	**NEW YORK, NY**	**1852**
COOPER (HENRY T.) & SON (ALBERT)	**NEW YORK, NY**	**1852-1857**
COOPER (ALBERT) & POND (CHARLES H.)	**NEW YORK, NY**	**1858-1867**
COOPER (ALBERT), HARRIS (EDWIN) & HODGKINS)	**NEW YORK, NY**	**1868-1874**

(Gun Makers, Pistol Makers, Military Goods, Dealers and Importers, Silversmiths)

GARRETT COOPER — **NEW YORK, NY** — **1833-1850**
Adv. silver-plated sword mountings (1848).

COOPER (GARRETT) & CAIRNS (JASPER) — **NEW YORK, NY** — **1850-1854**
(Military Ornamenter and Plater, Silversmith, Sword Hiltor)

THE CRADDOCK CO. — **KANSAS CITY, MO** — **1925-1935**
Sold M1902 sabers for all officers.
(Military Goods)

WILLIAM W. CRANE
HAROLD L. CRANE
(See W.H. Smith)

CHARLES H. CRUMP
(See John J. Low)

WILLIAM CURTIS — **PHILADELPHIA, PA** — **1846-D1867**
Succeeded by James Kelly (1867).

JOHN CURTIS — **PHILADELPHIA, PA** — **1867-1875**
Son of William Curtis.
Partner: Mrs. William Curtis.
(See James Kelly)
(Regalia)

H.N. DAGGETT
U.S. government purchasing agent in Europe. Purchased 5,031 cavalry sabers and 114 M1850 foot officer swords (1862).

BENJAMIN DARLINGTON	PITTSBURGH, PA	1800-1820

Adv. cutlery, saddles, and gunlocks (1816).
(Hardware, Military Goods)

THEODORE H. DAVIES & CO.	HONOLULU, HA	1975

Sold M1902 saber for all officers.
(Military Goods)

ELIAS DAVIS	NEWBURYPORT, RI	B1782-1801
S. (SAMUEL) & E. (ELIAS) DAVIS	BOSTON, MA	1802-1808
DAVIS (SAMUEL & ELIAS) &		
BROWN (ROBERT JOHNSON)	BOSTON, MA	1809-1821
ELIAS DAVIS	BOSTON, MA	1822-D1856

(See Samuel Davis)
(See Robert Johnson Brown-Silversmith listing)
(Jewelers, Silversmiths, Military Goods)

SAMUEL DAVIS	PROVIDENCE, RI	1780-1801
S. (SAMUEL) & E. (ELIAS) DAVIS	BOSTON, MA	1802-1808
DAVIS (SAMUEL & ELIAS),		
BROWN (ROBERT JOHNSON) & CO.	BOSTON, MA	1809-1821
DAVIS (SAMUEL) & WATSON (EDWARD E.)	BOSTON, MA	1822-1824
DAVIS (SAMUEL),		
WATSON (EDWARD E.) & CO.	BOSTON, MA	1825-1830

Partner: Bartlett M. Bramhill.

T. (THOMAS) A. (ASPINWALL) DAVIS & CO.	BOSTON, MA	1831-1836

Partner: A. Langford.

DAVIS (THOMAS ASPINWALL) &		
PALMER (JULIUS A.) & CO.	BOSTON, MA	1837-1845

Partner: Josiah G. Bachelders.

PALMER (JULIUS A.) & BACHELDERS		
(JOSIAH G., AUGUSTUS E.)	BOSTON, MA	1846-1862

U.S. contract for 370 cavalry sabers (1861).

PALMER (JULIUS A.), BACHELDERS		
(JOSIAH G., AUGUSTUS E.) & CO.	BOSTON, MA	1863-1881

Partner: J.A. Leighton.
Sold M1850 foot officer swords.

PALMER (JACOB P.) & LEIGHTON (J.A.)	BOSTON, MA	1881-1890

(See Edward E. Watson-Silversmith listings)
(See Elias David)
(See Robert Johnson Brown-Silversmith listings)
(Jeweler, Silversmith, Military Outfitter, Presentation Swords)

DEAN & CO.	SYRACUSE, NY	1875

Sold M1860 staff and field officer swords.
(Military Goods)

CHARLES H. DEANE	PEORIA, IL	1855-1862

Joined John A. Bush (1862).
(Regalia and Society Swords)

JOHN C.F. DEECKEN	GERMANY	1830-1852

J. (JOHN) C.F. DEECKEN   NEW YORK, NY   1852-1876
Adv. military goods in the *Army-Navy Journal* (1869).
DEECKEN (JOHN C.F.) & CO.   NEW YORK, NY   1876-1878
Partners and sons: George Deecken, Frederick Deecken.
J. (JOHN) C.F. DEECKEN   NEW YORK, NY   1878
Partners and sons: George Deecken, Frederick Deecken.

FREDERICK DEECKEN   NEW YORK, NY   1878-1882
Sold M1850 foot officer swords.

GEORGE DEECKEN   NEW YORK, NY   1878-1882
(Leather Goods, Hardware, Military Goods)

DAVID DELAPIERRE   NEW YORK, NY   1797-1818
BARTHOLOMEW & DAVID DELAPIERRE   NEW YORK, NY   1818-1831
BARTHOLOMEW DELAPIERRE   NEW YORK, NY   1831-1866
(Regalia, Society Swords, Laceman)

WILLIAM DENHAM   NEW YORK, NY   1860-1880
(Military and Fancy Goods)

DETROIT MASONIC REGALIA DEPOT
(See Thomas H. Armstrong-Maker listings)

DETROIT REGALIA CO.   DETROIT, MI   1890-1900
Partners: George D. Adams, William G. Bray
  (left in 1894), F.A. Updike (joined in 1894).
(Regalia and Society Swords)

**THE DETROIT SHEET
  METAL & BRASS WORKS**   DETROIT, MI   1895-1900
    President: Frank E. Kirby.
    Secretary: J.F. Kemp.
    Manager: G.N. McMillan.
(Society Goods and Swords, Railway and Marine Hardware)

A.N. DEWITT   BUFFALO, NY   1855-1860
(Regalia)

WILHELM D. DIETRICH   SOLINGEN, GERMANY   1830-1850
                                                    NEW YORK, NY   1850-1865
Adv. as an importer and hiltor of officer swords
  (1862-1865).
Displayed presentation swords at the New York
  Fair (1864).
Sold M1850 foot officer swords.
(Silversmith, Silver Plater, Sword Hiltor, Importer, Military Goods)

HORACE DIMICK   LEXINGTON, KY   1827-1847
                                                    ST. LOUIS, MS   1847-1853
Partner in Kittridge & Co.
DIMICK (HORACE) & CO.   ST. LOUIS, MS   1853-1859
Partner: Henry Folsom.

HORACE DIMICK CO.	ST. LOUIS, MS	1859-D1873

Victor and Thomas Rudolph bought Dimick Co. (1873).
Used Dimick name until 1881.
(Gun Store, Military Goods)

WILLIAM J. DINSMORE — BOSTON, MA — 1887-1900
(Regalia)

WILLIAM F. DOMINICK
(See Larrabee & North)

GARVEY DONALDSON — NEW YORK, NY — 1885-1890
(Regalia, Uniforms)

A.H. DONDERO — WASHINGTON, DC — 1910-1935
Sold M1902 saber for all officers.
(Military Outfitter)

DARIUS F. DRAKE — BOSTON, MA — 1861-1865
(Military Goods)

G. (GEORGE) W. DREW — CONCORD, NH — 1861-1865
(Jeweler, Military Goods)

GUSTAVUS DRUCKER — NEW YORK, NY — 1810-1858
Partner with Horstmann (1845-1850).
(See William Horstmann)
(Military Goods)

M.J. DRUMMOND — NEW YORK, NY — 1855-1860
(Regalia)

HENRY DUHRING — PHILADELPHIA, PA — 1825-1875
(Military Goods Store, Jeweler, Silversmith)

DUNN & SPENCER — PETERSBURG, VA — 1852
Adv. hardware, guns, cutlery, and edged tools.

DWELLY (R.E.) & PETTY (G.H.) — ALEXANDRIA, VA — 1865-1870
Successors to Hunt & Goodwin.
(Military Goods)

JOSEPH C. DYER (DEYER)	BOSTON, MA	1780-1800
DYER (JOSEPH C.) & EDDY	BOSTON, MA	1800-1804
JOSEPH C. DYER	BOSTON, MA	1804-1806
J. (JOSEPH C.) DYER	BOSTON, MA	1806-1818

Imported eagle-head swords from Joel Edward,
  London, England.
(Jeweler, Military Importer)

JOHN EARL	NEW YORK, NY	1790-1822
EARL (JOHN), LEE & CO.	NEW YORK, NY 115 Maiden Lane	1822-1824

JOHN EARL	NEW YORK, NY 15 Maiden Lane	1824-1825
	NEW YORK, NY 74 Maiden Lane	1825-1826
	NEW YORK, NY 70 Maiden Lane	1826-1828
	NEW YORK, NY 293 Maiden Lane	1828-1829

(Hardware, Military Goods, Importer)

JAMES EATON
(See Charles Folsom)

EDWARD EDERER — CHICAGO, IL — 1855-1880
Bought military goods from Horstmann Brothers
  & Co. and Shannon, Miller, & Co.
(See Horstmann Brothers & Co.)
(See Shannon, Miller, & Co.)
(Military Equipment and Goods, Military Decoration Maker)

EDRIDGE & ALDEN — BOSTON, MA — 1861-1865
(Presentation Swords)

J. HENRY EHRLICKER — PHILADELPHIA, PA — 1861-1870
Adv. West Point uniforms, military uniforms,
  and military goods in the *Army-Navy Journal* (1867).
(Uniforms, Military Goods)

EDWARD EICKE	NEW YORK, NY 42 John	1840-1855
	NEW YORK, NY 13 Maiden Lane	1855-1856
	NEW YORK, NY 118 William	1856-1860
	NEW YORK, NY 58 John	1860-1864
	NEW YORK, NY 4 Corllandt	1864-1868
	NEW YORK, NY 157 Canal	1868-1910

(Lace and Trim, Military Goods)

CHARLES A. EGGLESTON — WASHINGTON, DC — 1861-1865
(Military Goods and Clothing)

EMONS & MARSHALL — PHILADELPHIA, PA — 1861-1865
Sold M1860 staff and field officer swords.
(Military Goods, Swords)

GEORGE C. EVANS — PHILADELPHIA, PA — 1834-1859
Partner in Horstmann Bros. Co. (1854-1859).

EVANS (GEORGE) & HASSELL (WILLIAM S.) — PHILADELPHIA, PA — 1859-1866
Hassell also employed at Horstmann Bros.
Made presentation swords with blades from W.R.
  Kirschbaum, Solingen, Germany.

EVANS (GEORGE C.), **HASSELL (WILLIAM C.), & CO.**	PHILADELPHIA, PA	1866

Partners: Edward E. Hutchinson, James H. Wilson.

WILSON (JAMES H.) & **HUTCHINSON (EDWARD E.)**	PHILADELPHIA, PA	1866-1868
WILSON (JAMES H.) & **STELLWAGON (HENRY)**	PHILADELPHIA, PA	1868-1872
JAMES H. WILSON	PHILADELPHIA, PA	1872-1894

Sold M1860 staff and field officer swords and M1872 artillery officer swords.

WILLIAM H. WILSON	PHILADELPHIA, PA	1894-1900

Succeeded James H. Wilson.

J. (JAMES) H. WILSON CO.	PHILADELPHIA, PA	1900-1916

Sold out to William Lemberg (1916).
(See William H. Wilson & Henry Stellwagon)
(Military Outfitter, Military Importer, Silk Maker, Regalia, Presentation Swords)

GEORGE O. EVANS	LONDON, ENGLAND	1820-1860
	PHILADELPHIA, PA	1861-1866
EVANS (GEORGE O.) & LEACH (WILLIAM W.)	PHILADELPHIA, PA	1867-1872
GEORGE O. EVANS	PHILADELPHIA, PA	1873-1874
EVANS (GEORGE) & MAIZE (ELDRIDGE G.)	PHILADELPHIA, PA	1875
GEORGE O. EVANS & CO.	PHILADELPHIA, PA	1876-1899
GEORGE BOETTCHER & CO.	PHILADELPHIA, PA	1900-1909

Partner: George O. Evans.

GEORGE O. EVANS & CO.	PHILADELPHIA, PA	1910-1914

Partner: George C. Hudson.
(Tailor, Military Goods)

JAMES EYLAND	ENGLAND	B1795-1819

Immigrated to Charleston, SC (1819).

JAMES EYLAND & CO.	CHARLESTON, SC 330 King Street	1820-1827

Partners: William Carrington, W. & G. Chance.

JAMES EYLAND	CHARLESTON, SC	1827-1832
EYLAND (JAMES) & **HAYDEN (NATHANIEL N.)**	CHARLESTON, SC King and Wentworth Streets	1832-1835

Hayden was Eyland's accountant.
James Eyland died (1835).
(See William Carrington, Nathaniel N. Hayden)
(Silversmith, Jeweler, Military Goods, Swords, Pistols, Fancy Goods)

GEORGE W. FARRANT	NORFOLK, VA	1851-1852
H.F. LOUDON & CO.	NORFOLK, VA	1853-1857

Manager: George W. Farrant.

FARRANT (GEORGE W.) & LESTER (JOHN T.)	NORFOLK, VA	1858-1865

Partner: Thomas E. Bolster.
(See H.F. Loudon)
(Military Tailor)

F.B.Q. CLOTHING CO.	NEW YORK, NY	1925-1935

Sold M1902 saber for all officers.

A. (ABRAHAM) & M. (MARCUS) FECHEIMER	CINCINNATI, OH	1840-1846
FECHEIMER (ABRAHAM & MARCUS), GOLDSMITH (F.) & CO.	CINCINNATI, OH	1846-1850
FECHEIMER (ABRAHAM & MARCUS), GOLDSMITH (F.) & ELSAS	CINCINNATI, OH	1850
FECHEIMER (ABRAHAM & MARCUS) & GOLDSMITH (F.)	CINCINNATI, OH	1851-1854
FECHEIMER & BROTHER	CINCINNATI, OH	1855

Abraham died (1855).

MARCUS FECHEIMER	CINCINNATI, OH	1856-1865
FECHEIMER & CO.	CINCINNATI, OH	1865-1868
FECHEIMER, FRANKEL & CO.	CINCINNATI, OH	1868-1881
FECHEIMER BROTHERS & CO.	CINCINNATI, OH	1881-1910

Sold M1905 sword for all officers.
(Regalia, Military Uniforms, Clothier)

HERMAN FERSENHEIM WASHINGTON, DC 1861-1865

His company was called the
 Army-Navy Emporium.
J. Baronn was a sales representative.
(Military Goods)

A.D. FITCH ST. PAUL, MN 1861-1865
(Military Goods)

JAMES P. FITCH NEW YORK, NY 1834-1860

Worked for Schuyler, Hartley, & Graham (1854-1860).

NEW YORK, NY 1860-1861
19 John Street

Imported cavalry officer swords from Paul D.
 Luneschloss, Solingen, Germany.

NEW YORK, NY 1861-1862
15 Maiden Lane

U.S. contract for 193 musician's swords (1862).
Sold M1850 staff and field officers swords and
 cavalry officer sabers.

FITCH (JAMES P.) & WALDO (HOWARD)	NEW YORK, NY	1862-1864

Partner: Walter M. Smith.

FITCH (JAMES P.), WALDO (HOWARD), & BARRE (LEON)	NEW YORK, NY	1865-1870
FITCH (JAMES P.), VANVECHTON & CO.	NEW YORK, NY	1865-1870

Partners: E.C. Chamberlain, Howard Waldo.
(Military Goods, Presentation Swords, Pistols, Guns, Swords)

THOMAS FLETCHER	PHILADELPHIA, PA	D1787-1808
CHARLES FLETCHER	PHILADELPHIA, PA	1790-1808
FLETCHER (THOMAS & CHARLES) & GARDINER (BALDWIN & SIDNEY)	BOSTON, MA	1808-1811
	PHILADELPHIA, PA	1811-1830

Adv. horsemen's sabers and hangers (1809).
Bought blades from William Rose Jr.
Employee: Mathias Baldwin (1817-1819).

FLETCHER (THOMAS) & BAILEY (T.)	PHILADELPHIA, PA	1830-1838
FLETCHER (THOMAS) & BENNETT (JACOB)	PHILADELPHIA, PA	1838-1840

THOMAS FLETCHER	PHILADELPHIA, PA	1840-D1866

Adv. presentation swords (1840).
Designed sword presented to Gen. Winfield Scott (1816).
John Meer etched some blades.
(Silversmith, Goldsmith, Jeweler, Designer,
  Military Goods, Presentation Swords)

GEORGE A. FLODING	ATLANTA, GA	1875-1909

Sold M1872 cavalry officer swords.
(Regalia, Military Goods)

W.E. FLODING	ATLANTA, GA	1909-1920

Successor to George A. Floding.
Put out fraternal goods catalogs.
(Regalia, Military Goods)

THOMAS FLORENCE
(See Paul Bremond)

CHARLES FOLSOM	NEW YORK, NY	1831-1850
HENRY TOMES & CO.	NEW YORK, NY	1850-1856

Partners: Charles Folsom, James Eaton.

EATON (JAMES) & FOLSOM (CHARLES)	NEW YORK, NY	1856-1858
FOLSOM (CHARLES) & STEVENS (LOUIS)	NEW YORK, NY	1858-1862
TOMES, SON & MELVAIN	NEW YORK, NY	1862-1865

Buyer: Charles Folsom.

CHARLES FOLSOM	NEW YORK, NY	1865-1885
	33 and 38 Maiden Lane	

Adv. guns, pistols, rifles, and swords, and military,
  naval, and fancy goods to be sold to officers, cutlers,
  gunsmiths, and the general public at the lowest prices
  in the *Army-Navy Journal* (1864).
(See Henry Tomes)
(Military Goods Dealer and Importer)

HENRY FOLSOM	ST. LOUIS, MO	1830-1852

Brother of Charles Folsom.

DIMICK & CO.	ST. LOUIS, MO	1853-1859

Partner: Henry Folsom.

HENRY FOLSOM	ST. LOUIS, MO	1860-1864

Bought blades from Collins & Co.
Adv. military goods and presentation swords (1863).

HENRY FOLSOM & CO.	ST. LOUIS, MO	1865-1877

Son David Folsom entered the business.

H. (HENRY) & D. (DAVID) FOLSOM	ST. LOUIS, MO	1877-1933

Partner: James McCullough.
Branches
   Chicago: Folsom Brothers (1868-1871).
   New Orleans: Folsom Brothers (1868-1875).
   Memphis: Henry Folsom & Co. (1859-1864).
   New York: H. & D. Folsom & Co. (1877-1933).
(See Horace Dimick)
(Military Goods, Presentation Swords)

JOHN WESLEY FORBES
(See Maker listings)

GEORGE B. FOSTER	BOSTON, MA	B1810-1843
HARRIS & STANWOOD	BOSTON, MA	1843-1846

Partner: George B. Foster.

GEORGE B. FOSTER	BOSTON, MA 33 Tremont Street	1846-D1887

Adv. swords, belts, caps, and military articles
  for officers of the army and navy.
(See Harris & Stanwood)
(Military Goods)

GEORGE F. FOSTER	CHICAGO, IL	1837-D1879
GEORGE F. FOSTER & CO.	CHICAGO, IL	1879-1892

Owners and sons: Alonzo Foster, Benjamin F. Foster.

G.F. FOSTER SONS & CO.	CHICAGO, IL	1892-1900

Sold M1850 staff and field officer swords, M1840
  medical officer swords, and M1860 staff and field
  officer swords.

B. (BENJAMIN) F. FOSTER **UNIFORM & CAP CO.**	CHICAGO, IL	1900-1910

(Regalia, Military Goods, Swords)

JOHN SMITH FRAZER	NEW YORK, NY 85 Maiden Lane	1830-1847

Adv. engineer officer swords and topographical
  engineer officer swords.
(Tailor, Military Uniforms, Military Goods, Swords)

FROSTMANN (FROST, MANN) & CO.	NEW YORK, NY	1861

Probably Horstmann.
U.S. contract for 357 cavalry sabers, 100 foot officer
  swords, and 25 non-comm. swords.

FUNSTON (H.M.) & SCOFIELD (W.R.)	WASHINGTON, DC	1861-1865

(Military Goods)

LEOPOLD FURTWENGLER	GERMANY GREENBURG, PA Westmoreland County	B1823-1840 1840-D1900

Adv. knives, swords, and pistols (1864).
(Silversmith, Clock Maker, Watch Maker,
  Jeweler, Military and Fancy Goods)

T.D. GARD	WORCESTER, MA	1861-1865

Sold M1850 and M1860 staff and field officer swords.
(Military Goods)

JAMES GALT	RICHMOND, VA	B1741, 1765-D1800

(Silversmith)

JAMES GALT	ALEXANDRIA, VA	1794-D1847

Son of William Galt
(Silversmith)

M.W. GALT & BROTHER (WILLIAM)	WASHINGTON, DC	1847-1878

Sons of James Galt.
Adv. rich military swords, presentation swords, and army and navy officer requisites of every description in the *Army-Navy Journal* (1863).

M.W. GALT BROTHER & CO.	WASHINGTON, DC	1878-1892
GALT & BROTHER	WASHINGTON, DC	1892-1934
GALT & BROTHER, INC.	WASHINGTON, DC	1934-1991

(Silversmith, Watch Maker, Jeweler, Military Goods)

SAMUEL GALT	YORKTOWN, VA	B1700-1735
	MILLCREEK, VA	1735-1745
	HAMPTON, VA	1745-1751
	WILLIAMSBURG, VA	1751-D1761

(Silversmith)

WILLIAM GALT	YORKTOWN, VA	B1723-1751

Son of Samuel Galt.

	WILLIAMSBURG, VA	1751-1761
	ALEXANDRIA, VA	1761-1794

(Silversmith)

GELHAAR UNIFORM CO.	KANSAS CITY, MO	1910-1920

Sold M1902 saber for all officers.
(Uniforms and Military Goods)

HENRY GELSTON	BOSTON, MA	1827-1829

GELSTON (HUGH) & GOULD (JAMES)	BALTIMORE, MD	1816-1823
HUGH GELSTON	BALTIMORE, MD	1823-1833
	BALTIMORE, MD	1834-D1873

Company bought by Canfield & Brother (1834).
(See James Gould)
(See Canfield & Brother)
(Silversmith)

HUGH GELSTON	BOSTON, MA	B1794-1827

Partner in George I. Welles & Co. (1816-1827).

WELLES (ALFRED) & GELSTON (HUGH)	BOSTON, MA	1827-1829

(See George I. Welles & Co.-Silversmith listings)
(Jeweler, Silversmith, Fancy Goods, Military Goods)

GEM-SILVER CO. (GEMSCO)	NEWARK, NJ	1910-1930

Sold M1875 marine officer sabers
Sold M1902 saber for all officers made with blades imported from C.E. Eickhorn, Solingen, Germany.
Owned by Wilcox-Roth Co.
(Silversmith, Military Goods)

GEORGE S. GETHEN	PHILADELPHIA, PA	1920-1930

Sold M1902 sabers with German blades for all officers.
(Military Goods)

WILLIAM GETHEN	PHILADELPHIA, PA	1795-D1809

JOHN WARD GETHEN Son of William Gethen.	**PHILADELPHIA, PA**	**1809-1836**
JOHN WARD & ROBERT GETHEN (Silversmith, Military Goods)	**PHILADELPHIA, PA**	**1836-1840**
GEORGE H. GIBSON (Regalia, Military Goods)	**BOSTON, MA**	**1860-1865**
ALBERT A. GILBERT (Military Goods)	**PHILADELPHIA, PA**	**1861-1865**
WILLIAM GILEBRIST (Cutler)	**PHILADELPHIA, PA**	**1860-1865**
EDWARD GILES	**NEW YORK, NY**	**1840-1864**
PRICE (JOHN H.), GILES (EDWARD) & UNDERHILL (JOHN T.) (Silversmith, Military Goods)	**NEW YORK, NY**	**1864-1865**
GLAZE & RADCLIFFE (See Confederate Maker listing)		
T.C. GLEASON (Regalia, Fraternal Swords)	**CHICAGO, IL**	**1870-1880**
CHARLES J. GODFREY Issued military goods catalogs. (Military Goods, Sporting Goods)	**NEW YORK, NY**	**1890-1904**
AZRO GOFF (Regalia)	**NEW YORK, NY**	**1885-1890**
JAMES M. GOODALL JR. Sold M1860 staff and field officer swords. (Military Goods)	**CHICAGO, IL**	**1870**
DANIEL T. GOODHUE Adv. military goods, including swords, jewelry, and cutlery (1824-1826).	**PROVIDENCE, RI**	**1820-1860**
DANIEL T. GOODHUE & SON (GEORGE B.) (Silversmith, Jeweler, Military Goods, Swords, Cutlery)	**PROVIDENCE, RI**	**1861-1865**
JAMES GOULD	**BALTIMORE, MD**	**B1795-1817**
GELSTON (HUGH) & GOULD (JAMES)	**BALTIMORE, MD**	**1817-1820**
JAMES GOULD	**BALTIMORE, MD**	**1820-1851**
GOULD (JAMES) & WARD (WILLIAM H.)	**BALTIMORE, MD**	**1851-1855**
GOULD (JAMES) STOWELL (A. JR.) & WARD (WILLIAM H.)	**BALTIMORE, MD**	**1855-1860**
JAMES GOULD (Sword Hiltor, Silversmith, Jeweler, Military and Fancy Goods)	**BALTIMORE, MD**	**1860-D1874**
W.R. GOULDING & CO. (Cutler, Surgical Instruments)	**NEW YORK, NY**	**1850-1866**

MALCOLM GRAHAM	NEW YORK, NY	**1826-1853**
Partner in William H. Smith & Co. (1846-1853).		
SCHUYLER (JACOB), HARTLEY (MARCELLES), & GRAHAM (MALCOLM)		**1854-1878**
HARTLEY (MARCELLES) & GRAHAM (MALCOLM)		**1879-1899**
Malcolm Graham died (1899).		
(See Schuyler, Hartley, & Graham)		
(Military Goods Dealers)		
RENE L. GRAVELLE	PHILADELPHIA, PA	**1800-1809**
LEFEVRE (JOHN FELIX) & GRAVELLE (RENE L. & LOUISA M.)	PHILADELPHIA, PA	**1810-1811**
RENE L. GRAVELLE	PHILADELPHIA, PA	**1812-1831**
Partner: Louisa M. Gravelle.		
(See John Felix Lefevre)		
(Jeweler, Silversmith, Military Goods)		
ALONZO GRAVES	MORRISTOWN, NJ	**1900-1905**
(Regalia)		
GRAY (GEORGE P.) & POTTER (AUGUSTUS)	NEW YORK, NY	**1861-1865**
(Military Goods)		
WILLIAM GREGG	MONONGALIA CO., VA	**B1800-1811**
	ALEXANDRIA, VA	**1811-1818**
	LEXINGTON, KY	**1818-1821**
	PETERSBURG, VA	**1821-1824**
	COLUMBIA, SC	**1824-1831**
	CHARLESTON, SC	**1831-1838**
HAYDEN (NATHANIEL N. & H. SIDNEY) & GREGG (WILLIAM)	CHARLESTON, SC	**1838-1843**
WILLIAM GREGG	CHARLESTON, SC	**1843-1846**
GREGG (WILLIAM) & HAYDEN (H. SIDNEY & AUGUSTUS H.)	CHARLESTON, SC	**1846-1852**
Authorized dealer for Ames Mfg. Co.		
WILLIAM GREGG	CHARLESTON, SC	**1852-B1867**
Became a cotton broker.		
(See Nathaniel N. Hayden)		
(Jeweler, Silversmith, Military Goods)		
JACOB J. GRIFFEN	NEW YORK, NY	**1823-1850**
Employee of Horstmann, Son & Drucker (1843-1850).		
	NEW YORK, NY 24 Maiden Lane	**1850-1852**
	NEW YORK, NY 270 Water Street	**1852-1853**
WILSON & GRIFFEN (JACOB J.)	NEW YORK, NY 154 South Street	**1853-1854**
WILSON & GRIFFEN	NEW YORK, NY 24 Maiden Lane	**1854-1856**
	NEW YORK, NY 28 Maiden Lane	**1856-1857**
	NEW YORK, NY 23 Maiden Lane	**1857-1862**

ALEXANDER HAYS & CO.	NEW YORK, NY 19 John Street	1862-1863

Employee: Jacob J. Griffen.

JACOB J. GRIFFEN	NEW YORK, NY 35 Maiden Lane	1863-1869

(Military and Fancy Goods)

ARTHUR B. GRISWOLD
(See James E. Hyde)

GROOSMAN MILITARY & SOCIETY SUPPLY	CLEVELAND, OH	1875

(Regalia)

DANIEL GRUBB	MEADVILLE, PA Crawford County	1810-1825

(Gunsmith)

GEORGE GRUBB	PHILADELPHIA, PA	1790-1800

(Gunsmith, Cutler)

JOSEPH C. GRUBB & CO.	PHILADELPHIA, PA	1839-1886

U.S. contract for 248 cavalry sabers (1861).
Partners: John McLaughlin, Samuel Winchester.
Imported swords, knives, guns, and pistols.
(Military Goods, Importer)

TOBIAS GRUBB	ALLENTOWN, PA	B1792, 1812-D1872

(Gunsmith)

HENRY GUILD	BOSTON, MA	1852-1854
GUILD (HENRY) & STEVANS	BOSTON, MA	1855-1860
GUILD (HENRY) & DELANO	BOSTON, MA	1861-1888
HENRY GUILD & SON	BOSTON, MA	1888-1890

(Jeweler, Regalia)

JOHN G. HAAS	CARLISLE, PA	1876-1883
	LANCASTER, PA	1883-1890
	WASHINGTON DC	1900-1920

(Military Tailor and Uniforms)

HAGEMEYER CO.	NEW YORK, NY	1875

(Regalia)

GEORGE A. HAHN	BALTIMORE, MD	1867-1890

(Gunsmith, Military Goods)

J.H.F. HAHN	BALTIMORE, MD	1856-1902

Employee of Jacob Gminder (1876-1902).

	BALTIMORE, MD	1902-D1939

Partner and son: Irwin Hahn.
(Regalia, Military Goods)

WILLIAM HAHN	NEW YORK, NY	1858-1880

U.S. contract for 335 cavalry sabers (1861).
(Military Importer)

C. HALL
(See Confederate Dealer listings)

IVORY A. HALL (Silversmith, Jeweler, Military and Fancy Goods)	CONCORD, NH	B1795, 1825-D1880
M. HALL (Regalia)	HILLDALE, MI	1880
HANNIBAL G. HAMLIN JR. Employee of George W. Pohlman Co. (1853-1862).	CINCINNATI, OH	1833-1862
H. (HANNIBAL) G. HAMLIN JR. Sold M1850 foot officer swords. E.C.L. Mustin bought Hamlin Co. (1865). (Military Goods)	CINCINNATI, OH	1862-1865
CHARLES P. HARDING	BOSTON, MA	1860-1880
HARDING REGALIA CO.	BOSTON, MA	1880-1913
HARDING UNIFORM & REGALIA CO.	BOSTON, MA 22 School Street	1913-1993

Adv. in the 1925 Boston directory.
Uniforms and equipment for the army and navy.
Sold M1902 saber for all officers.
(Uniforms, Regalia)

NEWELL HARDING	BOSTON, MA	B1796-1830
NEWELL HARDING & CO. (Silversmith, Sword Hiltor)	BOSTON, MA	1830-D1862
B.F. HARLEY Sold M1860 staff and field officer swords. (Military Goods)	NEW MARKET, NH	1861-1865
HENRY W. HAROLD	ALLIANCE, OH	1872-1873
BICKEL (LOUIS) & HAROLD (HENRY W.)	AKRON, OH	1884-1887
HENRY W. HAROLD (See Louis Bickel) (Gunsmith, Cutlery)	AKRON, OH	1888-1892
SMITH B. HARRINGTON Had offices in the same location as the Ames Sword Co. at 45 Bromfield. (Regalia, Presentation Swords)	BOSTON, MA	1915-1925

HARRIS & STANWOOD
(See Henry Stanwood)

WILLIAM HARRIS
(See Henry B. Stanwood)

HART (JAMES M.), LEONORI & CO. (Regalia, Hatters)	ST. LOUIS, MO	1874-1875
CLARENCE A. HART	PHILADELPHIA, PA	1848-1868

ROBERT M. ROBINSON & CO.	**PHILADELPHIA, PA**	**1869-1870**
Partner: Clarence A. Hart.		
C. (CLARENCE) A. HART	**PHILADELPHIA, PA**	**1871-1896**
Succeeded Robinson.		
Sold M1860 staff and field officer swords.		
(See Robert M. Robinson)		
(Regalia, Military Goods)		
MARCELLUS HARTLEY	**NEW YORK, NY**	**1820-1853**
Employee of Frances Tomes & Son (1846-1849).		
SCHUYLER (JACOB R.), HARTLEY (MARCELLUS), & GRAHAM (MALCOLM)	**NEW YORK, NY**	**1854-1878**
Hartley managed the firearm department.		
Also purchased military goods for the U.S. government in Europe (1861-1863).		
(See Schuyler, Hartley, & Graham)		
(Military Goods)		
WILLIAM B. HARTLEY	**NEW YORK, NY** 9 Maiden Lane	**1855-1862**
U.S. contracts for 752 cavalry sabers (1861-1862).		
(Military Goods)		
FREDERICK F. HASSAM	**BOSTON, MA**	**1838-1856**
KINGMAN (LEVI C.) & HASSAM (FREDERICK F.)	**BOSTON, MA**	**1856-1861**
HASSAM BROTHERS	**BOSTON, MA**	**1861-1868**
Sold belt knives.		
(Importers and Dealers in Guns, Cutlery, and Military Goods)		
HATFIELD & SONS	**NEW YORK, NY**	**1833-1900**
Partners:		
Sampson Hatfield		
Charles W. Hatfield		
Lemuel F.B. Hatfield		
Albert S. Hatfield		
(Military Tailors)		
HENRY HAUSMANN	**NEW ORLEANS, LA**	**B1845, 1861-D1878**
Wife Theresa Hausmann ran company (1879-1889).		
T. (THERESA) HAUSMANN & SON	**NEW ORLEANS, LA**	**1890-1893**
T. (THERESA) HAUSMANN & SONS	**NEW ORLEANS, LA**	**1894-1905**
T. HAUSMANN & SONS LTD.	**NEW ORLEANS, LA**	**1906-1917**
T. HAUSMANN'S INC.	**NEW ORLEANS, LA**	**1819-1990**
(Silversmith, Military Goods, Fraternal Swords)		
NATHANIEL N. HAYDEN	**CHARLESTON, SC**	**B1805-1832**
EYLAND (JAMES) & HAYDEN (NATHANIEL N.)	**CHARLESTON, SC** Corner of King and Wentworth Streets	**1832-1835**
James Eyland died (1835).		
NATHANIEL HAYDEN	**CHARLESTON, SC**	**1835-1838**

HAYDEN (NATHANIEL N. & H. SIDNEY) &		
GREGG (WILLIAM) & CO.	CHARLESTON, SC	1838-1843

H. Sidney Hayden was Nathaniel's brother.

H. SIDNEY & AUGUSTUS HAYDEN	CHARLESTON, SC	1843-1846

Nathaniel N. Hayden moved to New York, NY (1843-D1875).

GREGG (WILLIAM) & HAYDEN		
(H. SIDNEY & AUGUSTUS H.)	CHARLESTON, SC	1846-1852

Gregg left in 1852.

HAYDEN BROTHERS & CO.		
(H. SIDNEY & AUGUSTUS H.)	CHARLESTON, SC	1852-1855

H. Sidney left and moved to Connecticut.

HAYDEN (AUGUSTUS H.) &		
WHILDEN (WILLIAM G.)	CHARLESTON, SC	1855-1863
	250 King Street at Hasel Street	

- Bought swords from Horstmann Brothers & Co. before the Civil War.
- Sold M1840 lt. artillery sabers.
- Adv. as dealers in watches, clocks, jewelry, silverware, military goods, cutlery, pistols, gas fixtures, house furnishings, and fancy articles (1861).

AUGUSTUS H. HAYDEN	CHARLESTON, SC	1863-1866
Served in the Confederate Army.		
A. (AUGUSTUS) H. HAYDEN	CHARLESTON, SC	1866-1879
	172 (later 255) King Street	

(See James Eyland and William Gregg)
(Silversmith, Jewelers, Military Goods, Swords and Pistols, Importer, Cutler)

PETER HAYDEN	NEW YORK, NY	1861-1865

U.S. contract for 1,500 cavalry sabers and 491 lt. artillery sabers (1862).
(Hardware and Military Importer)

HAYS & CO.	INDIANAPOLIS, IN	1861-1863
HAYS, KOHN (JOSEPH) & CO.	INDIANAPOLIS, IN	1864
HAYS, ROSENTHAL & CO.	INDIANAPOLIS, IN	1865

(See Joseph Kohn)
(Military and Fancy Goods, Clothier)

W. (WILLIAM) A. & B. (BETSY) HAYWOOD	NEW YORK, NY	1857-1880

(Jewelry, Insignia, Masonic and Military Swords)

NATHAN L. HAZEN	TROY, NY	B1809-1830
	CINCINNATI, OH	1831-1842
HAZEN (NATHAN L.) & COLLINS (PELEG)	CINCINNATI, OH	1843-1847
NATHAN L. HAZEN	CINCINNATI, OH	1848-D1851

(See Peleg Collins)
(Jeweler, Silversmith, Clock Maker)

JOHN C. HAZLETON	WASHINGTON, DC	1861-1864

(Military Goods and Equipment)

FRANCIS J. HEIBERGER	WASHINGTON, DC	1838-1857

Bought H.F. Loudon & Co. (1858).

ARMY & NAVY COOP	WASHINGTON, DC	1858-1861

Owner: Francis H. Heiberger.
Sold M1860 staff and field officer swords.

HEIBERGER (FRANCIS J.) & KING (HENRY)	WASHINGTON, DC	1862-1865

F. (FRANCIS) J. HEIBERGER	WASHINGTON, DC	1866-1910

Sold M1902 saber for all officers.
Adv. in the *Army-Navy Journal* (1869-1870).
(See Henry King)
(See H.F. Loudon & Co.)
(Military Tailors)

LOUIS HELWIG & CO.	CHICAGO, IL 165 Dearborn	1880-1885

(Regalia)

HILBORN & HAMBERGER	NEW YORK, NY	1861-1865

Imported M1852 naval officer swords.
(Military Goods)

HENRY A. HILL	WASHINGTON, DC	1861-1865

(Military Goods)

CARL HIRSCH & SONS	ST. LOUIS, MO	1800-1820

(Military Goods, Guns, Swords)

JAMES H. HIRSCH & SONS	CHICAGO, IL	1900-1930

Sold M1902 saber for all officers.
(Military Goods)

JOSEPH J. HIRSCHBUHL	LOUISVILLE, KY	1840-1858
HIRSCHBUHL (JOSEPH J.) & **DOLFINGER (JACOB)**	LOUISVILLE, KY	1858-1864

Sold M1860 staff and field officer swords.

JOSEPH J. HIRSCHBUHL	LOUISVILLE, KY	1864-1867

Adv. presentation swords and military goods (1864).
(See Jacob Dolfinger-Silversmith listings)
(Silversmith, Jeweler, Watch Maker, Military
  Goods, Swords)

HODGSON (ROBERT), NICHOLSON & CO.	BALTIMORE, MD	1790-1799
HODGSON (ROBERT), THOMPSON	BALTIMORE, MD	1800-1805

Sold cavalry sabers.
(Importer, Merchant, Military Goods, Guns, Swords)

JOHN HOEY	NEW YORK, NY	1861-1865

U.S. contract for 1,800 cavalry sabers and 700
  muskets (1861).
(Military Importer)

FREDERICK J.A. HORR	PHILADELPHIA, PA	1910-1930

(Military Goods)

THE HORSTMANN FAMILY

WILHELM (WILLIAM) H. HORSTMANN **CASSEL, GERMANY** B1785-1816
Province of Hesse-Nassau

- Three generations of the Horstmann family, including William H. Horstmann's father, William H. Horstmann Sr., were *passementiers*. His brother George Horstmann was a *passementier* also.
- A *passementier* was a weaver of narrow textile fabric used for dress trimming, coach lace, military epaulettes and aiguillettes, and sword knots.
- Many of these fabrics involved gold and silver thread. Silk, worsted, linen, or cotton were mixed with gold and silver thread to make highly decorative fabric called "bullion cloth."
- William and his brother George served the normal three-year apprenticeship with their father. Then they traveled for over four years as journeymen (journeymen traveled from shop to shop learning their trade). They both eventually became master *passementiers*.
- George went back to Cassel to work with his father after his journeyman training.
- William continued to travel in Germany, Austria, Switzerland, and finally France. In France he learned about and mastered the Jacquard loom (invented by Joseph Marie Jacquard). He later imported one to Philadelphia.
- William H. Horstmann immigrated to Philadelphia, PA (1816).

WILLIAM H. HORSTMANN **PHILADELPHIA, PA** 1816
- Worked for coach lace weaver Frederick Hoeckley.

PHILADELPHIA, PA 1817-1843
- Rented space at Arch and 12th Streets (1817-1819).
- Opened his own coach lace shop at 59 North 3rd Street (59 later changed to 51) from 1817-1860. Listed as a military store (1830-1842).
- Opened a branch in New York (1824).
- Imported a Jacquard loom (1824).
- Rented space at 53 North 3rd Street (1824-1829).
- Rented space at 48 North 3rd Street; listed as a military store (1829).
- Opened a four-story factory on Germantown Road and Columbia Avenue (1831-1852).
- Tore down the old shop and built a five-story factory at 51 (was 59 until 1830) North 3rd Street. Listed as a military store (1842-1860).
- Both factories (Germantown Road and 51 North 3rd Street) made coach lace, military woven cloth, trimming, and bullion fabric.
- Imported military goods and bullion fabric from his brother, George Horstmann, in Cassel, Germany.
- Turned over the company to his sons, William J. Horstmann (1819-1872) and Sigmund H. Horstmann (1820-1869), in 1843

WILLIAM H. HORSTMANN & CO. **PHILADELPHIA, PA** 1818-1824
- A separate division renting space at 45 North 3rd Street and 55 North 3rd Street.

WILLIAM H. HORSTMANN & SONS **PHILADELPHIA, PA** 1843-1893
- Military store and fringe factory.
- William H. Horstmann retired (1845).
- Authorized agent for Ames Manufacturing Co. (1843-1848).
- Bought the insignia-stamping equipment from John O'Hara (1848).
- Bought the complete stocks, tools, and machinery from the estate of Philadelphia armorer, metal worker, and sword hiltor Frederick W. Widmann for $300 (1848). Widmann had done work for Horstmann for years.
- The Horstmann company had been expanding its military business since the 1830 military store opened.
- The Horstmann company opened its own sword shop, employing Julius Knecke and Jacob Faser, former employees of Frederick W. Widmann (1849).
- William H. Horstmann died in Bethlehem, PA (1850).
- William H. Horstmann & Sons built a large five-story factory at 5th and Cherry Streets (1850-1954).

- The Germantown Road factory was then closed (1852).
- Opened a new showroom and distribution center at 723 Chestnut Street (1854-1868).
- A separate military division (Horstmann Bros. & Co.) was set up (1854).
- (See Horstmann Bros. & Co.)
- Bought the patents, stocks, and equipment of coach lace maker Clinton Co. of Clinton, MA (1857).
- William H. Horstmann & Sons enlarged the factory at 5th and Cherry Streets to include a new showroom (1860).
- The 723 North Chestnut Street factory and showroom and the 51 North 3rd Street factory and showroom were then closed (1861).
- Sigmond H. Horstmann died (1869).
- William J. Horstmann died (1872).
- William J. Horstmann's sons, F. Oden Horstmann Sr. and Walter Horstmann, took over the company (1872).
- Directors in 1872:
    Samuel Clarkson
    Albert Weihenmayer
    William Schultz Jr.
    George Schultz
    J. Howard Mecke

HORSTMANN BROTHERS & CO.   1854-1893

- William H. Horstmann & Sons set up a separate military division operating out of the 723 Chestnut factory (1854-1861) and at 5th and Cherry (1862-1893).
- The military division was called Horstmann Brothers & Co.
- William Hassell and George Evans joined Horstmann Brothers & Co. in 1854 and left in 1859 to start Evans & Hassel Co.
- (See Evans & Hassell)
- Joseph H. Lambert was a foreman (1869-1873).
- Bought M1860 cavalry officer swords from Gebruder Weyersberg, Solingen, Germany.
- Sold swords to Hayden & Whilden (1860).
- (See Hayden & Whilden)
- Bought the complete set of tools and equipment from the estate of insignia maker William Pinchin Jr. (1862).
- (See William Pinchin)
- Displayed presentation swords at the New York Fair (1864).
- Advertised regalia and society goods, military goods, regulation and presentation swords, Colt revolvers, flags, and guidons in many magazines and newspapers, including:
    Army-Navy Journal (1864-1870)
    Journal of the U.S. Cavalry Association
    Rough Ashlar (Richmond, VA)
    Voice of Masonry
    Masonic Review
    National Freemason
    Keystone
- Bought insignia die blocks from Henry H. Sinkler.
- (See Henry H. Sinkler)
- Sold military goods to Edward Ederer.
- (See Edward Ederer)

WILLIAM H. HORSTMANN CO.   1893-1954

- Authorized agent of the Boston Regalia Co.
- William H. Horstmann & Sons and Horstmann Brothers & Co. were reincorporated with a new company name (1893).

William H. Horstmann Co. Executives

1893	F. Oden Horstmann Sr.	Director (died 1894)
	Samuel Clarkson	President (died 1894)
	Walter Horstmann	Director
1894	Walter Horstmann	President
	Samuel Eckert	Vice President
1903-1912	F. Oden Horstmann Jr.	President
1916-1917	George Eiler Jr.	General Manager
	Edwin S. Dixon	Director
	Sidney Small	Director
	Walter Horstmann	President
	Samuel Eckert	Vice President
	Henry Freund	Treasurer
	Harry McManus	Secretary

William H. Horstmann Co. Divisions in 1916

- William H. Horstmann Co. had 600 employees (1916).
- Section A: Cloth and trimming sales; used Columbia trademark.
- Section B: Military equipment sales (uniforms, fraternal goods, regalia); used Knight in Armor trademark.
- Section C: Manufacturing.
- Purchasing branch in Paris, France.
- Manufacturing plant in Lyons, France.
- Sales agencies in New York, NY, Baltimore, MD, and Boston, MA.
- The production departments consisted of weaving factories, an embroidery department, uniform department, leather goods department, regalia manufacturing room, machine shop, foundry, plating shop, and wood products shop.
- Over the years, Horstmann companies issued over 80 catalogs, including 40 fraternal and regalia catalogs.

I.J. HORSTMANN PHILADELPHIA, PA 1954-1982
18th and Washington Avenue
- The final Horstmann company was called I.J. Horstmann & Sons (wool and hide business).

Horstmann Company Name Changes (Philadelphia and New York)

Philadelphia

William H. Horstmann	1817-1843
William H. Horstmann & Co.	1818-1824
A separate division was located at 45 North 3rd Street.	
William H. Horstmann & Sons	1843-1893

Horstmann Brothers & Co.	1854-1893
A separate military division.	
William H. Hortstmann Co.	1893-1954
I.J. Horstmann & Sons	1954-1982

New York

William H. Horstmann	1824-1836
9 Maiden Lane.	
William H. Horstmann & Co.	1837
36 Platt Street.	
William H. Horstmann & Co.	1838-1845
8 Maiden Lane.	
Jeweler Gustavus Drucker became a partner in 1838.	
Horstmann Sons & Drucker	1845-1850
8 Maiden Lane.	
Partners: Gustavus Drucker (left in 1850), John G. Franklin.	
Employee: Jacob J. Griffen.	
Bought swords from N.P. Ames, Cabotsville, MA.	
Horstmann Brothers & Co.	1850-1851
8 Maiden Lane	
Horstmann Brothers & Allien	1851-1869
8 Maiden Lane.	
Issued military catalogs.	
Partners: Henry V. Allien (left in 1870), Laurent Allien (son of Henry; left in 1870).	
Employee: Livingston A. Shannon.	
Horstmann Brothers & Allien	1869-1870
540 Broadway	
Adv. in the *Army-Navy Journal*.	
Listed a location in Paris, France, at 17 Rue Paradis Poissonniere.	
Horstmann Brothers & Co.	1871-1893
27 Maiden Lane.	

Horstmann Products

Military Products

Metal
Belt buckles
Buttons
Cap and hat insignia
Cap and hat ornaments
Flag pole ornaments
Bugles
Fifes
Drum major batons
Gorgets
Spurs
Cases for hats
Cases for chapeaus
Cases for swords

Wood
Drums
Drum sticks
Flag poles

Corded
Aiguillettes
Epaulettes
Hat and cap cords
Shoulder knots
Flag cords

Leather
Baltics
Belts
Holsters
Saddles
Cartridge boxes
Sword and bayonet scabbards
Bridles
Reins
Straps

Cloth
Enlisted and officer sword belts
Gloves
Gauntlets
Legging
Saddle blankets
Horsefly nets
Insignia
Chevrons
Banners
Flag
Guidons
Haversacks
Knapsacks
Shoulder harnesses
Hats
Caps
Chapeaus
Helmets
Shakos
Uniforms (military and fraternal)

Assorted Products
Hat plumes
Hat pompoms

Nonmilitary Products

Theatrical
Jewelry
Crowns

Swords
Brocades
Steel armor
Decorations
Trimmings
Stage hosier

Church
Embroideries
Bouillon
Spangles
Vestment materials

Trimmings
Upholstery
Ladies dress
Carriage
Blind
Sewing silk
Sewing yarns
Sewing spools

Coach
Lace
Fringe
Cords
Tassels

Cloth
Silk
Cotton
Worsted
Bouillon
Upholstery fabrics

Fraternal (Regalia)
Costumes
Uniforms
Jewelry
Swords
Lodge furniture

Police and Firemen
Hats
Caps
Belts
Badges
Gloves

The following Horstmann companies imported and fabricated swords:

WILLIAM H. HORSTMANN & SONS   **PHILADELPHIA, PA**   **1843-1848**
Authorized agent for Ames Manufacturing Co.

WILLIAM H. HORSTMANN & SONS   PHILADELPHIA, PA   1849
- Opened its own sword department (1849).
- Made every part of the sword except the blade.
- Blades were purchased locally, but most were imported from Solingen, Germany.
- Imported complete swords and blades from William Clauberg, Solingen, Germany.
- Imported blades from Gebruder Weyersburg, Solingen, Germany (including Damascus blades).
- Made a complete line of U.S. regulation swords, special-order officer swords, presentation swords, fraternal swords, fencing swords, and theatrical swords and daggers.
- Sold swords with silver hilts by Tiffany & Co.

HORSTMANN BROTHERS & CO.   PHILADELPHIA, PA   1854-1893
- U.S. Civil War enlisted sword contracts (swords were imported):
    13,440 M1840 and M1860 cavalry sabers
    6,734 non-comm. swords
    4,984 musician's swords
    30 lt. artillery sabers
    1,000 cavalry saber scabbards

HORSTMANN SONS & DRUCKER   NEW YORK, NY   1845-1850
Imported and sold:
    M1840 cavalry trooper sabers from Schnitzler & Kirschbaum, Solingen, Germany
    M1821 British-style cavalry sabers from Schnitzer & Kirschbaum, Solingen, Germany

HORSTMANN BROTHERS & ALLIEN   NEW YORK, NY   1851-1870
U.S. Civil War enlisted man sword contracts (swords were imported):
    1,043 M1840 and M1860 cavalry sabers
    1,143 non-comm. swords
    270 musician's swords
    87 artillery non-comm. swords

Horstmann Philadelphia Facilities

Shop and showroom   1817-1830
    59 North 3rd Street.
    Changed to 51 North 3rd Street (1830-1861).
    Military store.

Rented space   1818-1824
    45 and 55 North 3rd Street.

Rented space   1824-1829
    53 North 3rd Street.
    Still had 45 North 3rd Street.

Rented space   1829-1830
    48 North 3rd Street.
    Military store.

Four-story factory.   1831-1852
    Germantown Road at Columbia Avenue.

Shop and showroom   1842-1861
    51 (was 59) North 3rd Street.
    Torn down and a five-story factory and showroom built on the lot.

Five-story factory and showroom1852-1954
    5th and Cherry Street.
    Enlarged (1860).
    Military division moved here (1860).

Showroom and distribution center1854-1861
    723 Chestnut.
    Included military division.

BENJAMIN H. HOWELLBUFFALO, NY1835-1850
(Silversmith, Jeweler, Watch Maker, Military Goods)

MATTHEW HOWELLNEW YORK, NY1810-1825

CHARLES HOWELLNEW YORK, NY1825-1867
Son of Matthew Howell.
(Military Goods)

WILLIAM T. HOWELL & CO.PHILADELPHIA, PA1830-1835
Importer and dealer in hardware, cutlery,
  guns, saddlery, and fancy goods.
(Hardware, Guns, Cutlery)

HUNT (NEHEMIAH) &
GOODWIN (E. STONE)WASHINGTON, DC1861-1865
Branches in New York and Boston.
Sold presentation swords with blades imported
  from Wilhelm Clauberg, Solingen, Germany.
Succeeded by Dwelly & Petty.
(See Dwelly & Petty)
(Military Goods)

HENRY HUSTONNEW YORK, NY1835-1850
40 Maiden Lane
(Furrier, Hatter, Military Goods)

ISAAC & GEORGE HUTTON
(See Silversmiths listings)

A.W. HYATTNEW ORLEANS, LA1880-1885
Agent for J.H. Wilson swords.
(See George C. Evans)
(Regalia)

JAMES N. HYDE
(See Confederate listings)

J.E. HYDENEW YORK, NY1810-1815
Imported swords during War of 1812.
(Military Goods)

CHAPLIN & IHLINGKALAMAZOO, MI1852-1869
IHLING BROTHERS-EVERAND & CO.KALAMAZOO, MI1869-1921
(Uniforms and Military Goods)

INGRAM (ROBERT J.), KITCHEN (JOHN B. & ALFRED S.) & WILLIAMS (EDWARD)	CHICAGO, IL 79 Madison Street	1882-1884

Called Government Goods Depot.
Sold U.S. officer swords, M1840 lt. artillery officer swords, fraternal swords, and military and society uniforms and regalia.
(Military Goods, Military and Society Uniforms)

S. (SAUL) ISAACS & CO.	NEW YORK, NY	1861-1865

- Partners: Gun makers Benjamin J. Hart, B.F. Hart.
- Bought English navy-army outfitters S. Campbell, London, England.
- Imported British M1853 (variant) cavalry sabers and sold them to the Confederacy.
- Imported British M1822 foot officer swords (variant) and sold them to the Confederacy.
- Many marked "Isaac-Campbell" or "Isaacs & Co."

(Military Goods, Sword Importer)

D.C. JACCARD	ST. LOUIS, MO	1815-1829
JACCARD (D.C.) & CO.	ST. LOUIS, MO	1830-1861

(Silversmith)

EUGENE JACCARD	ST. LOUIS, MO	1820-1836
JACCARD (EUGENE) & RECORDON (CHARLES)	ST. LOUIS, MO	1836-1842
JACCARD (EUGENE) & CO.	ST. LOUIS, MO	1842-1847
EUGENE JACCARD & CO.	ST. LOUIS, MO	1847-1882

(See Charles Recordon-Silversmith listings)
(Silversmith, Jeweler, Watch Maker, Military Goods)

HENRY JACOBS	BROOKLYN, NY	1875

(Regalia)

S. JANOWITZ	WASHINGTON, DC	1861-1865

(Military Goods)

JOHN JEFFREY	LAWRENCEVILLE, PA Tioga County	1835-1845

(Gunsmith, Armorer, Military Goods)

J. (JOSEPH) A. JOEL & CO.	NEW YORK, NY	1890-1910

Adv. swords and military goods (1892).
(Military and Naval Goods, Swords)

JOHN JOERDANS	NEW YORK, NY 49 Nassau	1860-1863
	NEW YORK, 51 Maiden Lane	1863-1864

	NEW YORK, NY	1864-1872
	131 William	

(Military Goods, Fancy Goods, Military Importer)

ANDREW JOHNSON — MIDDLETOWN, CT — 1785-1800
Sold scythes made by Nathan Starr Sr.
(Cutler, Dealer)

DONNELLY JOHNSON & CO. — BOSTON, MA — 1900-1910
Sold M1902 sabers for all officers.
(Military Goods)

IVER JOHNSON — WORCHESTER, MA — 1867-1890
 — FITCHBURG, MA — 1891-1914
 — BOSTON, MA — 1915-1925

Sold M1860 staff and field officer swords.
(Military and Sporting Goods)

T. RODGERS JOHNSON — SAN FRANCISCO, CA — 1852-1880
A.J. Plate bought out Johnson (1880).
(See A.J. Plate)
(Military Goods and Regalia)

Firm	Location	Dates
JOHN B. JONES	BOSTON, MA	B1782-1809
JONES (JOHN B.), WARD (RICHARD) & PIERCE (JOHN)	BOSTON, MA	1809-1811
BALDWIN (JABEZ L.) & JONES (JOHN B.)	BOSTON, MA	1811-1837
JOHN B. JONES & CO.	BOSTON, MA	1837-1838

Partner: S.S. Ball.

JONES (JOHN B.) LOW (JOHN J.) & BALL (S.S.)	BOSTON, MA	1838-1840

Authorized dealer for Ames Mfg. Co.

LOW (JOHN J.), BALL (S.S.) & CO.	BOSTON, MA	1840-1846

Partner: John B. Jones.

JONES (JOHN B.) BALL (S.S.) & POOR	BOSTON, MA	1846-1852
JONES (JOHN B.), BALL (S.S.) & CO.	BOSTON, MA	1852-1854
JONES (JOHN B.) SHREVE (BENJAMIN), BROWN & CO.	BOSTON, MA	1854

John B. Jones died (1854).
(See Jabez L. Baldwin)
(See John J. Low)
(See Benjamin Shreve)
(See Nathaniel C. Poor)
(Silversmith, Jewelers, Importers, Military Goods)

TIMOTHY KEITH	BOSTON, MA	B1774-1805
T. (TIMOTHY) & W. (WILLIAM) KEITH	WORCHESTER, MA	1805-1856

Timothy Keith died (1856).
Had a branch in New York.
(Silversmith, Jeweler, Watch Maker, Military Goods)

JAMES KELLY — PHILADELPHIA, PA — 1850-1875
Bought out William Curtis (1871).
(Regalia)

WILLIAM KENDRICK (Regalia)	LOUISVILLE, KY	1865-1870
KENTON HAT & FUR CO. (Regalia)	ROCHESTER, NY	1871-1875
T. KESSMAN U.S. contract for 1,000 cavalry sabers (1861). (Military Importer)	NEW YORK, NY	1861-1865

THOMAS KETLAND
Son and successor to William Ketland Jr.
Immigrated to Philadelphia, PA (1789),
  but kept an interest in
  the British company.
	BIRMINGHAM, ENGLAND	1767-1789

THOMAS & JOHN KETLAND Imported gunlocks from William Ketland & Co., Birmingham, England. Also imported swords from William Ketland & Co. (Gun Maker, Lock Maker, Cutler)	PHILADELPHIA, PA	1789-1800
HENRY KING	WASHINGTON, DC	1840-1862
HEIBERGER (FRANCIS J.) & **KING (HENRY)**	WASHINGTON, DC	1862-1865
HENRY KING (See Francis J. Heiberger) (Military and Fancy Goods, Clothier)	WASHINGTON, DC	1865-1868
M.V. KINSEY Authorized agent for Henderson-Ames. (See Henderson-Ames listing) (Regalia)	ATLANTA, GA	1920-1925

W. (WILLIAM) S. (STOKES) KIRK
• Sold Civil War surplus, including
   Confederate pikes and lances.
• Sold M1902 saber for all officers.
• Imported swords from Eickhorn & Co.,
   Solingen, Germany.
• Issued military goods catalog.
(Military Goods and Surplus)
	PHILADELPHIA, PA	1870-1910

ANDREW B. KITCHEN (See J.T. Bailey)		
BENJAMIN KITTRIDGE	CINCINNATI, OH	1827-1847
B. (BENJAMIN) KITTRIDGE & CO. Sold M1850 foot officer swords made by Collins & Co. U.S. contract for 200 cavalry sabers (imported) (1861). Employee: Hans Frederick Koehler (gunsmith).	CINCINNATI, OH	1847-1865
KITTRIDGE (BENJAMIN) & **BENNETT (AUGUSTUS)** Sold Colt pistols.	CINCINNATI, OH	1866-1884

B. KITTRIDGE ARMS CO.	**CINCINNATI, OH**	**1884-1891**

- Branch in St. Louis, MO (1847-1853) called Kittridge (Benjamin) & Eaton (Daniel E.).
- Branch in New Orleans, LA, located at 55 St. Charles (1857-1865) called Kittridge (Benjamin) & Folsom (George).
- Branch in Madison, WI (1861-1865) called B. Kittridge & Co.
- (See Collins & Co.)

(Military Goods, Guns, Swords)

D. KLEIN & BROTHERS	**PHILADELPHIA, PA**	**1855-1905**

Sold M1902 sabers for all officers.
(Military Uniforms, Military Goods)

JOHN H. KNAPP	**NEW YORK, NY** 64 Maiden Lane	**1860-1864**
	NEW YORK, NY 21 Maiden Lane	**1864-1865**
	NEW YORK, NY 66 Maiden Lane	**1865-1866**

(Silversmith, Jeweler, Importer, Fancy Goods, Military Goods)

N.B. KNEASS	**PHILADELPHIA, PA**	**1800-1823**
MAGEE (MICHAEL) & KNEASS (N.B.)	**PHILADELPHIA, PA**	**1823-1848**
MAGEE (MICHAEL) & CO.	**PHILADELPHIA, PA**	**1848-1860**

Partner: N.B. Kneass.

MAGEE (MICHAEL), KNEASS (N.B.) & **GEORGE (JOHN B.)**	**PHILADELPHIA, PA**	**1860-1865**
N.B. KNEASS	**PHILADELPHIA, PA**	**1865-1866**
KNEASS (N.B.) MAYO & **DORMAN (ROBERT)**	**PHILADELPHIA, PA**	**1866-1867**
KNEASS (N.B.) & MAYO	**PHILADELPHIA, PA**	**1867-1872**

(See Michael Magee)
(Military Goods, Leather Goods, Saddlers)

JOSEPH KOHN	**INDIANAPOLIS, IN**	**1861-1863**
HAYS, KOHN (JOSEPH) & CO.	**INDIANAPOLIS, IN**	**1864**
JOSEPH KOHN	**INDIANAPOLIS, IN**	**1865-1870**

(See Hays & Co.)
(Military and Fancy Goods, Clothier)

H. (HENRY) KORN	**PHILADELPHIA, PA**	**1812-1860**

Sold military trim and goods.
Adv. military goods and army-navy furnishings, including swords (1843).
(Military Goods and Trimmings)

J. (JOSEPH) H. LAMBERT	**PHILADELPHIA, PA**	**1839-1853**
LAMBERT (JOSEPH H.) & **WHITE (JAMES W.)**	**PHILADELPHIA, PA**	**1854-1858**
JOSEPH H. LAMBERT	**PHILADELPHIA, PA**	**1859-1860**
LAMBERT (JOSEPH H.) & MAST (JOHN)	**PHILADELPHIA, PA**	**1861-1862**

Sold M1860 foot officer swords.

J. (JOSEPH) H. LAMBERT	PHILADELPHIA, PA	**1863-1882**

Employee of Horstmann Brothers & Co.
 (1869-1873).

JOSEPH H. LAMBERT &		
SON (EDWARD W.)	PHILADELPHIA, PA	**1883-1925**

Owner: Howard G. Lambert (1893).
Owner: Charles H. Sass (1897).
(Military Cap Dealer, Military Goods, Firemen
 Equipment, Leather Goods, Swords, Uniforms)

LANDSMANN, DIEDRICK & CO.	NEW YORK, NY &	**1807-1810**
	PHILADELPHIA, PA	

Imported and sold 98 German cavalry saber
 blades to the U.S. Philadelphia Armory (1808).
 (See U.S. Philadelphia Armory)
(Military Importer)

LANE & READ
LANE & HUNNEWELL
(See William Read)

W.H. LAPAINTE	BOSTON, MA	**1840-1845**

(Military Goods)

CHARLES R. LARRABEE	CHICAGO, IL	**1831-1851**
WILLIAM F. DOMINICK & CO.	CHICAGO, IL	**1851-1857**

Employee: Charles R. Larrabee.

LARRABEE (CHARLES R.) &		
NORTH (ROBERT L.)	CHICAGO, IL	**1857-1885**
	174 Lake Street	

Adv. military goods, presentation, dress,
 and service swords and sabers, fine cutlery,
 pistols, infantry trimmings, buttons and gold
 embroidery in the *Army-Navy Journal* (1863-1864).

CHARLES R. LARRABEE		**1885-1890**

(Hardware, Military Goods, Cutler, Swords, Guns)

R. (RALPH) P. LATHROP	ALBANY, NY	**1857-1861**

State of New York contract for 5,000
 hatchets (1861).

STEELE & LATHROP (RALPH P.)	ALBANY, NY	**1862-1867**

(Hardware, Guns, Edged Tools Military
 Goods, Cutlery)

GEORGE LAUTERER	CHICAGO, IL	**1875**

(Regalia)

JAMES LAUTERER	CHICAGO, IL	**1875**

(Regalia)

LAUTERSTEINS	SAN ANTONIO, TX	**1900-1910**

Sold M1902 saber for all officers.
(Military Goods)

WILLIAM LEHNBERG	PHILADELPHIA, PA	1900-1910

Sold M1902 sabers for all officers.
(Military Goods)

SAMUEL P. (PERKINS) LEIGHTON	BOSTON, MA	B1836-1865

Partner in the A.W. Pollard & Co. (1863-1865).

B. (BRYON) A. POLLARD &		
S. (SAMUEL) P. LEIGHTON	BOSTON, MA	1866-1873
B. (BRYON) A. POLLARD,		
LEIGHTON (SAMUEL P.) & CO.	BOSTON, MA	1874-1876
SAMUEL P. LEIGHTON & CO.	BOSTON, MA	1877-1890
BOSTON REGALIA CO.	BOSTON, MA	1890-1925

President: Samuel P. Leighton (retired in 1910).
Treasurer: William C. Remy.
Representative: Lester C. Bruce (1923).
Adv. uniforms and equipment for the army
  and navy in the Boston directory.
Agent for William Horstmann & Co.
(See A.W. Pollard)
(Regalia, Military Goods)

SAMUEL P. LEIGHTON	COLUMBUS, OH	1910-D1916
H. (HENRY) G. LEISENRING	PHILADELPHIA, PA	1859-1871

U.S. contract for 21,196 cavalry sabers (imported) (1861).

	NEW ORLEANS, LA	1872-1877

(Military Importer)

LEMUEL LELAND	SHERBORN, MA	1848-1860

Sold M1840 cavalry sabers.
(Military Goods)

JAMES INNES LEMON	LOUISVILLE, KY	B1804, 1828-1831
LEMON (JAMES INNES) &		
KENDRICK (WILLIAM)	LOUISVILLE, KY	1832-1858
JAMES I. LEMON & CO.	LOUISVILLE, KY	1859-1861

Partner: Edmund J. Daumont.

LEMON (JAMES INNES) & SON	LOUISVILLE, KY	1861-D1869

(See William Kendrick-Silversmith listings)
(See Edmund J. Daumont-Silversmith listings)
(Jeweler, Silversmith, Regalia, Military Goods)

F.C.K. LEMNAN	HAMPTON, MA	1850-1855

(Military Goods)

LEWECK (G.) & CAHN	NEW YORK, NY	1855-1870
G. LEWECK	NEW YORK, NY	1870-1877

(Regalia)

EDWARD J. LEWIS	BROOKLYN, NY	1851-1865

(Gunsmith, Military Goods)

WILLIAM T. L'HOMMEDIEU	MOBILE, AL	1810-1830
L'HOMMEDIEU BROS.	MOBILE, AL	1830-1834

Partners: William T. L'Hommedieu,
  John A. L'Hommedieu.

William T. L'Hommedieu died (1834).

J. (JOHN) A. L'HOMMEDIEU	MOBILE, AL	1834-D1867

(Clocksmith, Jeweler, Silversmith, Military Goods)

CHARLES LIBEAU	CINCINNATI, OH	1827-1829
VALENTINE G. & CHARLES LIBEAU	CINCINNATI, OH	1829-1831
CHARLES LIBEAU	CINCINNATI, OH	1831-D1862

(Gunsmith, Military Goods and Equipment)

VALENTINE G. LIBEAU	PHILADELPHIA, PA	1800-1825
	CINCINNATI, OH	1825-1829
VALENTINE G. & CHARLES LIBEAU	CINCINNATI, OH	1829-1831
VALENTINE G. LIBEAU	CINCINNATI, OH	1831-1832
	NEW ORLEANS, LA	1832-1848

(Gunsmith, Military Goods and Equipment)

J.A. LIMERICK	BALTIMORE, MD	1898-1940

Bought out Jacob Gminder business when Gminder died (1898).
(Military and Society Goods)

ROSE LIPP REGALIA CO.	BOSTON, MA 175 Tremont	1910-1925

Authorized agent for Ames Sword Co.
(Regalia, Fraternal and Military Swords)

JOSEPH M. LITCHFIELD	SAN FRANCISCO, CA	1849-1869
PURDY (CHARLES) & **LITCHFIELD (JOSEPH M.)**	SAN FRANCISCO, CA	1869-1874

Charles Purdy died (1874).

J. (JOSEPH) M. LITCHFIELD	SAN FRANCISCO, CA	1874-1880

Sold M1872 lt. artillery officer sabers and M1872 cavalry officer sabers.
(Military Goods, Clothiers, Importers)

LITTELS & CO.	NEW YORK, NY	1770-1775

(Military Goods)

CHARLES L. LOCKWOOD & CO.	WASHINGTON, DC	1861-1865

(Military Equipment, Clothier)

LODER & CO.	ROCHESTER, NY	1875

(Regalia)

L. LOMBARD	NEW YORK, NY	1861-1865

(Military Goods)

C. LOMBARDY & CO.	NEWARK, NY	1870-1875

(Military Goods)

H.F. LOUDAN	WASHINGTON, DC	1830-1853
H.F. LOUDAN & CO.	WASHINGTON, DC	1853-D1857

- Adv. army and navy swords (1853).

- Employee: Francis J. Heiberger.
- Had branch in Norfolk, VA, with George W. Farrant (manager).
- (See Francis J. Heiberger)
- (See George W. Farrant)

(Military Tailor)

JOHN J. LOW	BOSTON, MA	B1800-1822
PUTMAN (EDWARD) & LOW (JOHN J.)	BOSTON, MA	1822-1825
JOHN J. LOW	BOSTON, MA	1825-1828

Adv. swords and pistols from Birmingham, England (1825).

JOHN J. LOW & CO.	BOSTON, MA	1828-1838

Partners: Francis Low, Henry B. Stanwood.

JONES (JOHN B.), LOW (JOHN J.) & BALL (S.S.)	BOSTON, MA	1838-1840

Agent for Ames Mfg. Co. swords.

LOW (JOHN J.), BALL (S.S.) & CO.	BOSTON, MA	1840-1846

Partner: John B. Jones.

JOHN J. LOW	BOSTON, MA	1846-1869
SHREVE (BENJAMIN) CRUMP (CHARLES H.) & LOW (JOHN J.)	BOSTON, MA	1869-1888
SHREVE (BENJAMIN) CRUMP (CHARLES H.) & LOW (JOHN J.) CO. INC.	BOSTON, MA	1888-1891

John L. Low died (1876).
(See John B. Jones)
(See Henry Stanwood)
(See Benjamin Shreve)
(Silversmiths, Jewelers, Importers, Military Goods)

JAMES LUCKEY	NEW YORK, NY	1875-1890

Branch in Philadelphia, PA.
(Regalia)

EDMUND A. LUDLOW	FULTON, NY	1840-1850

(Military Goods, Leather Goods)

LYNCH & KELLY	UTICA, NY	1875

(Regalia)

JAMES S. LYONS	RICHMOND, VA	1835-1840

(Guns and Uniforms)

M.A. LYONS	RICHMOND, VA	1850-1852

(Regalia)

PELEG MACOMBER	PROVIDENCE, RI	1886-D1893

(Military Goods)

MACOY & SICKELS	NEW YORK, NY	1865-1870

(Regalia)

MACULLAR (ADDISON) & WILLIAMS (GEORGE B.)	BOSTON, MA	1850-1860

MACULLAR (ADDISON), WILLIAMS (GEORGE B.) & PARKER (CHARLES W.)	BOSTON, MA	1860-1880

Adv. army and navy uniforms in the *Army-Navy Journal* (1864).

MACULLAR (ADDISON), PARKER (CHARLES W.) & CO.	BOSTON, MA	1880-1885

(Military Uniforms)

JAMES S., THEODORE & LEOPOLD MAGNUS	NEW YORK, NY	1843-1865
LEOPOLD MAGNUS	NEW YORK, NY	1865-1900

(Lace Manufacturing, Military Goods)

MICHAEL MAGEE	PHILADELPHIA, PA	1800-1823
MAGEE (MICHAEL) & KNEASS (N.B.)	PHILADELPHIA, PA	1823-1848
MAGEE (MICHAEL) & CO.	PHILADELPHIA, PA	1848-1861

Partners: N.B. Kneass, John B. George.

MAGEE (MICHAEL) KNEASS (N.B.) & GEORGE (JOHN B.)	PHILADELPHIA, PA	1861-1865
MICHAEL MAGEE & CO.	PHILADELPHIA, PA	1865-1872

Partner: John B. George.
Had a branch in New Orleans, LA.
(See N.B. Kneass)
(Military Goods, Leather Goods, Regalia)

CHARLES G. MANNING	CINCINNATI, OH	1835-1854
ADDIS & CO.	CINCINNATI, OH	1855-1858

Partner: Charles G. Manning.

CHARLES G. MANNING	CINCINNATI, OH	1859-1863
C. (CHARLES) G. MANNING & CO.	CINCINNATI, OH	1864-1878
C.W. MANNING & CO.	CINCINNATI, OH	1879-1889
CHARLES G. MANNING JR.	CINCINNATI, OH	1890-1898

(Regalia, Military Goods)

J.H. MARSHALL	BOSTON, MA	1875

Sold fraternal swords.
(Regalia)

SEREPHIM MASI	WASHINGTON, DC	1822-1856

Partner: F. Masi.
(Jeweler, Silversmith, Military and Fancy Goods)

MASONIC EMPORIUM
(See John K. Moore)

MASONIC FURNISHINGS & CO.	NEW YORK, NY	1870-1875

(Masonic Regalia and Swords)

MASONIC PUBLISHING & MFG. CO.
(See Chandler & Darrow)

JOHN MAST	PHILADELPHIA, PA	1855-1860
LAMBERT (JOSEPH H.) & MAST (JOHN)	PHILADELPHIA, PA	1861-1862
JOHN MAST	PHILADELPHIA, PA	1863-1876

(See Joseph H. Lambert)
(Military Goods, Tassel Maker)

CHARLES W. MAY
(See Schuyler, Hartley, & Graham)

CHARLES MCBURNEY	BOSTON, MA	1825-1846
CHEEVER (SIMON G.) &		
MCBURNEY (CHARLES)	BOSTON, MA	1847-1848
CHARLES MCBURNEY	BOSTON, MA	1849-1851
BOSTON BELTING CO.	BOSTON, MA	1852-1855

(See Simon G. Cheever)
(Leather Goods, Saddler, Military Goods)

THOMAS MCCORMICK   BALTIMORE, MD   1861-1865
(Military Goods, Military Tailor)

EDWARD MCDONALD
MCDONALD & LYONS
(See Confederate listings)

J. (JOHN) B. MCFADDEN	PITTSBURGH, PA	1830-1849
JOHN B. MCFADDEN &		
SON (JAMES B.)	PITTSBURGH, PA	1850-1855
JOHN B. MCFADDEN & CO.	PITTSBURGH, PA	1856-1865

Partner and son: James B. McFadden.
(Silversmith, Jeweler, Watch Maker,
  Military and Fancy Goods)

JAMES H. MCKENNEY
(See John A. Baker)

I. MCLENE   INDIANAPOLIS, IN   1850
(Military Goods)

EDWARD EDMUND MEAD	ITHACA, NY	1810-1830
DEREIMER (CORNELIUS BROUWER)		
& MEAD (EDWARD EDMUND)	ITHACA, NY	1830-1831
MEAD (EDWARD EDMUND)		
ADRIANCE (EDWIN) & CO.	ST. LOUIS, MO	1831-1836
MEAD (EDWARD EDMUND)		
& ADRIANCE (EDWIN)	ST. LOUIS, MO	1836-1842
EDWARD EDMUND MEAD	ST. LOUIS, MO	1842-1864

(See C.B. DeReimer-Silversmith listings)
(Silversmith, Jeweler, Military Goods)

RODERICK MCLEOD	NEW YORK, NY	1837-1865
MCLEOD (RODERICK) &		
REMMY (WILLIAM)	NEW YORK, NY	1865-1880

Adv. uniforms for officers of the army, navy,
  and National Guard in the *Army-Navy
  Journal* (1869).
(Military Uniforms, Tailor)

ROBERT C. MELVAIN	NEW YORK, NY	1830-1858

Employee of Francis and Benjamin Tomes
  (1850-1858).

TOMES (FRANCIS JR.), SON (BENJAMIN) & MELVAIN (ROBERT C.)	NEW YORK, NY	1859-1865
TOMES (FRANCIS JR. & CHARLES H.), MELVAIN (ROBERT C.) & CO.	NEW YORK, NY	1865-1878

Employee of Schuyler, Hartley, & Graham
  (1874-1878).
(See Francis Tomes)
(See Schuyler, Hartley, & Graham)
(Military Goods, Importer, Guns, Swords)

MERRILL (J. AMBROSE) & QUIMBY (M.)	PORTLAND, ME	1853-1855

Bought out James Appleton Co. (1853).

J. AMBROSE MERRILL	PORTLAND, ME	1856-1869
J. MERRILL & CO.	PORTLAND, ME	1870-1905

Manager: Albion Keith.
(See James Appleton)
(Silversmith, Jewelers, Military Goods, Regalia)

BENJAMIN B. MERRILL	NEW YORK, NY 2 Maiden Lane	1854-1862
	NEW YORK, NY 9 Astor Lane	1862-1866
	NEW YORK, NY 142 Broadway	1866-1869
	NEW YORK, NY 285 Broadway	1869
	NEW YORK, NY 718 Broadway	1870-1873

(Military Tailor)

JAMES H. MERRILL	BALTIMORE, MD	1816-1855
MERRILL (JAMES H.), LATROBE (FERDINAND C. & JOHN H.B.) & THOMAS (PHILIP E. & L.W.)	BALTIMORE, MD	1855-1860
MERRILL (JAMES H.) & THOMAS (PHILIP E. & L.W.)	BALTIMORE, MD	

U.S. contract for 14,500 carbines (1861-1865).
Adv. rifles, pistols, cutlery and
  military goods (1863).
(Importer, Military Goods, Guns, Cutlery)

L. (LUKE) T. MERRILL	NEW YORK, NY	1861-1865

U.S. contract for hatchets during the Civil War.
(Edged Tools and Accoutrements)

JOHN C. METCALF	NEW YORK, NY 36 Maiden Lane	1843-1845
METCALF (JOHN C.) & SMITH (THOMAS)	NEW YORK, NY	1845-1846

(Military Equipment)

J. (JAMES) MEYER U.S. contracts for 12,260 cavalry sabers (imported). (Military Importer)	**NEW YORK, NY**	**1861-1865**

N.S. MEYER INC.
Branches in Los Angeles, CA, and
  Providence, RI.
Sold M1852 naval officer swords and
  M1902 swords for all officers.
(Military Goods)
	NEW YORK, NY	**1875-1992**

S.N. MEYER
Sold M1840 medical staff officer swords,
  M1872 mounted artillery officer swords,
  West Point cadet swords, and M1902 sabers
  for all officers.
(Military Outfitter)
	WASHINGTON, DC	**1861-1865**

JOHN P. MILNOR & CO. (Military Goods)	**BALTIMORE, MD**	**1860-1865**
MILITARY STORES & SPUNGE FACTORY Adv. military supplies, boarding pikes, and cutlasses (1798). (Naval Outfitter)	**PHILADELPHIA, PA**	**1795-1800**

ISAAC MILLER
Sold the governor of Maryland (1694-1699)
  pistols, muskets, carbines, powder, grenadier
  pouches, swords, bayonets, cartouche boxes,
  match boxes, fusees, bugles, hand grenades,
  carbine and sword belts.
(Military Goods)
	NEW YORK, NY	**1689-1699**

WILLIAM I. MILLER	**NEW YORK, NY**	**1813-1832**
FRANCIS TOMES & WILLIAM I. MILLER	**NEW YORK, NY** 6 Maiden Lane	**1833-1835**
TOMES (FRANCIS) & MILLER (WILLIAM I.)	**NEW YORK, NY** 6 Maiden Lane	**1836-1839**
WILLIAM I. MILLER	**NEW YORK, NY** 9 and 11 Maiden Lane	**1840-1854**
	NEW YORK, NY 15 Maiden Lane	**1855-1859**
	NEW YORK, NY 12 Maiden Lane	**1860-1862**
MILLER (JOHN) & CO.	**NEW YORK, NY** 9 Maiden Lane	**1863-1868**

Sold a complete line of military goods,
  including pistols and swords.
Sold M1850 foot officer swords and M1852
  naval officer swords.
Bought M1852 naval officer swords from Collins & Co.

Adv. military goods, foreign- and U.S.-made
swords, presentation swords, military
ornaments, revolvers, and holsters in the
Army-Navy Journal (1864-1868).

MILLER (JOHN) & WILSON (EVASTUS E.) NEW YORK, NY 1869-1871
Adv. a complete line of military and naval
goods, including swords, in the *Army-Navy Journal* (1869).
(See Francis Tomes)
(See Collins & Co.)
(Military Goods, Dealer and Importer)

WALSINGHAM A. MILLER
(See Livington A. Shannon)

PETER MINTZER PHILADELPHIA, PA 1818-1839

WILLIAM G. MINTZER PHILADELPHIA, PA 1840-1869
- Son of Peter Mintzer.
- Partner: Edward Hutchinson.
- During the Civil War, sold officer swords.
- Sold M1850 foot officer swords and presentation swords with blades imported from Wilhelm Hoppe, Solingen, Germany.
- William G. Mintzer died (1869).
- Robert M. Robinson bought the Mintzer Co. (1869).
- Edward Hutchinson joined Robinson.
- (See Robert M. Robinson)

(Military Goods, Regalia, Theatrical Equipment)

CHARLES MOELLER ST. LOUIS, MO 1861-1865
(Military Goods)

C. MOORE CINCINNATI, OH 1865-1870
JOHN K. MOORE CINCINNATI, OH 1870-1875
Company called Masonic Emporium.
(Regalia)

JOHN P. MOORE NEW YORK, NY 1823-1855
JOHN P. MOORE & SON (GEORGE) NEW YORK, NY 1855-1860
John P. Moore died (1860).
JOHN P. MOORE'S SON NEW YORK, NY 1860-1888
Partners: Henry M. Richard, John P. Richards.
Schoverling, Daly, & Gales bought Moore Co. (1888).
(Gunsmith, Saddler, Military Goods)

J.F. MORAN HARTFORD, CT 1905-1910
Sold M1902 saber for all officers.
(Military Goods)

ALEXANDER C. (CHASER) MORIN PHILADELPHIA, PA 1810-D1878
Son of John Morin.
(Jeweler, Silversmith, Military Goods)

ANTHONY C. (CHASER) MORIN Son of Alexander C. Morin. (Jeweler, Silversmith, Military Goods)	PHILADELPHIA, PA	1845-1866
AUGUSTUS MORIN (MORINEAU) (Silversmith)	PHILADELPHIA, PA	1830-1840
CHARLES C. (CHASER) MORIN (MORINEAU) Son of Alexander C. Morin. (Jeweler, Silversmith, Military Goods)	PHILADELPHA, PA	1860-1900
PHILIP MORIN (MORINEAU) (Silversmith)	PHILADELPHIA, PA	1830-1840
PIERRE MORIN (MORINEAU) (Silversmith)	PHILADELPHIA, PA	1790-1800
JOHN MORIN (MORINEAU) (Jeweler, Silversmith, Military Goods)	PHILADELPHIA, PA	1790-D1833
CHAUNCEY MORGAN Sold M1873 cavalry officer swords. (Silversmith, Military Goods)	HARTFORD, CT	1850-1900
JAMES G. MORGAN	DETROIT, MI	1868-1888
E.A. ARMSTRONG & CO. Employee: James Morgan.	DETROIT, MI	1888-1892
MORGAN (JAMES G.) PUHL (EMIL P.) & MORRIS (CHARLES P.)	DETROIT, MI GRAND RAPIDS, MI	1892-1903 1903-1910
Sold M1902 saber for all officers. (Regalia, Uniforms)		
I.M. MOSS & BROTHERS (Regalia)	PHILADELPHIA, PA	1855-1860
EBENEZER C.L. MUSTIN	CINCINNATI, OH	1835-1855
J.M. PICKERING & CO. Partner: E.C.L. Mustin.	CINCINNATI, OH	1855-1861
E. (EBENEZER) C.L. MUSTIN Bought out J.M. Pickering.	CINCINNATI, OH	1861-1871
THOMAS J. MUSTIN Partner: E.C.L. Mustin. Sold military goods business to James H. Pettibone (1873). (Regalia, Military Goods, Trimmings, Fancy Goods)	CINCINNATI, OH	1871-1875
GEORGE MYERS (Regalia)	ST. LOUIS, MO	1845-1856
CHARLES NAYLOR Authorized dealer for Ames Sword Co. (Regalia, Fraternal Swords)	PHILADELPHIA, PA	1870-1923

DANIEL NEILD (NEILL) (Cutler, Silversmith)	PHILADELPHIA, PA	1823-1860
NEWBOULD (JOHN A.) & **RUSSELL (A. THOMAS)** Adv. imported guns, pistols and cutlery (1844). (Importer, Pistols, Guns, Cutlery)	NEW YORK, NY	1843-1845
LOUIS NEWHOUSE (Military Goods, Gun Dealer)	CHARLESTON, SC	1775-1783
DAVID B. NICHOLS	SAVANNAH, GA	B1791-1820
D. (DAVID) B. NICHOLS & CO. Partner: John P. Smith.	SAVANNAH, GA	1820-1830
DAVID B. NICHOLS Adv. military goods (1848). (See John P. Smith-Silversmith listings) (Silversmith, Jeweler, Military Goods, Fancy Goods, Clocks)	SAVANNAH, GA	1830-D1860
WASHINGTON NOEL	LOUISVILLE, KY	1830-D1838
BEVERLY NOEL Wife of Washington Noel. (Military Goods, Fancy Goods, Silversmith, Jeweler)	LOUISVILLE, KY	1838-1840
NOELL & ALBERMANN U.S. contract for 357 non-comm. and musician's swords (1862). (Military Importer)	NEW YORK, NY	1861-1865
DANIEL NORCROSS	PHILADELPHIA, PA	1830-1849
DANIEL NORCROSS & CO. • Partner: Harriet Norcross. • Bought military goods and swords from Shannon, Miller, & Crane and Schuyler, Hartley, & Graham. • Partner: John Wolf • Wolf was the successor to the Norcross Company (1875). (See John Wolf) (Regalia, Military and Naval Goods)	SAN FRANCISCO, CA	1849-1875
OAK HALL CLOTHING • Sold M1840 variation artillery officer swords, M1860 staff and field officer swords, and M1872 mounted artillery officer sword. • Sold M1902 saber for all officers. (Tailor, Military Goods)	BOSTON, MA	1860-1910
FREDERICK OAKES	HARTFORD, CT	B1782-1806
GREENLEAF (DAVID J.) & **OAKES (FREDERICK)** Had silversmith and cutlery shop.	HARTFORD, CT	1806-1811

OAKES (FREDERICK) & SPENCER (JAMES)	HARTFORD, CT	1811-1820

James Spencer died (1820).

FREDERICK OAKES	HARTFORD, CT	1820-1842
FREDERICK & WILLIAM OAKES	HARTFORD, CT	1842-1848
FREDERICK OAKES & SON	HARTFORD, CT	1842-D1855

(See James Spencer-Silvesmith listings)
(See David Greenleaf Jr.-Maker listings)
(Goldsmith, Silversmith, Watch Maker, Jeweler, Cutler)

HENRY OAKES	HARTFORD, CT	1810-1842

Father of Frederick Oakes.
(Silversmith)

CHARLES OAKFORD	PHILADELPHIA, PA	1829-1833
CHARLES OAKFORD & SON (CHARLES JR.)	PHILADELPHIA, PA	1833-1862

Charles Oakford Sr. died (1862).

CHARLES OAKFORD & SONS	PHILADELPHIA, PA 834-836 Chestnut Street	1862-1865

Partners:
   Rebecca Oakford (wife of Charles Oakford Sr.)
   Charles Oakford Jr. (son of Charles Oakford Sr.)
   Isaac B. Oakford (son of Charles Oakford Sr.)
   William Oakford (son of Charles Oakford Sr.)
Adv. military goods for army and navy officers, including swords.
(Hatter, Military Goods)

E. (EDWARD) OWEN & CO.	WASHINGTON, DC 212 Pennsylvania Avenue	1831-1840
OWEN (EDWARD) & EVANS (JOHN D.) & CO.	WASHINGTON, DC	1840-1849

Partner and son: John S. Owen.
Edward Owen died (1849).

E. (EDWARD) OWEN & SON (SAMUEL W.)	WASHINGTON, DC	1849-1864

Adv. as military and naval tailors in the
  Army-Navy Journal (1864).

SAMUEL W. OWEN	WASHINGTON, DC	1864-1869

Adv. as military and naval tailors in the
  Army-Navy Journal (1865).

OWEN (SAMUEL W.) & PUGH	WASHINGTON, DC	1869-1875
S. (SAMUEL) W. OWEN	WASHINGTON, DC 1413 Pennsylvania Avenue	1870-1875

A second location called Owen House,
  owned by Samuel W. Owen.
Sold European-style clothing at Owen House.
(Military and Naval Tailors, Military Goods)

PALMER & BACHELDER
(See Samuel Davis)

J.C. PALMER	HARTFORD, CT	1851-1874

President of Sharps Rifle Mfg. Co.
U.S. contract for 150 lt. artillery sabers (1861).

JOHN PARKS	LONDON, ENGLAND	1830-1850
	NEW YORK, NY	1850-1865

(Silversmith, Silver Plater, Military Ornaments, Military Goods)

UNION STORE	ST. LOUIS, MO	1839-1863

Owner: Timothy P. Parson.

TIMOTHY P. & JOHN R. PARSON	ST. LOUIS, MO	1864-1865
TIMOTHY P., TIMOTHY T.,		
& WILLIAM PARSON	ST. LOUIS, MO	1866-1885

Branches in New York, NY, Chicago, IL, and Louisville, KY.
(Military Goods, Regalia)

B. (BENOIT) PASQUALE & SON (ERNEST)	SAN FRANCISCO, CA	1854-1867
B. (BENOIT) & E. (ERNEST) PASQUALE	SAN FRANCISCO, CA	1818-1878
B. (BENOIT) PASQUALE CO.	SAN FRANCISCO, CA	1879-1950

Sold M1860 staff and field officer swords, U.S. Public Health swords, and marine hospital swords
Sold M1902 sabers for all officers.
Put out a military goods catalog.
(Regalia, Military Goods, Importer, Flag and Uniform Maker, Toy Dealer)

PAYSON & NURSE	BOSTON, MA	1825-1845

Imported swords and firearms.
(Military Importer)

JAMES PECKHAM	COLUMBIA, SC	1815-1830
PECKHAM (JAMES & GEORGE) & CO.	CHARLESTON, SC	1830-1850

(Jeweler, Silversmith, Gun Dealer, Hardware)

JAMES S. PEMBERTON	ALBANY, NY	1810-1850

Imported swords from John Cooper, Birmingham, England.
(Silversmith, Sword Hiltor, Military Goods)

PERRY & STONE	NEW LONDON, CT	1870-1875

(Military Goods)

E.C. PHILLIPS	BOSTON, MA	1900-1915

Authorized dealer for Henderson-Ames.
(Regalia, Military and Fraternal Swords)

NATHANIEL PHILLIPS	ST. LOUIS, MO	1836-1845
NATHANIEL & JAMES PHILLIPS	ST. LOUIS, MO	1845-1859

(Military Goods, Regalia)

E. PIETRONGELL	ANNAPOLIS, MD	1900-1920

(Military Goods)

B. (BURTON) PIERCE CO.	BOSTON, MA	1890-1900

(Regalia)

PITTSBURGH UNIFORM & TAILORING CO.	PITTSBURGH, PA	1875-1910

Sold M1902 saber for all officers.
(Regalia, Military Equipment)

ADOLPHUS J. PLATE	SAN FRANCISCO, CA	1849-1862
A. (ADOLPHUS) J. PLATE & CO.	SAN FRANCISCO, CA	1863-1885

Partners: H.A. Plate, W.B. Cotrell, John Wolfe.
Bought out T. Rodgers Johnson (1880).
Adv. military goods and swords (1881).
(Gunsmith, Military Goods, Guns, Swords, Regalia)

E.M. PLATT	BOSTON, MA	1875

(Military Goods)

GEORGE POHLMAN	CINCINNATI, OH	1853-1865

Employee: H.G. Hamlin Jr.
(See H.G. Hamlin Jr.)
(Military Goods)

EDWARD POLE	PHILADELPHIA, PA	1760-1800

Adv. Cutteau de Chase and small swords (1775).
Adv. cannons, muskets, naval goods, poleaxes,
 boarding pikes, and cutlasses (1781).
(Ironmonger, Army and Navy Goods Dealer,
 Guns and Swords)

ABNER W. POLLARD	BOSTON, MA	1825-1830
TARBETT (LENDELL F.)		
& POLLARD (ABNER W.)	BOSTON, MA	1830-1833
ABNER W. POLLARD	BOSTON, MA	1833-1863
A. (ABNER) W. POLLARD & CO.	BOSTON, MA	1863-1866

- Partner and son: Byron A. Pollard.
- Authorized agent for Ames Mfg. Co. swords.
- Adv. military goods, regulation, and presentation swords, Masonic books, and regalia in the *Army-Navy Journal* (1863-1866).
- Abner W. Pollard died (1865).

POLLARD (BYRON A.)		
& LEIGHTON (SAMUEL P.)	BOSTON, MA	1866-1874

Adv. in the *Army-Navy Journal* (1866-1870).

B. (BYRON) A. POLLARD		
& LEIGHTON (SAMUEL P.) & CO.	BOSTON, MA	1874-1876
POLLARD (BYRON A.) ALFORD		
(FREDERICK) & CO.	BOSTON, MA	1876-1886

Byron A. Pollard died (1886).

FREDERICK ALFORD CO.	BOSTON, MA	1886-1890

(See Ames Mfg. Co.)
(See Samuel P. Leighton)
(Tailor, Hatter, Regalia, Fraternal and Regulation
 Swords, Fencing and Theatrical Goods)

JOHN PONDIR	PHILADELPHIA, PA	1861-1865

U.S. contract for 50 M1860 cavalry
 officer sabers (1862).
(Military Importer)

POOLE & SIMONS (Military Goods)	PHILADELPHIA, PA	1750-1770
NATHANIEL C. POOR	BOSTON, MA	B1808-1840
LOW, BALL & CO. Partner: Nathaniel C. Poor.	BOSTON, MA	1840-1846
JONES (JOHN B.), BALL (S.S.) & POOR (NATHANIEL C.)	BOSTON, MA	1846-1852
NATHANIEL C. POOR (See John B. Jones) (Jeweler, Silversmith, Military Goods)	BOSTON, MA	1852-D1895

HORACE PORTER
(See Silversmith listings)

JOSEPH S. PORTER	UTICA, NY	B1783-1808
PORTER (JOSEPH S.) & WHITE (PHILO)	UTICA, NY	1808-1811
BARTON (JOSEPH) & PORTER (JOSEPH S.)	UTICA, NY	1811-1817
JOSEPH S. PORTER	UTICA, NY	1817-1842
DOOLITTLE, NORRIS & CO. Partner: Joseph S. Porter.	UTICA, NY	1842-1846
JOSEPH S. PORTER (See Joseph Barton-Silversmith listings) (Silversmith, Goldsmith, Jeweler, Military Goods)	UTICA, NY	1846-D1862

J.B. PURDY & CO.
(See J.M. Litchfield)

PUTMAN & LOW
(See John J. Low)

THOMAS W. RADCLIFFE
(See William Glaze-Confederate listings)

CHARLES J. RAIBLE (Regalia)	LOUISVILLE, KY	1869-1874
GEORGE RAPHAEL	PHILADELPHIA, PA	1849-1862
GEORGE RAPHAEL & CO. (R. & C.)	PHILADELPHIA, PA	1862-1865

U.S. contract for 100 M1840 cavalry sabers
  (imported) and 1,000 artillery short swords (1862).
Also imported M1840 non-comm. and musician's swords.
Listed in Philadelphia city directory as a merchant.
(Sword and Gun Importer)

SOLOMAN RAPHAEL (Silversmith)	PHILADELPHIA, PA	1790-1800
BENJAMIN RANDOLPH Adv. pistols, carbines, and swords (1777). (Military Goods)	PHILADELPHIA, PA	1775-1783

EDWARD RANDOLPH
(See Joseph Richardson Jr.-Maker listings)

RAUCHERT & CO. (Military Goods)	PHILADELPHIA, PA	1860-1865
BENJAMIN RAWLS Gun and pistol repair. Cutlery and hardware dealer. (Goldsmith, Silversmith, Jeweler, Blacksmith)	COLUMBIA, SC	B1772, 1816-D1866
WILLIAM A. RAYMOLD	NEW YORK, NY	1830-1878
W. (WILLIAM) A. RAYMOLD	NEW YORK, NY	1878-1881
RAYMOLD (WILLIAM A.) & **WHITLOCK (BENJAMIN M.)**	NEW YORK, NY	1881-1891

- Both Raymold and Whitlock worked for Schuyler, Hartley, & Graham (1854-1878).
- Took over Hartley & Graham uniform business (1881).
- Sold M1860 staff and field officer swords.
- Authorized dealer for Ames Sword Co.

(See Benjamin Whitlock)
(See Hartley & Graham)
(Military Outfitters, Regalia, Uniforms)

JOSEPH RAYNES	LOWELL, MA	B1810-1835
JOSEPH RAYNES & CO.	LOWELL, MA	1835-1865, D1896

Adv. swords from U.S. makers (including C. Roby) and military goods (1862).
(See C. Roby)
(Regalia, Military Goods, Jeweler, Silversmith)

WILLIAM READ	BOSTON, MA	1804-1824
LANE (THOMAS W.) & READ (WILLIAM)	BOSTON, MA	1825-1849
WILLIAM READ	BOSTON, MA	1850-1854
WILLIAM READ & SON	BOSTON, MA	1855-1868

U.S. contract for 328 cavalry sabers (1861).
Sold M1860 staff and field officer swords.
Adv. bulletproof vests (1862).
Adv. rifles, carbines, muskets, revolvers, and swords (1864).

WILLIAM READ & SONS	BOSTON, MA	1869-1910

Sold M1860 staff and field officer sword.
Sold M1902 saber for all officers.
William Read died (1884)
(Military Goods, Musket Maker, Hardware, Swords, Firearm Importer)

REDDING (M.W.) & CO. Put out Masonic goods catalogs. Sold D.B. Howell fraternal swords. (Regalia, Fraternal Swords)	NEW YORK, NY	1859-1923
JACOB REED Sold M1860 staff and field officer swords.	PHILADELPHIA, PA	1824-1877

JACOB REED'S SONS	PHILADELPHIA, PA	1877-1880

Sold M1860 staff and field officer swords, M1875 Marine Corp officer swords, and M1872 lt. artillery officer sabers.

R.M.J. REED	PHILADELPHIA, PA	1880-1886

(Tailor, Military Goods)

JACOB REEDS & CO.	BOSTON, MA	1900-1915

Sold M1902 saber for all officers.
(Military Goods)

JOHN REIST	PHILADELPHIA, PA	1860-1865

(Cutler)

H. (HARMON) G. REYNOLDS	SPRINGFIELD, IL	1860-1870

(Regalia, Fraternal Swords)

STEPHEN & ASA RHODES
(See Bent & Bush)

WALTER A. RHODES	NEW YORK, NY	1905-1910

Sold M1902 saber for all officers.
Bought out John Boylan Company.
(Military Goods)

THOMAS RICHARDS
SAMUEL R. RICHARDS
(See Silversmith listings)

RICHARDS (STEPHEN),		
UPSON (GEORGE), & CO.	NEW YORK, NY	1808-1816

- Imported swords from Richards' relative, gun and sword maker Henry Richards, London, England
- Imported swords from Upson's relative, military exporter Henry Upson, London, England
- Imported swords from Osborne & Gunby, Richard D. Bolton, Thomas Gill, and John Salter (all from Birmingham, England).
- George Upson joined Clark, Pelletreau (1816).

RICHARDS (STEPHEN) &		
TAYLOR (RICHARD)	NEW YORK, NY	1817
RICHARDS (STEPHEN),		
TAYLOR (RICHARD) & WILDER	NEW YORK, NY	1818-1825

(See Maltby Pelletreau-Silversmith listings)
(Silversmith, Military and Naval Outfitter)

B. RICHARDSON & SONS	PHILADELPHIA, PA	1839-1849

(Military Goods)

JAMES A. RIDABOCK
(See John A. Baker)

HAROLD ROBINSON	PHILADELPHIA, PA	1861-1865

U.S. contract for 200 cavalry sabers (1862).
(Military Goods, Importer)

ROBERT M. ROBINSON & CO.	PHILADELPHIA, PA	1869-1870

Successor to William G. Mintzer.
Partners: Edward Hutchinson, Clarence A. Hart.
Clarence A. Hart was the successor to Robinson
  & Co (1870).
(See Clarence A. Hart)
(See Peter Mintzer)
(Military Goods, Regalia)

ROSENFIELD & RAPKIN	BOSTON, MA	1900-1910
ROSENFIELD UNIFORM CO.	BOSTON, MA	1910-1920

Sold M1902 saber for all officers.
(Uniforms, Military Goods)

EDWARD A.G. ROULSTONE	BOSTON, MA	1840-1843
EDWARD A.G. ROULSTONE & CO.	BOSTON, MA	1843-1853

Partner: Charles H. Roulstone.

WINSHIP (GUSTAVUS L.) & ROULSTONE (EDWARD A.G.)	BOSTON, MA	1853-1855
ROULSTONE (EDWARD A.G.) & SYFFERMAN (CHARLES F.)	BOSTON, MA	1856
EDWARD A.G. ROULSTONE	BOSTON, MA	1857-1880

(See Gustavus Winship)
(See Charles P. Syfferman)
(Saddler, Presentation Swords, Military Goods)

DANIEL CURTIS ROUNDY
(See B.A. & A.S. Wadhams)

THOMAS RUDOLPH & CO.
(See Horace Dimick)

RUGGLES & HASKELL	BOSTON, MA	1945

(Regalia)

CHARLES W. RUPRECHT	NEW YORK, NY	1861-1865

U.S. contract for 483 cavalry sabers (1861).
(Military Goods Importer)

BENJAMIN RUSSELL	BALTIMORE, MD	1861-1865

(Military Goods)

MICHAEL A. RUSSELL UNIFORM CO.	NEW YORK, NY	1874-1880

(Regalia, Clothier)

GUSTAVUS S. SACCHI	NEW YORK, NY	1860-1865

U.S. contract for 3,436 cavalry sabers (1860-1862).
(Military Importer)

SAINT & MEYER INC.	NEW YORK, NY	1902-1905

(Military Goods)

AMOS SANBORN & CO.	LOWELL, MA	1860-1870

Partner: H.B. Bacon.

Authorized agent for C. Roby swords.
(See C. Roby-Maker listings)
(Regalia, Hatter)

WILLIAM J. SAVAGE	**COLUMBUS, OH**	**1845-1880**

Partners: William M. Savage, Edward Savage.
(Silversmith, Clock Maker, Jeweler, Military Goods, Guns, Swords)

WILLIAM SAYERS	**NEW YORK, NY**	**1840-1852**
SAYERS (WILLIAM) & LENT (JAMES H.)	**NEW YORK, NY**	**1853-1855**
WILLIAM SAYERS	**NEW YORK, NY**	**1856-1858**

(See John Sayers-Silversmith listings)
(Gilder, Silversmith, Military Equipment)

PHILIP SCHAEFFER	**LANCASTER, PA**	**1790-1799**

Adv. cutlery, gunlocks, gunpowder, and saddlery (1797).
(Military Goods)

GARRETT SCHANCK	**NEW YORK, NY**	**1770-1791**
VAN VOORHIS (DANIEL) & SCHANCK (GARRETT)	**NEW YORK, NY**	**1791-1792**
VAN VOORHIS (DANIEL), SCHANCK (GARRETT) & MCCALL	**NEW YORK, NY**	**1792-1795**

Garrett Schanck died (1795).
(See Daniel Van Voorhis)
(Silversmith, Goldsmith, Sword Hiltor)

JOHN A. SCHANCK	**NEW YORK, NY**	**1790-1800**

(Silversmith, Goldsmith, Sword Hiltor)

V. SCHANCK	**ALBANY, NY**	**1835-1845**

(Silversmith, Regalia)

A. & E. (ERNEST) SCHEIDT	**NEW YORK, NY**	**1852-1858**
G.A. & E. (ERNEST) SCHEIDT	**NEW YORK, NY**	**1858-1862**

Imported 5,000 German-made cavalry sabers for James T. Ames (1862).
(See the Ames family)
(Military Importer and Dealer)

HENRY SCHICK & CO.	**WASHINGTON, DC**	**1900-1945**

(Army and Navy Uniforms)

PHILLIP & LEWIS SCHIFFLIN	**NEW YORK, NY**	**1861-1865**

- U.S. contract for 6,941 M1840 and M1860 cavalry sabers (1861-1862).
- U.S. contracts for non-comm., musician, staff and field officer, cavalry officer, foot officer, and mounted infantry officer swords (1861-1862).
- U.S. contract for 539 Austrian muskets and 2,000 Prussian muskets (1861).

(Hardware and Military Importer)

CHARLES F. SCHMIDT	NEW YORK, NY	**1861-1885**

U.S. contract for 1,800 cavalry sabers (1864).
(Military Importer)

WILLIAM SCHOONMAKER	NEW YORK, NY	**1830-1831**

(Military Cutlery, Hardware)

SCHULTZ MFG. CO.	CHICAGO, IL	**1870**

(Regalia)

JACOB SCHUYLER	NEW YORK, NY	**1813-1853**

Partner in Young, Smith & Co. (1833-1843).
Partner in Young & Smith (1844-1845).
Partner in William H. Smith & Co. (1846-1853).

SCHUYLER (JACOB), HARTLEY		
(MARCELLUS), & GRAHAM (MALCOLM)	NEW YORK, NY	**1854-1865**

- Locations: 13 Maiden Lane (1854-1856),
  22 St John and 19 Maiden Lane (1857-1876),
  and 17 and 19 Maiden Lane (1877-1878).
- Graham also worked for William H. Smith & Co. (1846-1853).
- One of the largest Civil War military outfitters.
- Issued extensive military catalogs.
- Displayed presentation swords at the New York Fair (1864).
- Sold a complete line of regulation swords.
- Had a very wide line of presentation swords, many with silver hilts.
- Imported blades from Paul D. Luneschloss and William Clauberg, Solingen, Germany.
- Imported M1840 cavalry sabers and many officer swords from William Clauberg, Solingen, Germany.
- Imported M1822 French foot officer swords (variation).
- Bought swords from Emerson & Silver.
- Bought blades and M1850 foot officer swords from Collins & Co.
- Bought swords from Henry Sauerbier.
- Adv. a complete line of military and naval goods, regulation and presentation swords, guns, uniforms, accessories, and regalia in the *Army-Navy Journal* (1863-1864).
- Issued a large illustrated catalog (1864).
- Had offices at 15 Rue D'Enghien in Paris, France, and 6 St. Mary's Row in Birmingham, England (1862 and early 1863).
- Had offices at 31 Rue Du Chateau D'Eau in Paris, France, and Sands Street in Birmingham, England (late 1863 to 1865).

(See William H. Smith)
(See Malcolm Graham)
(See Marcellus Hartley)
(See Emerson & Silver)
(See Collins & Co.)
(See Henry Sauerbier)

Schuyler, Hartley, & Graham U.S. Civil War Contracts

M1840 and M1860 cavalry sabers	3,424
M1840 lt. artillery sabers	567

M1840 non-comm. swords	1,620
M1850 foot officer swords	50
M1850 staff and field officer swords	26
Burnside rifles	719

SCHUYLER (JACOB), HARTLEY (MARCELLUS), & GRAHAM (MALCOLM) & CO.   NEW YORK, NY   1865-1867
- Had offices in London, England, and Paris, France (1865-1866).
- Adv. arms, military goods, presentation swords, and pistols in the *Army-Navy Journal* (1865-1866).
- Bought the Union Metallic Cartridge Co. (1866).
- Employee: Henry K. White (1865-1874).

SCHUYLER (JACOB), HARTLEY (MARCELLUS), & GRAHAM (MALCOLM)   NEW YORK, NY   1867-1878
- Adv. military, society, church, and theatrical goods in the *Army-Navy Journal* (1869).
- Sold military goods and swords to Daniel Norcross & Co. and Henry K. White (after 1874).
- Robert C. Melvain joined the company (1874).
- Salesman: Howard Waldo (1870-1878).
- Jacob Schuyler retired (1878).

(See Henry Tomes & Francis Tomes)
(See Charles W. May)
(See Henry K. White)
(See Daniel Norcross & Co.)
(Military Goods; Guns and Pistols; Presentation, U.S., Regulation, and Society Swords; Military, Church, and Theatrical Goods; Regalia)

HARTLEY (MARCELLUS) & GRAHAM (MALCOLM)   NEW YORK, NY   1878-1899
17-19 Maiden Lane
- Sold M1860 naval cutlasses.
- Sold weapons business to H.K. White (1881).
- Sold uniform business to Raymold & Whitlock (1881).
- Malcolm Graham died (1899).
- Bought controlling interest in Remington Arms Co. (1886).
- Made rifles and shotguns.
- Salesman: Howard Waldo (1878-1883).

HARTLEY (MARCELLUS) & CO.   NEW YORK, NY   1900-1902
- Marcellus Hartley died (1902).

(Military Goods, Guns, Swords)

R. (RICHARD) H. & W. (WILLIAM) H. SCOTT	ALBANY, NY	1842-1860
WILLIAM J. SCOTT	ALBANY, NY	1860-1867
RICHARD H. SCOTT	ALBANY, NY	1860-1867
R.H. & W.J. SCOTT	ALBANY, NY	1867-1871

RICHARD H. SCOTT	ALBANY, NY	1871-1881

Sold company to employee William Paddock and then relocated (1878).
(Gunsmith, Military Goods, Swords, Regalia)

OSCAR & EMIL SEEBASS	NEW YORK, NY	1840-1859
JOHN C. STADERMAN & CO.	NEW YORK, NY	1859-1863

Partners: Oscar Seebass, Emil Seebass.

SEEBASS BROTHERS — NEW YORK, NY — 1863-1865

Locations: 540 Pearl Street (1863), 2924 Broadway (1863-1864), 17 Maiden Lane (1864-1865).
Partners: Oscar Seebass, Emil Seebass.
Adv. swords and military and naval goods in the *Army-Navy Journal* (1863-1865).

OSCAR SEEBASS	NEW YORK, NY 17 Maiden Lane	1865-1876
EMIL SEEBASS	NEW YORK, NY 17 Maiden Lane	1865-1876

(See John C. Staderman)
(Military Goods)

A. SELDNER & CO.	WASHINGTON, DC	1850-1858
A. & L. (LEOPOLD) SELDNER	WASHINGTON, DC	1858-1860
L. (LEOPOLD) SELDNER & ADOLPH ROLLAND	WASHINGTON, DC	1860-1862
L. (LEOPOLD) SELDNER & CO.	WASHINGTON, DC	1862-1865

(Clothier, Regalia, Masonic Goods, Military Goods)

FRANK SELIGER	NEW YORK, NY	1861-1865

(Silver Plater, Military Ornaments, Swords Hiltor)

THOMAS SELLEW	PROVIDENCE, RI	1875

(Regalia)

W.S. SHAFFER	HARRISBURG, PA	1861-1865

Sold M1850 foot officer swords.
(Military Goods)

LIVINGSTON A. SHANNON	NEW YORK, NY	1830-1866

Worked for the Horstmann Brothers & Allien Co. (1852-1866).

SHANNON (LIVINGSTON A.), MILLER (WALSINGHAM K.) & CO.	NEW YORK, NY 32 Maiden Lane	1866-1867

- Bought out the complete military stocks (except pistols, banners, and badges) of the Tiffany Co. (1866).
- Sold military goods to Edward Ederer.
- Sold M1850 foot officer swords made by Henry Sauerbier.
- Imported M1860 cavalry officer sabers from F. Horster, Solingen, Germany.
- Sold M1872 artillery officer swords and Marine Corps swords.

SHANNON (LIVINGSTON A.), MILLER (WALSINGHAM A.) & CRANE (HAROLD L.)	NEW YORK, NY 32 to 46 Maiden Lane	1867-1896

- Adv. military goods for the army, navy, marines, and National Guard in the *Army-Navy Journal* (1869-1870).
- Sold military goods to Daniel Norcross & Co.
- Also sold police, fireman, and railroad uniforms; regalia; and church and theatrical trimmings.

MILLER (WALSINGHAM A.) & CO.	NEW YORK, NY	1896-1899

Partner: Harold L. Crane.
(See Tiffany & Co.)
(See Edward Ederer)
(See Daniel Norcross & Co.)
(Military Goods, Dealer and Importer)

GEORGE B. SHARPE	PHILADELPHIA, PA	1840-1848
WILLIAM H. & GEORGE B. SHARPE	PHILADELPHIA, PA	1848-1894

Silversmith and hiltor for Bailey & Co. (1850-1878).
Silversmith and hiltor for Bailey Banks & Biddle (1878-1894).
(See John Trowbridge Bailey)
(Silversmith, Sword Hiltor)

WILLIAM H. SHARPE	PHILADELPHIA, PA	1840-1848
WILLIAM H. & GEORGE B. SHARPE	PHILADELPHIA, PA	1848-1850

(Silversmith, Sword Hiltor)

HENRY SHELDON	HARTFORD, CT	1798-1818
SMITH, BEGELOW, & SHELDON (HENRY)	HARTFORD, CT	1818-1822
SHELDON (HENRY) & COLTON (NORMAND)	HARTFORD, CT	1822-1850
H. (HENRY) SHELDON & CO.	HARTFORD, CT	1850-1856

(See Normand Smith)
(Saddlers, Military Goods)

JOHN SHELDON
(See Simon G. Cheever)

SHEPPARD & BOYD	ALBANY, NY	1875

(Military Goods and Swords)

J.C. SHERWOOD	STANFORD, CT	1861-1865

(Military Goods)

SMITH J. SHERWOOD	BUFFALO, NY	1835-1838
	CHICAGO, IL	1839-1847
SHERWOOD (SMITH J.) & WHATLEY (ELI)	CHICAGO, IL	1847-1854

Employee: Harvey R. Caberay.
(See Harvey R. Caberay)
(Jewelers, Silversmith, Military Goods)

BENJAMIN SHIMWELL	PHILADELPHIA, PA	1860-1865

(Cutler)

SAMUEL SHIPP	CINCINNATI, OH	1819-1828
COLLINS (PELEQ) & SHIPP (SAMUEL)	CINCINNATI, OH	1829-1834
SAMUEL SHIPP	CINCINNATI, OH	1835-D1843

(Jeweler, Silversmith, Watch Maker, Military Goods)

SHOUNDS, ADCOCK & TEUFEL NEW YORK, NY 1896-1899
Sold presentation swords.
(Military Goods)

N. SAINT & MEYER INC. NEW YORK, NY 1902-1905
(Military Goods)

BENJAMIN SHREVE	BOSTON, MA	B1813-1853
JONES (JOHN B.), SHREVE (BENJAMIN) & BROWN	BOSTON, MA	1853-1854
SHREVE (BENJAMIN) BROWN & CO.	BOSTON, MA	1854-1861
SHREVE (BENJAMIN) STANWOOD (HENRY B.) & CO.	BOSTON, MA 226 Washington	1861-1869

Displayed presentation swords at the New York Fair (1864).
Adv. army and navy equipment, including presentation and regulation swords, belts, sashes, epaulettes, buttons, laces, caps, shoulder straps, camp chests, etc.

SHREVE (BENJAMIN), CRUMP (CHARLES H.), & LOW (JOHN L.)	BOSTON, MA	1869-1888
SHREVE (BENJAMIN), CRUMP (CHARLES H.), & LOW (JOHN L.) CO., INC.	BOSTON, MA	1888-1991

Benjamin Shreve died (1896).
(See John L. Low)
(See Henry B. Stanwood)
(See John B. Jones)
(Presentation Swords, Military Goods, Silversmith, Importer)

ABRAHAM SHUMAN	BOSTON, MA	1850-1870
PHILLIPS, SHUMAN (ABRAHAM) & CO.	BOSTON, MA	1870-1881
A. (ABRAHAM) SHUMAN & CO.	BOSTON, MA	1881-1916

Also called the Roxbury Clothing Co.
(Regalia, Military Goods)

GEORGE W. SIMMONS BOSTON, MA 1835-1868
Adv. swords and military equipment.
Sold M1850 foot officer swords and M1840 medical officer swords.

G. (GEORGE) W. SIMMONS BROS. & CO. BOSTON, MA 1869-1877
Sold M1860 staff and field officer swords and presentation swords.

G. (GEORGE) W. SIMMONS & CO.	BOSTON, MA	1878-1880
G. (GEORGE) W. SIMMONS & SON	BOSTON, MA	1881-1895

(Jeweler, Army and Navy Uniforms, Swords, Military Goods)

EDWARD SIMONS	NEWARK, NJ	1861-1865

Sold M1850 foot officer swords
(Military Goods, Military Ornaments, Saddlery)

GEORGE W. SIMONS	PHILADELPHIA, PA	1820-1839
GEORGE W. SIMONS & CO.	PHILADELPHIA, PA	1840-1864

- U.S. contracts for officer swords.
- Sold medical and pay department officer swords, M1850 foot officer swords, and M1850 staff and field officer swords.
- Bought sword blades from Collins & Co. and Emerson & Silver.
- Imported blades from William Clauberg, Solingen, Germany.
- Bought Paste enamel hilts from F.W. Bailey (Bailey & Co., Philadelphia, PA).

GEORGE W. SIMONS, BRO. & CO.	PHILADELPHIA, PA	1865-1869
GEORGE W. SIMONS, BRO. OPDYKE & CO.	PHILADELPHIA, PA	1870-1872
SIMONS BROTHERS & CO.	PHILADELPHIA, PA	1877-1906

- Issued military catalogs.
- Bought out Peter L. Krider & Co. (1903).

(See Collins & Co.-Maker listing)
(See Emerson & Silver-Maker listing)
(See Peter L. Krider & Co.)
(See Bailey & Co.)
(Silversmith, Jeweler, Sword Hiltor, Presentation Swords, Military Goods)

ABRAHAM SINK	PHILADELPHIA, PA	1785-D1831
ABRAHAM SINK JR.	PHILADELPHIA, PA	1831-D1836
ANN SINK	PHILADELPHIA, PA	1837-1840

(Military Goods Store, Hardware, Pistols, Swords, Dirks)

SAMUEL SINK	BEDFORD CO., PA	1810-1817

(Silversmith, Watch Maker)

WILLIAM SINK	CAMBRIA CO., PA	1810-1830

(Gunsmith)

A. SISCO	BALTIMORE, MD	1850-1864
CHARLES T. & JOHN E. SISCO	BALTIMORE, MD	1864-1921

Sons of A. Sisco.

SISCO BROS. (CHARLES T. & JOHN E.)	BALTIMORE, MD	1921-1925

Sold M1902 saber for all officers.
(Regalia, Military Equipment)

ARMY-NAVY STORE	PHILADELPHIA, PA	1860-1869
ALEXANDER SLOAN	PHILADELPHIA, PA	1869-1922

Bought Army-Navy Store and continued to use the name.
(Military Outfitter)

WARRINGTON L. SLOAT	MOBILE, AL	1819-1838

SMITH (CHASE) & SLOAT (WARRINGTON L.) (Clocksmith, Silversmith, Jeweler, Military Goods)	MOBILE, AL	1838-1842
MARTIN G. SLORTZ (Cutler)	PHILADELPHIA, PA	1860-1865

CHASE SMITH
(See L'Hommedieu Bros.)

JAMES S. SMITH	ENGLAND	B1807-1834
Immigrated to New York, NY (1834).		
JAMES S. SMITH & M. THIERS	NEW YORK, NY	1834-1838
JAMES S. SMITH	NEW YORK, NY	1838-1860
SMITH (JAMES S.) & SONS	NEW YORK, NY	1860-1863
Partners: George Smith (son;), James S. Smith Jr. (son; left in 1863), Benjamin F. Steward.		
SMITH (JAMES S.) & SPAULDING (GEORGE)	NEW YORK, NY	1863
Adv. military goods and swords (everything required by offices of the army and navy) in the *Army-Navy Journal* (1863).		
James S. Smith died (1863).		
JAMES S. SMITH & CO.	NEW YORK, NY	1864-1891
• Partners: Mary E. Smith (widow), George Smith (son).		
• Branches in Beauford, SC, Vicksburg, MS, and Newbern, NC.		
• Manufacturer of James S. Smith patented metallic shoulder straps.		
• Adv. military goods and swords in the *Army-Navy Journal* (1864).		
(Military Ornaments, Insignia, Sword and Military Goods Dealer)		
JAMES S. SMITH JR.	NEW YORK, NY	1840-1863
Partner in Smith & Sons (1860-1863).		
	NEW YORK, NY	1863-D1886
(Military Ornaments, Insignia, Sword and Military Goods Dealer)		
J.H. SMITH	COLUMBUS, OH	1861-1864
SMITH (J.H.) & CONRAD (P.T.)	COLUMBUS, OH	1864-1865
(Hatter, Military Goods)		
M.S. SMITH & CO. (Regalia)	DETROIT, MI	1865-1870
NORMAND SMITH	HARTFORD, CT	B1772-1818
SMITH (NORMAND), BIGELOW (RICHARD) & SHELDON (HENRY)	HARTFORD, CT	1818-1821
SMITH (NORMAND) & BIGELOW (RICHARD)	HARTFORD, CT	1821-1826
Partner: Normand Smith Jr.		
N. (NORMAND SR. & JR.) & T. (THOMAS) SMITH & CO.	HARTFORD, CT	1826-1834
Normand Smith Jr. died (1834).		

SMITH (THOMAS, CHARLES B., NORMAND SR.) & BOURN (BENJAMIN A.)	HARTFORD, CT	1834-1840
SMITH (THOMAS, CHARLES B., NORMAND SR.) & WORTHINGTON & CO.	HARTFORD, CT	1840-1975

Normand Smith Sr. died (1860).
(Military Goods, Saddlers, Leather Goods)

PETER SMITH & CO.	CINCINNATI, OH	1830-1857

Bought out by John Boner (1857).
(See John Boner)
(Military Goods, Regalia and Society Swords)

WILLIAM H. SMITH	NEW YORK, NY	1830-1832
YOUNG (HENRY), SMITH (WILLIAM H.) & CO.	NEW YORK, NY 2 and 4 Maiden Lane	1833-1843

Partner: Jacob Schuyler.

YOUNG (HENRY) & SMITH (WILLIAM H.)	NEW YORK, NY 2 and 4 Maiden Lane	1844-1845
WILLIAM H. SMITH & CO.	NEW YORK, NY 2 and 4 Maiden Lane	1846-1853

Partners: Henry Young, Jacob Schuyler (1835-1853),
  Malcolm Graham (1846-1853).
Schuyler and Graham left to form Schuyler,
  Hartley, & Graham (1853).
Agent for Ames Mfg. Co. swords.

SMITH (WILLIAM H.), YOUNG (HENRY) & CO.	NEW YORK, NY 2 and 4 Maiden Lane	1854-1858

Partner: Henry's son James H. Young.
Henry Young left (1855).

SMITH (WILLIAM H.), CRANE (WILLIAM W.) & CO.	NEW YORK, NY 4 Maiden Lane	1859-1866

- Partners:
    Harold L. Crane
    Walter M. Smith
    Charles N. Holmes
    Howard Waldo (1859-1862)
- U.S. contract for 482 M1840 and M1860 cavalry sabers (1861-1862).
- Imported from Schnitzler & Kirschbaum, Solingen, Germany.
- Became Shannon, Miller, & Crane (1866).

(See Henry Young)
(See Livingston A. Shannon)
(See Schuyler, Hartley, & Graham)
(Military Goods, Importer)

W.H. SMITH
(See Confederate listings)

SOHER (LOUIS) & REIMAN (HENRY A.)	SAN FRANCISCO, CA	1877-1880

(Regalia)

ADAM W. SPIES	**BIRMINGHAM, ENGLAND**	**1800-1819**
	NEW YORK, NY	**1819-1829**
	87 Maiden Lane	

Merchant and hardware dealer.
Imported swords from John Salter,
  Birmingham, England.
Shared same address as C. & J.D. Wolfe.

WOLFE (CHRISTOPHER),
  SPIES (ADAM W.), & CLARKE — **NEW YORK, NY** — **1830-1832**
  193 Pearl Street

ADAM W. SPIES — **NEW YORK, NY** — **1833-1838**
  192 Pearl Street

Partner and son: John J. Spies.

ADAM W. SPIES & CO. — **NEW YORK, NY** — **1839-1865**
- Locations: 192 Pearl Street (1839), 218 Pearl Street (1840-1845), 91 Maiden Lane (1846-1860), 187 Broadway (1860-1865).
- Partner and son: John J. Spies.
- Sold a complete line of regulation swords.
- Sold eagle-head-pommel naval officer swords.
- Displayed presentation swords at the New York Fair (1864).
- Sold six-shot Pepperbox pistols as well as other pistols and firearms.
- Adam W. Spies died (1860) and his son John J. Spies ran the company.

SPIES (JOHN J.) KISSAM (FREDERICK) & CO.
 — **NEW YORK, NY** — **1865-1880**

Locations: 16 Courtland
  (1865-1879), 279 Broadway (1879-1880).
(See Christopher Wolfe)
(See John D. Wolfe)
(Hardware, Military Goods, Importer, Swords and Firearms)

WILLIAM S. SPRATLEY — **NORFOLK, VA** — **1850-1855**
Adv. as imported and manufacturer of guns,
  pistols, and fine cutlery (1852).
(Gunsmith, Importer)

SPRENGER & EMRICH — **CINCINNATI, OH** — **1850-1860**
(Military Goods)

R. SPRINGE — **LEAVENWORTH, KA** — **1900-1920**
(Military Tailor and Outfitter)

JOHN C. STADERMAN	**NEW YORK, NY**	**1840-1855**
C. HENNING & JOHN C. STADERMAN	**NEW YORK, NY**	**1855-1859**
JOHN C. STADERMAN & CO.	**NEW YORK, NY**	**1859-1863**

Partners: Oscar Seebass, Emil Seebass.

STADERMAN (JOHN C.) & SHAPTER (JAMES D.)	NEW YORK, NY	1863-1865

Adv. as a military depot selling Solingen swords, silver-plated swords, and presentation swords in the *Army-Navy Journal* (1863-1865).
Displayed presentation swords at the New York Fair (1864).

JOHN C. STADERMAN & CO.	NEW YORK, NY	1865-1868
J. STADERMAN & CO.	NEW YORK, NY	1868-1878

(See Oscar & Emil Seebass)
(Military Goods, Military and Presentation Swords)

HENRY B. STANWOOD	BOSTON, MA	B1818-1838

Partner in John L. Low & Co. (1828-1838).

HARRIS (WILLIAM) & STANWOOD (HENRY B.)	BOSTON, MA	1838-1842
HARRIS (WILLIAM) STANWOOD (HENRY B.) & CO.	BOSTON, MA	1842-1848

Partner: George B. Foster.
Agents for Ames Mfg. Co. swords.

HARRIS (WILLIAM) & STANWOOD (HENRY B.)	BOSTON, MA	1848-1852
HENRY B. STANWOOD & CO.	BOSTON, MA	1852-1861
SHREVE (BENJAMIN), STANWOOD (HENRY B.) & CO.	BOSTON, MA	1861-1869

- Adv. presentation swords, belts, sashes, epaulettes, caps, and camp equipment.
- Displayed presentation swords at the New York Fair (1864).
- Henry B. Stanwood died (1869).

(See John L. Low & Co.)
(See Benjamin Shreve)
(See George B. Foster)
(Presentation Swords, Silversmith, Importer, Military Goods)

CHARLES K. STELLWAGON	PHILADELPHIA, PA	1840-1860
STELLWAGON (HARRY) & BROTHER (EDWARD)	PHILADELPHIA, PA	1860-1868
WILSON (JAMES) & STELLWAGON (HARRY)	PHILADELPHIA, PA	1868-1872

(See George C. Evans)
(See William Wilson)
(Jeweler, Silversmith, Watch Maker)

THOMAS STEPHENSON	BUFFALO, NY	1835-1839
THOMAS STEPHENSON & CO.	BUFFALO, NY	1839-1848

(Military Goods, Jeweler, Silversmith, Watch Maker)

JAMES R. STEVENS	HARTFORD, CT	1855-1865
STEVENS (JAMES R.) & ROGERS (ROBERT T.)	HARTFORD, CT	1866-1868
JAMES R. STEVENS & CO.	HARTFORD, CT	1869-1875

(Regalia, Military Goods, Jewelry, Silverware, Watches)

L. (LOUIS) E. STILZ & BROTHER	PHILADELPHIA, PA	1875-1915

(Regalia, Fraternal Swords)

HENRY STORMS	NEW YORK, NY	1815-1841
HENRY STORMS & SON (CHRISTIAN SCHAEFFER STORMS)	NEW YORK, NY	1842-1853

Adv. as a military and naval store selling muskets and swords (1846).

C. (CHRISTIAN) S. (SCHAEFFER) STORMS	ST. LOUIS, MO	1854-1862
	NEW YORK, NY	1863-1870

(Military Goods, Saddler, Leather Goods)

CHARLES STORRS	UTICA, NY	1800-1827
STORRS (CHARLES) & PARKER (GEORGE)	UTICA, NY	1828
STORRS (CHARLES) & DAVIES (THOMAS)	UTICA, NY	1829-1830
STORRS (CHARLES) & COOLEY (OLIVER B.)	UTICA, NY	1831-1839

Partners: Horace P. Bradley, David S. Rowland, Erastus Charles Starin.
Charles Storrs died (1839).
Succeeded by Tanner & Cooley.
(See Tanner & Cooley-Silversmith listings)
(Silversmith, Military Goods, Watch Maker)

MORTON C. STOUT & CO.	BALTIMORE, MD	1889-1896

(Military Goods)

CHARLES STRONG
(See Lemuel T. Wells)

WILLIAM B. STRONG	WASHINGTON, DC	1861-1865

Adv. swords, knives, saddles, and military ornaments (1864).
(Military Goods)

CHARLES SVENDSON & CO.	CINCINNATI, OH	1881-1885

(Regalia)

CHARLES F. SYFFERMAN	BOSTON, MA	1836-1855
ROULSTONE (EDWARD A.G.) & SYFFERMAN (CHARLES F.)	BOSTON, MA	1856
CHARLES F. SYFFERMAN	BOSTON, MA	1857-D1874

(See Edward A.G. Roulstone)
(Military Goods)

SAMUEL R. & WILLIAM J. SYMS	NEW YORK, NY	1828-1848
BLUNT (ORISON) & SYMS (SAMUEL R. & WILLIAM J.)	NEW YORK, NY	1848-1859
W. (WILLIAM) J. SYMS & BROTHER (SAMUEL R.)	NEW YORK, NY	1860-1865

U.S. contract for 13 lt. artillery sabers (1861).
(Military Goods)

LENDELL F. TARBETT
(See A.W. Pollard)

F.G. TISDALL	NEW YORK, NY	1855-1860

(Regalia, Fraternal Swords)

G. (GILBERT) R. TOBEY	**NEW YORK, NY**	**1861-1865**

U.S. contract for 2,573 non-comm. swords
  (1861-1862).
(Military Outfitter)

FRANCIS TOMES	**LONDON, ENGLAND**	**1800-1819**
LEWIS (EDWARD) & TOMES (FRANCIS)	**NEW YORK, NY** 27 Cortland	**1819-1824**

Edward Lewis was partner in London.

FRANCIS TOMES	**NEW YORK, NY** 98 Maiden Lane	**1825-1832**
FRANCIS TOMES & WILLIAM I. MILLER	**NEW YORK, NY** 6 Maiden Lane	**1833-1835**

Remained at 6 Maiden Lane until 1874.

TOMES (FRANCIS) & MILLER **(WILLIAM I.) & CO.**	**NEW YORK, NY**	**1836-1839**

(See William I. Miller)

FRANCIS TOMES & SONS	**NEW YORK, NY**	**1840-1849**

Partners and sons: Henry Tomes, Francis Tomes Jr.
Employee: Marcellus Hartley (1846-1849).
(See Henry Tomes)

FRANCIS (JR. & SR.) & BENJAMIN TOMES	**NEW YORK, NY**	**1850-1858**

Benjamin Tomes was the son of Francis Tomes Jr.
Employee: Robert C. Melvain.

TOMES (FRANCIS JR.) SON **(BENJAMIN) & MELVAIN (ROBERT C.)**	**NEW YORK, NY**	**1859-1865**

- Partner: Charles H. Tomes (1864-1865).
- Buyer: Charles Folsom (1862-1865).
- U.S. contracts for 3,289 M1840 cavalry sabers,
  plus 814 M1821 British cavalry sabers (1861).
- Sold cavalry officer sabers, mounted infantry
  officer swords, M1850 foot officer swords,
  presentation swords, and M1860 staff and field officer swords.
- Imported M1850 staff and field officer swords and sabers
  for mounted officers of infantry from William Clauberg, Solingen, Germany.
- Adv. military goods, swords, cutlery, and firearms
  in the *Army-Navy Journal* (1863-1864).
- Published pamphlet *Uniforms for Officers of
  the U.S. Navy* (1864).

TOMES (FRANCIS JR. & CHARLES H.), **MELVAIN (ROBERT C.) & CO.**	**NEW YORK, NY**	**1865-1874**

Adv. military goods, swords, cutlery, firearms
  in the *Army-Navy Journal* (1865-1870).
Melvain joined Schuyler, Hartley, & Graham (1874).
(See Robert C. Melvain)
(See Schuyler, Hartley, & Graham)
(See Warnock & Co.)

FRANCIS TOMES (JR.) & CO.	**NEW YORK, NY** 738 Broadway	**1875-1883**

Company went out of business (1883).
Some of Tomes' stock went to Warnock & Co.
(Military Goods Dealer and Importer, Guns and
  Swords, Hardware, Jewelry)

HENRY TOMES	NEW YORK, NY	1820-1840
FRANCIS TOMES & SONS	NEW YORK, NY	1840-1849

Partners: Henry Tomes, Francis Tomes Jr.

HENRY TOMES & CO.	NEW YORK, NY	1850-1856

Partners: Charles Folsom, James Eaton.

HENRY TOMES	NEW YORK, NY	1857-1870

London buyer for Schuyler, Hartley, & Graham (1865-1867).
(See Francis Tomes)
(See Henry Folsom)
(See Schuyler, Hartley, & Graham)
(Gun Dealer and Importer)

BENJAMIN C. TRUE	ALBANY, NY	1830-1831
TRUE (BENJAMIN C.) & DAVIS (WILLIAM)	ALBANY, NY	1832
BENJAMIN C. TRUE	ALBANY, NY	1833-1844
	CINCINNATI, OH	1845-1865

(Gunsmith, Silversmith, Die Cutter, Engraver, Military Goods)

TUNNEL CITY REGALIA CO.	FORT HURON, MI	1881-1898

Put out Fraternal Goods Catalogs
(Regalia)

P. (PHILLIP) H. TUSKA	NEW YORK, NY	1861-1863

U.S. contract for 2,877 cavalry sabers (1861-1862).
U.S. contract for 98 non-comm. swords (1861-1862).
(Military Outfitter)

UNION STORE
(See Timothy & William Parson)

STEPHEN & GEORGE UPSON
(See Silversmith listings)
(See Richards Upson)

ALBERT D. VAN COTT	MILWAUKEE, WI	1861-1875

(Military Goods, Silversmith, Jeweler, Watch Maker)

J. (JOSHUA) M. VARIAN & SONS (JACOB & JOSHUA JR.)	NEW YORK, NY	1864-1874

Adv. swords, military goods, and uniforms in the *Army-Navy Journal* (1869-1870).
Bought out Francis B. Baldwin (1864).
(See F.B. Baldwin)
(Military Goods)

DANIEL VAN VOORHIS	PHILADELPHIA, PA	B1751-1783
	PRINCETON, NJ	1783-1784
	NEW YORK, NY	1784-1786
VAN VOORHIS (DANIEL) & COLEY (WILLIAM)	NEW YORK, NY	1786-1787
DANIEL VAN VOORHIS	RUPERT, VA	1787-1791

Partner: Rueban Harmon.

VAN VOORHIS (DANIEL) & SCHANCK (GARRETT)	NEW YORK, NY	1791-1792
VAN VOORHIS (DANIEL), SCHANCK (GARRETT), & MCCALL	NEW YORK, NY	1792-1795
DANIEL VAN VOORHIS	NEW YORK, NY	1795-1797
VAN VOORHIS (DANIEL) & SON	NEW YORK, NY	1797-D1804

(See Garrett Schanck, William Coley, Reuban Harmon-Silversmith listings)
(Silversmiths, Goldsmiths, Jewelers, Engravers)

J.W. VICKERS	BUFFALO, NY	1876

(Regalia)

B. (BOYD) A. (ALEXANDER) & A. (ALVIN) S. WADHAMS	CHICAGO, IL	1868-1871

Burned out in Chicago fire (1871), but rebuilt.

A. (ALVIN) S. WADHAMS & CO.	CHICAGO, IL	1872-1874

Partner: Daniel C. (Curtis) Roundy.

WADHAMS (ALVIN S.) & ROUNDY (DANIEL CURTIS)	CHICAGO, IL	1875-1880
DANIEL C. (CURTIS) ROUNDY & SON	CHICAGO, IL	1881-1891

Authorized dealer for the Ames Sword Co.
Partner and son: Frank Curtis Roundy.

ROUNDY REGALIA CO.	CHICAGO, IL	1891-1925

Partners: Daniel Curtis Roundy (died 1907), Frank Curtis Roundy (son).
Authorized dealer for the Ames Sword Co.
(Military Goods, Masonic Goods, Regalia)

HOWARD WALDO	NEW YORK, NY	1839-1888

- Salesman at Smith, Crane, & Co. (1859-1862).
- Partner in Fitch, Waldo (1862-1864).
- Partner in Fitch, Waldo, & Barre (1864-1865).
- Partner in Fitch, VanVechton, & Co. (1865-1870).
- Salesman for Schuyler, Hartley, & Graham (1870-1878).
- Salesman for Hartley & Graham (1878-1883).
- Salesman for J.H. McKenney & Co. (1883-1888).

(Military Goods, Salesman, Dealer)

WILLIAM WALL	WASHINGTON, DC	1820-1840
SHANKS & WALL (WILLIAM)	WASHINGTON, DC	1841-1849
WILLIAM WALL	WASHINGTON, DC	1850-1852
WALL (WILLIAM) & STEPHENS (THOMAS K.)	WASHINGTON, DC	1853-1862
WALL, STEPHENS & CO.	WASHINGTON, DC	1863-1875

Adv. military goods, uniforms, and swords in the *Army-Navy Journal* (1863-1864).

WALL (WILLIAM) & ROBINSON (BUSHROD)	WASHINGTON, DC	1875-1880

(Army and Navy Goods, Clothier, Swords, Accessories)

MOSES A. WALLACH	BOSTON, MA	B1756, 1786-D1836

Called Wallach's Armory.
Adv. foils, hangers, cut-and-thrust swords, and small swords (1800).
Adv. swords, dirks, hangers, and foils (1809).
(Military Outfitter, Importer, Guns, Swords)

JAMES WARD	GUILFORD, CT	B1768-1789
BEACH (MILES) & WARD (JAMES)	HARTFORD, CT	1790-1796
JAMES WARD	HARTFORD, CT	1797-1803
WARD (JAMES) & BARTHOLOMEW (ROSWELL)	HARTFORD, CT	1804-1808

Adv. as a military store selling infantry and cavalry swords, guns, and military goods (1806).
Sold silver-mounted pillow pommel and hussar-hilt officer short sabers.

WARD (JAMES) BARTHOLOMEW (ROSWELL) & BRAINARD (CHARLES)	HARTFORD, CT	1809-1830

Roswell Bartholomew died (1830).
James Ward retired in 1830 and died in 1856.
James Ward was commissary general during the War of 1812.
(See Miles Beach)
(See Roswell Bartholomew & Charles Brainard-Silversmith listings)
(Silversmiths, Watch Makers, Military Goods, Guns, Swords)

JOSEPH W. WARNOCK	NEW YORK, NY	1818-1838
WARNOCK & CO.	NEW YORK, NY	1838-1866

Partners: Joseph W. Warnock (D1866), Robert E. Warnock (son).
Sold M1860 staff and field officer swords.
Adv. military hats and equipment in the *Army-Navy Journal* (1864-1869).

WARNOCK UNIFORM CO.	NEW YORK, NY	1866-1945

Partners: Robert E. Warnock, William A. Warnock (son of Robert E. Warnock).
Bought part of the military stocks of Francis Tomes & Co. (1883).
Sold M1902 sabers for all officers.
(See Franics Tomes)
(Military Goods)

WALTER WATSON	ENGLAND	1840-1861
	FAYETTEVILLE, NC	1861-1890

Gunsmith at Fayetteville Arsenal (1861-1864).
(Gunsmith, Gun Maker, Cutler)

M. (MARMADUKE) D. WAUD & CO.	BOSTON, MA 193 Washington Street	1861-1865

Adv. swords, pistols and military goods (1863).
Sold presentation swords.
(Military Goods, Presentation Swords)

ROBERT WEIR	BOSTON, MA	1850

Army and naval uniforms and a civilian costumer.

JAMES M. WELLS	NEW YORK, NY	1820-1836

(Silversmith)

JOSHUA T. WELLS (Military Tailor, Military Goods)	PHILADELPHIA, PA	1861-1866
LEMUEL WELLS	NEW YORK, NY	1770-1793
L. (LEMUEL) & H. (HORACE) WELLS	NEW YORK, NY	1794-1798
LEMUEL WELLS & CO.	NEW YORK, NY	1799-1807

LEMUEL WELLS
Imported swords from John Salter,
  Birmingham, England.
(See Lemuel T. Wells & Co.)
(Silversmith, Goldsmith, Jeweler, Military
  Goods, Hardware)
	NEW YORK, NY	1808-1840

LEMUEL T. WELLS CO.	HARTFORD, CT	1840-1841
WELLS (LEMUEL T.) & STRONG (CHARLES C.)	HARTFORD, CT	1842-1846
L.T. WELLS	HARTFORD, CT	1847-1850
L.T. WELLS & CO. Partner: James M. Loomis. (See Lemuel Wells) (Swords, Military Goods, Importer, Jeweler)	HARTFORD, CT	1851-1870
NATHANIEL WELLS & CO. (Silversmith)	NEW YORK, NY	1809-1820
SAMUEL WELLS	NEW YORK, NY	1790-1809
WELLS (SAMUEL) & UPSON (STEPHEN)	NEW YORK, NY	1810-1814
SAMUEL WELLS Imported swords from John Salter, Birmingham, England. (See Stephen Upson-Silversmith listings) (Silversmith, Jeweler, Military Goods, Importer)	NEW YORK, NY	1815-1870
WILLIAM WELLS (Silversmith)	HARTFORD, CT	B1766, 1786-D1828
THE WENDELL CO. (Regalia)	MINNESOTA, MN	1875
WESTERN REGALIA (Regalia and Society Swords)	CHICAGO, IL	1875
ELI WHATLEY (See Harvey R. Caberay)		
WHITE, WHITMAN & CO. Adv. military clothing in the *Army-Navy* *Journal* (1864). (Military Clothiers)	NEW YORK, NY	1841-1865
HENRY K. WHITE U.S. inspector of arms (1861-1865). Worked at Schuyler, Hartley, & Graham (1865-1874).	NEW YORK, NY	1840-1874

H. (HENRY) K. WHITE & SONS	NEW YORK, NY	1874-1964

- Bought military goods from Schuyler, Hartley, & Graham.
- Bought out Hartley & Graham's gun stock (1881). Had own gunsmith shop.
- The company was managed by Fred and Howard White (Henry's son) from 1900-1964.
- Sold M1902 saber for all officers.
- Turner Kirkland of Dixie Gun Works bought the White company when Fred White died (1964).

(See Hartley & Graham)
(See Schuyler, Hartley, & Graham)
(Military Goods)

JAMES E. WHITE	NEW YORK, NY	1850-1858
WHITE (ELIZABETH) &		
LOUGHRAN (MICHAEL)	NEW YORK, NY	1858-1868

Adv. naval swords, uniforms, and equipment and as a military and naval tailor in the *Army-Navy Journal* (1866-1867).

JAMES E. WHITE & CO.	NEW YORK, NY	1868-1870

Partner: James Lock.

WHITE & CO.	NEW YORK, NY	1870-1875

(Tailor, Military Goods)

JAMES R. WHITING	NEW YORK, NY	1860-1870

U.S. contract for 2,486 cavalry sabers and 280 Adams revolvers (imported) (1866).
(Military Importer)

BENJAMIN M. WHITLOCK	NEW YORK, NY	1830-1881

Worked for Schuyler, Hartley, & Graham (1854-1878).

RAYMOLD (WILLIAM A.) & WHITLOCK		
(BENJAMIN M.)	NEW YORK, NY	1881-1891
B. (BENJAMIN) M. WHITLOCK	NEW YORK, NY	1891-1895

Sold a complete line of swords.
Sold military uniforms and equipment.
(See William A. Raymold)
(See Schuyler, Hartley, & Graham)
(Military Outfitters)

THOMAS B. WHITLOCK	NEW YORK, NY	1796-1805
WILLIAM H. WHITLOCK	NEW YORK, NY	1805-1827

(Silversmith, Military Goods)

WHITMORE (M.) & WOLFF (C.H.) & CO.	PITTSBURGH, PA	1841-1854
WHITMORE (M.), WOLFF (C.H.),		
& DUFF (GEORGE J.)	PITTSBURGH, PA	1854-1872

Partner: T.H. Lane.
(Saddlery, Cutlery, Hardware, Importer)

MARINE T. WICKHAM
WICKHAM & CO.
(See Maker listings)

WILKES BARRE REGALIA FACTORY (Regalia)	WILKES BARRE, PA	1890
WILLIAM W. WILLARD	SYRACUSE, NY	1820-1833
WILLARD (WILLIAM W.) & STOKES (T.)	CAZENOVIA, NY	1833-1834
WILLIAM W. WILLARD	SYRACUSE, NY	1834-1840
WILLARD (WILLIAM W.) & HAWLEY (JOHN DEAN)	SYRACUSE, NY	1840-1872

Adv. military goods, presentation swords, and field officer swords (1862-1863).
(See John Dean Hawley-Silversmith listings)
(Silversmith, Watch Maker, Military Goods, Cutler, Presentation Swords)

WILLETT (JAMES P.) & RUAFF (CHARLES)	WASHINGTON, DC	1880-1884

Adv. military goods and swords (1884).
Sold M1860 staff and field officer swords.
(Military Goods, Regalia)

E.R. WILLIAMSON & CO. (Regalia)	MINNEAPOLIS, MN	1900-1920
JAMES ESHTON WILLIS	ARMSTRONG CO., PA	B1828, 1848-D1879

Sold muskets, rifles, pistols, gun supplies, knives, and sabers.
(Gunsmith, Gun and Sword Dealer)

WILLOUGHBY (C.L.), HILL (D.K.), & CO.	BOSTON, MA	1871-1888

Had a branch in Chicago.
(Regalia, Uniforms)

DANIEL H. WILSON & CO. (Military Goods, Regalia, Military Trimmings)	BOSTON, MA	1868-1886
JOHN WILSON (Silversmith)	PHILADELPHIA, PA	1750-D1787
NATHANIEL WILSON	EAST PENNBORO TOWNSHIP, PA Cumberland County	1735-1750
(Silversmith)		
ROBERT WILSON	NEW YORK, NY	1805-1810
	PHILADELPHIA, PA	1810-1825
ROBERT & WILLIAM WILSON	PHILADELPHIA, PA	1825-1846

Robert Wilson died (1846).
(Silversmith)

WILLIAM WILSON	PHILADELPHIA, PA	1810-1825
ROBERT & WILLIAM WILSON	PHILADELPHIA, PA	1825-1846
WILLIAM WILSON	PHILADELPHIA, PA	1846-1850
WILLIAM H. WILSON	PHILADELPHIA, PA	1850-1857
WILLIAM H. WILSON & SON	PHILADELPHIA, PA	1857-1866

Partner and son: James H. Wilson.
James H. Wilson left to join Evans & Hassell.

WILLIAM H. WILSON	PHILADELPHIA, PA	1866-1900

Partner: James H. Wilson (1895-1900).

J. (JAMES) H. WILSON CO.	PHILADELPHIA, PA	1900-1916

Sold out to William Lemberg (1916).
Sold M1872 artillery officer sabers and M1860 staff and field officer swords.
(See George C. Evans)
(Silversmith, Regalia, Military Goods)

WILLIAM W. WILSON	PITTSBURGH, PA	1835-1865

(Silversmith, Jeweler, Watch Maker, Military Goods, Regalia)

WILSON & HUTCHINSON
WILSON & STELLWAGON
JAMES H. WILSON
(See Evans & Hassell)

WILLIAM P. WILSTACH	PHILADELPHIA, PA	1855-1860
WILLIAM P. WILSTACH & CO.	PHILADELPHIA, PA	1861-1865

Partners: Charles Scott, Conrad B. Day.
U.S. contract for 937 cavalry sabers and 1,000 non-comm. swords (imported) (1861).
(Saddlers, Hardware, Military Goods, Insignia)

LOUIS WINDMULLER	NEW YORK, NY	1861-1865
	38 Maiden Lane	

U.S. contracts for 6,685 cavalry sabers (1861).
Contracts for staff and field officer, non-comm., foot officer, musician's, and lt. artillery swords.
Contract for 25 mounted infantry officers swords (all imported).
(Military Goods, Importer)

GUSTAVUS L. WINSHIP	BOSTON, MA	1833-1853
WINSHIP (GUSTAVUS L.)		
& ROULSTONE (EDWARD A.G.)	BOSTON, MA	1853-1856

(See Edward A.G. Roulstone)
(Presentation Swords, Military Goods, Guns)

WOLCOTT & MOORE	BOSTON, MA	1875

(Regalia)

GENERAL JAMES WOLF
(See Silversmith listings)

JOHN WOLF	SAN FRANCISCO, CA	1875-1880

Partner and successor to Daniel Norcross
(Military Goods, Regalia)

CHRISTOPHER WOLFE	NEW YORK, NY	1795-1815
C. (CHRISTOPHER) & J. (JOHN) D. WOLFE	NEW YORK, NY	1816-1829
	87 Maiden Lane	

Same address as A.W. Spies.
Imported swords from John Salter, London, England.
Sold cavalry and lt. artillery swords.

WOLFE (CHRISTOPHER), **SPIES (ADAM W.) & CLARKE**	NEW YORK, NY 193 Pearl Street	1830-1832
WOLFE (CHRISTOPHER) & CLARKE	NEW YORK, NY	1833-1880
WOLFE (CHRISTOPHER), **CLARKE & GILLESPIE**	NEW YORK, NY	1881-1885

(See John D. Wolfe)
(See Adam W. Spies)
(Hardware, Military Goods, Gun and Sword Importer)

JOHN D. WOLFE	NEW YORK, NY	1790-1812
D. (DAVID) & J. (JOHN) D. WOLFE	NEW YORK, NY 87 Maiden Lane	1812-1815
C. (CHRISTOPHER) & J. (JOHN) D. WOLFE	NEW YORK, NY 87 Maiden Lane	1816-1829

Imported swords from John Salter, London, England.
Sold cavalry and lt. artillery swords.

WOLFE (JOHN D.), BISHOP (JAPHET) & CO.	NEW YORK, NY	1830-1843
WOLFE (JOHN D.), BISHOP (JAPHET) & **COFFIN (JOHN P.)**	NEW YORK, NY	1844-1855

Partners: Thomas Bishop, Jesse B. Rogers.

COFFIN (JOHN P.), BRUCE (GEORGE W.) **& BISHOP (DAVID W.)**	NEW YORK, NY	1856-1862
COFFIN (JOHN P.), NEE & CO.	NEW YORK, NY	1863-1872

(See Christopher Wolfe)
(Hardware, Military Goods, Guns and
  Swords Importer)

ENOS WOODRUFF	CINCINNATI, OH	1800-1817

Partner: Ezra Woodruff.

WOODRUFF (ENOS) & DETERLY (JACOB)	CINCINNATI, OH	1817-1825
ENOS WOODRUF	CINCINNATI, OH	1825-1827
WOODRUFF (ENOS) & WHITE (GEORGE L.)	CINCINNATI, OH	1827-1834
ENOS WOODRUFF	CINCINNATI, OH	1834-1843

(See Jacob Deterly-Silversmith listings)
(Watch Maker, Silversmith, Jeweler, Brass
  Founder, Military Equipment)

L. WOODRUFF	CINCINNATI, OH	1843-1850
W.A. WOODRUFF	CINCINNATI, OH	1850-1860

(Silversmith)

ENOCH WOODS	CHICAGO, IL	1861-1870

(Military Goods, Guns and Knives)

YOUNG (JOSEPH W. & WILLIAM M.) **& HOSLEY**	SPRINGFIELD, MA	1893-1900
J. (JOSEPH) M. & W. (WILLIAM) M. YOUNG	SPRINGFIELD, MA	1900-1903
W. (WILLIAM) M. YOUNG REGALIA CO.	SPRINGFIELD, MA	1903-1910

(Regalia, Fraternal Swords)

ALEXANDER YOUNG	**BALTIMORE, MD**	**B1784-1810**
A. (ALEXANDER) YOUNG & CO.	**CAMDEN, SC**	**1810-1836**
A. (ALEXANDER) YOUNG & SON (EDWARD)	**CAMDEN, SC**	**1836-1838**

Bought swords from F.W. Widmann.

	COLUMBIA, SC	**1838-1845**
ALEXANDER YOUNG	**COLUMBIA, SC**	**1845-D1856**

(See Edward Young)
(Gunsmith, Silversmith, Gun Importer, Sword Dealer)

A.E. YOUNG	**ROCHESTER, NY**	**1875**

(Regalia, Military Goods)

EDWARD YOUNG	**CAMDEN, SC**	**B1816-1836**
A. (ALEXANDER) YOUNG & SON (EDWARD)	**CAMDEN, SC**	**1836-1838**
	COLUMBIA, SC	**1838-1845**
YOUNG (EDWARD) & CO.	**COLUMBIA, SC**	**1845-D1848**

(See Alexander Young)
(Gunsmith, Silversmith, Gun Importer)

HENRY YOUNG	**NEW YORK, NY**	**1820-1824**
HENRY YOUNG & CO.	**NEW YORK, NY**	**1825-1832**
YOUNG (HENRY),		
SMITH (WILLIAM H.) & CO.	**NEW YORK, NY**	**1833-1843**

(See William H. Smith)
(Hardware, Military Goods)

JOHN L. YOUNG	**PHILADELPHIA, PA**	**1872-1875**

(Regalia)

JESSE SHENTON ZANE
(See Maker listings)

CHAPTER 6

U.S. Silversmiths Who Mounted Swords

JOHN AITKINS PHILADELPHIA, PA 1754-1814
Apprenticed to William Taylor (1769-1771).
Sold as an indentured servant (1771-1775).
(Goldsmith)

ROBERT AITKINS PHILADELPHIA, PA 1757-1777
(Goldsmith, Engraver)

THOMAS AITKINS DELAWARE CO., PA 1660-1710

WILLIAM AITKINS PHILADELPHIA, PA 1800-1825
(Goldsmith)

SAMUEL ALFORD BARBADOS 1738-1858
 PHILADELPHIA, PA 1758-D1762

THOMAS ALFORD PHILADELPHIA, PA 1740-1765
Son of Samuel Alford.
(Goldsmith, Jeweler)

SAMUEL ALEXANDER
(See Maker listings)

JOHN ALLEN BOSTON, MA B1671-1700
ALLEN (JOHN) & EDWARDS (JOHN) BOSTON, MA 1700-1707

JOHN ALLEN (See John Edwards)	BOSTON, MA	1707-D1760
JOSEPH ANTHONY JR.	PHILADELPHIA, PA	B1762-1800
JOSEPH ANTHONY & SONS	PHILADELPHIA, PA	1800-D1814

Partners: Michael H. Anthony, Thomas Anthony.

M. (MICHAEL H.) & T. (THOMAS) ANTHONY (Goldsmith, Cutler)	PHILADELPHIA, PA	1814-1826

GEORGE ARMITAGE
(See Maker listings)

RALPH ATMAR
(See Maker listings)

SIMEON, JOHN, EMMOR, JOEL, SILAS NEWTON BAILEY
(See Maker listings)

BAILEY & KITCHEN
BAILEY, BANKS & BIDDLE
JOSEPH TROWBRIDGE BAILEY
(See Dealer listings)

EBENEZER BALCH	HARTFORD, CT	B1723-1744
	BOSTON, MA	1744-D1808

HORACE E. & JABEZ L. BALDWIN
ISAAC & HORACE E. BALDWIN
(See Dealer listings)

HENRY BALL	NEW YORK, NY	1812-1832
MARGUAND & CO.	NEW YORK, NY	1832-1839

Partners:
    Frederick Marguand
    Josiah Marguand
    Erastus O. Tomkins
    Henry Ball

BALL (HENRY), TOMKINS (ERASTUS O.) & BLACK (WILLIAM)	NEW YORK, NY	1839-1851
BALL (HENRY), BLACK (WILLIAM), & CO.	NEW YORK, NY	1851-1874

Adv. in the *Army-Navy Journal* as manufacturers
  and importers of presentation and U.S. regulation
  swords for the army and navy, plus other military
  swords (1863-1864).
Displayed presentation swords at the New York Fair (1864).

BLACK (WILLIAM), STARR & FROST	NEW YORK, NY	1874-1908
BLACK, STARR & FROST INC.	NEW YORK, NY	1908-1929
BLACK, STARR & FROST-GORHAM INC.	NEW YORK, NY	1929-1940
BLACK, STARR & GORHAM INC.	NEW YORK, NY	1940-1962
BLACK, STARR & FROST LTD.	NEW YORK, NY	1982-1990

(See Josiah & Frederick Marguand)
(See Erastus Tompkins)
(Jewelers, Military Goods, Regulation and Presentation Swords)

S.S. BALL
(See John L. Low-Dealer listings)

WILLIAM BALL SR.	PHILADELPHIA, PA	B1729, 1750-D1810

(Pewterer, Goldsmith, Brass Founder, Clock Maker, Jeweler, Military Goods)

WILLIAM BALL JR.	PHILADELPHIA, PA	B1763-1785

Bought blades from Samuel Harvey, Birmingham, England.
Imported blades from France and Germany.
Bought blades from William Rose.

JOHNSON (ISRAEL H.) & BALL (WILLIAM J.)	BALTIMORE, MD	1785-1790
WILLIAM BALL JR.	BALTIMORE, MD	1790-1811

Made eagle-head officer hangers and short sabers. 60 Market Street

BALL (WILLIAM JR.) & HEALD (JOHN S.)	BALTIMORE, MD	1811-D1815

William Ball Jr. died (1815).
(See Israel Johnson)
(See John S. Heald)
(See William Rose-Maker listings)
(Goldsmith, Clock Maker)

JOSEPH & GEORGE BANKS
(See Maker listings)

C.G. BARDECK	PHILADELPHIA, PA	1830-1836
GEORGE BARDECK	PHILADELPHIA, PA	1755-1802

Apprentice to Richard Humphreys (1772-1774).
(See Richard Humphreys)
(Goldsmith)

JOHN BARDECK	PHILADELPHIA, PA	1800-1810
JOSEPH J. BARRAS	PHILADELPHIA, PA	1830-1860
BARRAS (JOSEPH J.) & HEADLY	PHILADELPHIA, PA	1860-1865
JOSHUA L. BARRAS	PHILADELPHIA, PA	1835-1840
ROSWELL BARTHOLOMEW	HARTFORD, CT	B1781-1804
WARD (JAMES) & BARTHOLOMEW (ROSWELL)	HARTFORD, CT	1804-1809
WARD (JAMES), BARTHOLOMEW (ROSWELL) & BRAINARD (CHARLES)	HARTFORD, CT	1809-D1830

(See Charles Brainard)
(See James Ward-Dealer listings)

STANDISH BARRY	BALTIMORE, MD	B1763, 1784-D1844

Bought blades from William Rose.
Made eagle-head pommel swords.

ERASTUS BARTON	NEW YORK, NY	1790-1815
ERASTUS BARTON & CO.	NEW YORK, NY	1815-1820

Partner: Isaac Marguand.

MARGUAND (ISAAC) & BARTON (ERASTUS)	NEW YORK, NY	1820-1823

Erastus Barton died (1823).
(Jeweler, Military Goods)

JOSEPH BARTON	STOCKBRIDGE, MA	B1764-1804
	UTICA, NY	1804-1811
BARTON (JOSEPH) & PORTER	UTICA, NY	1811-1816
JOSEPH BARTON	UTICA, NY	1816-1826
BARTON (JOSEPH) & CLARK (WILLIAM)	UTICA, NY	1826-1829
BARTON (JOSEPH) & SMITH	UTICA, NY	1829-1831
BARTON (JOSEPH) & BUTLER (JAMES F.)	UTICA, NY	1831-D1832

(See Joseph S. Porter-Dealer listings)

WILLIAM BATEMAN	NEW YORK, NY	1755-1783

MILES BEACH
(See Dealer listings)

JOHN ANTHONY BEAU	NEW YORK, NY	1750-1770
	PHILADELPHIA, PA	1770-1775

(Engraver)

GEORGE W. BECHTEL & CO.	PHILADELPHIA, PA	1840-1861
BECHTEL (GEORGE W.) & SONS	PHILADELPHIA, PA	1861-1865
GEORGE BECHTEL	PHILADELPHIA, PA	1865
HENRY BECHTEL	PHILADELPHIA, PA	1815-1820

CHARLES FREDERICK BECKEL
(See Maker listings)

J.M. BEEBE & CO.	BOSTON, MA	1861-1865

Made presentation swords.

STANTON BEEBE	PROVIDENCE, RI	B1796-1825
GORHAM (JABEZ) & BEEBE (STANTON)	PROVIDENCE, RI	1825-1831
STANTON BEEBE	PROVIDENCE, RI	1831-1835

(See Jabez Gorham)

JAMES M. BENNETT	PHILADELPHIA, PA	1820-1843
BENNETT (JAMES M.)		
& CALDWELL (JAMES E.)	PHILADELPHIA, PA	1843-1848
JAMES E. CALDWELL & CO.	PHILADELPHIA, PA	1848-1881

Partner: James M. Bennett.
(See James E. Caldwell)
(Clock Maker)

JOHN BENNETT SR.	NEW YORK, NY	1815-1823
BENNETT (JOHN S.), COOKE (D.C.) & CO.		
	NEW YORK, NY	1823-1826
PELLETREAU (MALTBY),		
BENNETT (JOHN SR.) & COOK (D.C.)	NEW YORK, NY	1826-1827
PELLETREAU (MALTBY),		
BENNETT (JOHN SR.) & CO.	NEW YORK, NY	1827-1829

(See Malby Pelletreau)

JOSEPH BEST (Goldsmith)	PHILADELPHIA, PA	1700-1723
ROBERT BEST	PHILADELPHIA, PA CINCINNATI, OH	1790-1812 1812-D1831
SAMUEL BEST	PHILADELPHIA, PA CINCINNATI, OH	B1776-1802 1802-1806
BEST (SAMUEL) & DETERLY (JACOB)	CINCINNATI, OH	1806-1810
SAMUEL BEST (See Jacob Deterly)	CINCINNATI, OH	1810-D1859
OWEN BIDDLE (Clock Maker)	PHILADELPHIA, PA	B1737, 1764-D1799
SAMUEL BIDDLE	PHILADELPHIA, PA	1840-1861
KRIDER (PETER L.) & BIDDLE (SAMUEL)	PHILADELPHIA, PA	1861-1878
BAILEY (JOSEPH TROWBRIDGE), BANKS (GEORGE W.) & BIDDLE (SAMUEL)	PHILADELPHIA, PA	1878-1894

Made presentation swords.
(See Peter L. Krider-Dealer listings)
(See J.T. Bailey-Dealer listings)

BLACK, STARR & FROST
WILLIAM BLACK
BALL, TOMKINS & BLACK
(See Henry Ball)

JAMES & JOHN BLACK
(See Dealer listings)

ELIHU BLISS	NEWARK, NJ	1820-1842
BALDWIN (HORACE) & CO.	NEWARK, NJ	1842-1870

Partners: Isaac Baldwin, Elihu Bliss.
(See Isaac & Horace E. Baldwin)
(Jeweler)

ELIHU A. BLISS	NEWARK, NJ	1860-1875
CARPENTER (J.E.) & BLISS (ELIHU A.)	NEWARK, NJ	1875-1882
CARPENTER (J.E.) & BLISS (ELIHU A.) INC.	NEWARK, NJ	1882-1883
E. (ELIHU) A. BLISS & CO.	NORTH ATTLEBORO, MA	1883-1890
E. (ELIHU) A. BLISS INC.	MERIDEN, CT	1890-1920
NAPIER-BLISS CO.	MERIDEN, CT	1920-1922
NAPIER CO.	MERIDEN, CT	1922-1993
JONATHAN BLISS	MIDDLETOWN, CT	1785-1802
HART (JUDAH) & BLISS (JONATHAN)	MIDDLETOWN, CT	1803-1804
HUGHES (EDMUND) & BLISS (JONATHAN)	MIDDLETOWN, CT	1805-1806

(See Edmund Hughes)
(See Judah Hart)

STEPHEN BOARDMAN
(See Maker listings)

L.T. BOLAND
(See Dealer listings)

WILLIAM BOLTON (BOULTON)	**PHILADELPHIA, PA**	**1797-1808**
BOLTON (WILLIAM) & HORN (HENRY)	**PHILADELPHIA, PA**	**1808-1813**

(See Henry Horn)

ABRAHAM BOMPER	**BETHLEHEM, PA**	**B1705, 1725-D1793**
TIMOTHY BONTECOU SR.	**STRATFORD, CT**	**B1693, 1713-D1784**

Made silver-hilted colichemarde small swords.

TIMOTHY BONTECOU JR.	**STRATFORD, CT**	**B1723, 1743-D1789**
WILLIAM BOYD	**ALBANY, NY**	**B1775-1810**
SHEPHERD (ROBERT) & BOYD (WILLIAM)	**ALBANY, NY**	**1810-1830**
BOYD (WILLIAM) & HOYT (GEORGE B.)	**ALBANY, NY**	**1830-1832**
BOYD (WILLIAM) & MULFORD (JOHN K.)	**ALBANY, NY**	**1832-1840**

(See Robert Shepherd)
(See George Hunt)
(See John K. Mulford)

CHARLES BRAINARD	**HARTFORD, CT**	**B1787-1809**
WARD (JAMES) BARTHOLOMEW (ROSWELL) & BRAINARD (CHARLES)	**HARTFORD, CT**	**1809-1830**
C. (CHARLES) BRAINARD & SON (CHARLES H.)	**HARTFORD, CT**	**1830-D1850**

(See Roswell Bartholomew)
(See James Ward-Dealer listings)

EPHRIAM BRASHER	**NEW YORK, NY**	**B1744, 1766-1789**

Made silver-hilted hunting swords.
Made a dog-head pommel hunting sword
   for Ethan Allen.

E. (EPHRIAM) BRASHER & CO.	**NEW YORK, NY**	**1790-D1810**

Imported German blades.

JAMES BREARLEY
(See Maker listings)

CHARLES BREWER	**MIDDLETOWN, CT**	**B1778-1800**
HART (JUDAH) & BREWER (CHARLES)	**MIDDLETOWN, CT**	**1800-1803**
BREWER (CHARLES) & MANN (ALEXANDER)	**MIDDLETOWN, CT**	**1803-1805**
CHARLES BREWER	**MIDDLETOWN, CT**	**1806-D1860**

(See Judah Hart)
(See Alexander Mann)

NICHOLAS BROOKS
(See Dealer listings)

WILLIAM & ISAAC BROOME
(See Maker listings)

D. (DAVIS) BROWN	PHILADELPHIA, PA	1811-1815
EBENEZER BROWN	BOSTON, MA	1773-1816
JAMES BROWN (Goldsmith)	PHILADELPHIA, PA	1770-1785
LIBERTY BROWN	BALTIMORE, MD	1770-1794
BROWN (LIBERTY) & HOULTON (JOHN)	BALTIMORE, MD	1794-1798
LIBERTY BROWN	PHILADELPHIA, PA	1799-1809
BROWN (LIBERTY) & SEALE (WILLIAM)	PHILADELPHIA, PA	1810-1811
LIBERTY BROWN Bought blades from William Rose. Made presentation swords for War of 1812. (See William Seale) (See John Houlton) (Goldsmith)	PHILADELPHIA, PA	1811-1819
MATTHEW BROWN	EAST PENNSBORO TOWNSHIP, PA Cumberland County	1750
ROBERT JOHNSON BROWN	BOSTON, MA	1790-1809
DAVID (SAMUEL & ELIAS) **& BROWN (ROBERT JOHNSON)**	BOSTON, MA	1809-1821
R.J. BROWN	BOSTON, MA	1821-1833
R.J. BROWN & SON	BOSTON, MA	1833-1835
SETH E. BROWN (See Dealer listings)		
WILLIAM BROWN (Silver Plater)	ALBANY, NY	1830-D1859
WILLIAM BROWN (Jeweler, Watch Maker)	PHILADELPHIA, PA	1820-1840
CHARLES OLIVER, JAMES, JOSEPH SR. & JR. **& THOMAS BRUFF III** (See Maker listings)		
BENJAMIN BUCKMAN	WRIGHTSTOWN TOWNSHIP, PA Bucks County	1762-1782
ADRIAN, ABEL, JOHN, D.H. & SAMUEL BUELL (See Maker listings)		
GEORGE BURRELL (See Dealer listings)		
BENJAMIN BURT Made silver-mounted colichemarde small swords and court swords.	BOSTON, MA	B1727, 1750-D1805

JOHN BURT	BOSTON, MA	B1691, 1711-D1745
SAMUEL BURT	BOSTON, MA	B1724, 1744-D1754
WILLIAM BURT	BOSTON, MA	B1726, 1746-D1752

JAMES E. (EMOTT) CALDWELL　　　PHILADELPHIA, PA　　　1836-1839
Made presentation swords.
BENNETT (JAMES M.)
& CALDWELL (JAMES E.)　　　PHILADELPHIA, PA　　　1839-1848
J. (JAMES) E. CALDWELL & CO.　　　PHILADELPHIA, PA　　　1848-1992
Partners:
　　George W. Banks
　　Edwin Langton
　　James M. Bennett
　　Richard A. Lewis
James E. Caldwell died (1881).
Made a presentation sword for Admiral Schley (1898).
Sold M1902 saber for all officers.
(See James M. Bennett)
(See George W. Banks-Dealer listings)
(Jeweler, Watch Maker)

SAMUEL CALDWELL　　　PHILADELPHIA, PA　　　1810-1848
FILLEY (DAVID), MEAD (JOHN O.)
& CALDWELL (SAMUEL)　　　PHILADELPHIA, PA　　　1848-1875
(See John O'Mead)

CANFIELD BROTHER & CO.
(See Dealer listings)

MICHAEL CARIO　　　LONDON, ENGLAND　　　1708-1728
　　　　　　　　　　　　　　NEW YORK, NY　　　　　1728-1734
　　　　　　　　　　　　　　PHILADELPHIA, PA　　　1734-1748

(Goldsmith)

WILLIAM I. CARIO SR.　　　BOSTON, MA　　　　B1734-1741
　　　　　　　　　　　　　　NEW YORK, NY　　　1742-1763
　　　　　　　　　　　　　　PORTSMOUTH, NH　　1763-1789
　　　　　　　　　　　　　　NEW MARKET, NH　　1790-1808
　　　　　　　　　　　　　　NEWFIELDS, NH　　　D1809

Imported French blades.
Made silver-hilted small swords.

JOHN CARMAN (CARNAN)　　　PHILADELPHIA, PA　　　1751-1772
Adv. sword hilting (1771).
CHRISTOPHER HUGHES & CO.　　　BALTIMORE, MD　　　1773-1774
Partner: John Carman.
JOHN CARMAN　　　KINGSTON, NY　　　1774-1776
　　　　　　　　　　NEW YORK, NY　　　1776-1786

(See Christopher Hughes)
(Goldsmith)

JOHN M. CARTER
(See Maker listings)

OTIS G. CARTER
(See Harvey R. Caberay-Dealer listings)

THOMAS & JOSEPH CAVE
(See Maker listings)

THOMAS CHADWICK & HEIMS	ALBANY, NY	1800-1810
THOMAS CHADWICK	PHILADELPHIA, PA	1810-1825

LEWIS & CHARLES CHAMBERLAIN
(See Dealer listings)

JOHN, ISAAC, ELLIS, & BENJAMIN CHANDLEE
(See Maker listings)

CLAUDIUS & EASTON CHAP
(See Maker listings)

JOHN CHAPMAN
(See Maker listings)

BERIAH CHITTENDEN	NEW HAVEN, CT	B1751, 1770-D1827
EBENEZER CHITTENDEN	NEW HAVEN, CT	B1726-1764
BUELL (ABEL) & CHITTENDEN (EBENEZER)	NEW HAVEN, CT	1765
EBENEZER CHITTENDEN	NEW HAVEN, CT	1766-D1783

Musket and bayonet maker and arms repair
  for Committee of Safety (1776-1783).
(See Abel Buell-Maker listings)
(Gunsmith)

C. CHOUSO	HUDSON VALLEY, NY	1750-1780

Made silver-mounted hunting swords.

JOSEPH CHURCH	HARTFORD, CT	B1794, 1815-1825
CHURCH (JOSEPH)		
& ROGERS (WILLIAM & JOSEPH)	HARTFORD, CT	1825-1836
JOSEPH CHURCH	HARTFORD, CT	1836-D1876

BENJAMIN, EPHRAIM, ELLIS, EDWARD, CHARLES, JESSE & ELIAS CLARK
(See Maker listings)

CURTIS H. CLARK
CLARK, PELLETREAU & UPTON
(See Maltby Pelletreau)

FRANCIS C. CLARK	AUGUSTA, GA	1816-1821
F. (FRANCIS) C. CLARK & CO.	AUGUSTA, GA	1822-1829
F. (FRANCIS) C. & H. (HORACE) CLARK	AUGUSTA, GA	1830-1839
CLARK (FRANCIS C. & HORACE)		
& RACKETT (GEORGE) & CO.	AUGUSTA, GA	1840-1852

George Rackett died (1852).

A.W. & ISAAC COATS
(See Maker listings)

WILLIAM COLEY	NEW YORK, NY	1746-1766
WILLIAM & SIMEON COLEY	NEW YORK, NY	1766-1786
VAN VOORHIS (DANIEL) & COLEY (WILLIAM)	NEW YORK, NY	1786-1790

Partner: Reuban Harmon.
(See Daniel Van Voorhis-Dealer listings)

PELEG COLLINS
(See Dealer listings)

WILLIAM COLLINS
(See Maker listings)

JOHN CONEY
(See Maker listings)

WILLIAM A., JOHN G., & JAMES CONNING
(See Confederate Maker listings)

D.C. COOKE
(See Maltby Pelletreau)

OLIVER B. COOLEY	UTICA, NY	B1809-1830
STORRS (CHARLES) & COOLEY (OLIVER B.)	UTICA, NY	1831-1839
TANNER (PERRY G.) & COOLEY (OLVIER B.)	UTICA, NY	1840-1842
OLIVER B. COOLEY	UTICA, NY	1843-D1844

(See Charles Storrs-Dealer listings)
(See Perry G. Tanner)

GARRETT COOPER
BENJAMIN COOPER
JEREMIAH COOPER
B. & J. COOPER
HENRY T. COOPER
H.T. & A. COOPER
COOPER & POND
(See Dealer listings)

ABRAHAM CORK
(See Maker listings)

ABEL COTTEY
(See Maker listings)

ROBERT COWELL
(See Maker listings)

WILLIAM COWELL JR.	BOSTON, MA	1713-1761

Made silver-hilted small swords.

ALBION COX
(See Maker listings)

CHARLES H. CRUMP
(See John J. Low-Dealer listings)

JOHN N. DARBY
(See Confederate listings)

EDMUND J. DAUMONT	LEXINGTON, KY	1810-1820
E. (EDMUND) J. DAUMONT & CO.	LEXINGTON, KY	1820-1859
JAMES I. LEMON & CO.	LOUISVILLE, KY	1859-1861

Partner: Edmund J. Daumont.

JOHN DAVID SR.	PHILADELPHIA, PA	B1776-1763
	NEW YORK, NY	1763-1792
DAVID (JOHN SR. & JR.) & DUPUY		
(DANIEL SR., DANIEL JR. & JOHN)	PHILADELPHIA, PA	1792-1805

John David Sr. died (1793).

JOHN DAVID JR.	PHILADELPHIA, PA	1772-1792
DAVID (JOHN SR. & JR.) & DUPUY		
(DANIEL SR., DANIEL JR. & JOHN)	PHILADELPHIA, PA	1792-1805

(See Daniel Dupuy)

DAVIS & BROWN
DAVIS & WATSON
THOMAS ASPINWALL DAVIS
SAMUEL DAVIS
(See Samuel Davis-Dealer listings)

WILLIAM B. DEITRICH
(See Dealer listings)

CORNELIUS BROUWER DEREIMER	ITHACA, NY	B1804-1830
DEREIMER (CORNELIUS BROUWER)		
& MEAD (EDWARD & EDMUND)	ITHACA, NY	1830-1831
C. (CORNELIUS) B. (BROUWER) DEREIMER		
	ITHACA, NY	1831-1833
CORNELIUS BROUWER DEREIMER	ITHACA, NY	1833-D1872

(See Edward Edmund Mead-Dealer listings)

JACOB DETERLY	CINCINNATI, OH	B1786-1806
BEST (SAMUEL) & DETERLY (JACOB)	CINCINNATI, OH	1806-1810
WOODRUFF (ENOS) & DETERLY (JACOB)	CINCINNATI, OH	1810-1820
JACOB DETERLY	CINCINNATI, OH	1820-D1848

(See Enos Woodruff-Dealer listings)

ABRAHAM H. DEWITT
(See Confederate listings)

THOMAS & WILLIAM DICKEY
(See Maker listings)

JAMES A. DILLON
(See Maker listings)

SERIL DODGE	NORWICH, CT	B1757, 1777-1783
	PROVIDENCE, RI	1784-D1802

Used Sheffield plating.
Made silver shoe buckles.
(Clocksmith)

NEHEMIAH DODGE	PROVIDENCE, RI	1790-1824

Son of Seril Dodge.
(Clocksmith)

JACOB DOLFINGER	LOUISVILLE, KY	B1820, 1848-1855
DOLFINGER (JACOB) & HUDSON (HENRY)	LOUISVILLE, KY	1855-1858
HIRSHBUHL (JOSEPH J.)		
& DOLFINGER (JACOB)	LOUISVILLE, KY	1858-1864
JACOB DOLFINGER	LOUISVILLE, KY	1864-D1892

(See Henry Hudson)
(See Joseph J. Hirshbuhl-Dealer listings)

JOSEPH DRAPER	WILMINGTON, DE	B1800, 1816-1832
Made silver-hilted small swords.		
	CINCINNATI, OH	1832-D1864

GEORGE CHRISTOPHER DREWRY	PHILADELPHIA, PA	B1724, 1750-1775
	BALTIMORE, MD	1779-D1808

BENJAMIN DROWNE	PORTSMOUTH, NH	B1759, 1779-D1793

SAMUEL DROWNE	PORTSMOUTH, NJ	B1749, 1770-D1815

Made silver-hilted eagle-head hunting swords.

WILLIAM DUANE	PHILADELPHIA, PA	1810-1815

DANIEL DUPUY SR.	NEW YORK, NY	B1719-1783

Apprentice: Joseph Evans (1772-1779).
Made silver pillow-hilt swords.

DANIEL DUPUY & SONS	PHILADELPHIA, PA	1784-1791

Partners: Daniel Dupuy Jr., John Dupuy.

DAVID (JOHN SR. & JR.) & DUPUY		
(DANIEL SR., DANIEL JR. & JOHN)	PHILADELPHIA, PA	1792-1805
DANIEL DUPUY SR.	PHILADELPHIA, PA	1805-D1807

(Clock Maker)

DANIEL DUPUY JR.	NEW YORK, NY	B1753-1784
DANIEL DUPUY & SONS	PHILADELPHIA, PA	1784-1791

Partners: Daniel Dupuy Sr., John Dupuy.

DAVID (JOHN SR. & JR.) & DUPUY		
(DANIEL SR., DANIEL JR. & JOHN)	PHILADELPHIA, PA	1792-1805
DANIEL DUPUY JR.	PHILADELPHIA, PA	1805-D1826

JOHN DUPUY	NEW YORK, NY	B1747-1784
DANIEL DUPUY & SONS	PHILADELPHIA, PA	1784-1791
DAVID & DUPUY	PHILADELPHIA, PA	1792-1805
JOHN DUPUY	PHILADELPHIA, PA	1805-D1838

EAGLES & MORRIS
(See Perry & Eagles)

MOSES EASTMAN	CONCORD, NH	B1794-1826
J. PENFIELD & CO	CONCORD, NH	1825-1828

Partner: Moses Eastman.

MOSES EASTMAN	CONCORD, NH	1828-D1850
SETH EASTMAN	CONCORD, NH	B1801, 1821-D1885
JOHN EDWARDS	BOSTON, MA	B1671-1699
ALLEN (JOHN) & EDWARDS (JOHN)	BOSTON, MA	1700-1707
JOHN EDWARDS	ANNAPOLIS, MD	1708-D1746

Made silver-hilted small swords.
(See John Allen)

JACOB, JAMES & WILLIAM EGE
(See Confederate listings)

ANDREW & JOSEPH ELLICOTT
(See Maker listings)

C. (CHARLES) M. ENGLEHART	PHILADELPHIA, PA	1835-1865
M. ENGLEHART	PHILADELPHIA, PA	1835-1840

JOHN ENGLISH
(See Maker listings)

DAVID, JOSEPH, LEWIS & WILLIAM EVANS
(See Maker listings)

CHARLES EVERTZ (EBERTS)
(See Maker listings)

JAMES EYLAND
EYLAND & HAYDEN
(See Dealer listings)

WILLIAM FABER	PHILADELPHIA, PA	1820-1835
FABER (WILLIAM) & HOOPER (JOSEPH E.)	PHILADELPHIA, PA	1835-1840
WILLIAM FABER	PHILADELPHIA, PA	1840-1868
	NEW ORLEANS, LA	1868-1881
ROBERT FAIRCHILD	DURHAM, CT	B1738-1746
	STRATFORD, CT	1747-1779
	NEW YORK, NY	1780-D1794

Made silver-hilted hunting swords.

JACOB FASER
(See Confederate Maker listings)

WILLIAM P. FESSENDEN	PROVIDENCE, RI	1840-1857
WHITING, FESSENDEN & COWAN	PROVIDENCE, RI	1858

WILLIAM P. FESSENDEN & CO.	PROVIDENCE, RI	1858-1860
FESSENDEN & CO.	PROVIDENCE, RI	1860-1922

JACOB, JOHN SR. & JOHN FESSLER JR.
(See Maker listings)

JOHN FITCH
(See Maker listings)

THOMAS & CHARLES FLETCHER
FLETCHER & GARDINER
(See Dealer listings)

HENRY FLOWER
(See Maker listings)

FORBES FAMILY
(See Maker listing)

SAMUEL, PETER, JOHN SR., JOHN JR.,
  GEORGE SR., GEORGE JR. & WILLIAM FORD
(See Maker listings)

GEORGE B. FOSTER
(See Dealer listings)

JOHN FOSTER	NEW YORK, NY	1790-1811
FOSTER (JOHN) & RICHARD (THOMAS)	NEW YORK, NY	1811-1815
PHILLIPS & FOSTER (JOHN)	WINCHESTER, VA	1816-1824
JOHN FOSTER	WOODSTOCK, VA	1825
	MARTINBURG, VA	1826-1835

(See Thomas Richards)

JULIUS G. FRANCIS	MIDDLETOWN, CT	B1785-1801
HUGHES (EDMOND) & FRANCIS (JULIUS G.)	MIDDLETOWN, CT	1807-1809
JULIUS G. FRANCIS	MIDDLETOWN, CT	1810-D1858

(See Edmund Hughes)

THOMAS FURNIES	PHILADELPHIA, PA	1860-1865

LEOPOLD FURTWENGLER
(See Maker listings)

M.W., SAMUEL, JAMES & WILLIAM GALT
(See Dealers listings)

ROBERT & CHARLES GAMBLE
(See Maker listings)

SIDNEY GARDINER	BOSTON, MA	1790-1808
BALDWIN GARDINER	BOSTON, MA	1790-1808
FLETCHER (THOMAS & CHARLES)		
& GARDINER (BALDWIN & SIDNEY)	BOSTON, MA	1809-1811
	PHILADELPHIA, PA	1812-1825

BALDWIN GARDINER & CO. (See Fletcher & Gardiner-Dealer listings)	NEW YORK, NY	1825-1840

PHILIP, THOMAS GARRETT
(See Maker listings)

GEDDY FAMILY
(See Makers listings)

HUGH GELSTON
(See Dealer listings)

ROBERT, JOHN & WILLIAM GETHEN
(See Dealer listings)

CAESAR & WILLIAM GHISELIN (GISLING)
(See Maker listings)

JOHN GIBBS	PROVIDENCE, RI	B1751, 1780-D1797
CHRISTOPHER GIFFINGS Made silver-mounted eagle-head-pommel sabers.	NEW YORK, NY	1805-1835
WILLIAM GILBERT Made silver-hilted lion-head hunting swords.	NEW YORK, NY	B1746, 1767-D1818
JOHN WARD GILMAN	EXETER, NH	B1774, 1792-D1823

JACOB GMINDER
(See Maker listings)

DAVID GOBRECHT
(See Maker listings)

DANIEL T. GOODHUE
(See Dealer listings)

JABEZ GORHAM	PROVIDENCE, RI	B1792-1825
GORHAM (JABEZ) & BEEBE (STANTON)	PROVIDENCE, RI	1825-1831
GORHAM (JABEZ) & WEBSTER (HENRY L.)	PROVIDENCE, RI	1831-1837
GORHAM (JABEZ), WEBSTER (HENRY L.), & PRICE (WILLIAM G.)	PROVIDENCE, RI	1837-1841
J. (JABEZ) GORHAM & SONS Partners and sons: Henry Owen Gorham, John Gorham (B1820-D1898). Jabez Gorham retired (1850). Jabez Gorham died (1869).	PROVIDENCE, RI	1841-1850
GORHAM (JOHN) & THURBER (GORHAM)	PROVIDENCE, RI	1850-1852
GORHAM (JOHN) & CO. Partner: Lewis Dexter. Bought Collins blades. Sold M1850 foot officer swords.	PROVIDENCE, RI	1852-1865
GORHAM MANUFACTURING CO. Purchased Whiting Mfg. Co. (1926).	PROVIDENCE, RI	1865-1961

GORHAM CORPORATION Division of Textron Corp. since 1967. (See Whiting Mfg. Co.)	PROVIDENCE, RI	1961-1993

RENE GRAVELLE
(See Dealer listings)

WILLIAM H. GRAY
(See Maker listings)

WILLIAM GREGG
(See Dealer listings)

BENJAMIN GRIGNON	CHARLESTON, SC OXFORD, MA BOSTON, MA	1675-1685 1685-1696 1696-1708
RENE GRIGNON	OXFORD, MA BOSTON, MA NORWICH, CT	1691-1695 1696-1708 1708-D1715

ARTHUR BREEZE GRISWOLD
(See James E. Hyde-Dealer listings)
(See Confederate Maker listings)

HENRY BROWN GUEST
(See Maker listings)

CHARLES HALL Brother of David Hall Sr. (Clock Maker, Goldsmith)	LANCASTER, PA	B1742, 1755-D1795
DAVID HALL SR.	LANCASTER, PA PHILADELPHIA, PA	1740-1765 1765-1777
Made silver-mounted dog-head-pommel short sabers. Benjamin Franklin was an engraver partner. (Goldsmith)	BURLINGTON, NJ	1777-D1779
DAVID HALL JR. Son of Charles Hall.	LANCASTER, PA	B1767, 1786-D1814

IVORY HALL
(See Dealer listings)

BENJAMIN HALSTED	NEW YORK, NY	1744-1763
MYERS (MYER) & HALSTED (BENJAMIN)	NEW YORK, NY	1764-1768
BENJAMIN & MATTHIAS HALSTED	ELIZABETHTOWN, NY	1769
BENJAMIN HALSTED	PHILADELPHIA, PA	1770-1785
BENJAMIN HALSTED (Goldsmith)	NEW YORK, NY	1786-1814

SAMUEL, CROSBY, & PETER HAMMOND
(See Maker listings)

NEWELL HARDING
(See Dealer listings)

REUBEN HARMAN	NEW YORK, NY	B1750-D1806

Partner in Van Voorhis & Coley (1786-1790).

THOMAS HARPER	CHARLESTOWN, SC	1773-1782

(Goldsmith)

ORLANDO HARRIMAN
(See Marguand)

HARRIS & STANWOOD
(See Dealer listings)

GEORGE HARRIS
(See Maker listings)

ELIPHAZ HART	NORWICH, CT	B1787, 1807-D1866
FERDINAND HART	PITTSBURGH, PA	1800-1818
MORGAN (GIDEON) & HART (FERDINAND)	PITTSBURGH, PA	1818-1870

(See Gideon Morgan)

JOHN HART	PHILADELPHIA, PA	1755-1775

(Cutler)

JUDAH HART	BERLIN, CT	B1777-1800
HART (JUDAH) & BREWER (CHARLES)	MIDDLETOWN, CT	1800-1803
HART (JUDAH) & BLISS (JONATHAN)	MIDDLETOWN, CT	1803-1804
HART (JUDAH) & WILCOX (ALVAN)	NORWICH, CT	1804-1807
JUDAH HART	GRISWALD, MD	1807-D1824

Used Sheffield plating on some sword hilts.
(See Charles Brewer, Jonathan Bliss and Alvan Wilcox)

WALTER HART	PHILADELPHIA, PA	1830-1850
WILLIAM HART	BALTIMORE, MD	1790-1814
HART (WILLIAM) & SMITH (JOHN)	BALTIMORE, MD	1814-1818
WILLIAM HART	PHILADELPHIA, PA	1818-1824

(Clock Maker)

SAMUEL HARTLEY	PHILADELPHIA, PA	1818-1827
	PHILADELPHIA, PA	1827-1828
	PHILADELPHIA, PA	1828-1837
GARRETT (PHILIP) & HARTLEY (SAMUEL)	PHILADELPHIA, PA	1837-1839
CLARK (GEORGE) & HARTLEY (SAMUEL)	PHILADELPHIA, PA	1839-1841
SAMUEL HARTLEY	PHILADELPHIA, PA	1841-1865

(See Philip Garrett)

PHILIP HARTMAN	PHILADELPHIA, PA	1800-1815

Made silver-hilted eagle-head short sabers.

HENRY HAUSMAN
T. HAUSMAN
(See Dealer listings)

JOHN DEAN HAWLEY	SYRACUSE, NY	B1821-1840
WILLARD (WILLIAM W.) & HAWLEY (JOHN DEAN)	SYRACUSE, NY	1840-1872
JOHN DEAN HAWLEY	SYRACUSE, NY	1872-D1913

(See William W. Willard-Dealer listings)

NATHANIEL HAYDEN
(See Dealer listings)

EDEN HAYDOCK	PHILADELPHIA, PA	1820-1837
GARRETT (PHILIP) & HAYDOCK (EDEN)	PHILADELPHIA, PA	1837-1839
EDEN HAYDOCK	PHILADELPHIA, PA	1839-1852

(See Philip Garrett)
(Watch Maker)

ANDREW HAYS	NEW YORK, NY	1749-1769
HAYS (ANDREW) & MYERS (MYER)	NEW YORK, NY	1769-1770

(See Myer Myers)

NATHAN L. HAZEN
(See Dealer listings)

JOHN S. HEALD	BALTIMORE, MD	1790-1810
BALL (WILLIAM JR.) & HEALD (JOHN S.)	BALTIMORE, MD	1811-1815

(See William Ball Jr.)

DANIEL HENCHMAN	BOSTON, MA	B1736-1762
HENCHMAN (DANIEL) & POTWINE (JOHN)	BOSTON, MA	1762-D1775

Made silver-mounted hunting swords.
(See John Potwine)

ABASUERUS HENDRICKS
(See Maker listings)

EPAPHRAS HINSDALE	NEWARK, NJ	B1769-1881
E. (EPAPHRAS) HINSDALE & CO.		1881-D1910

Partner: John Taylor.

HORACE SEYMOUR HINSDALE	NEWARK, NJ	B1782-1820

Son of Epaphras Hinsdale.

TAYLOR (JOHN) & HINSDALE (HORACE SEYMOUR)	NEWARK, NJ	1810-1817
PALMER (JAMES) & HINSDALE (HORACE SEYMOUR)	NEWARK, NJ	1817-1823
HINSDALE (HORACE SEYMOUR) & ALKINS (JOHN H.)	NEWARK, NJ	1823-1838
HORACE SEYMOUR HINSDALE	NEWARK, NJ	1838-D1858

(See John Taylor)

JOSEPH HIRSCHBULH

HIRSCHBUHL & DOLFINGER
(See Dealer listings)

JOHN H., FREDERICK, WILLIAM & JAMES M. HOFFMAN
(See Maker listings)

WILLIAM HOMES SR.	BOSTON, MA	B1717, 1740-D1782
WILLIAM HOMES JR.	BOSTON, MA	B1742, 1765-D1825
HENRY HORN	PHILADELPHIA, PA	1790-1808
BOLTON (WILLIAM) & HORN (HENRY)	PHILADELPHIA, PA	1808-1813
HORN (HENRY) & KNEASS (WILLIAM)	PHILADELPHIA, PA	1813-1837
HENRY HORN	PHILADELPHIA, PA	1837-1840

(See William Kneass)
(See William Bolton)

JOHN HOULTON	BALTIMORE, MD	1774-1793
HOULTON (JOHN) & BROWN (LIBERTY)	BALTIMORE, MD	1794-1798
HOULTON (JOHN), OTTO (DAVID) & FALK	PHILADELPHIA, PA	1798-1809

(See Liberty Brown)

BENJAMIN H. HOWELL
(See Dealer listings)

SAMUEL & JAMES HOWELL
(See Maker listings)

GEORGE B. HOYT	ALBANY, NY	1820-1829
HOYT (GEORGE B.) & KIPPEN (GEORGE)	ALBANY, NY	1829-1830
BOYD (WILLIAM) & HOYT (GEORGE B.)	ALBANY, NY	1830-1832
GEORGE B. HOYT	ALBANY, NY	1832-1850

(See George Kippen)
(See William Boyd)

JOHN HUBB (HUB)   PHILADELPHIA, PA   1820-1837
Employee of Harvey Lewis.
Made silver hilts for swords designed by Lewis.
Made hilt for a sword presented
  to Colonel Jonathan W. Watmough.
(See Harvey Lewis)

JOHN & HENRY HUBER JR.
(See Maker listings)

HENRY HUDSON	LOUISVILLE, KY	1841-1855
DOLFINGER (JACOB) & HUDSON (HENRY)	LOUISVILLE, KY	1855-1858
HENRY HUDSON	LOUISVILLE, KY	1858-D1888

(See Jacob Dolfinger)

CHRISTOPHER HUGHES	BALTIMORE, MD	B1744-1773
CHRISTOPHER HUGHES & CO.	BALTIMORE, MD	1773-1774

Partner: John Carman.

CHRISTOPHER HUGHES (See John Carman)	BALTIMORE, MD	1774-D1824
EDMUND HUGHES	HAMPTON, CT	B1781-1804
WARD (JOHN) & HUGHES (EDMUND)	MIDDLETOWN, CT	1804
HUGHES (EDMUND) & BLISS (JONATHAN)	MIDDLETOWN, CT	1805-1806
HUGHES (EDMUND) & FRANCIS (JULIUS C.)	MIDDLETOWN, CT	1807-1809
EDMUND HUGHES (See John Ward) (See Julius C. Francis) (See Jonathan Bliss)	MIDDLETOWN, CT	1809-D1852
HENRY HUGHES	BALTIMORE, MD	B1756-1781
WILLIAM HUGHES	BALTIMORE, MD	B1744, 1780-D1791

RICHARD HUMPHREYS   PHILADELPHIA, PA   B1749-D1831
- Apprentice to Philip Syng Jr. (1766-1771).
- Adv. silver-mounted small swords, officers hangers, Couteaus de Chasses (1777-1781).
- Apprentices: Christian Wiltberger (1788-1793), George Bardeck (1772-1774), John Myer (1773-1778).
- Made a Congressional presentation sword for Colonel Tench Tilghman (1785).

(See Christian Wiltberger)
(See George Barbeck)
(See John Myer)
(See Philip Syng Jr.)
(Goldmsith)

EDWARD HUNT
(See Maker listings)

PHILLIP & ROSWELL HUNTINGTON
(See Maker listings)

BENJAMIN HURD   BOSTON, MA   B1739, 1760-D1787
Son of Jacob Hurd.

JACOB HURD   BOSTON, MA   B1702, 1720-D1758
Made silver-hilted colichemarde small swords and court swords.
Made swords for Colonel Richard Hazen and Colonel Thomas Noyes.

NATHANIEL HURD   BOSTON, MA   B1729, 1750-D1777
Son of Jacob Hurd.
Made silver-hilted small swords.

GEORGE HUTTON   ALBANY, NY   B1729-1799
GEORGE & ISAAC HUTTON   ALBANY, NY   1799-1806
Imported blades from Schimmelbusch (Carl) & Joest (Abraham), Solingen, Germany.
George Hutton died (1806).
(Military Goods)

ISAAC HUTTON	ALBANY, NY	1767-1799

Son of George Hutton.
Made silver-hilted eagle-head short sabers.

GEORGE & ISAAC HUTTON	ALBANY, NY	1799-1806
ISAAC HUTTON	ALBANY, NY	1806-D1855

JAMES E. HYDE
HYDE & GOODRICH
(See Confederate Dealer listings)

D.C. & EUGENE JACCARD
(See Dealer listings)

EPHRAIM, THOMAS, JOSEPH, SAMUEL, GEORGE, ISAAC, JOHN W. JACKSON
(See Maker listings)

GEORGE W. JACOBS	BALTIMORE, MD	B1775-1838
	PHILADELPHIA, PA	1839-D1846

Adv. silver-hilted swords.

JAMES, THOMAS & JOHN JENKINS
(See Maker listings)

ISRAEL A. JOHNSON	BALTIMORE, MD	1766-1785
JOHNSON (ISRAEL A.)		
& BALL (WILLIAM JR.)	BALTIMORE, MD	1785-1790
ISRAEL A. JOHNSON	EASTON, MD	1790-1793

(See William Ball Jr.)

REUBAN JOHNSON	BALTIMORE, MD	B1782-1809
JOHNSON (REUBAN) & REAT (JAMES)	RICHMOND, VA	1810-1814

During the War of 1812, they made an exquisite
  hilt for a sword designed at the Virginia
  Manufactory by John Clark. The sword was
  presented to U.S. Marine hero Lt. Presly N. O'Bannon.
Made silver-hilted short sabers.

REUBAN JOHNSON	RICHMOND, VA	1815-D1820

(See James Reat)

WILLIAM BLACKSTONE JOHNSTON
EDMUND J. JOHNSTON
(See Confederate listings)

JOHN B. JONES
(See Dealer listings)

JOHN, JAMES & DANIEL JONES
(See Dealer listings)

T. & W. KEITH
(See Dealer listings)

CHARLES & GEORGE KELLER
(See Maker listings)

WILLIAM KENDRICK	LOUISVILLE, KY	B1810-1829
HARRIS (JOHN C.) & KENDRICK (WILLIAM)	LOUISVILLE, KY	1830-1831
LEMON (JAMES INNES) **& KENDRICK (WILLIAM)**	LOUISVILLE, KY	1832-1858
WILLIAM KENDRICK	LOUISVILLE, KY	1859-D1880

Made a presentation sword for Colonel Robert Anderson.
(See James Innes Lemon-Dealer listings)
(Jeweler)

ROBERT KEYWORTH — WASHINGTON, DC — 1830-1858
(Jeweler)

JOHN & WILLIAM KING
(See Maker listings)

GEORGE KIPPEN	BRIDGEPORT, CT	B1790-1830
HOYT (GEORGE B.) & KIPPEN (GEORGE)	ALBANY, NY	1830
GEORGE KIPPEN	MIDDLETOWN, CT	1830-D1845

(See George B. Hoyt)

PETER KIRKWOOD
(See Maker listings)

JOHN H. KNAPP
(See Dealer listings)

CHRISTIAN KNEASS — PHILADELPHIA, PA — 1811-1837

WILLIAM KNEASS	PHILADELPHIA, PA	1792-1813
HORN (HENRY) & KNEASS (WILLIAM)	PHILADELPHIA, PA	1813-1837
WILLIAM KNEASS	PHILADELPHIA, PA	1837-1842

(See Henry Horn)

HENRY F. KRAFT
PETER W. KRAFT
KRAFT, GOLDSCHMIDT & KRAFT
(See Confederate Maker listings)

PETER L. KRIDER	PHILADELPHIA, PA	1850-1860
KRIDER (PETER L.) & BIDDLE (SAMUEL)	PHILADELPHIA, PA	1860-1878

Imported blades from C.R. Kirschbaum, Solingen, Germany.

PETER L. KRIDER — PHILADELPHIA, PA — 1878-1903

Simons Bros. & Co. bought Krider (1903).
(See Samuel Biddle)
(See George W. Simmons-Dealer listings)

JACOB KUCHER (KUCHLER) — PHILADELPHIA, PA — 1805-1835

Bought blades from William Rose.
Made half-basket-hilted sabers
   with helmet pommels.

PIERRE LAMOTHE	SANTIAGO, CUBA	1803-1809
	NEW ORLEANS, LA	1809-1822

PIERRE LAMOTHE & SON	NEW ORLEANS, LA	1822-1825

Imported blades from Peter William Knecht, Solingen, Germany.
Made French-style silver-hilted sabers and eagle-head swords.

PETER LANDRY
(See Maker listings)

JACOB GERRITSE LANSING	ALBANY, NY	B1681, 1736-D1767
JOHN LATCHA	READING, PA Berks County	1771-1781

FELIX, THEODORE & JOHN FELIX LEFEVRE
(See Maker listings)

JAMES INNES LEMON
(See Dealer listings)

GODFREY LEONARD
(See Maker listings)

PETER LERRETT	CARLISLE, PA Cumberland County	1775-1783

JOHN LETELIER SR.
(See Maker listings)

CURTIS, JOHN I. & THEOPHILUS LEWIS
(See Maker listings)

HARVEY LEWIS	PHILADELPHIA, PA	1785-1805
LEWIS (HARVEY) & SMITH (JOSEPH D.)	PHILADELPHIA, PA	1805-1811
HARVEY LEWIS	PHILADELPHIA, PA	1811-D1835

Hilt designer and maker.
Employee: John Hubb (silversmith).
Bought blades from William Rose.
Designed sword for Gen. Winfield Scott,
  Col. Jonathan G. Watmough, and Capt.
  Lewis Warrington ordered by the Virginia Assembly.
(See John Hubb)
(See Joseph D. Smith)
(Goldsmith)

MICHAEL LEWIS	PHILADELPHIA, PA	1790-1820
GEORGE LINDNER	PHILADELPHIA, PA	1835-1865
WILLIAM C. LITTLE	NEWBURYPORT, MA	B1745, 1765-D1816

Made silver-hilted small swords.

JAMES LOCK
(See Maker listings)

JOHN A. & WILLIAM T. L'HOMMEDIEU
(See Dealer listings)

H. LORD & CO.
(See Isaac Marguand)

JOHN L. LOW
(See Dealer listings)

**EDWARD, CALEB, DAVID, JOSEPH &
JOSEPH H. LOWNES**
(See Maker listings)

JOSEPH LUKEY	PITTSBURGH, PA	1790-D1822
Hilted dirks and swords.		
MRS. JOSEPH LUKEY	PITTSBURGH, PA	1822-1840
(Watch Maker, Goldsmith)		
JOHN LYNCH	BALTIMORE, MD	B1761, 1786-D1848
Imported Spanish blades.		
ALEXANDER MANN	MIDDLETOWN, CT	B1777-1802
BREWER (CHARLES) & MANN (ALEXANDER)	MIDDLETOWN, CT	1802-1805
BROWN & MANN (ALEXANDER)	MIDDLETOWN, CT	1805
(See Charles Brewer)		

JOSEPH MANNING
(See Maker listings)

SIMEON MARBLE	NEW HAVEN, CT	B1776-1800
SIBLEY (MARK) & MARBLE (SIMEON)	NEW HAVEN, CT	1800-1807
SIMEON MARBLE	NEW HAVEN, CT	1807-D1856
(See Clark Sibley)		
FREDERICK MARGUAND	SAVANNAH, GA	B1799-1826
J. (JOSIAH) PENFIELD & CO.	SAVANNAH, GA	1826-1828
Partners: Frederick Marguand, Moses Eastman.		
MARGUAND & BROTHER	NEW YORK, NY	1828-1831
Partners: Isaac Marguand, Frederick Marguand.		
MARGUAND & CO.	NEW YORK, NY	1831-1839
Partners:		
Frederick Marguand		
Josiah P. Marguand		
Henry Ball		
Erastus O. Tomkins.		
FREDERICK MARGUAND	NEW YORK, NY	1839-D1882
(See Erastus O. Tomkins)		
(See Henry Ball)		
(See Josiah Penfield)		
(Jeweler)		
JOSIAH P. MARGUAND	SAVANNAH, GA	1812-1832
MARGUAND & CO.	NEW YORK, NY	1832-1839
Succeeded Henry Ball.		

Partners:
    Frederick Marguand
    Josiah P. Marguand
    Henry Ball
    Erastus O. Tomkins.
Succeeded by Ball, Tomkins & Black.
(See Henry Ball)
(See Ball, Tomkins & Black)
(See Erastus Tompkins)
(Jeweler)

ISAAC MARGUAND	FAIRFIELD, CT	B1766-1786
WHITING (BRADFORD)		
& MARGUAND (ISAAC)	FAIRFIELD, CT	1786-1791
ISAAC MARGUAND	EDENTON, NC	1791-1796
	SAVANNAH, GA	1796-1801
MARGUAND (ISAAC)		
& PAULDING (CORNELIUS)	SAVANNAH, GA	1801-1805
H. (HEZEKIAH) LORD & CO.	SAVANNAH, GA	1805-1808

Partners: Isaac Marguand, Cornelius Paulding.

MARGUAND (ISAAC),		
HARRIMAN (ORLANDO) & CO.	NEW YORK, NY	1808-1812

Partner: Cornelius Paulding.

MARGUAND (ISAAC), PAULDING (CORNELIUS)		
& PENFIELD (JOSIAH) (M.P. & P.)	SAVANNAH, GA	1812-1815

Made eagle-head infantry officers swords.

ERASTUS BARTON & CO.	NEW YORK, NY	1815-1820

Partner: Isaac Marguand.

MARGUAND (ISAAC) & BARTON (ERASTUS)	NEW YORK, NY	1820-1823
ISAAC MARGUAND	NEW YORK, NY	1823-1828
MARGUAND & BROTHER	NEW YORK, NY	1828-1831

Partners: Isaac Marguand, Frederick Marguand.

ISAAC MARGUAND	NEW YORK, NY	1831-D1838

(See Bradford Whiting)
(See Cornelius Paulding)
(See Josiah Penfield)
(See Erastus Barton)
(Jeweler)

SEREPHIM MASI
(See Dealer listings)

JOHN B. MCFADDEN
(See Dealer listings)

JOHN MCMULLEN	PHILADELPHIA, PA	B1765-1795
ERWIN (HENRY) & MCMULLEN (JOHN)	PHILADELPHIA, PA	1796-1810
MCMULLEN (JOHN) & BLACK (JOHN)	PHILADELPHIA, PA	1811-1816
JOHN MCMULLEN	PHILADELPHIA, PA	1817-D1843

(See Henry Erwin)
(See John Black)

MEAD ADRIANCE & CO.
(See Dealer listings)

EDWARD EDMUND MEAD
(See Dealer listings)

JOHN O. MEAD	CHICOPEE, MA	1800-1834
Silver plater and hiltor for N.P. Ames (1829-1834).		
	LONDON, ENGLAND	1834-1839
Learned electroplating.		
	HARTFORD, CT	1839-1846
Partner in William Rogers & Co. (1840-1846).		
MEAD (JOHN O.) & SONS	PHILADELPHIA, PA	1846-1847
FILLEY (DAVID) & MEAD (JOHN O.)	PHILADELPHIA, PA	1847-1848
FILLEY (DAVID), MEAD (JOHN O.), & CALDWELL (SAMUEL)	PHILADELPHIA, PA	1848-1875

(See Samuel Caldwell)
(See William Rogers & Co.)
(See N.P. Ames-Maker listings)

WILLIAM MEADOWS
(See Maker listings)

ANTHONY H. MENKENS
(See Charles Recordon)

JOSEPH P. MEREDITH   BALTIMORE, MD   1824-1881
Partner in Canfield, Brother & Co. (1849-1881).
(See Canfield, Brother & Co.)

J. AMBROSE MERRELL
(See Dealer listings)

JOHN G.D. MEURSET	CHARLESTON, SC	1778-1804
MONK (JAMES) & MEURSET (JOHN G.D.)	CHARLESTON, SC	1805-1807
JOHN G.D. MEURSET	CHARLESTON, SC	1807-1810

(See James Monk)

PETER, GEORGE & WILLIAM MILLER
(See Maker listings)

EDMUND MILNE   PHILADELPHIA, PA   B1724, 1757-D1820
Made a sword presented to a Captain Barney (1782).
Had William Squibb as apprentice (1773-1775).
(Goldsmith)

ROBERT MILNE   PHILADELPHIA, PA   1800-1818
(Clock Maker)

SAMUEL MILNE   PHILADELPHIA, PA   1750-1770
Apprentices: James Logan, James Samuel Gordon (1769).
(Goldsmith)

MITCHELL & TYLER
(See Confederate listings)

THOMAS MIX   NEW HAVEN, CT   1764-1782

BUEL (ABEL) & MIX (THOMAS)	NEW HAVEN, CT	1783
THOMAS MIX	PHILADELPHIA, PA	1784-1801

(See Abel Buel-Maker Listing)

JAMES MONK	CHARLESTON, SC	1780-1797
ATMAR (RALPH J.) & MONK (JAMES)	CHARLESTON, SC	1797-1799
JAMES MONK & CO.	CHARLESTON, SC	1799-1805
MONK (JAMES) & MEURSET (JOHN G.D.)	CHARLESTON, SC	1805-1807
JAMES MONK	CHARLESTON, SC	1807-1810

(See John G.D. Meurset)
(See Ralph Atmar Jr.-Maker listings)
(Goldsmith, Engraver)

JOHN C. MOORE	LONDON, ENGLAND	1812-1832
JOHN C. MOORE & CO.	NEW YORK, NY	1832-1847
JOHN C. MOORE & SON (EDWARD C.)	NEW YORK, NY	1848-1854

John C. Moore retired (1854).
Edward took over the company.

EDWARD C. MOORE	NEW YORK, NY	1854-1868

John Chandler Moore (Edward's son) joined the company (1865).
Tiffany & Co. absorbed the Moore Co. (1868).
The Moores had been doing work for Tiffany & Co. since 1843.
Edward C. Moore died (1891).
(See Tiffany & Co.)

WILLIAM V. MOORE	MOBILE, AL	1835-1854
WILLIAM V. MOORE & CO.	MOBILE, AL	1854-1865

Employee of James Conning (1861-1865).
(See James Connings-Confederate listings)

CHAUNCER MORGAN
(See Dealer listings)

JOHN, GIDEON & THOMAS MORGAN
(See Maker listings)

ALEXANDER, JOHN, ANTHONY, CHARLES, AUGUSTUS, & PIERRE MORIN
(See Dealer listings)

ABEL MOULTON	NEWBURYPORT, MA	B1784-D1840
EBENEZER MOULTON	NEWBURYPORT, MA	B1768-D1824
EDWARD MOULTON	NEWBURYPORT, MA	B1846-D1907
JOSEPH MOULTON I	NEWBURYPORT, MA	B1694-D1756
JOSEPH MOULTON II	NEWBURYPORT, MA	B1724-D1795
JOSEPH MOULTON III	NEWBURYPORT, MA	B1744-D1816
JOSEPH MOULTON IV	NEWBURYPORT, MA	B1814-D1903
WILLIAM MOULTON I	NEWBURYPORT, MA	B1617-D1664
WILLIAM MOULTON II	NEWBURYPORT, MA	B1664-D1732
WILLIAM MOULTON III	NEWBURYPORT, MA	B1720-D1793

Made silver-hilted lion- and dog-head hunting swords and hangers.

WILLIAM MOULTON IV	NEWBURYPORT, MA	B1772-D1861
WILLIAM MOULTON V	NEWBURYPORT, MA	B1851-D1940
JOHN H. MULFORD	ALBANY, NY	1822-1832
BOYD (WILLIAM) & MULFORD (JOHN H.)	ALBANY, NY	1832-1842
MULFORD (JOHN H.) & WENDELL (WILLIAM)	ALBANY, NY	1843-1856

(See William Boyd)
(See William Wendell)

AMOS MUNSON
(See Makers listings)

JOHN MYERS	PHILADELPHIA, PA	B1756-1810

Made D-guard pillow-hilt short sabers.
Apprenticed to Richard Humphreys (1773-1781).

JOSEPH MYERS	LANCASTER, PA	1750-1775
MYER MYERS	NORWALK, CT	B1723-1745
	UNDERHILL, VT	1745-1764

Made silver-hilted small swords.

MYERS (MYER) & HALSTED (BENJAMIN)	NEW YORK, NY	1764-1768
HAYS (ANDREW) & MYERS (MYER)	NEW YORK, NY	1769-1770
MYER MYERS	NEW YORK, NY	1771-D1795

(See Benjamin Halsted)
(See Andrew Hays)
(Goldsmith)

DANIEL NEILD
(See Dealer listings)

DAVID B. NICHOLS
(See Dealer listings)

WASHINGTON & BEVERLY NOEL
(See Dealer listings)

JOHN NOLL SR. & JR.
(See Maker listings)

GEORGE NUNGESSOR	EASTON, PA Northampton County	1786-1796

FREDERICK OAKES
(See Dealer listings)

JONATHAN OTIS	SANDWICH, MA	B1723-1775
	MIDDLETOWN, CT	1775-1778
	NEWPORT, RI	1778-D1791

Made silver-hilted Colicheinarde small swords.

PALMER & BACHELDORS
JACOB P. PALMER
(See S. & E. Davis-Dealer listings)

JAMES PALMER	NEW YORK, NY	1798-1817
PALMER (JAMES)		
& HINSDALE (HORACE SEYMOUR)	NEW YORK, NY	1817-1823
PALMER (JAMES) & CLAPP (H.W.)	NEW YORK, NY	1823-1831
JAMES PALMER	PHILADELPHIA, PA	1831-1835
PALMER (JAMES)		
& DAVIS (JOSHUA GEORGE)	BOSTON, MA	1835-1855

WILLIAM & RICHARD PARKER
(See Maker listings)

JOHN PARKS
(See Dealer listings)

ROWLAND PARRY
THOMAS PARRY
PARRY & SMITH
JOHN J. PARRY
JOHN PARRY
(See Maker listings)

CORNELIUS PAULDING	SAVANNAH, GA	1780-1800
MARGUAND (ISAAC)		
& PAULDING (CORNELIUS)	SAVANNAH, GA	1801-1804
H. (HEZEKIAH) LORD & CO.	NEW YORK, NY	1805-1808

Partners: Cornelius Paulding, Isaac Marguand.

MARGUAND (ISAAC),		
HARRIMAN (ORLANDO) & CO.	NEW YORK, NY	1809

Partner: Cornelius Paulding.

CORNELIUS PAULDING & CO.	NEW ORLEANS, LA	1810-1811
MARGUAND (ISAAC),		
PAULDING (CORNELIUS)		
& PENFIELD (JOSIAH)	SAVANNAH, GA	1812-1815

(See Josiah Penfield)
(See Isaac Marguand)

JAMES PECKHAM
(See Dealer listings)

ELIAS PELLETREAU	SOUTH HAMPTON, NEW YORK	B1726, 1746-D1810

Made silver-mounted Colichemarde small swords.
(Jeweler)

MALTBY PELLETREAU	NEW YORK, NY	1815-1816
CLARK (CURTIS H.)		
& PELLETREAU (MALTBY)	NEW YORK, NY	1816-1817
CLARK (CURTIS H. & GREGORY),		
PELLETREAU (MALTBY)		
& UPSON (GEORGE)	NEW YORK, NY	1817-1824

MALBY PELLETREAU	NEW YORK, NY	1824-1826
PELLETREAU (MALTBY), BENNETT (JOHN SR.) & COOKE (D.C.)	NEW YORK, NY	1826-1827
PELLETREAU (MALTBY), BENNETT (JOHN SR.) & CO.	NEW YORK, NY	1827-1829

Partner: D.C. Cooke.
(See Richards Upson-Dealer listings)
(See John Bennett Sr.)
(See D.C. Cooke)

WILLIAM SMITH PELLETREAU	SOUTH HAMPTON, NY	B1786-1814
PELLETREAU (WILLIAM SMITH) & UPSON (STEPHEN)	NEW YORK, NY	1815
PELLETREAU (WILLIAM SMITH) & RICHARD (THOMAS)	NEW YORK, NY	1816-1825
PELLETREAU (WILLIAM SMITH) & VAN WYCK (STEPHEN)	NEW YORK, NY	1826-D1842

(See Thomas Richard)
(Jeweler)

JAMES S. PEMBERTON
(See Dealer listings)

JOSIAH PENFIELD	SAVANNAH, GA	B1785-1811
MARGUAND (ISAAC), PAULDING (CORNELIUS) & PENFIELD (JOSIAH)	SAVANNAH, GA	1812-1826
J. (JOSIAH) PENFIELD & CO.	SAVANNAH, GA	1826-D1828

Partners: Moses Eastman, Frederick Marguand.
(See Moses Eastman)
(See Cornelius Paulding)
(See Isaac & Frederick Marguand)

PETER PERDRIAUX (PERREAUX-PERRAUX)	PHILADELPHIA, PA	1795-1800
PETER G. PERDRIAUX	PHILADELPHIA, PA	1856-1865
S. PERDRIAUX	PHILADELPHIA, PA	1825-1833

THOMAS & JACOB PERKINS
(See Maker listings)

EAGLES & MORRIS (JOHN)	NEW YORK, NY	1799-1805
PERRY & EAGLES	NEW YORK, NY	1805-1806

JOHN PHILLIPS
(See Maker listings)

WILLIAM PINCHIN SR. & JR.
(See Maker listings)

JOHN H. PIPPEN
(See James Conning-Confederate listings)

HORACE PORTER	BOSTON, MA	1805-1827
Employee at George I. Welles & Co. (1825-1827).		
HORACE PORTER & CO.	BOSTON, MA	1827-1833
(See George I. Welles)		
(Military Goods)		

JOSEPH S. PORTER
(See Dealer listings)

JOHN POTWINE	HARTFORD, CT	B1698-1735
POTWINE (JOHN) & WHITING		
(CAPTAIN CHARLES)	HARTFORD, CT	1735-1762
HENCHMAN (DANIEL)		
& POTWINE (JOHN)	BOSTON, MA	1762-1775
JOHN POTWINE	BOSTON, MA	1775-D1792

Made a silver-mounted sword for
 Massachusetts Governor Roger Wolcott.
(See Daniel Henchman)
(See Captain Charles Whiting)

JAMES POUPARD
(See Maker listings)

EDWARD PUTMAN
PUTMAN & LOW
(See John J. Low-Dealer listings)

THOMAS W. RADCLIFFE
(See Confederate listings)

SOLOMAN RAPHAEL
(See Dealer listings)

BENJAMIN RAWLS
(See Dealer listings)

JOSEPH RAYNES & CO.
(See Dealer listings)

JAMES REAT	RICHMOND, VA	B1782-1809
JOHNSON (REUBAN) & REAT (JAMES)	RICHMOND, VA	1810-1814
JAMES REAT & CO.	RICHMOND, VA	D1815

Made presentation swords for the War of 1812.
(See Reuban Johnson)

CHARLES RECORDON	ST. LOUIS, MO	1820-1836
JACCARD (EUGENE)		
& RECORDON (CHARLES)	ST. LOUIS, MO	1836-1842
MENKENS (ANTHONY H.)		
& RECORDON (CHARLES)	ST. LOUIS, MO	1842
ANTHONY H. MENKENS	ST. LOUIS, MO	1842-1866

(See Eugene Jaccard-Dealer listings)

JOHANN REID	WURTEMBERG, GERMANY	B1784-1805
	CHAMBERSBURG, PA	1805-1815
	ALLEGHENY CO., PA	1815-1820
TEMPLETON REID	MILLEDGEVILLE, GA	B1765-1812
T. (TEMPLETON) & E. (ELISHA) REID	MILLEDGEVILLE, GA	1813-1815
TEMPLETON REID	COLUMBUS, GA	1816-D1851
ELISHA REID	COLUMBUS, GA	1816-1836
PAUL REVERE SR.	BOSTON, GA	B1702, 1720-D1754
PAUL REVERE II	BOSTON, MA	B1735, 1755-D1818

Made silver hilts for militia officer swords.
Learned powder making in Philadelphia during the Revolutionary War.
Bought a rolling and slitting mill from Leonard (Jonathan) and Kinsley (Adam) of Canton, MA (1799), and turned it into a powder mill.
(See Leonard Family-Maker listings)

PAUL REVERE III	BOSTON, MA	B1760, 1780-D1813
GEORGE E. RICHARD & CO.	NEW YORK, NY	1810-1832
SAMUEL R. RICHARDS JR.	PHILADELPHIA, PA	1791-1794
RICHARDS (SAMUAL R. JR.) & WILLIAMSON (SAMUEL)	PHILADELPHIA, PA	1794-1800
SAMUEL R. RICHARDS JR.	PHILADELPHIA, PA	1800-1818

(See Samuel Williamson)

THOMAS RICHARDS	NEW YORK, NY	1780-1801
SAYRE (JOHN) & RICHARDS (THOMAS)	NEW YORK, NY	1802-1811
FOSTER (JOHN) & RICHARDS (THOMAS)	NEW YORK, NY	1811-1815
PELLETREAU (WILLIAM SMITH) & RICHARDS (THOMAS)	NEW YORK, NY	1815-1825
THOMAS RICHARDS	NEW YORK, NY	1825-1834

(See William S. Pelletreau)
(See John Foster)
(See John Sayre)

FRANCIS SR. & JR., JOSEPH SR. & JR., THOMAS, JOHN, NATHANIEL RICHARDSON
(See Maker listings)

GEORGE RICHARDSON	RICHMOND, VA	B1757-1782
CAPT. WILLIAM & GEORGE RICHARDSON	RICHMOND, VA	1782-1793
GEORGE RICHARDSON	RICHMOND, VA	1793-D1809
CAPT. WILLIAM RICHARDSON	RICHMOND, VA	B1757-1782
CAPT. WILLIAM & GEORGE RICHARDSON	RICHMOND, VA	1782-1793
W. (WILLIAM) H. RICHARDSON	RICHMOND, VA	1808-1850

Authorized dealer for Ames Mfg. Co. swords.

BARTON & CHARLES RICHMOND
(See Confederate listings)

JOHN, JOHN FREDERICK, BENJAMIN
  & GEORGE RIECKE
(See Maker listings)

GEORGE W. RIGGS	BALTIMORE, MD	B1777-1816
RIGGS (GEORGE W.)		
& GRIFFITH (HENRY)	BALTIMORE, MD	1816-1818
GEORGE W. RIGGS	BALTIMORE, MD	1818-D1864
AUGUSTUS ROGERS	NEW YORK, NY	1810-1831
LEONARD (ALLEN)		
& ROGERS (AUGUSTUS)	NEW YORK, NY	1831-1840
AUGUSTUS ROGERS	BOSTON, MA	1840-1865

(Presentation Swords)

JOSEPH ROGERS	NEWPORT, RI	B1753-1770
TANNER (JOHN) & ROGERS (JOSEPH)	NEWPORT, RI	1770-1785

John Tanner died (1785).

JOSEPH ROGERS	NEWPORT, RI	1785-1825
CHURCH (JOSEPH)		
& ROGERS (JOSEPH & WILLIAM)	NEWPORT, RI	1825-1836

Joseph Rogers died (1825).
(See Joseph & William Rogers)
(See John Tanner)

WILLIAM ROGERS	NEWPORT, RI	B1801-1824

Son of Joseph.

CHURCH (JOSEPH)		
& ROGERS (JOSEPH & WILLIAM)	HARTFORD, CT	1824-1835
WILLIAM ROGERS & CO.	HARTFORD, CT	1836-1846

Partners: Asa Rogers, John O. Mead.

WILLIAM ROGERS & SON	HARTFORD, CT	1846-1865

Son and partner: William Henry Rogers.

WILLIAM ROGERS MFG. CO.		1865-1898

William Rogers died (1873).
(See Joseph Rogers)
(See John O. Mead)
(See Joseph Church)

JOHN A. ROHR
(See Maker listings)

JOHN RUSSELL
(See Dealer listings)

HARRY SAFFORD
(See Maker listings)

JOHN & DANIEL SALLADE
(See Maker listings)

ISAAC SANFORD	HARTFORD, CT	1765-1785
BEACH (MILES) & SANFORD (ISAAC)	LITCHFIELD, CT	1785-1792
ISAAC SANFORD	HARTFORD, CT	1792-1823
	PHILADELPHIA, PA	1823-D1842

(See Miles Beach-Dealer listings)
(Clock Maker)

ENSIGN SARGEANT	HARTFORD, CT	B1761, 1790-D1843

(Jeweler, Clock Maker)

H. (HENRY) SARGEANT	HARTFORD, CT	B1796, 1820-D1864

(Jeweler, Clock Maker)

JACOB SARGEANT	HARTFORD, CT	B1761, 1785-D1843

Adv. sword hilting (1799).
(Jeweler, Clock Maker)

JOHN SAYRE	NEW YORK, NY	B1771-1801
SAYRE (JOHN) & RICHARDS (THOMAS)	NEW YORK, NY	1801-1811
JOHN SAYRE & CO.	NEW YORK, NY	1811-D1852

(See Thomas Richards)
(Importer and Jeweler)

BARTHOLOMEW SCHAATS	NEW YORK, NY	B1670, 1690-D1758

Made silver-hilted court swords.

J. (JEREMIAH) SCHAFFIELD	PHILADELPHIA, PA	1785-1800

Made silver-hilted hunting swords.

NATHAN SCOTHORN JR. & SR.
(See Maker listings)

JOHN SCOTT	MONTGOMERY TOWNSHIP, PA	
	Cumberland County	1775-1783

JACABUS SCOUT
(See Maker listings)

WILLIAM SEALE JR.	PHILADELPHIA, PA	1790-1810
BROWN (LIBERTY)		
& SEALE (WILLIAM JR.)	PHILADELPHIA, PA	1810-1811
WILLIAM SEALE JR.	PHILADELPHIA, PA	1811-1822

(See Liberty Brown)

GEORGE B. & WILLIAM H. SHARPE
(See Dealer listings)

ROBERT SHEPHERD	ALBANY, NY	B1781-1800
SHEPHERD (ROBERT)		
& BOYD (WILLIAM)	ALBANY, NY	1800-1810
ROBERT SHEPHERD	ALBANY, NY	1810-D1853

(See William Boyd)

SMITH J. SHERWOOD
SHERWOOD & WHATLEY
(See Harvey R. Caberay-Dealer listings)

SAMUEL SHIPP
(See Dealer listings)

BENJAMIN SHREVE
(See Dealer listings)

CLARK SIBLEY	NEW HAVEN, CT	B1778-1806
SIBLEY (CLARK) & MARBLE (SIMEON)	NEW HAVEN, CT	1801-D1807

Adv. silver- and brass-mounted swords (1801).
(See Simeon Marble)

ANTHONY SIMMONS	PHILADELPHIA, PA	1770-1793
SIMMONS (ANTHONY) **& WILLIAMSON (SAMUEL)**	PHILADELPHIA, PA	1793-1794
SIMMONS (ANTHONY) **& ALEXANDER (SAMUEL)**	PHILADELPHIA, PA	1795-1804
ANTHONY SIMMONS	PHILADELPHIA, PA	1804-D1808

(See Samuel Alexander-Maker listings)
(Goldsmith)

JOSEPH SIMMONS
(See Maker listings)

WARRINGTON L. SLOAT
(See John L'Hommedieu-Dealer listings)

JOHN P. SMITH	SAVANNAH, GA	1799-1835

Partner in D.B. Nichols & Co. (1820-1830).
(See David B. Nichols-Dealer listings)

JOSEPH D. SMITH	PHILADELPHIA, PA	1780-1805
LEWIS (HARVEY) & SMITH (JOSEPH D.)	PHILADELPHIA, PA	1805-1811
JOSEPH D. SMITH	PHILADELPHIA, PA	1811-D1818

(See Harvey Lewis)

JEREMIAH SNOW JR. & SR.
(See Maker listings)

THOMAS SPARROW SR.	PHILADELPHIA, PA	1720-D1753

Made silver-mounted small swords.

THOMAS SPARROW JR.	PHILADELPHIA, PA	B1746-1765
	ANNAPOLIS, MD	1765-1784

Son of Thomas Sparrow Sr.

JAMES SPENCER	HARTFORD, CT	B1775-1810
OAKES (FREDERICK) & SPENCER (JAMES)	HARTFORD, CT	1811-1820

James Spencer died (1820).
(See Frederick Oakes)

CHRISTIAN STAKEL	YORK, PA	1775-1783

HENRY B. STANWOOD
(See John L. Low-Dealer listings)

EDWARD, CHARLES & HENRY STELLWAGON
(See Dealer listings)

THOMAS STEPHENSON
(See Dealer listings)

JAMES R. STEVENS
STEVENS & ROGERS
(See Dealer listings)

HENRY STILES
(See Maker listings)

CHARLES STORRS
(See Dealer listings)

ELI A. STORRS	UTICA, NY	1820-1833
HENRY S. STORRS	UTICA, NY	B1826-D1862
SHUBAEL STORRS	UTICA, NY	1803-D1847
A. STOWELL JR.	BALTIMORE, MD	1835-1855
GOULD (JAMES), STOWELL (A. JR.) & WARD (WILLIAM H.) (See James Gould)	BALTIMORE, MD	1855-1860

WILLIAM STRONG
(See Maker listings)

ROBERT SWAN (SWAINE)	WORCHESTER, MA	1765-1795
	ANDOVER, MA	1795-1799
	PHILADELPHIA, PA	1799-1831

Made silver-hilted eagle-head short sabers.

DANIEL SYNG Son of Philip.	CORK, IRELAND	B1713-1720
	PHILADELPHIA, PA	1720-1734
	LANCASTER, PA	1734-D1745
(Goldsmith)		
JOHN SYNG Son of Philip.	PHILADELPHIA, PA	1734-1772
	WILMINGTON, DE	1772
(Goldsmith)		
PHILIP SYNG SR.	CORK, IRELAND	B1676-1720
	PHILADELPHIA, PA	1720-D1739
(Goldsmith, Brass Founder)		
PHILIP SYNG JR.	CORK, IRELAND	B1703-1720
	PHILADELPHIA, PA	1720-1771
	MERION TOWNSHIP, PA Montgomery County	1771-D1789

Employees: Engraver Lawrence Herbert (1748), apprentice Richard Humphreys (1766-1771).
(See Richard Humphreys)
(Goldsmith)

JOHN TANNER	NEWPORT, RI	B1713-1769
TANNER (JOHN) & ROGERS (JOSEPH)	NEWPORT, RI	1770-1785

John Tanner died (1785).
(See Joseph Rogers)

PERRY G. TANNER	UTICA, NY	B1822-1840
TANNER (PERRY G.) & COOLEY (OLIVER B.)	UTICA, NY	1840-1842

Partners:
    Horace P. Bradley
    Nathan M. Christian,
    William Gaylord Doud
    Charles Seager

PERRY G. TANNER	UTICA, NY	1842-D1878

(See Oliver B. Cooley)

JOHN TARGEE	NEW YORK, NY	1777-1798
JOHN & PETER TARGEE	NEW YORK, NY	1798-1811
JOHN TARGEE	NEW YORK, NY	1811-1841

Made 12 presentation swords for War of 1812 heroes ordered by the city of New York (1815).

PETER TARGEE	NEW YORK, NY	1770-1798
JOHN & PETER TARGEE	NEW YORK, NY	1798-1811
PETER TARGEE	NEW YORK, NY	1811-1820
WILLIAM TARGEE	NEW YORK, NY	1807-1810

(Goldsmith)

GEORGE W. TAYLOR	PHILADELPHIA, PA	1810-1830
TAYLOR (GEORGE W.), LAWRIE (ROBERT D.) & WOOD (J.E.)	PHILADELPHIA, PA	1830-1845
TAYLOR (GEORGE) & LAWRIE (ROBERT D.)	PHILADELPHIA, PA	1845-1865

(See J.E. Wood)

JOHN TAYLOR	NEWARK, NJ	1780-1801
E. (EPAPHRAS) HINSDALE & CO.	NEWARK, NJ	1801-1810

Partner: John Taylor.

TAYLOR (JOHN) & HINSDALE (HORACE SEYMOUR)	NEWARK, NJ	1810-1817

Horace Hinsdale was the son of Epaphras.

TAYLOR (JOHN) & BALDWIN (ISAAC)	NEWARK, NJ	1817-1840

(See E. Hinsdale)
(See Horace Seymour Hinsdale)
(See Isaac Baldwin-Dealer listings)

BARENT TEN EYK	ALBANY, NY	B1714, 1735-D1795
JACOB TEN EYK	ALBANY, NY	B1705, 1725-D1793

Made silver-hilted small swords.

KEONRAET TEN EYK	ALBANY, NY	B1678, 1695-D1753
GEER TERRY	ENFIELD, CT	B1775-1800
	WORCHESTER, MA	1801-1807

Adv. silver-hilted officer swords (1801).
Made silver-hilted hussar-hilt officer short sabers.

	ENFIELD, CT	1808-1858
L.B. TERRY	ENFIELD, CT	1810-1820
WILBERT TERRY	ENFIELD, CT	1785-1810

THOMAS, GRISWALD
(See Arthur Breeze Griswald-Confederate listings)

TIFFANY & CO.
(See Maker listings)

ERASTUS O. TOMPKINS	NEW YORK, NY	1812-1832
MARGUAND & CO.	NEW YORK, NY	1832-1839

Partners:
    Frederick Marguand
    Josiah P. Marguand
    Henry Ball
    Evastus O. Tompkins

BALL (HENRY) TOMPKINS (ERASTUS O.) & BLACK (WILLIAM)	NEW YORK, NY	1839-1851

(See Marguand & Co.)
(See Henry Ball)

BENJAMIN & DANIEL TRUE
(See Dealer listings)

GEORGE UPSON	NEW YORK, NY	1790-1807
RICHARDS (STEPHEN), UPSON (GEORGE) & CO.	NEW YORK, NY	1808-1816

Imported swords from London, England.

CLARK (CURTIS H. & GREGORY JR.) PELLETREAU (MALTBY) & UPSON (GEORGE)	NEW YORK, NY	1817-1824
GEORGE UPSON	NEW YORK, NY	1825-1830

(See Malby Pelletreau)
(See Richards Upson-Dealer listings)

STEPHEN UPSON	NEW YORK, NY	1790-1809
WELLS (SAMUEL) & UPSON (STEPHEN)	NEW YORK, NY	1800-1814
PELLETREAU (WILLIAM S.) & UPSON (STEPHEN)	NEW YORK, NY	1815
STEPHEN UPSON	NEW YORK, NY	1816-1820

(See William S. Pelletreau)
(See Wells & Upson-Dealer listings)

PETER VALET	NEW YORK, NY	1787-1797
Made a silver-mounted sword for Maj. James Duane.		

ALBERT D. VAN COTT
(See Dealer listings)

PETER VAN DYCK	NEW YORK, NY	B1664, 1684-D1751
RICHARD VAN DYCK	NEW YORK, NY	B1717, 1737-D1770

STEPHEN VAN DYCK
(See William Smith Pelletreau)

DANIEL VAN VOORHIS
(See Dealer listings)

JOHN VEAL SR.	COLUMBIA, SC	1820-1838
VEAL (JOHN SR.) & GLAZE (WILLIAM)	COLUMBIA, SC	1838-1841
JOHN VEAL SR.	COLUMBIA, SC	1841-1851
(See William Glaze-Confederate listings)		
GEORGE VOGELER	WURTEMBERG, GERMANY	B1767-1805
	PHILADELPHIA, PA	1805-1810
(Goldsmith)		

JOHN WALLACE
WALLACE & BEGGS
WALLACE & WILSON
(See Maker listings)

JAMES WARD
(See Dealer listings)

WILLIAM H. WARD
(See James Gould)

JONATHAN WARNER	PHILADELPHIA, PA	1770-1780
(Watchmaker)		
JOHN S. WARNER	BALTIMORE, MD	1795-1825
J. (JOHN) S. WARNER	PHILADELPHIA, PA	1825-1865
JOSEPH P. WARNER	PHILADELPHIA, PA	B1811-1840
	BALTIMORE, MD	1840-D1862
(Watchmaker)		
EDWARD E. WATSON	BOSTON, MA	1800-1821
DAVIS (SAMUEL)		
& WATSON (EDWARD E.)	BOSTON, MA	1822-1824
DAVIS (SAMUEL)		
& WATSON (EDWARD E.) & CO.	BOSTON, MA	1825-1830
Partner: Bartlett M. Bramhill.		

EDWARD E. WATSON (See S.E. Davis-Dealer listings)	BOSTON, MA	1831-D1839
JOSHUA & EMMOR TREGO WEAVER (See Maker listings)		
JEDIDIAH WEISS Son of John George Weiss. Apprenticed to John S. Krause (1810-1815).	BETHLEHEM, PA	B1796, 1815-D1873
JOHN GEORGE WEISS	CHRISTIAN SPRINGS, PA	
		B1758-1795
	BETHLEHEM, PA	1795-D1811
(Gunsmith, Clock Maker, Cutler)		
ALFRED WELLES	BOSTON, MA	B1783-1807
ALFRED & GEORGE I. WELLES **(WELLES & CO.)** Adv. imported swords (1809).	BOSTON, MA	1807-1816
GEORGE I. WELLES & CO. Partners: Alfred Welles, Hugh Gelston, Horace Porter.	BOSTON, MA	1816-1827
WELLES (ALFRED) & GELSTON (HUGH)	BOSTON, MA	1827-1829
ALFRED WELLES & CO. Authorized agent for Ames Mfg. Co. swords. Imported J. Salter (London, England) swords. Sold eagle-head-pommel swords. (See George I. Welles) (See Hugh Gelston) (Jeweler)	BOSTON, MA	1829-D1860
GEORGE I. WELLES	BOSTON, MA	B1784-1807
ALFRED & GEORGE I. WELLES **(WELLES & CO.)**	BOSTON, MA	1807-1816
GEORGE I. WELLES & CO. Partners: Alfred Welles, Hugh Gelston (1816-1820), Horace Porter. (See Horace Porter) (See Alfred Welles) (See Hugh Gelston) (Jeweler)	BOSTON, MA	1816-1827
JAMES M. WELLS **LEMUEL WELLS** **LEMUEL & HORACE WELLS** **WILLIAM WELLS** **SAMUEL WELLS** (See Dealer listings)		
WILLIAM WENDELL	ALBANY, NY	1820-1839
MULFORD (JOHN H.) **& WENDELL (WILLIAM)**	ALBANY, NY	1840-1850
WENDELL (WILLIAM) & ROBERTS (See John Mulford)	ALBANY, NY	1850

WILLIAM WHETCROFT
(See Maker listings)

TIFFT & WHITING	NORTH ATTLEBORO, MA	1840-1858
WHITING MANUFACTURING CO.	NORTH ATTLEBORO, MA	1858-1910
	BRIDGEPORT, CT	1910-1926
	PROVIDENCE, RI	1926-1992

Made presentation swords in the 1890s.

Became division of Gorham Manufacturing Co. (1926).

BRADFORD WHITING	FAIRFIELD, CT	B1751-1786
WHITING (BRADFORD) **& MARGUAND (ISAAC)**	FAIRFIELD, CT	1787-1791
BRADFORD WHITING	NORWICH, CT	1791-1800

(See Isaac Marguand)

CAPT. CHARLES WHITING	NORWICH, CT	B1725-1735
POTWINE (JOHN) & WHITING **(CAPT. CHARLES)**	HARTFORD, CT	1735-1762
CAPT. CHARLES WHITING	HARTFORD, CT	1762-D1765

(See John Potwine)

EDWARD & AMOS WHITTEMORE
(See Maker listings)

FREDERICK W. WIDMANN
(See Maker listings)

ALVAN WILCOX	NORWICH, CT	B1783-1805
HART (JUDAH) & WILCOX (ALVAN)	NORWICH, CT	1805-1807
ALVAN WILCOX	FAYETTEVILLE, NC	1807-1823
ALVAN WILCOX	NEW HAVEN, CT	1824-D1870

(See Judah Hart)

WILLIAM W. WILLARD
WILLARD & STOKES
WILLARD & HAWLEY
(See Dealer listings)

DEODAT WILLIAMS	HARTFORD, CT	1750, 1776-D1781

Adv. silver-mounted officer hangers with lion, eagle, panther, or plain pommels (1776).

SAMUEL WILLIAMSON	PHILADELPHIA, PA	B1772-1792

Apprenticed to Joseph Lownes (1787-1792).

SIMMONS (ANTHONY) **& WILLIAMSON (SAMUEL)**	PHILADELPHIA, PA	1792-1794
RICHARDS (SAMUEL. R. JR.) **& WILLIAMSON (SAMUEL)**	PHILADELPHIA, PA	1794-1800
SAMUEL WILLIAMSON	PHILADELPHIA, PA	1800-D1843

(See Anthony Simmons)
(See Samuel R. Richards Jr.)
(Goldsmith)

ROBERT WILSON-NATHANIEL WILSON
JAMES H. WILSON
WILLIAM W. WILSON-WILLIAM WILSON
WILLIAM H. WILSON
JOHN WILSON
(See Dealer listings)

CHRISTIAN WILTBERGER JR.	PHILADELPHIA, PA	B1766-1793

Apprenticed to Richard Humphreys (1788-1793).

WILTBERGER (CHRISTIAN) & **ALEXANDER (SAMUEL)**	PHILADELPHIA, PA	1793-1795
CHRISTIAN WILTBERGER JR.	PHILADELPHIA, PA	1795-1811
	WASHINGTON, DC	1811-D1851

Bought blades from Lewis Prahl.
Made silver-mounted lion-head hunting swords.
(See Samuel Alexander-Maker listings)
(Goldsmith, Jeweler)

EDWARD WINSLOW	BOSTON, MA	B1669, 1690-D1753
ALEXANDER WISHART	NEW YORK, NY	1808-1818
B. WISHART	PHILADELPHIA, PA	1839-1846
DANIEL WISHART	NEW YORK, NY 45 Maiden Lane	1822-1845

Made military buttons.

HUGH WISHART	NEW YORK, NY 45 Maiden Lane	1784-1819

Made military buttons
Made silver-mounted officer short sabers.

JOHN WISHART	NEW YORK, NY	1849-1859
WILLIAM WISHART	NEW YORK, NY	1800-1820
(G.J.) GEN. JAMES WOLF	WILMINGTON, DE	1780-1828
GEN. JAMES WOLF	PHILADELPHIA, PA	1828-1858

Bought blades from Joseph Rose.
(Swordsmith)

JOHN WOOD	MIDDLETOWN, CT	1784-1806
WARD (JOHN) & HUGHES (EDMUND)	MIDDLETOWN, CT	1806-1811
WARD (JOHN) & COX (JOHN)	PHILADELPHIA, PA	1811-1813
WARD (JOHN) & GARRETT (PHILIP)	PHILADELPHIA, PA	1813-1822
WARD (JOHN) & MILLER (WILLIAM)	PHILADELPHIA, PA	1822-1824
JOHN WARD	PHILADELPHIA, PA	1824-1839

(See Edmund Hughes)
(See Philip Garrett)
(See William Miller)

J.E. WOOD	PHILADELPHIA, PA	1810-1830
TAYLOR (JOHN) LAWRIE **(ROBERT D.) & WOOD (J.E.)**	PHILADELPHIA, PA	1830-1845

J.E. WOOD PHILADELPHIA, PA 1845-1865
(See John W. Taylor)

ENOS WOODRUFF
(See Dealer listings)

WILLIAM WRIGHTMAN
(See Maker listings)

JOSEPH WYATT PHILADELPHIA, PA 1797-1798

JAMES YOULE
(See Dealer listings)

JESSE S. ZANE
(See Maker listings)

M.Z. ZIMMERMAN
M.Z. & J.F. ZIMMERMAN
C.H. ZIMMERMAN
(See Confederate listings)

CHAPTER 7

Confederate Armories and Arsenals Making, Repairing, or Storing Edged Weapons

Atlanta Arsenal, Atlanta, GA

- In operation from 1862-1864.
- Located on the northwest corner of Walton and Peachtree Streets.
- Contracted with a Colonel Green for cavalry sabers (1862).
- Contracted with A.H. Dewitt for 3,000 cavalry sabers (1862).
- Contracted with H. Marshall & Co. for 6,194 cavalry sabers and 1,000 lt. artillery sabers (1862).
- The Confederacy added to the facility by purchasing the John C. Peck and Francis Day armory and converted it to an arms repair and storage facility (1863).
- Made ammunition with machinery brought from the Nashville Armory.
- Also made rifled guns, parrott gun ammunition, haversacks, knapsacks, cavalry saddles, and infantry leather accoutrements.
- The arsenal was closed when Atlanta fell (1864).

    Arsenal Commander: Maj. Moses Hanibal Wright.
    Assistant Arsenal Commander: Capt. R.M. McCall.
    Military Storekeeper: Capt. C.C. Campbell.
    Ordnance Agent: H.W. Broxton.

(See John C. Peck)
(See A.H. DeWitt)
(See H. Marshall & Co.)

Augusta Arsenal, Augusta, GA

- Georgia took over the U.S. arsenal at Augusta (1861).
- Converted it into an artillery, ammunition, gun powder, and ordnance manufactory.
- Horseshoes, artillery caissons, and wagons were also made at Augusta.
- Pikes were made in 1862.
- Francis Bannerman bought many pikes that had been stored at Augusta in an auction (1904).

   First Commander: Col. G.W. Rains.
   Second Commander: Col. W.C. Gill.
   Military Storekeeper: Capt. John W. Ansley (1861-1862).
   Military Storekeeper: Capt. J.P. Girardey (1862-1865).

Briarfield Armory and Arsenal, Columbus, MS

- Established in 1862 with machinery and tools from the Memphis, TN, Arsenal (when Memphis fell to Union troops in 1862).
- Made and repaired guns and cavalry sabers.
- Made ammunition, cannonballs, and shot.
- Jacob Faser, formally superintendent of a sword factory owned by James Conning of Mobile, AL, became master gunsmith at Briarfield (1862-1863). Faser also was a consultant to the gun and sword makers Leech & Rigdon, who moved to Briarfield when Memphis fell to Union troops in 1862.
- The Briarfield Armory was closed and all machinery and tools were moved to the Selma, AL, Arsenal (1863).

   Commander: Maj. W.R. Hunt (1862).
   Commander: Maj. W.R. Chambliss (1862-1863).
   Military Staff: Capt. James Harding (1862-1864).

(See Memphis Armory)
(See James Conning)
(See Thomas S. Leech)

Fayetteville Armory and Arsenal, Fayetteville, NC

- Originally a U.S. arsenal seized by North Carolina (1861).
- Captured rifle-making machinery from the U.S. arsenal at Harpers Ferry, VA, was sent to Fayetteville (1861).
- Made and repaired saber bayonets, cavalry sabers, and rifles.
- When the armory was captured by Union troops (1865), there were 500 cavalry sabers on hand.

   Commander: Lt. Col. J.A. D'Lagnel (1861-1864).
   Commander: Lt. Col. F.L. Childs (1864-1865).
   Military Staff: Capt. J.E. Dangerfield (1863-1865).

Georgia State Armory, Milledgeville, GA

- In operation from 1862-1864.
- Known as the Milledgeville Armory.
- The Georgia State Penitentiary was converted to an armory (1862).
- Made and repaired muskets, bayonets, and pikes.

- Most of the pikes and bowie knives contracted for by Georgia Governor Joseph E. Brown in February 1862 were stored at the Georgia State Armory.
- When General Sherman's cavalry unit, Wilson's Raiders, destroyed the arsenal in 1864, 2,300 muskets, 5,000 pikes, and 1,500 cutlasses (bowie knives) were also destroyed.

    Chief of Ordinance: Maj. Lachland H. McIntosh.
    Master Armorer: Peter Jones.
    Military Storekeeper: Capt. T.M. Bradford.

(See Joseph E. Brown)

Lynchburg Ordnance Depot, Lynchburg, VA

- The 5,000 cavalry lances ordered by the Pocahontas Virginia County Court were stored here.

    Commander: Capt. G.T. Getty (1862-1864).
    Commander: Capt. E.S. Hutter (1864-1865).

Macon Arsenal, Macon, GA

- In operation from 1862-1865.
- Located at the end of 3rd Street.
- The Confederacy took over the D.C. Hopkins & Sons gun factory and J.N. & C.D. Findlay iron works and cannon factory and converted them into the Macon Arsenal.
- Additional land was obtained from W.B. Johnston.
- The complete stocks plus some machinery and tools from the Savannah Ordnance depot were also moved to the arsenal. Steam hammers were obtained from the Central Railroad and gun-stocking machinery from the H.R. Richmond Armory.
- Repaired and stored cannon, muskets, rifles, carbines, and edged weapons (cavalry sabers).
- Made cavalry sabers, pikes, cannon, ammunition, gun powder, knapsacks, and canteens.
- Contained a blacksmith shop, machine shop, carpentry shop, foundry, laboratory, and cannon factory.

    Arsenal Commander: Capt. Richard M. Cuyler.
    Laboratory Superintendent: Capt. J.W. Mallett.
    Purchasing Agent: R.B. Findlay.
    Machinists:
        F. Gibson.
        A.J. Hogan.
        James Mitchell.
        John O'Connell.
        J.P. Parker.
        William Wallace.
        Thomas Lackee.
    Ordnance Agents:
        Peter C. Sawyer.
        M.J. Edgerly.
        C.W. Ellis.
        J.E. Kelley.
        A.T. Acosta.
        J.E. Bryan.
    Clerk: John Allen.
    Superintendent of Rifle-Stocking Department: John W. Krepps.

Foreman of Carpenters: B.F. Perry.
Foreman of Laborers: Oliver Porter.
Mechanic: Andrew I. Youngblood.
Master Machinist: William D. Copeland.

Memphis Armory, Memphis, TN

- Located at the corner of Monroe and 3rd Streets.
- The complex contained an ordnance station, the Confederate Saber Manufactory (made cavalry sabers), and an ammunition manufactory.
- Made cannon balls, shells, canister and grape shot, cartridges, fuses, rockets, and signal lights.
- When Memphis fell in 1862, all equipment and stores were moved to the Briarfield Armory.

    Armory Commander: Col. William Richardson Hunt (1861).
    Armory Commander: Maj. R. Grindred (1862).
    Commander of the Saber Manufactory: Capt. J.T. Trezevant.
    Commander of the Ammunition Manufactory: Lieutenant Sengstock.

Nashville Armory and Arsenal, Nashville, TN

- Known as the Nashville Gun Factory.
- Located on the corner of Mulberry and 3rd Streets.
- Operated as a Confederate ordnance station.
- Made and stored ammunition, arms, and accoutrements.
- Contracted with the Nashville Plow Works for 909 cavalry sabers (1861-1862).
- Closed when Nashville occupied (1862).

    Commander: Capt. M.H. Wright (1861).

(See Nashville Plow Works)

Richmond Armory, Richmond, VA

- In operation from 1860-1865.
- The state of Virginia contracted with the Tredegar Iron Works to restore the Virginia Manufactory (1860).
- James Henry Burton supervised.
- The manufactory was taken over by the Confederacy (1861) and the name changed to the Richmond Armory.
- It was fitted with the machinery captured by the Confederacy at the U.S. arsenal at Harpers Ferry, VA.
- It was actually a complex made up of an armory, arsenal, artillery works, and laboratory, as well as the Confederate Ordnance Department headquarters.
- Had up to 450 workmen.
- The armory was located at the south end of 5th Street between the James River and the Kanawaha Canal.
- Repaired and refitted approximately 4,500 swords and cavalry sabers.
- Converted flintlock muskets to percussion.
- The laboratory was located on Browns Island at the foot of 7th Street.
- The artillery works was located on 7th Street south of the Kanawaha Canal.
- The arsenal was located on Byrd Island between Canal and River Streets. Its fronting was on 7th Street.
- Had 3,350 cavalry sabers on hand (April 1861).

- Issued 7,863 cavalry sabers by October 1863.

    Armory Commander: Col. Charles Dimmock (1860-1861).
    Armory Commander: Col. James H. Burton (1861-1862).
    Armory Commander: Col. Benjamin Sloan (1862).
    Armory Commander: Capt. W.S. Downer (1862-1864).
    Armory Commander: Maj. F.F. Jones (1864-1865).
    Military Storekeeper: Capt. Robert White.
    Master Armorer: S. Adams.
    Master Armorer: E. Persignon.
    Ordnance Inspector: T.S. Rhett.
    Foreman-Bayonet Department: Reese H. Butler.
    Ordnance Agent: W.F. Mitchell.
    Laboratory Commander: W. Leroy Brown.
    Artillery Works Commander: James D. Brown.
    Arsenal Commander: Captain W.N. Smith (1860).
    Arsenal Commander: Major Smith Stanburg (1861-1865).
    Arsenal Storekeeper: O.W. Edwards (1861-1865).

- Ordnance Department Headquarters:
    Chief of Ordnance: Col. J. Gorgas.
    Assistant Chief of Ordnance: Maj. E.B. Smith.
    Bureau of Foreign Supplies: Maj. T.L. Bayne (in charge of importing arms and ordnance from Europe through the Union blockade).

(See The Virginia Manufactory-U.S. Armory listing)
(See The Tredegar Iron Works)

Selma Arsenal, Selma, AL

- Established in 1862 with machinery from the Mt. Vernon and Briarfield Arsenals.
- Had 24 buildings.
- Made artillery seige guns, caissons, shot, shell, cartridges, rifles, pistols, knapsacks, clothing, ammunition boxes, and cavalry sabers.
- Also repaired arms.

    Superintendent: Capt. N.D. Cross.
    Commander: Lt. Col. J.L. White.
    Military Storekeeper: John E. Logwood.
    Armorer: Jacob Faser (from the Briarfield Armory).
    Executive Officer: W.R. Chambliss (1862-1864).
    Arms Inspector: Capt. R.M. Nelson.
    Military Staff: Capt. A.R. Jones, Capt. Samuel D. Vance.

(See Briarfield Armory)

CHAPTER 8
Confederate Sword Makers

A.L. ABBOTT
(See J.N. Hyde)

B.B. ALFORD   ATLANTA, GA   1861-1865
Sold the state of Georgia 18 pikes (1862).

MAJOR EDWARD C. ANDERSON
Confederate purchasing agent in Europe.
Ran 500 cavalry sabers and 13,341 Enfield
  muskets through the Union Blockade (1861).

JESSE ANSLEY
(See Charles H. Rigdon)

ARNOLD & COOLEY (EARLE)   WADESBOROUGH, NC   1861-1865
                                                            West Wade Street

- Both men were from Middletown, CT.
- They probably worked for or were familiar with Nathan Starr of Middletown, CT, who made cavalry sabers during and after the War of 1812.
- Arnold and Cooley's Civil War sabers are identical to Starr sabers.
- Originally set up a bayonet factory.
- Also made guns, cavalry sabers, bowie knives, and metal military goods.
- Had a North Carolina contract for guns and cavalry sabers. North Carolina supplied the steel.

- Employees:
    - Hiram Brown Braswell
    - Alfred Baucom
    - Peter Swink
    - Gaston Huntley
    - Daniel Luther Saylor
    - Samuel Flake
- Baucom and Braswell also set up a gun and gun powder factory at Baucom's flour and corn mill on the north fork of Jones Creek.
- Employee: Cabinetmaker Daniel Luther Saylor.

(Gun and Edged Weapon Maker)

ATHENS FOUNDRY   ATHENS, GA   1861-1865
Owner: Reuban Nickerson.
Made bayonets for shotguns.
Made one double-barreled cannon designed by John A. Gilleland.

ATLANTA SWORD FACTORY
(See H. Marshall)

JOHN BAKER   MASON, GA   1861-1865
     Bibb County

Sold the state of Georgia 300 bowie knives and 296 pikes (1862).

MAYOR BAUGH   MEMPHIS, TN   1861-1865
Had 64 pikes made for the defense of Memphis (1861).

BAYSER, STEBBINS & CO.   COLUMBIA, SC   1861-1865
South Carolina contract for 215 bayonets (1864).

BELL & DAVIS   ATLANTA, GA   1861-1865
Made bowie knives.

SAMUEL BELL   KNOXVILLE, TN   1850-1865
Made bowie knives.

C. (CHARLES) BELLENOT   NEW ORLEANS, LA   1850-1861
     Exchange Alley and Bienville Streets

Sword blade engraver for local sword makers such as Pradel, Dufilho, Voitier, Cook & Brother, and Hyde & Goodrich.
Die sinker and button and insignia maker.

BELLENOT (CHARLES) & ULRICH (FREDERICK)   NEW ORLEANS, LA   1861
Ulrich was a silver plater and button maker for state of Louisiana.
(Blade Engraver and Military Ornaments)

WILLIAM BERRY   ATLANTA, GA   1861-1865
Sold the state of Georgia 1 bowie knife and 37 pikes (1862).

W.G. BETTERTON & J.E. CHALARD
Confederate purchasing agents in Cuba.
Ran 500 cavalry sabers through the Union
  blockade (1861).

BENNINE BISSONNET	PARIS, FRANCE	1815-1856

Brother of Louis.

BENNINE & LOUIS BISSONNET	NEW ORLEANS, LA	1856-1859
BENNINE BISSONNET	HOUSTON, TX	1859-1865
BENNINE & LOUIS BISSONNET	HOUSTON, TX	1865-1882

Bennine Bissonnet died (1882).
(Gunsmith, Blacksmith, Machinist)

LOUIS BISSONNET	PARIS, FRANCE	B1819-1856

Brother of Bennine.

BENNINE & LOUIS BISSONNET	NEW ORLEANS, LA	1856-1859
LOUIS BISSONNET	MOBILE, AL	1859-1862
	83 South Wilk	

- Made staff and field officer swords.
- Made a sword for Gen. Braxton Bragg.
- Made cavalry officer swords.
- Made naval officer swords.
- Made a sword for Capt. James D. Johnston, commander of the CSS *Tennessee*.
- Worked as a gunsmith doing arms repair at the Mobile Arsenal.

LOUIS BISSONNET	MOBILE, AL	1862-1865

Worked for James Conning.

BENNINE & LOUIS BISSONNET	HOUSTON, TX	1865-1882
LOUIS BISSONNET	HOUSTON, TX	1882-D1885

Partner and son: Laurent Louis Bissonnet.
(See James Conning)
(Gunsmith, Sword Maker, Jeweler)

LAURENT LOUIS BISSONNET	HOUSTON, TX	1885-1895

Son of Louis.
(Gunsmith)

JOSEPH G. BLOUNT
(See the Haimon Family)

JAMES BOATWRIGHT	CHESTER CO., SC	B1773-1816
GLAZE (MIDDLETON)		
** & BOATWRIGHT (JAMES)**	CHESTER CO., SC	1816-1838

Made wagons, carriages, sugar mills,
  and cotton gins.

GLAZE (MIDDLETON)		
** & BOATWRIGHT (JAMES)**	COLUMBIA, SC	1838-1851
WILLIAM GLAZE & CO.		
** (PALMETTO ARMORY)**	COLUMBIA, SC	1851-1852

Partners: James Boatwright, Benjamin Flagg.
(Musket Maker, Sword Maker)

PALMETTO IRON WORKS   COLUMBIA, SC   1852-1861
Partner: James Boatwright.
Foreman: George A. Shields.
James Boatwright died (1857).
Made farm implements, boilers, and saw
  and sugar mills.
(See Middleton Glaze)
(See William Glaze)

CHARLES BORUM   NORFOLK, VA   1861-1865
Made shotgun bayonets.

R. (ROBERT) H. BOSHER   RICHMOND, VA   1861-1875
                                  10 South 9th Street and corner of Main

Partners: E.J. Bosher, Jeter Bosher.
Operated a carriage factory.
Made leather scabbards for Boyle, Gamble,
  & MacFee swords.
Had Confederate contracts for wood, planking,
  and wagon and ambulance parts.

STEPHAN BOUIS   RICHMOND, VA   1857-1858
Employee of tinners Charles D. Yale & Co.
STEPHAN BOUIS   RICHMOND, VA   1858-1861
                                  32 Main Street

Employee of tinners J & F Heffley.
STEPHEN BOUIS & CO.   RICHMOND, VA   1861-1865
                                  28 Main Street

Adv. military goods manufactured and
  for sale (1861).
Made belt buckles and knives.
(Military Goods and Tinner)

EDWARD BOYLE   RICHMOND, VA   1840-1859
BURGER (PETER & HENRY R.)
& BOYLE (EDWARD)   RICHMOND, VA   1859-1861
                                  8th and Arch Streets

Saw makers.
Adv. for blacksmith and grinders to make
  knives, bayonets, and swords (1861).
Made swords, bayonets, and bowie knives (1861).
Employee: saw maker Thomas Gamble.
BOYLE (EDWARD)
& GAMBLE (THOMAS)   RICHMOND, VA   1861-1865
- Factory was on South 7th near the
  Tredegar Iron Works and the Richmond Armory.
- Gamble was a former employee of Burger & Boyle
- Blade polisher: John Ege.
- Blade etcher: William T. Ege.
- Swords produced:
    Staff and field officer swords
    Foot officer swords
      (shortened model used as Naval officer swords)
    Cavalry officer sabers

        Cavalry sabers
        Non-comm. swords
        Bowie knives
        Bowie bayonets
        Saber bayonets
- Imported German blades.
- Mitchell & Tyler were agents for Boyle & Gamble swords.
- Patented a sword bayonet adapter (1861).

BOYLE (EDWARD),
  GAMBLE (THOMAS)
  & MCFEE (EDWARD P.)   **RICHMOND, VA**   **1861-1865**

- The retail branch of Boyle & Gamble.
- Sold swords to the Confederate government.
- R.H. Bosher (carriage factory) made many
    of the leather scabbards.
- Swords sold:
        Cavalry sabers
        Cavalry officers sabers
        Foot officer sword
        Non-comm. swords
        Bowie bayonets
        Saber bayonets

BOYLE (EDWARD) & GAMBLE (THOMAS)   **RICHMOND, VA**   **1866-1870**
                                                               13th Street

(Saw Maker)

MCFEE (EDWARD D.) & SIEGLE
  (CHRISTIAN F.)   **RICHMOND, VA**   **1866-1870**

After the war, McFee started his own
  company and continued to make swords.
(See Mitchell & Tyler Dealer listings)
(See P. Burger)
(See William T. Ege)
(Saw Maker, Sword Maker, Blacksmith, Cutler)

T.M. BRENNAN   **NASHVILLE, TN**   **1861-1865**

- Confederate contract for artillery,
    including 6-pound smooth-bore cannon
    and 12-pound howitzers.
- Contract for cavalry sabers (1861).
- Given a $4,000 advance (at approximately
    $10 a saber, this would mean 400 were made).

A.D. BROWN (SR. & JR.)   **COLUMBUS, GA**   **1861-1865**
                                             Broad St. near Thomas St.

- Wood products maker.
- Originally worked in the Farish Carter
    cotton mill making wooden mill products.
- Rented the first floor of the now vacant
    Farish Carter Cotton Mill (Front Street near
    Franklin) and set up a wood products factory (January 1861).
- Made wooden barrel canteens, wooden mill shuttles,
    and wooden sword grips for L. Haiman & Brother and
    Abram H. DeWitt (both had sword factories in the Farish Carter Mill).
- A.D. Brown Sr. was a machinist.

- A.D. Brown Jr. was a mechanic.

(See Farish Carter Cotton Mill)

JOSEPH E. BROWN   1862

- Governor of the state of Georgia.
- Issued a proclamation to the "mechanics" of Georgia (February 20, 1862) requesting 10,000 pikes and 10,000 long side knives (Confederate bowie knives) to be made in one month (see Pike & Bowie Knife Maker listings for fabricators).
- The patterns for the pike and knife were to be obtained at the Ordnance Office of the Georgia State Armory, Milledgeville, Georgia (Maj. L.H. McIntosh, Chief of Ordnance).
- Master armorer Peter Jones inspected the pikes and knives.
- Military storekeeper Capt. T.M. Bradford inventoried the pikes and knives.
- Specifications for pike ($5.00 each):
    6-foot staff of ash, white oak, or hickory; well-seasoned, straight (not cross grained); a cloverleaf-style head to be made of well-tempered steel
- Specifications for knife ($4.60 each):
    3 pounds, 18-inch blade, with scabbard (tipped), belt, and clasp
- Brown sent 827 pikes and 321 knives to the Chattanooga quartermaster and 400 pikes to Confederate troops in Augusta.

(See Georgia State Armory)

WILLIAM RILEY BROWN
(See Columbus Iron Works)

WILLIAM BUCHANON	**LAUREL HILL, NC** Rockingham County	1755-1785
JOHN BUCHANON	**LAUREL HILL, NC**	1775-1865

Son of William Buchanon.
Partner: Murdock Morrison (1863-1865).
Made pistols, rifles, and bowie knives.
(See Murdock Morrison)
(Gun Maker, Knife Maker)

PETER BURGER	**RICHMOND, VA**	1839-1859
HENRY R. BURGER	**RICHMOND, VA**	1839-1859
BURGER (PETER & HENRY R.) **& BOYLE (EDWARD)**	**RICHMOND, VA**	1859-1861

Saw makers.
Adv. for grinders and blacksmiths to make knives, bayonets, and swords (1861).
Employees (all saw makers):
    Michael Cardey
    Stephen Flohr
    Thomas Gamble
    Berry Grubbs
    William Kinstry
    Samuel Kirk

John Kreagle
James Massey
Andrew McNeice
Isaac Neal

**BURGER (PETER)
& BROTHER (HENRY R.)** RICHMOND, VA 1861-1865
Made bayonets, bowie knives, and foot
 officer swords.
(See Edward Boyle)
(Saw Maker, Blacksmith, Edged Weapons)

ANTHONY CADMAN
(See H. Goldbeck)

A.J. CAMERON COBBVILLE, GA 1840-1861
CAMERON (A.J.) & WINN (D.W.) COBBVILLE, GA 1861-1862
Sold the state of Georgia 458 bowie knives
 (1862).
A.J. CAMERON COBBVILLE, GA 1863-1885
(Gunsmith)

THOMAS W. CHANDLER
(See H. Marshall)

J.H. CARR
(See James Conning)

J.E. CHALARD
(See W.C. Betterton)

C.J. CHRISTOPHER ATLANTA, GA 1863-1864
Located on Bridge Street near the bridge.
Made and repaired swords.
Adv. as a sword maker and a repairer of
 swords of every description.
Spur maker, gilder, and burnisher (1864).

C.B. CHURCHILL & CO. NATCHEZ, MS 1861-1865
Operated a foundry.
Manager: George Peacock.
Made shot, shell, and edged weapons.

NELSON CLEMENTS HOUSTON, TX 1861-1865
- Contracted with the Confederate Secretary
 of War Benjamin to act as a purchasing agent
 in Europe (1861).
- The contract was for 20,000 stands (musket, rod,
 bayonet) of muskets, 5,000 revolvers, additonal
 ammunition, and 5,000 cavalry sabers (not to exceed
 $1,000,000 in cost).
- Nelson purchased 7,000 rifles and 2,840 muskets from
 Sinclair, Hamilton & Co., London, England.
- Shipped via the *Carolina Goodyear* to the Mexican port
 of Matamoras (later to be ferried across the river to Brownsville, TX).
- Other goods were shipped via the *Blanche* to Matamoras, Mexico.

MARION CLEVELAND	ATLANTA, GA	1861-1865

Sold the state of Georgia 10 pikes (1862).
(Pike Maker)

THE COLLEGE HILL IRON WORKS	NASHVILLE, TN	1860

Owner: L.(Lee) T.(Thomas) Cunningham.
L.T. Cunningham and Robert E. Dury
  offered to buy muskets, pistols, and sabers
  for the Confederate government in June 1861,
  before Cunningham equipped and opened his armory.

THE COLLEGE HILL ARMORY	NASHVILLE, TN	1861-1862

- Corner of Mulberry and College Streets (on College Hill).
- Owner: L.(Lee) T. (Thomas) Cunningham (probably a relation of G.W. Cunningham of Hamilton & Cunningham, who were successors to Nashville Plow Works).
- Its three-story building measured 176 by 48 feet.
- Had a state of Tennessee contract for cavalry officer sabers, cavalry sabers, staff and field officer swords, and foot officer swords (1861).
- Also converted flintock muskets to percussion.
- The armory was closed when Union troops under General Rosecrans occupied Nashville (1862). It then became part of a Union hospital complex. The Third Presbyterian Church, next door over, was also part of the complex.
- The city was occupied until the end of the war (1865).
- The company continued to do business after the war but used the original name of College Hill Iron Works.

THE COLLEGE HILL IRON WORKS	NASHVILLE, TN	1865-1872

After the war, the armory was reconverted
  to an iron forge and foundry.
Owner: L.(Lee) T.(Thomas) Cunningham (died 1872).
The works were sold to S.E. Jones & Son (1872).
The College Hill Iron Works became part
  of the Franklin Street Foundry.

THE FRANKLIN STREET FOUNDRY	NASHVILLE, TN	1872-1875

Owners: S.E. Jones, Griffen T. Jones (son of S.E.).
Adv. in the Nashville city directory as selling
  castings of all kinds.
(See the Nashville Plow Works)

COLUMBUS IRON WORKS	COLUMBUS, GA Muscogee County	1848-1882

- Located at Thomas Street at the corner of Short Steet.
- Owner: William Riley Brown.
- Employed over 100 people.
- Main building was two stories, 300' x 40'.
- The blacksmith shop was 100' long.
- The machine shop had 12 lathes.
- The cannon foundry (separate building) was 60' x 60'.

- The rolling mill made iron for gun barrels and sword blades.
- The brass foundry made guns and sword parts (some sold to Louis Haiman & Brother).
- Louis Haiman & Brother occupied the complete second floor with their sword factory. (See Louis Haiman & Brother)
- Adv. in the Mears & Co. Columbus city directory as the Columbus Iron Works, making a large variety of metal products, including saw, sugar, and grist mills; portable steam engines; gears; cauldrons; plates; balls; pullies; spiders; and ovens (1859-1860).

Columbus Iron Works Civil War Production

- Naval breech-loading brass cannon
- Iron rifled cannon
- 12-pound mortars
- Shot and shell (Confederate contract)
- Mississippi rifles
- Brass gun and sword parts
- Rolled iron for gun barrels and sword blades, etc.
- Railway car wheels

- The Confederate Navy leased the Columbus Iron Works (June 1862).
- It became part of the Confederate Naval Works commanded by Maj. James H. Warner.
- Haiman still operated his sword factory on the second floor.
- The Columbus Iron Works was burned down by Union General James C. Wilson's Cavalry Corps (April 17, 1865).
- It was still in business on Thomas Street and the corner of Bay Street (1882).
- Superintendent: George J. Golden.

CONFEDERATE SABER MANUFACTORY
(See the Memphis Armory-Armory listings)

CONFEDERATE STATES ARMORY
(See Louis Froelich)

CONFEDERATE STATES SWORD FACTORY
(See the Haiman Family)

JAMES CONNING NEW YORK, NY B1813-1840
MOBILE, AL 1840-1846
12 Dauphin Street, below Water Street
MOBILE, AL 1846-1861
26 Dauphin and corner of Water Street

- Partners: Nephew William A. Conning (B1835), John H. Pippen (joined 1855).
- Employees:
    George Taylor (jeweler and silversmith)
    F.V. Mathew (watch maker and silversmith)
    William V. Moore (jeweler and silversmith)

- Charles Colin (silversmith)
- John Hand (silversmith)
- John T. Huggins (silversmith)
- H.R. Procter (silversmith)
- James M. Williams (silversmith).
• Made silver- and gold-mounted swords.
• Bought swords from the Ames Mfg. Co.
• Bought swords and military goods from W.H. Horstmann.
• Agent for S.P. Amory & Co. rifles.

MOBILE, AL   1861-1865
26 Dauphin and corner of Water Street

• Partners: William A. Conning (nephew), William V. Moore, John H. Pippen.
• Built a sword factory at 41 St. Francis Street (1861).
• Jacob Faser set up and tooled the sword factory and acted as superintendent (1861-1862).
• Faser also etched, polished, and ground blades.
• Some products marked "Conning & Faser."
• Faser designed Conning's staff and field officer sword.
• The factory had up to 14 workmen, including gun and sword maker Louis Bissonnet (1862-1865) and blade etcher J.H. Carr.
• Had Alabama contracts for cavalry sabers, lt. artillery sabers, and buttons.
• Bought brass sword hilts and mountings and buckles from brass founders Skates & Co., Tuscaloosa, AL.
• Bought sword blades from Parks, Lyons, Mobile, AL.

JAMES CONNING & CO.   MOBILE, AL   1866-1873
• 26 Dauphin Street and corner of Water Street.
• Partners: William A. Conning (nephew), John H. Pippen.
• James Conning died (1871).
• Partners following Conning's death: Mrs. James Conning (widow), William A. Conning (nephew), John G. Conning (son of James Conning), John H. Pippen.

(See Louis Bissonnet)
(See Parks, Lyons)
(See Jacob Faser)
(See William V. Moore-Silversmith listings)
(See William H. Horstmann-Dealer listings)
(See Ames Mfg. Co.-Maker listings)
(Silversmith, Jeweler, Watch Maker, Sword Maker, Military and Fancy Goods, Regalia, Cutlery, Guns, Pistols)

JOHN H. PIPPEN   MOBILE, AL   1873-1881
26 Dauphin and corner of Water Street

Partners: William A. Conning, John G. Conning (son of James A. Conning).
(Watch Maker, Silversmith, Jeweler, Guns, Military Goods)

James Conning Merchandise List

Sword Factory Products
Cavalry sabers (Alabama contract)
Lt. artillery sabers (Alabama contract)
Foot officer swords
Staff and field officer swords

Military Goods Sold
Chapeaus
Plumes
Epaulettes
Sword belts
Sashes
Buttons
Cartridges
Caps and wads
Double-barreled shotguns
Sharps rifles
Colt revolvers
Allen revolvers
Swords (imported from Germany)
Swords (Horstmann Brothers)
Swords (Ames Mfg. Co.)
Derringer pistols
Pocket, belt, and hunting knives

Fancy Goods Sold
Gold- and silver-handled canes
Gold and silver dress trimmings
Tassels
Feathers
Masonic regalia
Jewelry
Watches
Clocks
Gilt hairpins
Silver combs
Feathered fans
Card cases
Gold pencils
Fine paintings
Womens head ornaments
General cutlery
Plated tableware
Silverware
Flutes
Accordians
Repaired clocks, watches, and jewelry

FERDINAND W.C. COOK **& FRANCIS L. COOK**	ENGLAND	1825-1845
	NEW YORK, NY	1845-1852
	NEW ORLEANS, LA	1853-1860

Worked as engineers for Benton & Hercules.

COOK (FERDINAND W.C.) **& BROTHER (FRANCIS L.)**	NEW ORLEANS, LA	1861-1862

- Opened an armory at 1 Canal Street (1861).
- Bought the Fulton Warehouse at Fulton and South Market Streets (1862).
- Had a Confederate contract for 4,000 Enfield-type rifles (1862).

- Had a Louisiana contract for 1,400 pikes (1862).
- When New Orleans fell (April 1862), the Cooks moved their machinery down the Mississippi on barges to Vicksburg, MS, and then overland to Selma, AL, and finally to Athens, GA.

ATHENS, GA   1863-1864

- Bought the Hodgson Brothers cotton mill and 45 acres in Athens (August 20, 1862).
- Then bought the William A. Carr cotton mill and 200 acres in Athens.
- Also bought 16 acres from the Athens Manufacturing Co.
- Opened a new armory (December 25, 1862). It was a three-story brick and stone building, 300' x 150', with a large central turret.
- Located at the foot of Broad Street on the North Branch of the Oconee River.
- The complex contained a blacksmith shop, smokehouse, saw and planning mill, wood finishing room, and employee dwellings.
- Bought iron from the Shelby Iron Works and Colin T. McRae of Selma, AL.
- Employed 200 workmen.
- Could make 600 guns a month.
- Made some iron-hilted foot artillery swords and cavalry sabers, but they were of poor quality.
- Military production stopped in the summer of 1864 because of slow payment by the Confederate government.
- Maj. Ferdinand W.C. Cook then formed a home guard (23rd Battalion of Georgia Volunteers). Francis L. Cook was captain. Many of the Athens Armory workmen joined the unit.
- Ferdinand W.C. Cook was killed at the battle in Hardeeville, SC (December 11, 1864).
- The Confederacy leased the armory and bought the machinery and began military production again (March 17, 1865).
- The Confederacy was to pay the Cooks 10 percent yearly of the armory value of $650,000. The armory was under the direction of master armorer Charles Henry Ford of Richmond, VA. Francis L. Cook worked with Ford.
- Production stopped when the war ended (April 9, 1865).
- After the war, Francis L. Cook continued making farm machinery, syrup mills, sorghum mills, and sugar boilers.
- The armory was sold at auction to the Athens Manufacturing Co. (1870). It was converted back to a cotton mill.

(Engineers; Gun, Cannon, Sword, Pike, and Bayonet Makers)

Cook & Brother Product Line

Musketoons
Enfield-type rifles
Artillery rifles
Cavalry horseshoes
Syrup mills
Sorghum mills
Sugar boilers
Farm machinery
Carbines

Saber bayonets
Triangular bayonets
Bayonet scabbards
Pikes
Foot Artillery swords (iron hilted)
Cavalry sabers (iron hilted)
Naval cutlasses (two types)
Belts
Cartridge boxes

COOPERS IRON WORKS   CARTERSVILLE, GA   1861-1885
- Located on the Etowah River, 6 miles from Cartersville, GA.
- Also called Etowah Iron Works.
- Owner: Mark Anthony Cooper (B1800-D1885).
- Partner: William Rushton.
- Employed up to 500 men.
- Major output was iron.
- Supplied the Confederacy with iron, iron rails, and cannon.
- Sold five pikes to the state of Georgia (1862).
- Made three types of bowie knives (some for the Atlanta Greys).
- Floring Herzog etched many of the bowie knife blades.
- The Iron Works was completely destroyed by Gen. William T. Sherman's troops (1865).

(See Foring Herzog)
(Metallurgist, Edged Weapon Maker, Steel Maker)

CRUSH & WADE   CHRISTIANBURG, VA   1861-1865

Had Confederate contracts for cavalry sabers.
(Sword Makers)

JOHN N. DARBY   NASHVILLE, TN   1861-1865

Sword hiltor.
(Silversmith)

ABRAM HENRY DEWITT   NEW YORK, NY   B1817-1847
                                                     COLUMBUS, GA   1847-1862
                                                     99 Broad Street

- Bought the jewelry shop of Henry E. Dibble (1847).
- Employees:
    - J.H. Bramhall (watch maker).
    - John Seats (clerk).
    - H. Goldbeck (engraver).
    - L.W. Cabell (clerk).
- Adv. watches, watch repair, and silverware (1848).
- Adv. gold and silver watches, jewelry, diamonds, silver pitchers and tableware, clocks, Masonic keys, and walking canes in the Columbus city directory (1859).
- Adv. guns, pikes, bowie knives, service swords with belts, navy pistols, cavalry spurs, military buttons, and field officer swords with metallic scabbards in the *Daily Inquirer* (1861-1862).
- Rented the basement of the Vacant Farish Carter Cotton Mill (Front

Street near Franklin Street) and set up a sword factory (January 1861). (See Farish Carter Cotton Mill)
- Made foot officer swords with a rattlesnake-design hilt (counterguard). By October 1861, he had already made over 500.
- Local craftmen working with DeWitt:
    Goldbeck & Cadman made his buttons (see H. Goldbeck).
    John P. Murray made some guns (see John P. Murray).
    Hall, Moses, & Co. made his pikes (see Hall, Moses, & Co.).
    Jacob H. Moshell made his sword blades (see Jacob H. Moshell).
    James B. Jaques & Brother made his sword scabbards (see James B. Jaques & Brother).
    A. Ingmire etched his blades (see A. Ingmire).
    N.B. Love made the rattlesnake pattern for DeWitt's foot officer swords (see N.B. Love).
- DeWitt offered to make cavalry sabers, artillery swords, cutlasses, and saber bayonets in correspondence with Georgia Governor Joseph Brown (October 1861).
- He then set up a company called A.H. DeWitt & Co. to manufacture swords and built a sword factory.

A. (ABRAM) H. (HENRY) DEWITT & CO.   COLUMBUS, GA   1862

- Greenwood (Elridge) & Gray (William C.), cotton brokers and warehousemen, agreed to finance DeWitt's company and owned one-third interest).
- Greenwood & Gray bought city lot 188 (January 17, 1862), and DeWitt built his sword factory there (two-story brick building).
- The sword factory was on Oglethorpe Street in the middle of the block, between Franklin and Bryan Streets.
- (Greenwood & Gray also financed John P. Murray's rifle plant, which was attached to DeWitt's factory on a rear cutoff facing Warren Street).
- Mr. Kean was the sword shop foreman.
- On May 22, 1862, DeWitt received a contract from Maj. M.H. Wright of the Atlanta Arsenal for at least 3,000 cavalry sabers with belts for $20 each (a sample had been sent to Wright earlier).
- Artillery swords were also contracted for (1862).
- DeWitt's factory employed over 130 men and could make 75 sabers a day.
- The sabers were inspected by Frederick C. Humphrey.
- The results of an inspection of DeWitt's sword factory by W. Leroy Brown (August 5, 1862) were disclosed in a letter to Col. Josiah Gorgas Chief of Ordnance for the Confederacy):
    1. 1,543 cavalry sabers had already been delivered.
    2. 300 cavalry sabers were on hand.
    3. 830 cavalry sabers were under way.
    4. Steel for approximately 327 more was available.
    5. The sabers were strong and well made but were not well finished.
    6. No artillery swords had been made.
    7. 3,000 cavalry sabers were to be made.
    8. No more cavalry sabers could be made unless they got steel from the government.
- In late 1862, steel did run out, and to keep his men busy, DeWitt began to make M1841 Mississippi rifles, but they were of poor quality (approximately 200 made).
- On December 31, 1862, DeWitt's shop at 99 Broad Street was destroyed by fire (Greenwood & Gray's cotton warehouse on Randolph Street between Broad and Front was also destroyed). DeWitt's son Clinton DeWitt was badly burned and died.

- Overcome with grief and despondent over the loss of his shop and the lack of help from the Confederate government, DeWitt sold his sword factory to John P. Murray for rifle manufacturing in early 1863. He then joined the Alabama infantry.
- In 1865, DeWitt sold his holdings in Columbus and settled in Russell County, Alabama (just across the border). (Jacob H. Moshell also lived there.) DeWitt's property (jewelry and military goods shop that was burned down) at 99 Broad Street must have been sold to T.S. Spear, because Spear is listed at that address in Haddock's Columbus Directory (1873).

(See Greenwood & Gray)
(See T.S. Spear)

WILLIAM DICKSON	DICKSON, AL	1840-1860
OWEN O. NELSON	TUSCUMBIA, GA	1860

Gunsmith who made bowie knives and converted flintocks.

DICKSON (WILLIAM)
& NELSON (OWEN O.) — DICKSON, AL — 1861

Partner: Louis H. Sadler.
Called the Shakanoosa Arms Company.

	ROME, GA	1862
	ADAIRSVILLE, GA	1863
	DAWSON, GA	1864-1865

Made Mississippi rifles, carbines, bayonets, and bowie knives.
Bought iron from the Shelby Iron Work, Selma, AL.
(Gunsmiths, Cutlers)

DIXIE WORKS — CANTON, MS — 1861-1863

Owners: James Wales, Mr. Barlow (farm tool maker from Charon, MS).
Made farm tools, muskets, rifles, pistols, and cavalry sabers.
Had 400 employees.
It was a large facility covering 100 acres.
Destroyed (1863).

DOG RIVER FACTORY — MOBILE, AL — 1861-1865

Located on Fulton Road and the Dog River, 5 miles south of Mobile, AL.
Started as the Mobile and Dog River Manufacturing Co., a textile mill and warehouse.
Converted to a Confederate depot, storage facility (arsenal), and military staging area.
The staging area was called Camp Good.
The depot stored arms and swords and made edged weapons for the state of Alabama.

JOHN R. DORSETT — HARRIS, GA — 1861-1865

Sold 232 pikes to the state of Georgia (1862).
(Gunsmith, Pike Maker)

T.D. DORSETT — HARRIS, GA — 1870-1883
(Gunsmith)

B. (BENJAMIN) DOUGLAS & CO.	COLUMBIA, SC	1861-1865

Made brass military goods in their brass foundry
  as well as cavalry sabers and staff and field officer swords.
(Brass Founder, Sword Maker)

J.D. DOUGLAS
(See John D. Gray)

T.D. DRISCOLL	HOWARDSVILLE, VA	1861-1865

Made 28 cavalry sabers a week (1862).

ALFRED H. DUFILHO SR.	PARIS, FRANCE	B1833-1853
A. (ALFRED) H. DUFILHO SR.	NEW ORLEANS, LA	1853-D1907
	21 Royal Street between Custom House and Canal Streets	

- Partner and brother: Louis Dufilho.
- Made surgical instruments.
- Had a Confederate contract for amputating kits (1861).
- Edged Weapon Production:
    200 Naval cutlasses (1861 Confederate contract)
    Foot officer swords
    Staff and field officer swords
    Lt. artillery sabers
    Cavalry sabers
    Bowie knives
    Belt knives
    Push daggers
- The New Orleans foundry cast many of the
  brass sword hilts for Dufilho.
- Dufilho also repaired surgical instruments and cutlery.

(See Blaise Pradel Jr.)
(See J.F. Zimmerman)
(See Charles Bellenot)
(Sword Maker, Knife Maker, Surgical Instrument Maker)

T.B. DUNLAP	MACON, GA	1861-1865

Made staff and field officer swords.
Sold 29 pikes to the state of Georgia (1862).
(Sword Maker, Pike Maker)

ROBERT E. DURY
(See College Hill Iron Works)

EAGLE FOUNDRY	MEMPHIS, TN	1861-1862

Located in the Memphis Navy Yard.
Owners: Mr. Streeter, Mr. McDaniel.
Superintendent and master machinist: Mr.
  Chamberlain.
Installed cavalry saber making and pistol
  making machinery (1861).

COL. BENJAMIN EASTVAN
(See Confederate State Armory)

JACOB EGE (Silversmith, Sword Hiltor)	RICHMOND, VA	B1754, 1775-D1795
JAMES L. EGE	FREDERICKSBURG, VA	1832-1845
JAMES L. EGE Salesman for Mitchell & Tyler.	RICHMOND, VA	1845-1866
JAMES H. TYLER CO. Partner: James L. Ege. (See Mitchell & Tyler-Confederate Dealer listings) (Silversmith, Watch Maker)	RICHMOND, VA	1866-1883

JOHN EGE
WILLIAM T. EGE
(See Mitchell & Tyler-Confederate Dealer listings)

WILLIAM J. ELDER	WALKINSVILLE, GA Clark County	1840-1862
WILLIAM J. ELDER & D.W. WINN Sold 50 pikes to the state of Georgia (1862).	WALKINSVILLE, GA	1862
WILLIAM J. ELDER (Gunsmith, Cutler)	WALKINSVILLE, GA	1862-1865
JOHN ESPER	GRIFFEN, GA Spaulding County	1861-1865

Sold 815 pikes to the state of Georgia (1862).
(Blacksmith, Gunsmith)

ETOWAH IRON WORKS
(See Coopers Iron Works)

J.C. EVE	ATLANTA, GA	1861-1865

Sold 126 pikes to the state of Georgia (1862).

B. FALLON
Confederate purchasing agent in Europe.
Ran 6,000 cavalry sabers through the Union blockade (1862).

THE FARISH CARTER COTTON MILL	COLUMBUS, GA Front Street near Franklin Street	1849-1865

- Established by Col. Farish Carter
  (1849-closed 1860).
- Made yard and cloth on 100 looms with
  5,000 spindles.
- Four Columbus companies rented space
  in the now vacant mill (January 1861).
    Basement: A.H. DeWitt (sword factory).
    First Floor: A.D. Brown Jr. & Sr. (a wood
      products factory making canteens,
      cotton mill shuttles, and sword handles).
    Second and third floor: E.S. Greenwood & W.C. Gray
      (rope factory, sword grip windings).
    Fourth Floor: L. Haiman & Son (sword factory).
(See A.H. DeWitt)
(See A.D. Brown Jr. & Sr.)

(See E.S. Greenwood & W.C. Gray)
(See L. Haiman & Son)

JACOB FASER   **WURTEMBERG, GERMANY**   **B1823-1828**

The Faser family immigrated to Philadelphia, PA (1828).

                                                                     PHILADELPHIA, PA   **1828-1838**

                                                                    PHILADELPHIA, PA   **1838-1848**

Faser became an apprentice and valued employee of the famous Philadelphia metalworker and sword maker F.W. Widmann.

Widmann bequeathed his pattern (sword) book to Faser when he died (1848).

                                                                     PHILADELPHIA, PA   **1848-1850**

William H. Horstmann bought the Widmann stock and equipment for $200 (1848).

Faser went to work for Horstmann and helped set up his sword shop (1849).

                                                                     PHILADELPHIA, PA   **1850-1854**

John Goodman helped Faser set up his own gun and sword shop.

Faser designed a staff and field officer sword.

                                                                     MACON, MS   **1854-1861**

Operated a silversmith shop.

                                                                     MOBILE, AL   **1861-1862**

- Set up a sword factory at 41 St. Francis Street for James Conning.
- Tooled the factory and became superintendent.
- Also etched, polished, and ground sword blades.
- Designed a staff and field officer sword for Conning.

                                                                     COLUMBUS, MS   **1862**

- Worked as a sword maker and gun maker at the Confederate Briarfield Arsenal.
- Also did special order work for local officers.
- Acted as a consultant to the Leech & Rigdon Sword Factory located near the arsenal.
- Made a brace of dueling pistols for Confederate President Jefferson Davis.
- Moved to Selma, AL, when the Briarfield Arsenal machinery and equipment was moved to the Selma, AL, Arsenal after Union troops had gotten too close (1863).

                                                                     SELMA, AL   **1863-1864**

- Worked at the Selma Arsenal.
- Parks, Lyons & Co. (Mobile, AL) offered Faser a job, but he declined (1863).

                                                                     MACON, MS   **1864-D1891**

- Opened a silversmiths shop.
- Continued to make guns and swords.
- Became mayor and later an alderman.
- Jacob Faser died (1891).

(See Briarfield Arsenal)
(See F.W. Widmann)
(See W.H. Horstmann)
(See John Goodman)
(Silversmith, Sword Maker, Gun Maker, Blade Etcher, Designer)

CYRUS FISHER	STRASBURG, VA	B1814-1856
WILLIAM B. FISHER	STRASBURG, VA	B1820-1856
W. (WILLIAM) B. AND C. (CYRUS) FISHER	LYNCHBURG, VA 176 Main Street	1856-1865

Called Lynchburg Gun & Pistol Emporium.
Adv. as importers, manufacturers, and dealers in guns, pistols, and fine cutlery (1856).
Partners and brothers: Levy Fisher, George Fisher.

CYRUS FISHER	LYNCHBURG, VA 176 Main Street	1865-D1877

Partner and son: Samuel O. Fisher.

L. (LOUIS) FITZPATRICK	NATCHEZ, MS	1845-1885

Son of Rees.
(Gunsmith)

REES FITZPATRICK	CINCINNATI, OH	B1809-1831

Probably apprenticed under one of the many German knife makers in Cincinnati.

	BATON ROUGE, LA	1831-1838

- Purchased a lot on St. Louis Street behind Daniel Searles' house (1833).
- Probably did work for Daniel Searles.
- Made a bowie knife for Col. James Bowie, which was ordered by his brother Rezin Pleasant Bowie.
- Silversmith C. Moore moved into Fitzpatrick's shop when he left for Natchez, Mississippi (1838).

(See Daniel Searles)

	NATCHEZ, MS	1838-D1868

- Union Street, between Main and State (1838-1858), then on Market Street, north side of Court House Square (1858-1868).
- Adv. making and repairing guns, mathematical instruments repaired, steel-type and stamp cutting, and canes mounted (1840).
- Adv. watch and clock repair, mathematical instrument repair, cane mounting, gunsmithing, rifle making and repairing, and burnishing and polishing of arms of every description, including edged weapons (1858).
- During the Mexican War, outfitted a Natchez Infantry Co. with bowie bayonets.
- Made presentation swords for Maj. Gen. John Anthony Quitman (1848) and for Maj. Earl Van Dorn (1860), both with Damascus blades.

(Gun Maker, Sword Maker, Knife and Bayonet Maker, Watch Maker, Clock Maker, Silversmith, Goldsmith, Jeweler)

BENJAMIN FLAGG	MILLBURY, MA	B1807-1849

Employee and later partner at Asa H. Waters & Co. (1843-1849).

B. (BENJAMIN) FLAGG & CO.	MILLBURY, MA	1849-1850

Bought musket- and bayonet-making machinery from Asa H. Waters.

Sold 760 muskets and 274 rifles to Glaze
  & Radcliff (1849).

BENJAMIN FLAGG   MILLBURY, MA   1851-1852
Partner at William Glaze & Co.

B. FLAGG & CO.   MILLBURY, MA   1852-D1882
(See Andrus Waters-Maker listings)
(See William Glaze)
(Gunsmith)

FORD (J.J.) & DUMAS   ATHENS, GA   1861-1862
Sold the state of Georgia 90 pikes (1862).

J.J. FORD   ATHENS, GA   1862-1865
Sold the state of Georgia 136 bowie knives (1862).
(Gunsmith, Cutler)

C. (CHARLES) H. (HENRY) FORD   ATHENS, GA   1865
Master armorer for Cook & Brother.
(See Ferdinand W.C. Cook)
(Gunsmith)

B.P. FREEMAN   MACON, GA   1861-1865
Blade etcher and sword maker for E.J.
  Johnston and W.J. McElroy.
(Made a cavalry saber in his blacksmith shop).
(See E.J. Johnston)
(See W.J. McElroy)
(Etcher, Blacksmith, Sword Maker)

LOUIS FROELICH   WILMINGTON, NC   1840-1861
WILMINGTON SWORD FACTORY   WILMINGTON, NC   1861-1862
Owners: Louis Froelich, Col. Benjamin
  Eastvan (left 1862).
Froelich moved to Kenansville, NC.

CONFEDERATE STATES ARMORY   KENANSVILLE, NC   1862-1864
- Owner: Louis Froelich.
- North Carolina contracts:
    - 3,700 cavalry lances
    - 6,500 saber bayonets
    - 11,700 cavalry sabers
    - 2,700 foot officer swords
    - 600 naval cutlasses
    - 800 artillery short swords
    - ? non-comm. swords
    - ? bowie knives
- Also made 300 saber belts, 300 knapsacks, 800 gross military buttons, 1,700 sets of infantry accoutrements.
- Roman numerals are found on many of their sword hilts and scabbards.
- The factory was burned by Union troops (1864).

GARRETT & O'HARA   MEMPHIS, TN   1861-1862
Operated a brass foundry.
Made brass sword and gun parts for Leech & Rigdon (Thomas S. Leech & Co.).
Made brass military goods, including brass buttons, spurs, and stirrups.

Adv. sword and gun trimmings (1862).
(See Thomas S. Leech)

JOHN H. GILLELAND ATHENS, GA 1861-1865
Sold the state of Georgia 40 bowie knives (1862).
Designed a double-barreled cannon (one
  made at the Athens Foundry).
(House Builder, Blacksmith, Knife Maker)

HENRY GINDER
(See J.N. Hyde)

GITTER & MOSS MEMPHIS, TN 1861-1865
  Beal Street

Adv. swords, knives, and army cutlery of
  all kinds (1861).

CONRAD GLAZE HAMPSHIRE CO., VA 1831
(Gunsmith)

GEORGE GLAZE HAMPSHIRE CO., VA 1782-D1823
(Gunsmith)

GEORGE W. GLAZE SHENANDOAH VALLEY, VA
  1820-1830
(Gunsmith)

MIDDLETON GLAZE CHESTER CO., SC 1780-1812
Father of William Glaze.
GLAZE (MIDDLETON) & PRESCOTT CHESTER CO., SC 1812-1816
Made muskets and swords for War of 1812.
GLAZE (MIDDLETON)
  & BOATWRIGHT (JAMES) CHESTER CO., SC 1816-1838
  COLUMBIA, SC 1838-1851
Made sugar mills, cotton gins, carriages
  and wagons.
Built a factory on Laurel and Lincoln Streets (1850).
The factory was taken over by William Glaze
  (Middleton Glaze's son) (1851).
(See William Glaze)
(See James Boatwright)

WILLIAM GLAZE CHESTER CO., SC B1815-1838
Son of Middleton Glaze.
Probably worked in his father's business.
(See Middleton Glaze)
VEAL (JOHN SR.) & GLAZE (WILLIAM) COLUMBIA, SC 1838-1841
(See John Veal-Silversmiths listings)
(Silversmith, Jeweler, Clock and Watch Repair)
WILLIAM GLAZE COLUMBIA, SC 1841-1848
(Silversmith, Jeweler, Hardware, Guns and
  Swords, Military Goods, Clocks and Watches)

GLAZE (WILLIAM) & RADCLIFFE (THOMAS W.)	**COLUMBIA, SC**	**1848-1851**

- Ames Mfg. Co. authorized agents.
- Sold two presentation swords to state of South Carolina for Col. A.H. Gladden and Major Butler, heroes of Mexican War (1848). The swords were made by Ames Mfg. Co.
- State of South Carolina contract for 660 M1842 muskets (1849).
- Second contract for 100 muskets and 274 M1841 rifles (1849). Rifles and muskets made by B. Flagg & Co., Millbury, MA.

(See Thomas W. Radcliffe)
(Gun Makers, Sword Makers, Pistol Makers, Silversmiths, Clocks, Watches)

WILLIAM GLAZE & CO.	**COLUMBIA, SC**	**1851-1852**

- Called Palmetto Armory.
- Corner of Laurel and Lincoln Streets in the old Middletown Glaze-James Boatwright factory.
- Partners: Benjamin Flagg, James Boatwright (former partner of Middleton Glaze).
- Flagg brought his gun and bayonet machinery from Millbury, MA.
- The machinery was installed in the old Middleton Glaze-James Boatwright factory.
- The company was formed to fulfill a South Carolina contract (1851) for:
    - 1,000 M1841 rifles
    - 6,000 M1842 muskets and bayonets
    - 1,000 pair of M1842 pistols
    - 1,000 M1840 cavalry sabers
    - 1,000 M1840 lt. artillery sabers
- The cavalry saber contract was increased to 2,000 (1852) and the lt. artillery saber contract was cancelled (526 lt. artillery sabers had already been delivered).
- Glaze brought 600 brass gunlocks and bands from Balls Brass Foundry in Charleston, SC.
- Glaze also made single- and double-barrelled shotguns.
- Over 40 armorers worked at the factory.
- The Palmetto Armory name was changed to The Palmetto Iron Works (1852).

(See James Boatwright)
(See Benjamin Flagg)
(See Middleton Glaze)

WILLIAM GLAZE & CO.	**COLUMBIA, SC**	**1852-1861**

- Called Palmetto Iron Works.
- Partner: James Boatwright (died 1857).
- Foreman of the brass foundry: George A. Shields.
- Made steam engines, sugar boilers, farm implements, ornamental iron railings, iron and brass castings, saw and sugar mills, cotton gins, balls, and gears.
- James Boatwright died (1857).
- Annual production of over 500 tons (1860).
- Adv. as an iron founder and machinist in Columbia city directory (1860).
- Thomas E. McNeill, with the backing of William

Glaze and Thomas W. Radcliffe, attempted to set up a Confederate armory and foundry at Macon, GA, but it was never built (1861).

GLAZE (WILLIAM) & SHIELDS (GEORGE)   COLUMBIA, SC   1861-1868
- Palmetto Iron Works.
- George Shields operated the foundry.
- Had a state of Georgia contract for 5,000 bayonets (1861).
- Rifled and refurbished 3,720 muskets, made 54,000 Minnie Balls, and sold 1,000 shell casings (1861).
- Made rollers for the Confederate powder mills at Raleigh and Columbia, SC (1861).
- Offered to make cartridges for the state of South Carolina (1861) but was refused.
- Offered 200 old bayonets to the state of South Carolina (1861), which were refused.
- Sold castings and crucibles to the South Carolina State Military Works at Greenville (1861).
- South Carolina contract for 275 saber bayonets and 4,800 musket and rifle appendages (nipples, screws, etc.) (1862).
- Made seven prototype Asa George Revolving Cannons (1867).
- The Palmetto Iron Works was destroyed by Union General William T. Sherman (1865).
- Glaze & Shields partially rebuilt their factory (late 1865).
- Made Utley cotton presses.
- Glaze & Shields went bankrupt (1868).

WILLIAM GLAZE   COLUMBIA, SC   1868-1883
126 Richardson Street
- Palmetto Iron Works.
- Partner: R.N. Richbourg.
- Made brass military goods.
- William Glaze died (1883).
- R.N. Richbourg succeeded Glaze (1883-1930).

(Jewelers, Silversmiths, Cutlers, Gun Dealers)

THOMAS W. GODWIN   PORTSMOUTH, VA   1861-1865

Called the Virginia Iron Works.
Invented a nine-shot revolver with a bowie knife bayonet.

H. GOLBECK   GERMANY   1830-1852
   COLUMBUS, GA   1852-1861

Goldbeck worked for A.H. DeWitt as a jeweler and engraver.
Etched sword blades for DeWitt and L. Haiman & Bro.

CADMAN (ANTHONY) & GOLDBECK (H.)   COLUMBUS, GA   1861-1865
- Cadman was an English gunsmith who also immigrated to Columbus (1852).
- Made Georgia coat-of-arms buttons.
- Made Confederate eagle buttons under contract.
- Made percussion revolvers and also worked at the Columbus Arsenal (1864).
- Goldbeck was on Crawford Street (1866).
- Goldbeck was at 34 Broad Street (1873).

WILLIAM M. GOODRICH
C.W. GOODRICH
(See J.N. Hyde)

JOHN D. GRAY	GRAYSVILLE, GA Whitehall Street.	1850-1861
	GRAYSVILLE, GA	1861-1865

Gray was originally from England.
Operated a furniture factory.

- Converted his furniture factory to a military arms and equipment factory.
- Also had a foundry and gun factory in Columbus, GA, located on the Chattahoochee River at the foot of Franklin Street on Broad Street.
- Gray was the brother of William C. Gray (Greenwood & Gray).
- Foremen at the Graysville factory:
    K.A. Buzzell
    W.C. Davidson
    J.D. Douglas
    C.F. Miller
    W.J. Page
    J.H. Webb
    P.L. Webb

John D. Gray Military Production

Confederate contract for 200 Mississippi rifles.
Confederate contract for 1,000 carbines.
Alabama contract for 177 Mississippi rifles.
Georgia contract for 600 bowie knives.
Georgia contract for 1,445 pikes.
Georgia contract for 2,000 cavalry sabers.
Tennessee contract for 2,000 wooden canteens.
Virginia contract for 2,000 wooden buckets.
Confederate contract for up to 20,000 Enfield rifles.
Contract with White & Co., Dalton, GA, for 1,000 wooden tent poles, slides, and buttons.

COLONEL GREEN
(See Atlanta Arsenal)

GREENWOOD (ELDRIDGE S.) **& GRAY (WILLIAM C.)**	COLUMBUS, GA	1861-1865

- Cotton warehousemen and brokers.
- Warehouse location: Randolph Street between Broad and Front Streets.
- Gray was brother of John D. Gray.
- Greenwood & Gray rented the second and third floors of the vacant Farish Carter Cotton Mill (Front Street near Franklin Street) and set up a rope factory (January 1861).
- Financed and owned one-third interest in Abram

H. DeWitt & Co. sword factory (two-story factory on Oglethorpe Street, midway between Franklin and Bryan Streets).
- Also financed the J.P. Murray rifle factory (attached to the rear of the DeWitt sword factory on a cutoff facing Warren Street).
- Greenwood & Gray purchased City Lot 188 as a site for the factories (January 17, 1862).
- Signed contracts with the state of Alabama for 358 M1841 Mississippi rifles and 153 carbines (Murray made both).
- Cotton warehouse burned down (December 31, 1862).

(See A.H. DeWitt)
(See J.P. Murray)
(See L. Haiman & Brother)
(See John D. Gray)

GRIER (COLONEL E.C.) & MASTERSON	GRISWOLDVILLE, GA	1862

Sold the state of Georgia 113 pikes (1862).

ARTHUR BREEZE GRISWOLD	POUGHKEEPSIE, NY	B1829-1842
	NEW ORLEANS, LA	1842-1853

Partner at Hyde & Goodrich.

THOMAS (HENRY J.), GRISWOLD (ARTHUR BREEZE)	NEW ORLEANS, LA	1861-1865
ARTHUR BREEZE GRISWOLD & CO.	NEW ORLEANS, LA	1865-1866
A. (ARTHUR) B. (BREEZE) GRISWOLD & CO.	NEW ORLEANS, LA	1866-1906

Arthur Breeze Griswold died (1877).

A.B. GRISWOLD & CO. LTD.	NEW ORLEANS, LA	1906-1924

(See J.N. Hyde)
(Jewelers, Silversmith, Military Goods)

SAMUEL GRISWOLD	WINDSOR, CT	B1790-1814
	GRISWOLDVILLE, GA	1814-1861

Founded Griswoldville (10 miles from Macon).
Set up a factory and machine shop making cotton gins.
H. Stevens built Griswold a sawmill.
Also had a planing mill, gristmill, and soap and candle factory.
(See H. Stevens)

GRISWOLD (SAMUEL) & GUNNISON (ARVIN W.) (GRISWOLD & GRIER)	GRISWOLDVILLE, GA	1861-1864

- Partners: Son Giles G. Griswold (died 1861), Colonel E.C. Grier.
- Griswold converted his cotton gin factory to an armory.
- Sold the state of Georgia 804 cloverleaf pikes (1862).
- Made 3,600 brass-frame Colt-type revolvers for the Confederacy (100 a month).
- Gunnison was a cotton gin and revolver maker in New Orleans.
- Gunnison started as a foreman in Griswold's Cotton Gin Factory (1855) and became superintendent.

- The factory was burned down by Kilpatrick's Union Cavalry (November 1864).
(Pistol Maker, Pike Maker)

GROSPORT NAVY YARD (NYG)   **GROSPORT, VA**   1861-1865
The state of Virginia took over the yard (1861)
  and found 2,111 boarding pikes in inventory.

GUILBAUX & GIEFFERS (FRANZ)   **NEW ORLEANS, LA**   1861-1865
Sold bowie knives.
(Military Goods, Saddlery)

R.W. HABERSHAM   **CHARLESTON, SC**   1861-1865
Patented a saber lance (1861).
Sent a sample artillery saber to state of South Carolina.
(Cutler)

THE HAIMAN FAMILY

HERMAN HAIMAN   **COLMAR, PRUSSIA**   1800-1845

LOUIS HAIMAN   **COLMAR, PRUSSIA**   B1828-1845
Son of Herman Haiman.

ELIAS HAIMAN   **COLMAR, PRUSSIA**   B1842-1845
Son of Herman Haiman.
The Haiman family immigrated to Columbus, GA (1845).

HAIMAN (HERMAN) & SON   **COLUMBUS, GA**   1845-1860
- Partner and son: Louis Haiman.
- Operated a hardware shop (tinners by trade).
- Located on Front Street between Crawford
  and Thomas Streets (next to the Columbus Iron Works).
- Employees (all tinsmiths):
    Stelly Polk
    Theodore Bleier
    M.E. Costan
    Nathan Crun
    A. Huntley.

L. (LOUIS) HAIMAN & BROTHER   **COLUMBUS, GA**   1860-1865
- Partners: Elias Haiman (brother), Joseph
  Guy Blount.
- The Haimans converted their tin shop
  into an armory.
- Expanded rapidly, eventually covering most
  of a city block and employeeing over 400 workers.
- The armory and adjacent buildings eventually
  included blacksmith shop with trip hammers
  and 30 forges, iron and brass foundries, a machine
  shop, sewing shop, leather shop, pistol factory
  (Old Muscogee Iron Works), and sword factories
  (in Columbus Iron Works and the Farish Carter Building).
- In January 1861, Haiman rented the fourth floor of the
  vacant Farish Carter Cotton Mill and set up a sword
  factory (Front Street near Franklin Street).
  (See Farish Carter Cotton Mill)

- In 1861, Haiman rented the upper floor of the Columbus Iron Works (Thomas Street and corner of Short Street, next door to the Haiman Armory).
- Set up a large sword factory.
- Bought brass gun and sword parts from the Columbus Iron Works.

Haiman Associates

W.K. Harris—wooden sword handles.
Operated the Novelty Works (furniture factory) on Front Street, corner of Few Street.

John W. King—hiltor.
Operated the Columbus Glass Works.

Thomas S. Spear—engraver.

James H. Moshell—blade maker.

H. Golbeck—engraver.

David Wolfson—engraver.

A. Ingmire—engraver.

- Elias Haiman spent much of his time in Europe, purchasing materials (especially steel). He purchased sword blades in Solingen, Germany.
- The Haiman sword factory, located on the upper floor of the Columbus Iron Works, was called the Confederate States Sword Factory.
- It could make 250 swords a week and had over 160 employees.
- The Haimans sent a complete sword price list to Chief of Ordnance Capt. Richard Cuyler, Savannah, GA (October 22, 1861).
- (See Price List)
- The Haimans bought the Muscogee Iron Works (Oglethorpe Street and the corner of Franklin Street) from Lockhart (Henry) & Moses (Isaac) in April 1862.
- It had a foundry, machine shop, and blacksmith shop with 30 forges.
- Converted it into a pistol factory (Columbus Firearm Company) and added a three-story building (65' x 85').
- A leather shop was added later.
- Made navy revolvers (Confederate contract for 10,000).

Louis Haiman & Brother Military Production

- Had Confederate contracts (Atlanta Arsenal) for 8,000 cavalry sabers.
- Made 80 sabers a day.
- The first group of sabers went to Clanton's Alabama cavalry regiment.
- Had a Confederate contract for 50,000 M1842 sword bayonets (delivered 3,150).
- Had a Confederate contract for 10,000 navy revolvers.
- Also made shotguns, rifles, and shotgun bayonets.

Other Sword Production
Artillery officer swords
Foot officer swords
Naval officer swords
Lt. artillery sabers
Artillery short swords
Non-comm. swords
Presentation swords, including those made for Col. Peyton H. Colquitt (first sword made by the Haimans), Gen. Henry D. Clayton, Gen. Archibald Gracie, Gen. Alpheus Baker, Capt. Edgar G. Dawson, and Capt. E.V. White

Military Equipment Production
Brass plates
Brass buckles
Oil cloth
Haversacks
Cartridge boxes with straps
Sword bayonets
Leather scabbards
Tassels
Leather sword belts
Saddles
Bridles
Sheet metal camp equipment, including cooking utensils

L. Haiman & Brother Sword Price List
Sent to Confederate Ordnance Department (October 22, 1861)
Capt. Richard Cuyler, Chief of Ordnance, Savannah, GA

$25 each
Officers
Plain

$35-$50 each
Officers
Figured blades and gilted mountings

$23 each
Cavalry sabers
36-inch blade, basket hilt of brass, metal scabbard, black leather belt, shoulder strap and tassel on sword guard

$20 each
Artillery sabers
32-inch blade, single strap guard, metal scabbard, black leather belt

$14 each
Artillery sword (short)
19-inch blade, leather scabbard (brass mounted), black leather belt, heavy brass handle

- Adv. brass buckles, plates, bayonet scabbard mountings, camp furniture of tin or iron, officer and non-comm. swords, cavalry sabers (September 1861).

- Adv. quality swords made at the Confederate States Sword Factory, Columbus, GA, by L. Haiman & Company (November 1861).
- The Haiman complex was burned down by Union General James C. Wilson's Cavalry Corps after Louis Haiman refused to take the oath of allegiance (April 17, 1865).

L. (LOUIS) HAIMAN & CO.   COLUMBUS, GA   1865-1868
- Partners: Joseph G. Blount, Elias Haiman.
- Employee: James H. Moshell (blacksmith).
- Operated the Phoenix Foundry & Machine Shop (Oglethorpe between Bridge Street and Franklin Street).
- Manufactured ovens, pots, plows, grist and saw mills, as well as brass castings.

BLOUNT (JOSEPH G.)
& HAIMAN (ELIAS & LOUIS)   COLUMBUS, GA   1868-1875

Operated the Southern Agricultural Works.
Employee: James H. Moshell (blacksmith).
Major production was plows.
Joseph G. Blount died (1875).

LOUIS & ELIAS HAIMAN   ATLANTA, GA   1875-1894
Louis Haiman died (1878).

ELIAS HAIMAN   CLEVELAND, OH   1875-D1914
Vice-president of the Empire Plow Co.
Elias Haiman died in Germany (1914).

HALL (H.T.) & DEXTER (C.E.)   COLUMBUS, GA   1861-1865
                                                 44 Broad Street

Cotton brokers.
Had a branch in Montgomery, AL.
Supplied arms and accoutrements
  to the Confederacy.

HALL, MOSES & CO.   COLUMBUS, GA   1861-1865
                                 96 Broad Street
- Partners:
    Hervey Hall
    Simeon T. Hall
    J.J. Moses
    William A. Beach
- Bookkeeper: E.I. Moses.
- Clerks: Moultrie Moses, F.R. Matthews, R.H. Lockhart.
- A hardware manufacturer.
- Made pikes sold by A.H. DeWitt.
- Had a Georgia contract for rifles (March 1862).

BEACH (WILLIAM A.) & MOSES (J.J.)   COLUMBUS, GA   1865-1875
                                                   96 Broad Street

Hardware makers.

JAMES H. HALL   ATLANTA, GA   1861-1865
Sold the state of Georgia 15 bowie knives and 6 pikes (1862).

F.M. HALL	ATLANTA, GA	**1861-1865**

Sold the state of Georgia 49 bowie knives (1862).
(Knife Maker)

HAMILTON & CUNNINGHAM
(See Nashville Plow Works)

HANNON & M.C. ALIER	MOBILE, AL	**1861-1865**

Made foot officer swords.
(Cutler)

W.K. HARRIS	COLUMBUS, GA	**1839-1865**

- Owned the Novelty Works (1860-1865).
- Furniture manufacturer.
- Factory location: Front Street, corner of Few Street.
- Shop location: 148 Broad Street.
- Made wooden sword grips for L. Haiman & Brother.

(See L. Haiman & Brother)

NASON HATCH	ATLANTA, GA	**1861-1865**

Made pikes during the Civil War.
(Pike Maker)

O.S. HAYNES	ATLANTA, GA	**1861-1865**

Sold the state of Georgia 49 bowie knives (1862).

HECK (COL. J.M.), BRODIE & CO.	RALEIGH, NC	**1861-1865**

Called Raleigh Bayonet Factory.
Confederate contract for 1,000 bayonets (1864).
Foreman: Reese H. Butler.

CHARLES HEINZ SR.	COLUMBIA, SC	**1840-1861**

Made bowie knives.

	ATLANTA, GA	**1861-1867**
	8 Whitehall Street at Alabama Street	

Atlanta Arsenal contract to convert flintlocks
   during the Civil War.
Had 12 employees.

HEINZ (CHARLES SR. & JR.)
  & BERKELE (JOHN)   ATLANTA, GA   **1867-1890**
        8 Whitehall Street and Alabama Street

Sold cutlery, hardware, guns, rifles, pistols,
   and ammunition.

HEINZ (CHARLES SR.)
  & SON (CHARLES JR.   ATLANTA, GA   **1890-1905**
(Gunsmith, Cutler, Hardware)

A.G. & F.J. HERRINGTON
(See W.J. McElroy)

FLORINA HERZOG	MACON, GA	**1835-1855**
BOLSHAW & HERZOG (FLORINA)	MACON, GA	**1855-1861**
	11 Colton Avenue	

(Crockery Maker)

FLORINA HERZOG	MACON, GA	**1861-1865**

Etched blades for E.J. Johnston & Co. (swords),
  W.J. McElroy & Co. (swords), and Coopers Iron
  Works (knives) during the Civil War.
(Blade Etcher)

JAMES M. HIGGINS	LA GRANGE, GA	**1861-1865**

Sold 191 pikes to the state of Georgia (1862).
(Gunsmith, Cutler)

HILLMAN & BROTHER	MEMPHIS, TN	**1861-1865**

49 Front Row at Court Street on the Tennessee River.
Made bayonets for Mississippi rifles and shotguns.
Operated a rolling mill.
Also made rifle barrels.

D.C. HODGKINS & SONS	MACON, GA 507 Mulberry Street	**1858-1862**

- Partners and sons: John C. Hodgkins, Walter C. Hodgkins.
- Ordered arms for the state of Georgia from northern manufacturers (1860).
- Had Georgia contracts for 700 Colt revolvers, 700 cavalry sabers, and 250 rifles.
- Made rifled carbines, surgical instruments, and bowie knives for the state of Georgia.
- Confederate contract to alter over 2,000 flintlock muskets to percussion.
- Also made cotton samplers and farm equipment.
- The Confederate government took over the company, and with the Findlay Iron Works, established the Macon Armory (1862).

E.R. HODGSON & BROTHER	ATLANTA, GA	**1861-1865**

Sold the state of Georgia 28 pikes (1862).

R.J. HUGHES	MONROE, GA Walton County	**1861-1865**

Sold the state of Georgia 1,469 bowie knives (1862).
(Gunsmith, Carriage Maker)

JOHN R. HUNT	MACON, GA	**1861-1865**

Made brass moldings for W.J. McElroy.
Company name was McElroy & Hunt Co.
(See W.J. McElroy)

JAMES HURT	MACON, GA	**1861-1865**

Sold the state of Georgia 17 pikes (1862).

MAJ. CALEB HUSE
- Born in Newburyport, MA.
- Attended and taught at West Point Military Academy.
- Served in the U.S. artillery and ordnance department before the Civil War.

- Served in the Confederate ordnance department under Colonel Gorges (Chief of Ordnance) during the Civil War as a captain (later a major).
- Inspected many imported LeMat revolvers.
- Went to Europe as a Confederate purchasing agent.
- Bought over 18,000 rifles and carbines, 16,178 cavalry sabers, and huge amounts of military goods.
- Made large purchases from the Imperial Austrian Arsenal, including sabers.
- Bought M1853 (variation) cavalry sabers from Isaac Campbell & Co., London.
- A relative of brass founder Samuel Huse, Newburyport, MA.

(See Samuel Huse-U.S. listings)

JAMES N. HYDE	NEW YORK, NY	1780-1798
HYDE (JAMES N.) & NEVINS (RUFUS)	NEW YORK, NY	1798-1814
J. (JAMES) N. HYDE	NEW ORLEANS, LA	1814-1819
	58 Chartres Street	

Partner: Charles W. Goodrich.

HYDE (JAMES N.) & GOODRICH (CHARLES W.)   NEW ORLEANS, LA   1819-1861
58 Chartres Street (1819-1838)
15 Chartres Street (1838-1858)

- Factory and foundry at Canal and Royal Streets (1858-1861).
- Partners: Henry Thomas Jr., Arthur Breeze Griswold (1853-1861), William M. Goodrich (1853-1861).
- Authorized agent for Ames Mfg. Co. swords.
- Sold Deringer pistols.
- Hilted and assembled swords.
- James N. Hyde left (1861).
- The company continued as Thomas, Griswold & Co.

THOMAS (HENRY JR.), GRISWOLD (ARTHUR BREEZE) (T.G. & CO.)   NEW ORLEANS, LA   1861-1862

- Factory and foundry at the corner of Canal and Royal Streets.
- Partners: Henry Ginder, A.L. Abbott, William M. Goodrich.
- Adv. as importers of pistols, Enfield rifles, swords, caps, cartridges, bowie knives, and military and sporting goods.
- Made presentation swords, staff and field officer swords, foot officer swords, lt. artillery officer swords, cavalry sabers, lt. artillery sabers, brass-hilt naval cutlasses, and cavalry lances (French style).
- Made presentation swords for Gen. Sterling Price and Capt. J.F. Girault.
- Published *The Lancers Manual* (1861).
- Sword production stopped when New Orleans fell to Farragut's naval squadron (April 1862).

(See Arthur Breeze Griswold)
(Silversmith, Jeweler, Sword Makers, Importers, Military Goods)

FREDERICK HYER   RICHMOND, VA   1855-1860

Machinist for Talbot & Brother, engine and car builders at 1529 E. Cary Street.

F. (FREDERICK) HYER	RICHMOND, VA	1861-D1881

Made 80 pikes for the state of Georgia (1862)
  and for the Confederacy.
Made naval cutlasses (two types) with solid brass hilts.
(Machinist, Sword Maker, Pike Maker)

A. INGMIRE	COLUMBUS, GA	1860-1865
	31 Broad Street	

Engraver.
Blade Etcher for A.H. DeWitt and L. Haiman & Brother.
(See A.H. DeWitt)
(See L. Haiman & Co.)

J. (JAMES) B. JAQUES & BRO.	COLUMBUS, GA	1861-1865
	Oglethorpe Street, corner of Bryan Street	

Partner and brother: R.W. Jaques.
Bookkeeper: S.R. Jaques.
Employee: Henry Hawthorn.
They were carriage makers.
The Jaques were associates in A.H. DeWitt & Co (1862).
Made leather scabbards for DeWitt swords.

EDMUND J. JOHNSTON	PUTNAM CO., GA	B1819-1832
Brother of William.	MACON, GA	1832-1838

WILLIAM BUTLER JOHNSTON	PUTNUM CO., GA	B1809-1831

Apprenticed as a jeweler (1824-1831).

	MACON, GA	1831-1838

Opened a jewelry and silverware shop.
Expanded rapidly.
Sold imported watches and pistols.

WILLIAM B. JOHNSTON & CO.	MACON, GA	1838-1850

- Partner and brother: Edmund J. Johnston.
- Started to sell military equipment at the beginning of the Mexican War (1846-1848).
- Sold guns, pistols, and swords.
- Repaired clocks and watches.
- Edmund took over the shop (1850).

E. (EDMUND) J. JOHNSTON	MACON, GA	1850-1860
E. (EDMUND) J. JOHNSTON & CO.	MACON, GA	1860-1887

- Located on Mulberry Street next to the telegraph office, two doors down from the Lanier House Hotel.
- Partner: William B. Johnston (died 1887).
- Edmund J. Johnston died (1879).
- Made foot officer swords, cavalry sabers, lt. artillery sabers, naval cutlasses, foot artillery swords (French style).
- Made 40 foot officers swords, 40 lt. artillery sabers, 40 cavalry sabers, and 40 naval cutlasses a week (1862).
- Made a presentation sword for Gen. W.H.T. Walker (1861).
- Made a sword presented to Jefferson Davis (1862).
- Made officer swords for Col. E.W. Chastains and his officers (8th Georgia Infantry Regiment).
- Blade engravers: Florina Herzog, B.P. Freeman.

- Also made havelocks, belt buckles, capes of enameled cloth, and cartridges.
- Confederate contract for Colt cartridges (1862).
- Purchased a brass-rolling machine from T.C. Nisbet, Macon, GA.

(See T.C. Nisbet)

V.J. KARNES	**NASHVILLE, TN**	**1856-1866**

Made bowie knives.
(Cutler, Knife Maker)

MR. KEAN	**COLUMBUS, GA**	**1861-1865**

Was a shop foreman in A.H. DeWitt's sword
  factory on Oglethorpe Street.
In early 1863, when J.P. Murray bought DeWitt's
  sword factory, Kean stayed on.
It was thought he continued some cavalry saber production.
(See A.H. DeWitt)
(See J.P. Murray)

A. (ALFRED) KENT	**ATLANTA, GA**	**1861-1865**

Sold 126 pikes to the state of Georgia (1863).
(Gunsmith)

D. KERNAGHAN & CO.	**NEW ORLEANS, LA** 65 Canal Street	**1855-1858**

Partner: M.J. Kernaghan.

	NEW ORLEANS, LA 21 Camp Street	**1858-1861**

Sold Tranter revolvers.
Partner: M.J. Kernaghan.
(Jeweler, Military Goods)

PETER KIND & SON	**COLUMBIA, SC** Sumpter Street	**1861-1865**

Partner and son: Yawcob Kind.
Operated a brass foundry.
Made brass sword mountings for Kraft, Goldsmith & Kraft.
(See Kraft, Goldsmith & Kraft)

JOHN W. KING	**COLUMBUS, GA**	**1839-1859**
KING (JOHN W.), ALLEN) **(A.M.) & CAMAK (THOMAS**	**COLUMBUS, GA** Front and Crawford Streets	**1860-1865**

Called Columbus Glassworks.
Did contract work for Louis Haiman &
  Brother as a sword hiltor.
(See Louis Haiman & Brother)

KITTRIDGE (BENJAMIN)) **& FOLSOM (GEORGE**	**NEW ORLEANS, LA** 55 St. Charles	**1857-1865**

(See Benjamin Kittridge-U.S. listings)

KNIGHTS BLACKSMITH SHOP	**AMELIA, VA**	**1861-1865**

Confederate contract for bowie knives.

HENRY F. KRAFT	**GERMANY**	B1828-1855
	COLUMBIA, SC	1855-1862

Master etcher.
Adv. as a gold and silver plater in the
 Columbia business directory (1861).
(Silversmith, Goldsmith, Jeweler, Etcher)

PETER W. KRAFT	**GERMANY**	B1831-1855
Brother of Henry F. Kraft.		
	COLUMBIA, SC 184 Main Street	1855-1862

Adv. bowie knives and imported and
 American-made guns, rifles, and pistols (1861).
Employees: Windhorn Deterick (gunsmith), H.
 Reckling (gunsmith), Lipmann
 Goldsmith (Goldsmidt) (company clerk).
(Gunsmith, Gun and Pistol Dealer)

KRAFT (PETER W.), GOLDSMITH **(LIPMANN) & KRAFT(HENRY F.) (K.G.K.)**	**COLUMBIA, SC** 181 Richardson Street	1862-1865

- Made bowie knives.
- Imported German sword blades.
- Made foot officer swords.
- Made very unusual cavalry officer swords
 (using some old triple-fullered, double-edged
 straight blades made by Schimelbush & Joest,
 Solingen, Germany, in the early 1800s).
- Made staff and field officer swords.
- Bought sword mountings from Peter King & Son.

PETER W. KRAFT	**COLUMBIA, SC**	1865-1884
P. (PETER) W. KRAFT & SONS	**COLUMBIA, SC**	1884-1890

(See Peter King & Son)
(Sword Maker, Jeweler, Silversmith, Goldsmith)

LAN & SHERMAN (See Lau & Shuman)

LAU (T.A.) & SHUMAN (LEWIS)	**RICHMOND, VA** Corner of 9th and Cary Streets	1855-1865

- Operated the Southern File Manufactory.
- Employees:
    John Boothroyd (file maker)
    Henry Deubel (file maker)
    George Gerersdorfer (file maker)
    John Slinn (file maker)
    John H. Paulding (file maker)
    Henry S. Whitfield (file maker)
    A.J. Bowers (Founder)
- Made bowie knives during the Civil War.
- Adv. bowie knives of the finest steel (1861).

(File Maker, Knife Maker)

THOMAS S. LEECH	**MEMPHIS, TN**	B1825-1857

Leech was a cotton broker (1855-1857.

THOMAS S. LEECH & CO.	MEMPHIS, TN	1857-1861
Partner: John Burgess Leech.		
Agents for Henry Deringer Jr. pistols.	MEMPHIS, TN Main and McCall Streets	1861-1862

- Called Memphis Novelty Works.
- Partners: John Burgess Leech, Charles H. Rigdon, brother W. Rigdon (master engraver).
- The Rigdons were machinists, scale makers, and revolver makers on Poplar between Main and 2nd Avenue.
- The Rigdons brought some revolver-making equipment with them when they joined Leech.
- Leech & Co. made swords, revolvers, bayonets, knives, and military equipment.
- Bought brass sword parts from Garrett & O'Hara.
- Adv. in the *Memphis Daily Appeal* (1861-1862) as mfg. of army cutlery, including infantry swords, cavalry swords and sabers, artillery cutlasses and knives, bowie knives of every description, and bayonets for shotguns and rifles.
- Memphis fell to Union troops (1862).
- Leech & Co. moved to Columbus, MS.

	COLUMBUS, MS	1862

- Called Novelty Works.
- Partners: Charles H. and W. Rigdon.
- Moved to a location next to the Briarfield Armory, Columbus, MS.
- Jacob Faser was a consultant to Leech.
- Moved to Greensboro, GA, in mid-December.

(See Charles H. Rigdon)
(See Garrett & O'Hara)
(See Jacob Faser)
(Gun Dealer, Gun Maker, Pistol Maker, Sword Maker, Military Equipment Maker, Blacksmith, Cutler)

THOMAS S. LEECH & CO.	GREENSBORO, GA	1863-1864

- Set up a revolver factory in the Greensboro Steam Factory (February 1863).
- Bought from John Cunningham.
- Also bought a lot at Bush and South Streets.
- Stopped sword production and sold the sword machinery and materials. They adv. the sale in April 1863.
- Charles H. & W. Rigdon left Leech (1864) and joined Jesse Ansley in Augusta, GA (Rigdon-Ansley & Co., revolver factory, on Marbury Street).

LEECH & CO.	GREENSBORO, GA	1864-1865
Partners: Thomas S. Leech, John Burgess Leech.		
Had a Confederate revolver contract (1864).		
THOMAS S. LEECH	MEMPHIS, TN	1866-D1885

Leech Products Markings

Thomas S. Leech & Co.
Leech & Rigdon

Memphis Novelty Works
Novelty Works

Thomas S. Leech Product Line

Confederate contract for 5,000 cavalry sabers (1862); 1,500 are known to have been delivered
Cavalry officer swords
Staff and field officer swords
Foot officer swords
Artillery short swords
Lt. artillery sabers
Bowie bayonets for rifles and shotguns
Bowie knives
Percussion revolvers (.36-caliber iron-framed Navy revolvers)
Bullet molds
Brass castings
Sword belts
Military drums
Brass belt buckles
Brass spurs and stirrups
Brass mountings for gunsmiths
Also repaired light machinery and printing presses and did general blacksmithing

---

A. LINDE **MEMPHIS, TN** **1855-1867**
217 Main Street

Maker of Deringer-type pistols and guns.
Dealer in cutlery, watches, clocks, guns, rifles,
  pistols, gun equipment, gunsmithing materials,
  and silverware.
Also did gun repairs.

N.B. LOVE **COLUMBUS, GA** **1861-1865**
Thomas Street between Short and
Front Streets

Called Love's Variety Shop.
Made wood products such as buttons.
Also was a pattern maker (wooden prototypes
  used to make foundry castings).
Made the rattlesnake-hilt pattern for A.H.
  DeWitt's foot officer sword.

LOWRY & WILDER **ATLANTA, GA** **1861-1865**
Sold 193 pikes to the state of Georgia (1862).

MACFEE & SIEGLE
(See Edwin Boyle)

MARSELLES MCKENNIE & CO. **CHARLOTTESVILLE, VA** **1860-1865**
Made foot officer swords.
Had four employees.
Made six swords a week.

MARSHALL, BEACH & CO.   WILMINGTON, NC   1861-1865
Sold 250 bayonets to the city of Wilmington (1864).

MARSHALL & RICE
(See Hammond Marshall)

HAMMOND MARSHALL   MAINE   B1814-1861
Became a dentist.

H. (HAMMOND) MARSHALL & CO.   ATLANTA, GA   1861-1862
Mariella Street between Simpson and Latimer Streets

- Partners: Lemuel Dean, Thomas W. Chandler (factory superintendent; B1823-D1880), William W. Johnson (foundry superintendent).
- Had a contract with the state of Georgia for cavalry sabers but they were rejected because of inferior scabbards made from burned iron.
- Had Confederate contracts with Lt. Moses Hanibal Wright at the Atlanta Arsenal for 100 cavalry sabers at $12 each (February 17, 1862), 94 cavalry sabers at $12 each (April 5, 1862), 3,000 cavalry sabers at $14 each (May 22, 1862), and 1,000 lt. artillery sabers at $13 each (May 22, 1862).
- Advanced $10,000 by the Confederate government to start saber production on 4,000 sabers (May 22, 1862).
- Marshall was to deliver 170 sabers a week, all of which were to be delivered in 8 months.
- Had a Confederate contract for 3,000 cavalry sabers at $18.50 each (June 5, 1862). The contract was not completed because of a shortage of materials.
- Some saber scabbards were refused by the Atlanta Arsenal because they were made of burned iron. Marshall corrected the problem in two months.

ATLANTA SABER MANUFACTORY   ATLANTA, GA   1862-1864
- President: Hammond Marshall.
- Partners: Lemuel Dean, Thomas W. Chandler, William W. Johnson.
- Had 30 factory workers.
- Formed a partnership with one of his workers (James Rice) and made 418 pikes delivered to the Atlanta Arsenal (July 1862).
- Made two presentation swords, which were delivered to the Atlanta Arsenal in August 1862.
- Adv. ("Old rifle barrels and axes wanted") in the *Atlanta Daily Intelligence* (November 1862).
- Made a presentation sword for Gen. Braxton Bragg (1863).
- Also made staff and field officers swords sold locally.
- Had Confederate contracts for:
    Belt plates
    Horseshoes
    Horseshoe nails
    Grind stones
    Portfire tubes
    Portfire tube molds
    Tent spikes and plates

  Screwdrivers
  Bullet molds
  Brass boxes
  Sheet brass
  Cartridge box knobs
  Cast copper bars
  Axes
  Wrenches
- Adv. in the *Daily Intelligence* (May 1863) for blacksmithing, carriage, buggy and wagon repair, and horse and mule shoeing.
- Adv. in the *Southern Confederacy* (June 1864) for old sheet iron.
- Began making scythes (1864).
- Returned to dentistry after the war.
- Hammond Marshall died (1874).

Atlanta Saber Manufactory List of Workers (1862)

E.T. Allen	W. Johns
Robert Arrent	A.J. Luttrell
G.W. Bailey	E.B. Marshall
J.M. Barney	W.L. McCool
W.D. Black	T.J. McGarie
J.M. Blankenship	Edward E. Murphy
Joshua R. Browing	Samuel A. Orr
J.W. Callaway	James Rice
John W. Cason	Charles Shepherd
Joshua Condon	Isaac O. Shields
Joab Curtis	D.J. Strode
John Farrell	E.R. Tucker
R.W. Garner	E. Walker
J.L. Griffin	Richard Warswick
D.Y. Hicks	J.B. Wilson

(Sword Maker, Pike Maker, Tool Maker, Military Equipment)

J. (JOSEPH) J. (JOHN) MARTIN **MARTHASVILLE, GA** B1813-1854
Marthasville became Atlanta, GA.
Partner: David Thurman.

                TILTON, GA 1854-D1884

- Partners and sons: William Henry Martin (B1842-D1895), Micajah David Martin (B1851-D1909).
- Called Tilton Armory.
- Sold 12 pikes to the state of Georgia (1862).
- Employee: William H.C. Cowan.
- Had a sword factory making cavalry sabers.
- Made rifles also.

(Gunsmith, Blacksmith, Pike Maker, Sword Maker)

O.W. MASSEY   **ATLANTA, GA** 1861-1865
Sold 63 pikes to the state of Georgia (1862).

M.E. MATTHEWS   ATLANTA, GA   1861-1865
Sold 10 pikes to the state of Georgia (1862).

ANTHONY L. MAXWELL   SARATOGA, NY   1840-1860
A. (ANTHONY) L. MAXWELL & CO.   KNOXVILLE, TN   1861-1862
Tennessee contract for muskets (1861).
Altered flintlocks and repaired arms.
Had a foundry, machine shop, and blacksmith shop.

SHEPHARD, MAXWELL
   (ANTHONY L.) & HOYT   KNOXVILLE, TN   1863
Became part of the Confederate Knoxville
   Arsenal (5,000 pikes were found in the arsenal
   when Union troops burned it down in 1863).
(Gunsmith, Blacksmith, Machinist, Pike Maker)

MCDONALD (EDWARD)
   & LYONS (ASHER)   RICHMOND, VA   1850-1855
Southern Regalia and Banner Emporium.

EDWARD MCDONALD   RICHMOND, VA   1855-1875
    9th Street between Main and Cary Streets
(Regalia)

MCDONALD & CO.   RICHMOND, VA   1875-1880
Owner: Rachel McDonald (wife of Edward).

WILLIAM JOHN MCELROY (M'ELROY)   COEYMANS, NY   B1824-1844
    Green County

WILLIAM JOHN MCELROY   SAVANNAH, GA   1844-1845
(Tinsmith, Coppersmith)

WILLIAM J. MCELROY   MACON, GA   1845-1860
    Poplar between 3rd and 4th Streets
Opened a tin shop.

W. (WILLIAM) J. (JOHN)
   MCELROY (& CO.)   MACON, GA   1860-1870
- Converted his tin shop into an armory.
- Added a building on 3rd Street (1861) as a brass foundry and an ornamental iron foundry.
- Set up a three-story sword factory (32' x 68') on 4th Street in the fall of 1862. It included a blacksmith shop, polishing and grinding shop, and machine shop.
- Bought a brass-rolling machine from T.C. Nisbet.
- Partners:
    - James Thompson (sales)
    - Alexander S. Reynolds (brass founder, 1860-1861)
    - Cornelius D. Wall (machinist, 1860-1861)
    - J.E. Wells Jr. (blade etcher)
    - S.E. Thues (blade etcher)
- Reynolds and Wall went to work for the Macon Armory (1861).
- William John McElroy died (1888).

(See T.C. Nisbet)
(See S.E. Thues)
(See J.E. Wells Jr.)

W. (WILLIAM) J. MCELROY HERRINGTON (A.G. & F.J.) & CO.   1862-1863
A separate company making foot officer swords.
The Herringtons were machinists.

MCELROY (WILLIAM J.) & HUNT (JOHN R.) 1862-1863
A separate company making brass buckles.
Hunt was a brass molder.
McElroy adv. swords, sabers, and bowie knives of
  all descriptions in the *Macon Telegraph* during the Civil War.

McElroy Products

Tinware (Japanware)
Copperware
Ornamental brass castings (general brasswork)
Brass mounts for guns, knives, and swords
Ornamental iron
Farm tools
Brass cavalry bits
Brass cavalry spurs (50 a week)
Brass cap insignia
Plated cap insignia
Brass belt buckles
Sword belts and straps
Tin canteens

McElroy Edged Weapons Production

Infantry non-comm. swords (20 a week)
Naval cutlasses (20 a week)
Staff and field officer swords
Foot officer swords (20 a week)
Foot artillery swords
Lt. artillery officer sabers
Cavalry officer sabers
Cavalry trooper sabers
French foot officer swords (imported)
Bowie (belt) knives (20 a week)
Lasso knives
Bayonets
Infantry pikes (1862 state of Georgia contract for pikes)

EDWARD D. MCFEE
(See Edwin Boyle)

ALEXANDER MCKINSTRY   AUGUSTA, GA   B1823-1836
                               MOBILE, AL   1836-1875
Alabama contract for 1,000 bowie knives
  and 1,000 bowie shaped pikes to outfit the 48th Infantry
  Regiment of Alabama from Mobile, probably made
  by Dickson & Nelson (1861).
McKinstry was colonel of the 32nd Infantry Regiment
  of Alabama from Mobile (1862).

(See Owen W. Dickson)
(Lawyer, Edged Weapon Dealer)

MEMPHIS NOVELTY WORKS
(See Thomas S. Leech)

J.W. & L.L. MOORE	ATLANTA, GA	1861-1865

Sold the state of Georgia 853 bowie knives (1862).

MURDOCK MORRISON	WENTWORTH, NC	1821-1863
	Rockingham County	
	LAUREL HILL, NC	1863-1865

Partner: William Buchanan.
Made pistols, rifles, and bowie knives.
(See John Buchanan)

JACOB H. MOSHELL	COLUMBUS, GA	B1829-1862

Blacksmith by trade (later a carpenter also).
Adv. as a gun-barrel maker (1862).
Did work for the Columbus Arsenal as barrel maker.

A.H. DEWITT & CO.	COLUMBUS, GA	1862

Jacob H. Moshell was an associate of DeWitt.
Made sword blades (marked "J.H. Moshell-Columbus, GA")
  for DeWitt.

L. HAIMAN & BROTHER	COLUMBUS, GA	1863-1865

Jacob H. Moshell was an employee and
  blade maker.

L. HAIMAN & CO.	COLUMBUS, GA	1865-1868

Jacob H. Moshell was a blacksmith.

BLOUNT (JOSEPH G.)		
& HAIMAN (ELIAS & LOUIS)	COLUMBUS, GA	1868-1875

Jacob H. Moshell was a blacksmith.
After the war, Moshell lived in Russell County,
  AL, right across the state line.
Abram H. DeWitt also lived there after the war.
Jacob H. Moshell died (1898).
(See A.H. DeWitt)
(See L. Haiman & Brother)

SLOCUM (J.C.) & MURRAY (DANIEL)	MOBILE, AL	1855-1858
D. (DANIEL) MURRAY	MOBILE, AL	1859-1874

Maine Street between Hamilton and Lawrence Streets.
Made foot officer swords.
(Blacksmith, Sword Maker)

JOHN P. MURRAY	LONDON, ENGLAND	B1825-1850
HAPPOLDT (BENJAMIN G.)		
& MURRAY (JOHN P.)	CHARLESTON, SC	1850-1859
	45 State Street	

(Gun Makers)

J. (JOHN) P. MURRAY	COLUMBUS, GA	1859-1889
	46 Broad Street	

- Adv. in the Columbus directory as successor
  to Happoldt & Murray, making shotguns, rifles,
  and pistols (1860).

- Greenwood & Gray, cotton brokers and warehousemen, financed the building of a sword factory for Abram H. DeWitt and a rifle factory for John P. Murray (January 1861).
- Bought city lot 188 for that purpose (January 17, 1862).
- DeWitt's sword factory was on Oglethorpe St. midway between Franklin and Bryon Streets.
- Murray's rifle factory was attached to DeWitt's sword factory on a rear cutoff facing Warren Street.
- Contracted to convert 200 flintlocks to percussion for the state of Georgia (August 1861).
- Advertised as a maker and dealer in shotguns, rifles, pistols, powder and drum flasks, bowie knives, shot pouches and belts, powder, shot, caps, gun material, and everything in the sporting line (July 1862).
- Made M1841 Mississippi rifles, sharpshooter rifles, musketoons, and M1855 carbines (1862).
- Bought the sword factory of A.H. DeWitt after a fire on December 31, 1862, destroyed DeWitt's shop at 99 Broad Street, killing his son Clinton. He converted it into a rifle factory (early 1863).
- Between October 1, 1863 and November 1, 1864, Murray delivered 358 M1841 Mississippi rifles and 153 M1855 carbines under a contract to the state of Alabama (signed by Greenwood & Gray).
- Jacob H. Moshell made gun barrels for grindstone makers Murray Robinet & Co. (located at Murray's factory).
- It is believed that a Mr. Kean, sword shop foreman for A.H. DeWitt, continued making cavalry sabers after Murray bought DeWitt out in early 1863.
- Murray also did work for the Columbus Arsenal, such as restocking and repairing guns.
- Employed over 150 men.
- Employee: G.W. Blythe (gunsmith).
- Murray's factory was burned down by Union General James C. Wilson's cavalry corps (April 17, 1865).
- Haddock's Columbus Directory listed J.P. Murray's factory as located on Oglethorpe St. below Randolph Street (1873).
- He moved back to Charleston, SC (1889).

JOHN P. MURRAY   **CHARLESTON, SC**   **1889-D1910**
(See Greenwood & Gray)
(See A.H. DeWitt)
(See Jacob H. Moshell)

NASHVILLE PLOW WORKS

ALBIGENCE WALDO PUTNAM   **BELPRE, OH**   **B1799-1856**
Also lived in Mississippi.
Became a wealthy lawyer.
Descendant of Gen. Israel Putnam
  (Revolutionary War hero).
Bought a three-story factory and lot in
  Nashville, TN, from John M. Lawrence
  for $6041.80 (1856).

AGRICULTURAL
  MANUFACTURING CO.   **NASHVILLE, TN**   **1856-1859**
Owner: A.W. Putnam.
Made plows, plowshares, wagons, wheelbarrows,
  cultivators, and harrows.

He was unsuccessful in the venture and sold out
for $4,600 to Thomas A. Sharp and
James M. Hamilton (1859).

SHARP & HAMILTON
PLOW FACTORY   **NASHVILLE, TN**   **1859-1861**

- Located at 8th Avenue (south) near the Franklin Pike, just north of Nashville and Chattanooga Railroad Bridge.
- Owners: Thomas A. Sharp (B1823-D1865), James M. Hamilton (B1821-D1895).
- Foreman: Daniel Campbell.
- Made 150 plows a week.
- Made other farm implements also.
- Adv. in the Nashville City and Business Directory (1860-1861).

NASHVILLE PLOW WORKS   **NASHVILLE, TN**   **1861-1862**

- Owners: Thomas A. Sharp, James M. Hamilton.
- Sold the state of Tennessee $12,710.18 worth of swords.
- Offered to make the following swords for the state of Tennessee (May 30, 1861):
  - Cavalry sabers–$7.00 each.
  - Horse artillery sabers–$5.00 each.
  - Artillery short swords–$4.00 each.
  - Musketoon sword bayonets–$5.00 each.
  - Non-comm. swords–$5.50 each.
  - Musician's swords–$4.00 each.
  - (All complete with scabbard).
- Sold to the state of Tennessee:
  - Cartridge boxes
  - Plates and belts
  - Sword and saber belts and plates
  - Pistol holsters
  - Gun slings
  - Bayonet scabbard and frog waist belts and plates for non-comms. and musicians
  - Sappers belts with frog bullet pouches
  - Bullet pouch belts
  - Powder flasks
- Sold $493.50 worth of cavalry sabers (50) to the state of Tennessee (September 1861).
- Had a Confederate contract for cavalry sabers ($11,078.68 advanced), which were stored at the Nashville Armory.
- Delivered 55 at $10.50 each (September 1861).
- Delivered 357 at $10.50 each (October 1861).
- Delivered 100 at $11.00 each (November 1861).
- Delivered 213 at $11.00 each (December 1861).
- Delivered 239 at $11.00 each (January 1862).
- The sabers were stamped "Sharp & Hamilton-Nashville, Tennessee" or "Nashville Plow Works."
- Sharp & Hamilton also made cavalry officer sabers, staff and field officer swords, and foot officer swords.
- The Nashville Plow Works was closed when Union troops under General Rosecrans occupied Nashville (February 16, 1862).
- Sharpe and Hamilton were arrested and charged with treason and put under a $3,000 bond each.
- Since none of the Nashville Confederates arrested were ever

brought to trial, we presume they either took the oath of allegiance or had their cases continued, which is what happened to all who were arrested. Union troops occupied Nashville until the war ended (1865).
- Thomas A. Sharpe died (1865).

HAMILTON (JAMES M.)
& CUNNINGHAM (GEORGE W.)   NASHVILLE, TN   1865-1895
23 Public Square
- G.W. Cunningham was probably a relation of Lieutenant Cunningham of the College Hill Iron Works (College Hill Armory).
- Dealers in wholesale and retail hardware and agricultural implements (plows).
- Adv. in the Nashville city directory (1872).
- James M. Hamilton died (1895).
- Maj. George W. Cunningham was in charge of the Quartermaster Clothing Department of the Atlanta Supply Depot in Atlanta, GA (1863-1864).

(See College Hill Armory)

OWEN O. NELSON
(See William Dickson)

NEW ORLEANS FOUNDRY
& ORNAMENTAL WORKS   NEW ORLEANS, LA   1861-1865
Corner of Magnolia and Erastostes Streets
- Also known as the Phoenix Iron Works.
- Owners: B.K.T. Bennett, Francis Lurges, Sylvester Bennett.
- Made brass rifle parts, brass sword hilts, cavalry sabers, naval cutlasses, and artillery sabers.
- Made brass sword hilts for New Orleans sword makers such as Pradel, Dufilho, Vortier, Cook & Brother, and Hyde & Goodrich.

T.C. NISBET   MACON, GA   1861-1865
- Sold 66 pikes to the state of Georgia (1862).
- Operated an iron works and machine shop.
- Made sheet brass-rolling machines for Edmund J. Johnston and William J. McElroy of Macon, GA.
- Made steam engines, boilers, sawmills, and ornamental iron.

(See E.J. Johnston)
(See W.J. McElroy)

L. OPPLEMAN   LYNCHBURG, VA   1861-1865
Made bowie knives.

PARKS, LYONS (THOMAS B.) & CO.   MOBILE, AL   1861-1865
State and Water Streets
- Had a machine shop, blacksmith shop, iron foundry, and brass foundry.
- Alabama contract for 1,000 cavalry sabers (1861).
- Also made naval cutlasses.
- Sold sword blades to James Conning.
- Offered Jacob Faser a job (1863); he refused.
- Made the Confederate submarine *Huntley*.

LYONS (THOMAS B.) **& KEYLAND (WILLIAM)**	MOBILE, AL State and Water Streets	1866-1869

Called Southern Iron Works.
Employees:
- James Kiernan (machinist)
- William Koeppel (machinist)
- George Krantz (molder)
- R. Magee (molder)
- Mathew McKeever (machinist)

LYONS, KEYLAND & ALEXANDER	MOBILE, AL	1870

Called Southern Iron Works.
Owners: Thomas B. Lyons, William Keyland, William A. Alexander.

SOUTHERN IRON WORKS	MOBILE, AL	1871-1872

Owners: Thomas B. Lyons, William Keyland.
(See James Conning)

HIRAM PEABODY	RICHMOND, VA	1861-1865

Made bowie knives.
(Cutler)

JOHN C. (CALVIN) PECK	SHARON, CT	B1830-1858
BROWN (A.H.), PRIEST (EDWIN) & **PECK (JOHN C.)**	ATLANTA, GA	1858-1860
PECK (JOHN C.) & BOWMAN (JOHN T.)	ATLANTA, GA	1860-1861
PECK (JOHN C.) & DAY (FRANCIS)	ATLANTA, GA Decatur and Pratt Streets	1861-1863

- Had a planning mill, lumberyard, and woodworking shop.
- Converted to an armory (1861).
- Made rifles and rampart guns.
- Contracted with the state of Georgia to grind the blades and supply handles for 10,000 pikes being made at the Western & Atlantic Railroad Machine Shop in Atlanta (1861).
- The Confederacy bought the Peck & Day Armory and added it to the Atlanta Arsenal complex (1863).
- John C. Peck was made superintendent of the wood works at the arsenal (1863).

JOHN C. PECK	THOMASVILLE, GA	1863-1865
	ATLANTA, GA	1865-1870
PECK (JOHN C.) & SCHOFIELD	ATLANTA, GA	1870-1873
J. (JOHN) C. PECK & CO.	ATLANTA, GA	1873-1885

(See Atlanta Arsenal)
(See Western & Atlantic Railroad Machine Shop)
(Carpenter, Gunsmith, Blacksmith, Pike Maker)

PETERSBURG IRON WORKS
(See Uriah Wells)

GEORGE PIELERT	CATONSVILLE, KY	1861-1865

Made bowie knives while a private in the 3rd Virginia Artillery.
(Blacksmith, Knife Maker)

T.A. POTTS NEW ORLEANS, LA 1861-1865
Made bowie knives.

BLAISE C. PRADEL PARIS, FRANCE 1825-1849
  NEW ORLEANS, LA 1849-1862
  68 St. Charles Street

Surgical instrument maker and blade grinder.
Sold fancy goods.
Employees: Louis De Compte, Peter Villian
  (instrument makers).

BLAISE PRADEL JR. PARIS, FRANCE B1829-1857
Stepbrother to Blaise C. Pradel.
  NEW ORLEANS, LA 1857-1862

Worked at brother's shop (1857).
Opened a shop at 134 Chartres (1858-1861).
Moved to 121 Chartres (1861-1863).
Made surgical instruments and foot officer swords.
Engraved blades for his swords and some for Alfred H. Dufilho.

PRADEL (BLAISE JR.)
  & BROTHER (BLAISE C.) NEW ORLEANS, LA 1863-1868
  44 and 54 St. Charles Street

Made surgical and dental instruments and
  general cutlery.
Blaise C. Pradel returned to France (1868).

BLAISE PRADEL JR. NEW ORELANS, LA 1868-D1884
  54 St. Charles Street

Expanded into barber's instruments and guns.
(Cutlers, Instrument Makers, Sword Makers, Engravers)

T.L. PRUETT PRATTVILLE, AL 1861-1865
Made bowie knives.
(Cutler)

THOMAS W. RADCLIFFE COLUMBIA, SC 1812-1833
  CAMDEN, SC 1833-1848
Radcliffe apprenticed to silversmith William Gregg.

GLAZE (WILLIAM)
  & RADCLIFFE (THOMAS W.) COLUMBIA, SC 1848-1851
T. (THOMAS) W. RADCLIFFE & CO. COLUMBIA, SC 1851-1856
RADCLIFFE (THOMAS W.)
  & GUIGNARD (JAMES S.) COLUMBIA, SC 1856-1858
Dealer in pistols, shotguns, and presentation swords.

T. (THOMAS) W. RADCLIFFE & CO. COLUMBIA, SC 1856-1870
  Richardson and Plains Streets

Partners: son Lewis Radcliffe, Richard Davis.
Sold English Tranton revolvers to the
  Confederacy during the Civil War.
Thomas W. Radcliffe died (1870).

T.W. RADCLIFFE & CO. COLUMBIA, SC 1870-1896
Partners: son Lewis Radcliffe, Richard Davis.
Sold out to the Sylvan Brothers (1896).
(See William Glaze)
(Silversmith, Goldsmith, Gunsmith, Jeweler, Military Importer)

THOMAS W. RADCLIFFE JR. Son of Thomas Sr. (Silversmith, Goldsmith, Watch Maker)	COLUMBIA, SC	1860-1870
CHARLES J. RAIBLE (Masonic Regalia)	LOUISVILLE, KY	1851-1874
W.L. RAINEY Sold 11 pikes to the state of Georgia (1862).	ATLANTA, GA	1861-1865
RALEIGH BAYONET FACTORY (See Heck, Brodie)		
BENJAMIN RAWLS (See U.S. Dealer listings)		
READ & DICKSON (BENJAMIN) Mississippi contract for 300 cavalry lances (1862). Made foot officer swords	NATCHEZ, MS	1861-1865
HUMPHREY REID Sold the state of Georgia 76 pikes (1862.	COLUMBUS, GA	1841-1865
TEMPLETON & ELISHA REID (See Silversmith listings)		
CAPT. FRANZ REUTER Invented a pike with a scythe blade (1862).	NEW ORLEANS, LA	1861-1865
RICHMOND (CHARLES R.) **WOLTERING (JOSEPH W.)**	MEMPHIS, TN Memphis Navy Yard at 96 Front Row Street	1858-1861
Partner: Peter Gross. Manufacturer and dealer in copper, tin, and ironware. (Stove Maker)		
C. (CHARLES R.) RICHMOND & CO. Partners: Joseph W. Woltering, Peter Gross. Adv. the manufacturing of cavalry and infantry swords (1863).	MEMPHIS, TN	1861-1863
CHARLES H. RIGDON Scale maker and machinist.	CINCINNATI, OH	1824-1844
	ST. LOUIS, MO	1844-1859
Partner and brother: W. Rigdon. Worked for and made revolver machinery for Shauk (William Abel) & McLanahon (J.K.).		
	MEMPHIS, TN	1859-1861
Partner and brother: W. Rigdon. Scale maker and machinist on Poplar Street between Main and 2nd Streets.		
THOMAS S. LEECH & CO. Partners: Charles H. Rigdon, W. Rigdon.	MEMPHIS, TN	1861-1864

Sword and pistol makers who made navy
  revolvers for the Confederacy.

**RIGDON (CHARLES H. & W.)
& ANSLEY (JESSE A.)**   AUGUSTA, GA   1864-1865
                                    Marbury Street

- Partners: Andrew J. Smith, Charles R. Kent.
- Factory was 50' x 150'.
- Many of the factory workmen belonged
  to a militia company called Rigdon's Guard.
- Confederate contract for 1,500 navy revolvers.

(See Thomas S. Leech)
(Scale Makers, Pistol Makers, Machinists)

SHARP & HAMILTON
(See Nashville Plow Works)

WILLIAM SCHLEY   ATLANTA, GA   1861-1865
Sold 83 pikes to the state of Georgia (1862).

SHEPHARD, MAXWELL & HOYT
(See Anthony L. Maxwell)

SMITH J. SHERWOOD
(See Dealer listings)

SHAKANOOSA ARMS CO.
(See Owen O. Nelson)

SKATES & CO.
(See James Conning)

J. (JOHN) C. SMITH   AUGUSTA, GA   1861-1865
Sold 105 bowie knives to
  the state of Georgia (1862).
(Knife Maker)

ARMAND SOUBIEL   NEW ORLEANS, LA   1853-1862
                                    160 Chartres Street
Importer, dealer, and maker of arms.
Closed when New Orleans was occupied (1862).

SOUTHERN IMPORTING HOUSE
(See Samuel Sutherland)

T. (THOMAS) S. SPEAR   COLUMBUS, GA   1838-1865
                                    67 Broad Street, corner of Randolph
                                    Street

- Successor to S.B. Purble.
- Adv. as a jeweler and watch maker
  in the 1860 city directory.
- Also adv. silverware, canes, and spectacles.
- Spear did blade etching for Louis
  Haiman & Brother during the Civil War.

- Employees
    - Charles Fogg (jeweler)
    - George K. Saylor (jeweler)
    - George Jordan (watch maker)
    - W.B. Langdon (clerk)
    - D. McArthur (clerk)
    - J.S. Arnold (clerk)
    - T.M. Barnard (clerk)
    - Clifford Coleman (clerk)
    - J.D. Slade (bookkeeper)

COLUMBUS, GA 1865-1875
99 Broad Street

- When A.H. DeWitt sold off his property in Columbus (1865), T.S. Spear bought the property at 99 Broad.
- He is listed at that location in the 1873 Haddock City Directory

(See A.H. DeWitt)
(See Louis Haiman & Brother)

JOHN N. STATON SCOTTVILLE, VA 1861-1865
Albermarle County

Adv. bowie knives and swords of all kinds (1861).

HENRY STEVENS CORNWALL, ENGLAND B1813-1836
NEW YORK, NY 1836-1843
AUGUSTA, GA 1843-1854
Greene County

Built and sold sawmills.
Sold a sawmill to Samuel Griswold.

STEVENS (HENRY) MILL & POTTERY WORKS BALDWIN CO., GA 1854-1876
- Located near the Milledgeville, GA, Arsenal.
- Built sawmills.
- Opened a pottery works.
- Made pottery, stoneware, sewer pipe, and firebrick.
- During the Civil War, made 1,428 cloverleaf pikes for the state of Georgia.
- Pikes marked: "H. Stevens PO. CO." (pottery company).
- Also made bowie knives for the state of Georgia and firebrick for the Macon, GA, armory furnaces.
- Henry Stevens retired (1876).

STEVENS POTTERY CO. BALDWIN CO., GA 1876-1883
Partners and sons: W.C. Stevens, J.H. Stevens, William Stevens.
Henry Stevens died (1883).

STEVENS BROTHERS & CO. BALDWIN CO., GA 1883-1890
Partners: W.C. Stevens, J.H. Stevens, William Stevens.
(Pike Maker, Knife Maker)

SAMUEL SUTHERLAND RICHMOND, VA 1850-1865
132 Main Street

- Called Southern Importing House.

- Gunsmiths:
    - Thomas W. Lyons
    - Owen O'Malley
    - George Place
    - Miles Bott
    - David Schiver
    - Benjamin Guthright
    - William Hancock
    - John W. Lipscomb
    - William Allen
- Altered Virginia Manufactory muskets for the Confederacy.
- Made bowie knives.
- Importer, dealer, and maker of guns, pistols, rifles, sporting goods, cutlery, powder flasks, and accessories.

RICHMOND, VA   1865-1905
1406 E. Main Street

Samuel Sutherland died (1875).
Samuel's son, A.B. Sutherland, became owner of the company.
(Gunsmith, Importer, Knife Maker)

TEXAS (STATE OF)
Ordered 200 cavalry lances, made at an unknown factory at Chappell Hill, TX (1861).

THOMAS, GRISWOLD & CO.
(See James N. Hyde)

JAMES THOMPSON
(See W.J. McElroy)

S.E. THUES   MACON, GA   1861-1865
Mulberry Street near 2nd Street

Blade etcher for W.J. McElroy.
(See W.J. McElroy)
(Blade Etcher)

TILTON ARMORY
(See J.J. Martin)

TREDEGAR IRON WORKS   RICHMOND, VA   1838-1869
- The official name was J.R. Anderson & Co.
- Owner: Joseph Reid Anderson.
- Located on the south side of the Kanawaha Canal, west of the Virginia Manufactory (Richmond Armory).
- Adv. in the 1860 Richmond directory as machinists and founders making locomotive and stationary engines, saw and grist mills, railroad machinery, brass and iron, guns, shot, and shell.
- Employees:
    - William P. Ayres: Superintendent, Bolt Factory
    - Thomas D. Burley: Superintendent, Spike Factory
    - Alexander Delany: Superintendent, Machine Shop

- Edward Taylor: Foreman, Blacksmith Shop
- P.S. Derbyshire: Foreman, Foundry
- Charles Hagan: Foreman, Machine Shop
- John Reid: Foreman, Pattern Shop
- William E. Tanner: General Superintendent, Machine Shops
- Restored the Virginia Manufactory (1860).
- James H. Burton was employed to supervise the restoration.
- Supplied revolvers and gun carriages to the Confederacy (from northern sources) until April 1861.
- Had a rolling mill, cannon foundry, and gun foundry.
- South Carolina contract for thirty-two 24-pounder cannons, eight 10-inch mortars, four 8-inch Columbiads, and ten 8-inch howitzers (1851).
- Made naval cutlasses, Brooks guns, William's breech-loading cannon (under Confederate contract), munitions, military equipment, and armor plate for iron-clad ship *Virginia*.

THE TREDEGAR COMPANY　　　　RICHMOND, VA　　　　1869-1950
Made projectiles during World War II.

TURNER & WEBB　　　　COLUMBUS, GA　　　　1861-1865
Sold the state of Georgia 11 pikes (1862).

FREDERICK ULRICH
(See Charles Bellenot)

UNION CAR WORKS　　　　PORTSMOUTH, VA　　　　1861-1865
Made bowie knives, bayonets, and cutlasses. Major production was railroad cars.

UNION MFG. CO.　　　　RICHMOND, VA　　　　1850-1865
- Machine shop.
- Makers of Sloat's sewing machines and other industrial machines.
- President: James S. Kent.
- Stockholder: Horace L. Kent.
- Foreman: Archibald McCurdy.
- Superintendent: George B. Sloat.
- Called Sloat's Rifle Factory.
- Had Confederate contracts for:
  - Torpedo parts
  - Submarine batteries
  - Ambulance axles
  - Milling machines
  - Platform scales
  - Pipes
  - Portable forges
  - Lathes and drills
  - Bone buttons
  - Camping equipment
  - Sewing machines and parts
  - Musket parts
  - Rifles
  - 3-inch rifle shells
  - Bayonets

- Had a Confederate contract to clean and repair 765 Virginia Manufactory muskets and rifles (1862).
- Had a Confederate contract to grind and polish 10 pikes and drill and rivet 229 pikes (1862).

JOHN VEAL SR.	**COLUMBIA, SC**	**1800-1838**
VEAL (JOHN SR.) & GLAZE (WILLIAM)	**COLUMBIA, SC**	**1838-1841**
JOHN VEAL SR.	**COLUMBIA, SC**	**1841-1857**

Veal retired (1857) and sold out to Samuel Townsend.
(See William Glaze)
(Silversmith)

JOHN VEAL JR.   COLUMBIA, SC   1860-1861
Son of John Sr.
(Silversmith)

VIRGINIA IRON WORKS
(See Thomas W. Godwin)

LEON VOITIER   NEW ORLEANS, LA   1861-1865
Made staff and field officer swords.

JAMES WALES
(See Dixie Works)

DANIEL WALLIS (WALLACE)   TALLADEGA, AL   1840-1860
WALLIS (DANIEL) & RICE (SAMUEL F.)   TALLADEGA, AL   1861-1865
Alabama contract for Mississippi rifles and
  1,000 bayonets (1862).
Made cavalry sabers.
(Gunsmith, Cutler)

ASA WATERS
(See William Glaze)

WILLIAM M. WATKINS   MONROE, GA   1861-1865
Sold the state of Georgia 12 pikes (1862).
(Blacksmith, Gunsmith)

J. (JOSEPH) E. WELLS JR.   MACON, GA   1861-1865
                                           Colton and Cherry Streets

Blade etcher for W.J. McElroy.
(See W.J. McElroy)
(Blade Etcher)

URIAH WELLS   PETERSBURG, VA   1861-1864
Called Petersburg Iron Works.
Made cavalry sabers and bowie knives.

WESTERN & ATLANTIC
  RAILROAD MACHINE SHOP   ATLANTA, GA   1861-1864
Made 10,000 infantry pikes and bowie knives
  for the state of Georgia (1861).
Peck (John C.) & Day (Francis) contracted to
  grind the blades and make handles for the pikes.

The machine shop's major production was railroad supplies.
(See John C. Peck)

JOHN G. WHITE   **PERRY, GA**   **1861-1863**
- Sold the state of Georgia 303 pikes (1862).
- Nathan Weed was an agent for White's products.
- White made shoe lasts and pegs, dies, spokes, rims, hubs, gun carriages, artillery parts, and weapons.
- Had a Confederate contract for gun carriages (caissons).

(See Nathan Weed-Dealer listings)
(Blacksmith, Pike Maker, Iron Products)

E.P. WILLIAMS   **MILLEDGEVILLE, GA**   **1861-1865**
Had a contract with Maj. John M. Brown of
   Georgia (brother of Georgia Governor Joseph
   E. Brown) for 240 infantry pikes (140 with gun
   stock handles, 100 with regular straight shafts).
The pikes were stored at the Milledgeville, GA, Arsenal.
The pikes were made for a company of
   pikemen to defend the city of Savannah.

WILMINGTON SWORD FACTORY
(See Louis Froelich)

J.C. WILSON   **HOUSTON, TX**   **1862-1865**
Made very heavy hilted foot officer swords
   and M1840-style cavalry swords.
(Sword Maker)

ROSS WINAN   **BALTIMORE, MD**   **1861-1865**
Called Winan's Works (locomotive makers).
Made 2,000 pikes for the city of Baltimore (1861),
   ordered by Marshall Kane of the
   Baltimore Police Department.
Also invented a steam-powered armored railroad cannon.

D.W. WINN	**COBBVILLE, GA**	**1840-1860**
CAMERON (A.J.) & WINN (D.W.)	**COBBVILLE, GA**	**1861-1862**
Sold the state of Georgia 458 bowie knives (1862).		
WILLIAM J. ELDER & D.W. WINN	**WATKINSVILLE, GA**	**1862**
Sold the state of Georgia 50 pikes (1862).		
D.W. WINN	**WATKINSVILLE, GA**	**1862-1865**

(See William J. Elder)
(See Cameron & Winn)
(Gunsmiths and Cutlers)

D.B. WOODRUFF   **ATLANTA, GA**   **1861-1865**
Sold the state of Georgia 314 pikes (1862).

G. (GEORGE) N. WYMAN	**AUGUSTA, GA**	**1839-1859**
Partner in May & Co. carriage works (1859).		
	AUGUSTA, GA 208 Broad Street	**1859-1865**

Made and repaired carriages.
Sold saddles and harness.
Sold the state of Georgia 116 pikes (1862).
Also made leather cartridge boxes and
  percussion cap boxes.

WYMAN (GEORGE N.) & MAY	AUGUSTA, GA 208 Broad Street	1865-1866
C. (CHARLES) H. ZIMMERMAN & CO.	NEW ORLEANS, LA 94 and 96 Canal Street	1865-1871

(Silversmith)

J.G. ZIMMERMAN & CO.   ATLANTA, GA   1861-1865

Sold the state of Georgia 209 bowie knives
  and 152 pikes (1862).

M. ZIMMERMAN	NEW ORLEANS, LA	1836-1856
ZIMMERMAN & SON	NEW ORLEANS, LA 93 Canal Street	1856-1858

Partners: M. Zimmerman, son J.F. Zimmerman.

M. ZIMMERMAN & SON   NEW ORLEANS, LA   1858-1865
                                        96 Canal Street

Partner and son: J.F. Zimmerman.
J.F. Zimmerman etched some blades for
  A.H. Dufilho during the Civil War.
(See A.H. Dufilho)
(Silversmiths, Watch Makers, Jewelers,
  Engravers, Blade Engravers)

P. (PETER) ZIMMERMAN   NEW ORLEANS, LA   1865-1871
(Silversmith)

CHAPTER 9

European Sword Makers and Dealers Who Exported Swords to Confederate Dealers during the Civil War

GERMAN FIRMS

Wilhelm Clauberg
Carl Brock Jr.
W.R. Kirschbaum
Paul D. Luneschloss
Schnitzer & Kirschbaum
Carl Joseph Falkenberg
Wilhelm Walsheid

FRENCH FIRM

F.P. Devisme (Paris)
- Made swords for Gen. Robert E. Lee and Gen. John B. Hood.

ENGLISH FIRMS

Firmin & Sons (London)
- Sold Marine Corps swords with M1821 British lt. cavalry hilts (marked "C.M." for Confederate Marines on back of blade) to Courtney & Tennent.
- Sold dolphin-head naval officer swords made by Robert Mole to Courtney & Tennent.

Robert Mole & Son (Birmingham)
- Swords marked "RM & SB."
- Sold brass-hilted variant of the British M1853 cavalry saber (issued to the 4th Kentucky Cavalry).

- Sold dolphin-head naval officer swords.
- Sold M1854 gothic-hilt foot officer swords.
- Sold two types of naval cutlasses to Courtney & Tennent; one had a two-branch brass hilt, and one had a sheet-iron hilt.

Isaac, Campbell, & Co. (London)
- Sold a variant of the British iron-hilted M1853 cavalry saber (Caleb Huse purchased large quantities).
- Sold M1854 gothic-hilt foot officer swords to Halfmann & Taylor.
- Products marked "Isaac's & Co."

(See U.S. Dealer listings)

Joseph Rogers & Sons (Sheffield)
- Sold British M1841 naval officer swords to C. Hall (dealer).

Henry Wilkinson (London)
- Sold M1822 British staff officer swords.

CHAPTER 10

Confederate Sword Dealers

ALLEN (JOHN M.) & DIAL (J.C.)	**COLUMBIA, SC**	**1860-1865**

Adv. wholesale and retail weapons and agricultural
  implements (1860).
Adv. rifles and pistols for mounted men (1861).
Sold and imported edged weapons.
(Gun Dealers, Farm Implements, Military Goods)

JOHN STILES BIRD	**CHARLESTON, SC**	**B1794-1850**
J. (JOHN) S. (STILES) BIRD & CO.	**CHARLESTON, SC**	**1850-1860**

Partner: Charlton H. Bird.

CHARLTON H. BIRD	**CHARLESTON, SC**	**1860-1887**

Partner: John Stiles Bird.
John S. Bird died (1887).
(Silversmith, Surveying Equipment, Military
  and Fancy Store)

H.B. BROWN'S SON	**CHARLESTON, SC**	**1862-1865**

Sold naval officer swords.

CANFIELD & BROTHER
(See U.S. Dealer listings)

CLARKSON (JOSEPH A.) & ANDERSON		
(J.M. & L.C.)	**RICHMOND, VA**	**1850-1861**
	106 Main Street	

Hardware makers.
Employees: H. Brownell, R.B. Gunn, J.H. Anderson, A.A. Brandt.

CLARKSON (JOSEPH A.) & CO.	RICHMOND, VA	1861-1865

Adv. bowie knives and pistols (1861).

WILLIAM CROCKER COURTNEY	RICHMOND, VA	B1818-1849
	CHARLESTON, SC	1849-1852
COURTNEY (WILLIAM C.) **& TENNENT (GILBERT B.) & CO.**	CHARLESTON, SC 35 Hayne Street	1852-1865

- Partners:
    - James B. Evans (left 1859)
    - James S. Murdock
    - Robert Murdock
    - J. Waring Axson
    - Jasper W. Lillard
- Financed by H.W. Conner; also leased property to them.
- Courtney & Tennent maintained offices in Leamington, England.
- Imported naval officer swords and naval cutlasses from Robert Mole & Son, Birmingham, England.
- Imported Marine Corps officer swords from Firmin & Sons, London.
- Murdock & Tennent also purchased large quantities of naval goods for the Confederate Navy and acted as agents for John Fraser & Co. in England.
- Gilbert B. Tennent died (1879).

W. (WILLIAM) C. (CROCKER) **COURTNEY & CO.**	CHARLESTON, SC	1865-1878

Partners: Robert Murdock, James S. Murdock.

CHARLESTON BAGGING MFG. CO.	CHARLESTON, SC	1878-1885

President: William C. Courtney.
William C. Courtney died (1885).
(Cotton Merchants)

W.J. DELANO	MEMPHIS, TN	1861-1865

Adv. 500 cavalry sabers for sale made by a New Orleans maker (1862).
(Military Goods)

ROBERT J. DENNY	RICHMOND, VA 205 Main Street	1855-1865

Clerk: D.P. Denny.
Adv. in 1860 city directory as dealer in foreign and domestic hardware, cutlery, guns, edged tools, and house furnishings.

SIMON F. DODGE	WINCHESTER, VA	1861-1865

Sold bowie knives.
(Military Goods)

J. (JOSEPH) F. EISENMANN & CO. (Military Tailors)	COLUMBIA, SC	1850-1865
ENGLISH, CASTLEMAN & CO. Partners: James A. English, Charles M. Castleman, Charles A. Baldwin. Adv. as importers and dealers in hardware and English and German guns and cutlery. (Guns, Military Outfitter, Cutlery, Importer)	ALEXANDRIA, VA	1855-1865
ETHELBERT HALFMANN (Clothing)	PHILADELPHIA, PA	1830-1861
	MONTGOMERY, AL	1856-1860
(Tailor and Clothing Dealer) **HALFMANN (ETHELBERT) & TAYLOR (HENRY)**	MONTGOMERY, AL	1861-1863

- Imported M1854 British foot officer swords from Isaac Campbell & Co., London (marked "S. Campbell & Co.").
- Halfmann was a purchasing agent in Europe and Cuba for the Confederacy.
- Imported buttons from England also.
- Ethelbert Halfman died (1863).

(Military Goods, Importer)

C. HALL Imported M1841 naval officer swords from Joseph Rodgers & Sons, Sheffield, England. (Military Goods, Fancy Goods, Importer, Gun Dealer)	NORFOLK, VA	1852-1865
HARRIS, NICHOLS (BARAK J.) & CO. (Military Goods)	CHARLESTON, SC	1861-1867
HAYDEN & WILDEN (See U.S. Dealer listings)		
A. (AARON) MILES (Military Tailor, Military Equipment)	COLUMBIA, SC	1850-1865
SAMUEL PHILLIPS MITCHELL	RICHMOND, VA	B1815-1845
JOHN HENRY TYLER	BOSTON, MA	1820-1845
MITCHELL (SAMUEL PHILLIPS) & TYLER (JOHN HENRY)	RICHMOND, VA 108 Main Street	1845-1866

- Employees:
    - John Ege (blade polisher)
    - William T. Ege (blade etcher)
    - John Tyler (clerk)
    - Edward McConnell (jeweler)
    - James M. Baker (bookkeeper)
    - James L. Ege (salesman)
    - C.K. Chapin (salesman)
    - James Evans (salesman)
    - F. Adams (watch maker)

        H.C. Hicks (watch maker)
        G. Honneger (watch maker)
- Imported French cavalry sabers (M1822) and British M1854 foot officer swords.
- Sold Boyle & Gamble swords, navy pistols, French Minnie muskets, and English Enfield rifles.
- Adv. as dealers in clocks, watches, jewelry, silver, silverware, spectacles, military, and fancy goods in the 1860 Richmond directory.
- Adv. English and American guns, navy pistols, French cavalry sabers, a large variety of officer swords, belts, sashes, epaulettes, gloves, spurs, buttons, laces, and uniform trimmings in the March 25, 1861, edition of the *Richmond Dispatch*.
- Samuel Phillips Mitchell died (1866).

(See James L. Ege)
(See Boyle & Gamble-Maker listings)
(Silversmith, Jeweler, Watch Makers, Military Goods, and Importer)

JOHN H. TYLER & CO.	**BOSTON, MA**	**1866-1883**

Partner: James L. Ege.
John H. Tyler died (1883).
(Jeweler, Watch Maker)

P.I. MOORE & CO.	**RICHMOND, VA** 24 Pearl Street	**1855-1863**

Adv. in the 1860 city directory as importers and dealers in foreign and domestic hardware, cutlery, guns, and edged tools.

J. (JULIUS) A. PALMER	**ALEXANDRIA, VA**	**1861-1865**

(Military Goods)

JAMES H. RICE	**ALEXANDRIA, VA**	**1861-1865**

(Military Goods)

ROBINSON, ADAMS & CO.	**RICHMOND, VA**	**1861-1865**

Agents: James E. Riddick, L.A. Gegan.
Adv. military goods, light and heavy cavalry sabers, lt. artillery sabers, muskets, and bayonets (all imported) in 1862 and 1863.
(Gun Maker, Sword and Gun Importer)

SMITH (THOMAS M.), **RHODES (EDWARD) & CO.**	**RICHMOND, VA** 22 Pearl Street	**1852-1861**

Partners: George W. Wilson, William S. Hurt.
Salesmen: Robert A. Mason, Henry V. Pecor, William H. Winn.
Adv. as dealers and importers of hardware, saddlery, guns, and cutlery (1861).

W.H. SMITH	**AUGUSTA, GA**	**1840-1861**

Authorized dealer for Ames Mfg. Co. swords.
(Military Goods)

DANIEL L. SWETT	**VICKSBURG, MS**	**1855-1860**

Sold Deringer revolvers.

D. (DANIEL) L. SWETT & CO.	**VICKSBURG, MS**	**1861-1865**

(Military Goods)

W.W. WALKER	**COLUMBIA, SC**	**1850-1865**

(Military Tailor, Military Equipment)

JAMES WALSH	**RICHMOND, VA**	**1860-1875**
	60 Main Street at St. Charles Street	

Adv. as importer and maker of guns in the 1860 directory.
Adv. bowie knives, dirks, sword canes, guns, and military goods (1861).
Sold Colt pistols.
Employees: Thomas J. Adams (gunsmith), Robert Dunaway (gunsmith), James C. Wharton (gunsmith).
(Military Goods)

THOMAS WATSON	**FAYETTEVILLE, NC**	**1861-1870**

Immigrated from England (1861).
Worked part-time in the Fayetteville Arsenal
Had his own gunshop
Also a dealer in pistols, cutlery, and edged tools.
(Gun Maker, Arms Dealer)

C. (CASPAR) WEDLINGER	**RICHMOND, VA**	**1861-1865**
	146 Main Street	

Salesman: R.A. Saunders.

CASPAR WEDLINGER	**RICHMOND, VA**	**1865-1880**
	916 Main Street	

Partners: Anthony Wedlinger, Rudolph Wedlinger.
(Tailor, Military Outfitter)

NATHAN WEED	**MACON, GA**	**1840-1861**
WEED (NATHAN), CORNWALL & CO.	**MACON, GA**	**1861-1864**

- Sold 196 bowie knives and 174 pikes to the state of Georgia (1862).
- Importer and dealer in hardware, iron, farm implements, gun carriages, artillery parts, and weapons.
- Agent for John G. White, Macon, GA. White was a maker of shoe lasts and pegs, dies, spokes, rims, hubs, and gun carriges.
- Cornwall was owner of Cornwall Iron Works, Cherokee County, AL.
- Sold currier knives, pruning knives, tools, and old blacksmith bellows.

(See John G. White-Maker listings)
(Hardware and Weapons Dealer)

W. (WILLIAM) WING	**MOBILE, AL**	**1861-1863**
	168 Dauphin Street	

Adv. officer swords (1861).
(Military Goods)

APPENDIX A

Sword Markings

MARKS ON U.S. CAVALRY SABERS

Date	Marks
1798-1806	"U.S." and date in script
1807-1817	"V" and/or "P" and inspector's initials
1818-1831	"U.S.", "P", and inspector's initials
1832-1931	"U.S.", date, and inspector's initials

V = Verification
Sword checked for correctness of design according to contract specifications.

P = Proof
Sword checked for quality of hilt, blade, and scabbard.

U.S. ARMS INSPECTORS AND THEIR INITIALS

A list of U.S. government military arms inspectors and their initials can be a great help to collectors. Many times, the sword maker or dealer name and date of fabrication cannot be read, as continuous use, rust, and pitting can make this information illegible. Since inspector initials are found on the hilt and scabbard as well as on the blade, the chance of finding them is greater. If you know the inspector, his initials, and when he worked, you can determine within a few years the date your sword was made.

Much of this information is from the Arms Inspector listings in the Dixie Gun Works Inc. catalog. A special thanks to George Winter, Editor.

Initials	Inspector	Years Worked
A.A.H.	Andrew A. Harwood	1818-1864
A.A.W.	A.A. White	1905-1906
A.B.	A. Buckminster	1860-1861
A.B.B.	A.B. Blackington	1860-1862
A.B.F.	Archibald B. Fairfax	1823-1861
A.C.D.	Albert C. Dillingham	1889-1890
A.C.M.	Alfred C. Manning	1863
A.C.T.	A.C. Trego	1918
A.D.K.	A.D. King	1831-1865
A.F.	Abonijad Foot	1818-1822
A.F.C.	A.F. Cameron	1875
A.G.B.	A.G. Bennett	1868-1879
A.G.P.	Anson G. Perkins	1859-1863
A.H.	Asabel Hubbard	1813-1847
A.H.C.	A.H. Clark	1859-1879
A.H.C.	Archibald H. Ceiley	1862-1863
A.H.F.	Andrew H. Forsythe	1917
A.H.G.L.	A.H.G. Lewis	1906
A.H.K.	Albert H. Kirkham	1862-1865
A.H.N.	A.H. North	1862
A.H.T.	Albert H. Thompson	1862-1864
A.J.B.	A.J. Bristol	1870-1879
A.J.H.	A.J. Hall	1904
A.L.	A. Lavigne	1894-1909
A.L.K.	Albert L. Koones	1862-1865
A.L.W.	A.L. Woodworth	1905-1928
A.P.C.	A.P. Casey	1859-1861, 1875-1877
A.P.C.	A.P. Cobb	1874
A.R.	Adam Rhulman	1835-1854
A.R.	Alexander Reuben	1862-1863
A.R.W.	Abraham R. Woolley	1813
A.S.G.	Albert S. Granger	1862
A.W.E.	Arthur W. Evans	1917-1918
A.W.H.	A.W. Hatch	1903
B.B.L.	B.B. Lombard	1898
B.F.J.	B.J. James	1904-1906
B.F.L.	B.F. Lougharin	1906
B.H.	Benjamin Hannis	1861
B.H.	Benjamin Huger	1854-1858
B.L.	B. Lyon	1875
B.L.	Benjamin Lamphear	1798
B.M.	Benjamin Moore	1810-1815
B.R.W.	B.R. Whitcomb	1899
B.S.	B. Syrett	1898
C.A.B.	Charles A. Brand	1899-1900
C.A.W.	C.A. White	1904-1905
C.B.	Charles Boarman	1847

C.B.	Cyrus Buckland	1841
C.B.C.	Calvin B. Cross	1862-1863
C.C.H.	C.C. Hubbard	1906-1907
C.C.M.	Charles C. Morrison	1879-1882
C.D.	C. Davis	1905-1906
C.D.	C. Drommer	1898-1910
C.E.	Charles Eberle	1807
C.E.B.	C.E. Buckland	1859
C.E.E.	C.E. Evans	1905-1906
C.E.S.	Charles E. Sherman	1842-1847
C.E.W.	Charles E. Wilson	1862-1864
C.F.	C. Foot	1829-1841
C.F.L.	C.F. Lewis	1863
C.F.R.	Charles F. Rogers	1917
C.F.U.	C.F. Ulrich	1905-1906
C.G.	Calvin Gay	1818-1831
C.G.C.	C.G. Chandler	1861-1863
C.G.C.	Charles G. Chapman	1863-1864
C.G.C.	Charles G. Curtis	1862-1863
C.G.H.	Charles G. Howe	1917
C.H.H.	C.H. Hunt	1864
C.H.P.	C.H. Parker	1902
C.H.W.	C.H. Wicker	1904
C.J.	Catesby Jones	1805-1858
C.L.B.	C.L. Barlett	1904-1818
C.M.B.	C.M. Bayington	1901-1910
C.N.G.	Charles N. Goodrich	1862-1863
C.P.	Charles Packard	1818-1819
C.P.H.	Charles P. Hill	1874
C.P.L.	C.P. Lynn	1906
C.R.	Cadwalader Ringold	1849-1866
C.R.B.	C.R. Bunker	1875-1876
C.R.S.	Curtis R. Stickney	1871
C.S.	Clark Swallow	1862
C.S.C.	Charles S. Cotton	1858-1877
C.S.L.	C.S. Leonard	1875
C.S.L.	Charles S. Lowell	1858-1864
C.T.J.	C.T. Judd	1863
C.V.	C. Valentine	1848-1905
C.W.	Charles Williams	1807-1814
C.W.	Charles Woodman	1876-1877
C.W.B.	C.W. Bacon	1875
C.W.H.	C.W. Hartwell	1831-1850
C.W.S.	C.W. Snook	1876
D.A.	Daniel Ammen	1836-1878
D.A.L.	David A. Lyle	1876-1880
D.A.P.	Dwight A. Perkins	1862
D.A.T.	D.A. Turner	1914-1915
D.C.	Daniel Cotton	1798
D.D.	Daniel Dunsmore	1861-1868
D.F.C.	David F. Clark	1861-1886
D.F.M.	Dexter F. Mosman	1862-1863
D.J.D.	D.J. Davis	1904-1906

D.L.	D. LeGro	1826-1850
D.M.K.	David M. King	1898-1905
D.M.T.	Daniel M. Taylor	1892
D.P.	Daniel Pettibone	1808-1809
D.P.S.	Daniel P. Strong	1862
D.R.	Daniel Reynolds	1861-1864
D.R.	David Rice	1835-1863
D.T.	Daniel Tyler	1831-1850
D.W.	Decius Wadsworth	1799-1821
D.W.M.	D.W. Massey	1909
D.W.T.	D. Waldo Tyler	1862
E.A.	Epuphroditus Allis	1818-1841
E.A.E.	E.A. Elliott	1894-1910
E.A.G	E.A. Gowrie	1902-1909
E.A.G.	E.A. Graves	1894-1902
E.A.H.	E.A. Hendrick	1894
E.A.K.	E.A. Kingsbury	1904-1906
E.A.M.	E.A. May	1819-1850
E.A.W.	E.A. Williams	1875
E.B.	Edmund Byrne	1814-1850
E.B.	Edward Barrett	1871
E.B.	Elizur Bates	1841-1846
E.B.B.	E.B. Boutwell	1828-1850
E.B.B.	Edgar B. Boyd	1862
E.B.P.	E.B. Peck	1898-1902, 1909-1913
E.C.B.	Edmund C. Bailey	1862
E.C.W.	E.C. Wheeler	1862-1882
E.E.C.	E.E. Chapman	1918-1919
E.F.	E. Farrar	1860-1868
E.F.	Edgar Freeman	1811-1828
E.F.	Edward Flather	1862-1863
E.F.D.	E.F. Dunbar	1875
E.H.	Edward Hocker	1861-1884
E.H.P.	E.H. Pearson	1898
E.H.P.	Edwin H. Perry	1862
E.J.F.	E.J. Frost	1864
E.J.K.	E.J. Kernan	1909-1910
E.J.S.	E.J. Schoch	1904-1906
E.K.C.	E.K. Colton	1860-1864
E.L.B.	E.L. Bolles	1902
E.L.W.	E.L. Wunder	1903
E.M.	Edward McCue	1862
E.M.	Edwin Martin	1862
E.M.C.	E.M. Camp	1860-1863
E.M.D.	Edward M. Dustin	1862-1863
E.M.L.	E.M. Lovering	1909-1910
E.M.T.	E.M. Tinkham	1898-1906
E.S.	Elisha Shaw	1796
E.S.A.	E.S. Allin	1850-1865
E.S.F.	Edward S. Frost	1862-1863
E.T.	Edwin Tyler	1813-1819
E.T.	Elisha Tobey	1816-1832
E.W.B.	E.W. Blake	1818

E.W.B.	E.W. Bruce	1875
E.W.C.	E.W. Clarke	1870-1879
F.A.M.	F.A. Massey	1905-1906
F.A.R.	Francis A. Roe	1841-1885
F.B.	Frank Baker	1907-1917
F.B.A.	Francis B. Austin	1917
F.C.	F. Chillingworth	1875
F.C.	Francis Camp	1859-1861
F.C.W.	Frank C. Warner	1863-1869
F.E.R.	F.E. Randall	1906-1907
F.E.W.	F.E. Wilson	1901-1906
F.E.W.	F.E. Wyman	1909
F.F.H.	F.F. Hull	1905-1906
F.G.F.	F.G. Fisher	1899-1902
F.H	Fred Harvey	1862
F.H.	Frank Heath	1883-1884
F.H.E.	F.H. Elwell	1894-1910
F.H.S.	Frank H. Schofield	1897-1901
F.L.H.	F.L. Hosmer	1898-1923
F.M.C.	F.M. Chapin	1898-1899
F.M.K.	F.M. Kelsey	1904-1906
F.M.R.	Francis M. Ramsay	1850-1897
F.R.	Frank Richards	1871
F.R.	Franklin Root	1862-1863
F.R.	Frederick Rodgers	1857-1899
F.R.B.	F.R. Bull	1860
F.S.L.	F.S. Leonard	1899-1902
F.S.N.	F.S. North	1862-1863
F.S.S.	Frederic S. Strong	1862-1863
F.T.C.	Frank T. Cleveland	1875
F.W.A.	F.W. Adams	1904-1906
F.W.M.	F.W. Macher	1906
F.W.S.	F.W. Sanderson	1862-1879
G.A.L.	George A. Lawrence	1862-1863
G.A.M.	George A. Magruder	1817-1861
G.A.S.	G.A. Spooner	1899-1910
G.A.W.	George A. White	1875
G.A.W.	George A. Wood	1929-1932
G.B.A.	G.B. Allen	1894-1902
G.B.C.	G.B. Cruzen	1861
G.B.F.	George B. Foote	1862-1863
G.B.R.	George B. Russell	1862-1863
G.C.	George Curtis	1861
G.C.S.	G.C. Schnell	1905
G.D.	G. Dillingham	1875
G.D.	G. During	1898-1910
G.D.F.	G.D. Fisk	1875
G.D.G.	Gilbert D. Greason	1862
G.D.L.	George D. Little	1862-1865
G.D.R.	G.D. Ramsay Jr.	1863-1865
G.D.S.	G.D. Shattuck	1855-1860
G.E.C.	George E. Chamberlain	1862-1879

G.E.M.	G.E. Miller	1905-1906
G.E.S.	George E. Saunders	1862-1863
G.E.W.	G.E. Worder	1905-1906
G.F.	George Flegel	1812-1823
G.F.	George Flyn	1824-1825
G.F.B.	George F. Bowen	1878
G.F.G.	G.F. Gray	1904-1906
G.F.M.	George F. Morrison	1849-1860
G.F.T.	George F. Tucker	1862
G.G.	Guert Gansvoort	1850-1864
G.G.B.	George G. Bowe	1862-1863
G.G.S.	G.G. Saunders	1856-1870
G.H.	George Haines	1860
G.H.	George Hosmer	1862-1889
G.H.D.	George H. Dupee	1862-1863
G.H.G.	George H. Graham	1862
G.H.H.	George H. Hubbard	1862-1863
G.H.M.	G.H. Munroe	1899-1900
G.H.S.	Gilbert H. Stewart	1918-1919
G.H.S.	Gustavus H. Scott	1828-1873
G.J.M.	G.J. McCallin	1902
G.K.C.	George K. Charter	1861-1864
G.K.J.	G.K. Jacobs	1875
G.L.P.	G.L. Prentice	1875
G.M.C.	George M. Colvocoresses	1849-1867
G.M.R.	George M. Ransom	1839-1882
G.P.	George Palmer	1862
G.P.	Giles Porter	1862-1875
G.R.G.	G.R. Goring	1908-1910
G.R.H.	George R. Harrington	1901
G.S.M.	G.S. Morse	1862
G.T.	George Talcott	1836-1838
G.T.A.	G.T. Allen	1848
G.T.B.	George T. Balch	1861-1862
G.T.W.	G.T. Weaver	1894-1899
G.W.	George Wells	1833-1862
G.W.	George Wright	1850-1852
G.W.C.	George W. Chapin	1862-1864
G.W.H.	George W. Hagner	1845-1846
G.W.H.	George W. Hamlin	1846-1852
G.W.M.	George W. McKee	1874-1878
G.W.P.	G.W. Patch	1846-1858
G.W.R.	George W. Rodgers	1839-1863
G.W.S.	G.W. Sherman	1858-1860
G.W.S.	G.W. Shuman	1858-1860
G.W.S.	G.W. Smith	1857
G.W.S.	G.W. Sword	1856
H.B.B.	Hanson B. Bullock	1862-1863
H.B.C.	H.B. Cooley	1862-1863
H.B.H.	H.B. Hart	1875
H.B.J.	H.B. Johnson	1862
H.C.W.	H.C. Washburn	1904-1906
H.D.	H. Dana	1862-1863

H.D.H.	Henry D. Hasting	1862-1864
H.D.J.	Henry D. Jennings	1862-1863
H.D.W.	H.D. White	1899
H.E.	Henry Erven	1871
H.E.H.	H.E. Hollister	1862-1863
H.E.M.	H.E. Madden	1902
H.E.V.	Henry E. Valentine	1862
H.E.W.	H.E. Wallenberg	1906
H.F.L.	Harry F. Lynch	1839-1840
H.G.F.	H.G. Firmin	1868-1882
H.G.G.	H.G. Gould	1898
H.H.D.	H.H. Denny	1898
H.H.E.	Harold H. Eames	1889-1890
H.H.G.	John H. Griffith	1862
H.H.P.	Henry H. Perkins	1808-1817
H.J.M.	H.J. Meldrun	1898
H.K.	H. Kane	1902-1903
H.K.	Henry Kirk	1862-1863
H.K.C.	Henry Knox Craig	1835-1861
H.K.H.	Henry K. Hoff	1862-1868
H.K.W.	H.K. White	1861-1865
H.L.L.	H.L. Lathrop	1862
H.M.	H. Murdock	1875
H.M.	Henry Metcalfe	1869-1875
H.M.B.	H.M. Brooks	1902-1906
H.N.	Henry Nettleton	1876-1880
H.S.	H. Saunders	1875
H.S.	H. Stephens	1816
H.S.	H. Syrett	1904-1906
H.S.	Harris Smith	1862-1879
H.S.	Horace Scott	1878-1885
H.S.	Howard Stockton	1868
H.S.H.	H.S. Hill	1875
H.S.L.	Homer S. Lathe	1862
H.T.	H. Tracy	1831-1850
H.W.	Henry Walke	1827-1871
H.W.H.	Harry W. Hunt	1899-1902
H.W.W.	Henry W. Wilcox	1862
I.A.	Isaac Arnold	1870
I.B.	Isack Bartlett	1808
I.H.	Isaac Hull	1808
I.R.	I. Randall	1904-1906
J.A.	J. Arnold Jr.	1869-1871
J.A.	Joel Abbot	1812-1855
J.A.	John Avis	1837-1838
J.A.B.	John A. Bell	1902-1903
J.A.G.	James A. Greer	1848
J.A.W.	J.A. Woodward	1905-1906
J.B.	James Bell	1827-1828
J.B.C.	J.B. Cooley	1898
J.B.C.	J.B. Craig	1896-1902
J.B.K.	John B. Kirkham	1823-1841

J.B.T.	J.B. Tyler	1894-1910
J.C.	J. Clancy	1905-1907
J.C.	James Carrington	1803-1845
J.C.	James Chattaway	1862-1863
J.C.A.	J.C. Ayers	1881-1882
J.C.B.	John C. Beaumont	1852-1853
J.C.B.	Joseph C. Bragg	1841-1849
J.C.P.	J.C. Parker	1905-1906
J.C.S.	John C. Sharpe	1825-1840
J.C.S.	Joseph C. Stebbins	1834-1842
J.C.S.	Joseph C. Symmes	1847-1861
J.D.	J. Dowlar	1811-1862
J.D.	Joseph Dale	1815-1818
J.D.J.	J.D. Johnson	1819-1822
J.E.C.	J.E. Connolly	1902
J.E.C.	J.E. Cummings	1862-1863
J.E.C.	Joseph Edgar Craig	1861-1906
J.E.G	John E. Greer	1876-1883
J.E.H.	J.E. Hitchcock	1862-1863
J.E.H.	Jay E. Hoffer	1903-1904
J.F.B.	J.F. Riley	1898-1910
J.F.E.C.	J.F.E. Chamberlain	1875
J.F.S.	J.F. Sullivan	1898-1908
J.G.	John Garvin	1865-1874
J.G.B.	J.G. Benton	1866-1881
J.G.B.	John G. Butler	1886
J.G.F.	J.G. Flagg	1894-1900
J.G.L.	J.H. Lyons	1898
J.G.W.	J.G. Woodbury	1904
J.H.	James Harris	1837-1851
J.H.	James Hawkins	1848
J.H.	John Hannis	1862
J.H.	John Hawkins	1840-1852
J.H.	John Hill	1813-1835
J.H.	Joseph Hannis	1838-1862
J.H.	Joseph Harniss	1841-1844
J.H.C.	J.H. Coope	1870-1879
J.H.D.	J.H. Doyle	1894
J.H.E.	J.H. Ewig	1898
J.H.F.	J.H. Fletcher	1909
J.H.H.	J.H. Howarth	1899-1910
J.H.H.	Joseph H. Hubbard	1862
J.H.M.	James H. McGuire	1862
J.H.W.	J.H. Wowarth	1898
J.J.A.B.	James J.A. Bradford	1833-1835
J.J.C.	John J. Cornwell	1847-1867
J.J.L.	J.J. Lee	1898
J.J.M.	J.J. Murphy	1898
J.K.	J. Kimball	1875
J.K.B.	J.K. Burbank	1901-1910
J.L.	J. Lippold	1876
J.L.	Joseph Lanman	1819
J.L.	Joseph Lombard	1819-1841
J.L.	Joseph Lumbard	1818

J.L.C.	Joseph L. Cottle	1863-1875
J.L.H.	James L. Henderson	1828-1861
J.L.S.	J.L. Sticht	1895-1904
J.L.S.	J.L. Strong	1896-1902
J.M.	J. Mills	1875
J.M.	John Maggs	1862
J.M.	John McLean	1799-1802
J.M.	Joseph Morgan	1798-1802
J.M.	Julian McAllister	1865
J.M.	Justice Murphy	1841-1842
J.M.	Justin Murphy	1813-1833
J.M.B.C.	J.M.B. Clitz	1870
J.M.C.	J.M. Crighton	1895-1910
J.N.	John Newbury	1818-1826
J.N.	John Nicholson Jr.	1799-1807
J.N.	John Nicholson Sr.	1797-1798
J.N.	John Norman	1830
J.N.B.	J.N. Boyer	1905-1906
J.N.H.	J.N. Hemenway	1907
J.N.J.	John N. Jordan	1891-1898
J.N.S.	J.N. Sollace	1831-1850
J.O.	J. O'Malley	1896-1902
J.O.B.	J.O. Bush	1864
J.P.	Jacob Perkins	1819-1821
J.P.	James Perkin	1815
J.P.	John Pope	1843
J.P.	Joseph Perkin	1798
J.P.C.	James P. Chapman	1848
J.P.M.	J.P. McGuinness	1905
J.P.O.	J.P. O'Neil	1904-1910
J.P.O.	James P. Oeller	1813-1849
J.P.W.	Joseph P. Wells	1863
J.R.	J. Reid	1904-1910
J.R.	James Rockwell Jr.	1874-1876
J.R.D.	J.R. Dearborn	1894
J.R.E	John R. Esleek	1898-1910
J.R.E.	John R. Edie	1874
J.R.G.	J.R. Graham	1875-1877
J.R.G.	John R. Goldsborough	1864-1865
J.R.M.	John R. McGuinness	1868-1869
J.R.M.M.	J.R.M. Mullaney	1832-1879
J.S.	Jacob Shough	1808-1811
J.S.	James Stillman	1831-1850
J.S.	James Stubblefield	1807-1821
J.S.	John Stahl	1868
J.S.	John Stebbins	1819-1835
J.S.	John Symington	1832-1863
J.S.	Joseph Smith	1809-1837
J.S.	Josiah Snell	1800-1801
J.S.B.	J.S. Burns	1898-1910
J.S.C.	J.S. Chauncey	1812-1869
J.S.C.	J.S. Cooley	1898
J.S.D	John S. Duston	1862-1863
J.S.D.	James S. Dudley	1861-1876

J.S.D.	John S. Dexter	1798
J.S.P.	James S. Palmer	1825-1867
J.T.	Jerome Towne	1862-1863
J.T.	John Taylor	1861-1862
J.T.	Joseph Tarbell	1798-1815
J.T.	Josiah Tatnal	1858
J.T.B.	James T. Baden	1862-1864
J.T.C.	John T. Cleveland	1856-1877
J.T.T.	John T. Thompson	1896-1902
J.W.	John Wilder	1868
J.W.	John Williamson	1838-1849
J.W.	Joseph Weatherhead	1821-1830
J.W.A.	J.W. Alden	1905-1906
J.W.E.	J.W. Ewig	1898-1910
J.W.K.	John W. Keene	1862-1863
J.W.K.	John W. Kelly	1853-1864
J.W.R.	James W. Reilly	1849-1895
J.W.R.	James W. Ripley	1830-1863
J.Y.	Jonathan Young	1841-1881
K.M.D	K.M. Dennon	1896
K.S.M.	Kelly S. Morse	1893-1916
L.A.B.	Lester A. Beardslee	1850-1898
L.B.C.	Luke B. Chase	1861-1862
L.C.	Lyman Converse	1863
L.C.A.	Lucius C. Allin	1859
L.C.B.	L.C. Brown	1874
L.D.	L. Duston	1861-1867
L.D.	Lewis Draper	1876
L.F.	J.P. Farley	1874-1876
L.G.	Lewis Ghriskey	1811
L.G.G.	L.G. Gilmore	1896-1904
L.J.M.	L.J. Megette	1898
L.L.	Luther Luge	1841-1842
L.L.K.	L.L. Kuralt	1905-1910
L.M.	L. Menz	1907
L.M.F.	Lewis Foster Jr.	1837
L.N.	L. Newell	1876-1885
L.O.H.	L.O. Hale	1902-1906
L.P.	L. Papanti	1898
L.P.D.	L.P. Dustin	1894
L.S.	Luther Sage	1812-1838
L.W.	Leicester Wheeler	1818
M.E.H.	M.E. Hawkins	1898
M.H.	Michael Hayes	1860
M.L.	N. LeClair	1905-1906
M.L.M.	Moses L. Morse	1822-1824
M.M.	M. Moulton	1861
M.M.J.	Martin M. Johnson	1862-1863
M.P.B.	M.P. Benjamin	1899-1910
M.P.L.	Mann Paige Lomax	1836-1848
M.R.M.	M.R. Marsh	1898

M.T.K.	Marian T. Krepps	1862-1863
M.T.W.	Marine T. Wickham	1811-1816
M.W.C.	M.W. Carr	1862-1863
M.W.M.	M.W. Morley	1862
N.B.	Nehemiah Baden	1813-1820
N.C.T.	Nathan C. Twining	1885-1897
N.F.	Lewis M. Ferry	1863
N.F.	Nathan Forbes	1798-1804
N.F.	Noah Foot	1824
N.L.B.	N.L. Benoit	1900-1904
N.O.	Noble Orr	1798-1802
N.W.	Nathaniel Whiting	1862
N.W.P.	Nahaun W. Patch	1831-1850
O.A.	Oliver Allen	1816-1818
O.B.G.	O.G. Graham	1875
O.D.	Otis Dudley	1830
O.H.P.	Oliver H. Perry	1829-1849
O.S.	Oliver Sexton	1841
O.W.A.	O.W. Ainsworth	1831-1870
P.B.	Peter Barrett	1862-1870
P.B.	Pomeroy Booth	1862
P.B.B.H.	P.B.B. Havens	1875
P.C.	P. Chapman	1844
P.C.	Pierce Crosby	1838-1883
P.G.	Peter Getz	1803, 1806-1808
P.J.K.	P.J. Kiley	1901-1906
P.K.	P. Keller	1904-1906
P.T.C.	Patrick Thomas Cunningham	1863-1872
P.T.S.	P.T. Safford	1874
P.V.	P. Valentine	1862
R.A.C.	Rinaldo A. Carr	1889-1909
R.B.	Robert Beals	1862
R.B.	Robert Blanchard	1831
R.B.	Rogers Birnie Jr.	1879-1880
R.B.C.	R.B. Chamberlain	1906-1907
R.B.H.	Robert B. Hitchcock	1851-1853
R.C.	Robert Corbit	1798
R.C.	Rufus Chandler	1831-1850
R.C.	Russel Curtis	1818
R.D.D.	R.D. Draper	1905-1906
R.E.	R. Ellis	1818
R.H.B.	R.H. Bailey	1870-1885
R.H.K.W.	Robert Henry Kirkwood Whitely	1838-1875
R.J.	Robert Johnson	1822-1826
R.K.A.	Remick K. Arnold	1862-1877
R.L.	Roswell Lee	1818-1819
R.L.B.	R.L. Buckland	1860
R.M.	R. Matthews	1906
R.M.D.	R.M. Dennon	1895-1902
R.M.H.	R.M. Hill	1875-1876

R.N.S.	R.N. Stannard	1906
R.O.	Robert Orr	1798-1808
R.P.	Richard Paine	1839-1848
R.P.	Richard Parker	1838-1847
R.P.B.	Robert P. Barry	1860-1865
R.P.B.	Robert P. Beales	1862-1879
R.P.P.	Robert P. Parrott	1836-1837
R.S.	Richard Smith	1806-1830
R.S.L.	Robert S. LaMotte	1861-1869
R.T.S.	R.T. Safford	1862-1885
R.W.M.	Richard W. Meade	1850-1895
R.W.M.	Robert W. McNeely	1890
S.A.	S. Adams	1860-1861
S.A.	Samuel Alexander	1808-1830
S.A.D.	S.A. Dinsmore	1862-1863
S.B.	Samuel Barron	1812-1861
S.B.L.	Samuel B. Lathrop	1818
S.C.	Silas Crispin	1862
S.C.R.	S.C. Rowan	1826-1889
S.D.	Samuel Dale	1817-1818
S.D.	Stephen Danks	1863
S.E.B.	S.E. Bugbee	1901-1910
S.E.B.	Stanhope English Blunt	1889-1890
S.H.	Samuel Hawkins	1862
S.H.B.	S.H. Broughton	1899-1910
S.J.	Seth Janes	1818-1824
S.K.	S. Knows	1846-1852
S.K.	Samuel Keller	1848
S.L.	Samuel Leonard	1862-1875
S.L.T.	S.L. Tuttle	1894
S.L.W.	Samuel L. Worsley	1862-1863
S.M.	Samuel Marcy	1838-1862
S.M.	Stillman Moore	1846-1852
S.P.	S. Priestly	1904-1906
S.P.B.	Samuel P. Baird	1861-1873
S.T.B.	Samuel T. Bugbee	1862
S.W.P.	S.W. Porter	1859-1860
T.A.	Thomas Annely	1797
T.A.B.	Theodore A. Belkap	1862-1863
T.B.H.	Thomas B. Hawks	1862-1863
T.D.	Thomas Dale	1796
T.H.R.	T.H. Rogers	1896
T.H.S.	Thomas H. Stevens	1816
T.J.F.	T.J. Fitzpatrick	1898
T.J.L.	T.J. Lovett	1904-1906
T.J.S.	T.J. Stevenson	1870-1879
T.P.	Thomas Palmer	1808-1809
T.P.M.	T.P. Maroney	1898
T.S.	Thomas Sangster	1812
T.S.	Thomas Stockton	1812-1825
T.S.	Thomas Stuart	1813
T.S.	Townsend Stith	1810

T.T.S.L.	Theodore T.S. Laidley	1864-1866
T.V.	Thomas Valentine	1863
T.W.	Thomas Warner	1833-1837
T.W.B.	T.W. Booth	1861-1865
T.W.R.	Thomas W. Russell	1862
U.P.S.	Urial P. Strong	1862
V.L.B.	V.L. Bennett	1875-1879
W.	Marine T. Wickham	1811-1816
W.A.B.	W.A. Benjamin	1898
W.A.B.	W.A. Bennett	1898
W.A.T.	William Anderson Thornton	1840-1861
W.A.W.	W.A. Walker	1905-1907
W.B.	William Blanchard	1831
W.B.	William Bradbury	1860-1861
W.B.	William Brown	1862
W.B.S.	William B. Shubrick	1806-1861
W.B.W.	William B. Whittelsey	1898
W.C.	William Cadwell	1860-1861
W.C.	William Chapman	1860-1864
W.C.F.	W.C. Fielding	1898-1907
W.D.	William Dickinson	1848-1850
W.D.E.	W.D. Earl	1863
W.D.N.	William D. Nicholson	1862-1871
W.E.	W. Easley	1902
W.E.B.	W.E. Benjamin	1898
W.E.B.	W.E. Boynton	1902-1910
W.E.H.	W.E. Hosmer	1905-1915
W.E.S.	W.E. Strong	1915-1916
W.F.	William Foster	1863
W.F.B.	W.F. Bradbury	1898-1902
W.F.F.	W.F. Fennyery	1904-1906
W.G.	W. Ganeard	1901-1902
W.G.C.	W.G. Chamberlain	1859-1875
W.H.B.	W.H. Brundrett	1898-1902
W.H.B.	William H. Barber	1862
W.H.B.	William H. Bulkley	1898-1900
W.H.C.	W.H. Clayton	1898-1901
W.H.C.	William H. Carver	1862-1863
W.H.C.	William H. Chandler	1862-1863
W.H.G.	W.H. Greene	1901-1902
W.H.H.	W.H. Hayden	1901-1906
W.H.M.	W.H. Morley	1898-1902
W.H.R.	William H. Roberts	1863-1864
W.H.R.	William H. Russell	1862-1863
W.J.C.	W.J. Clark	1898
W.J.H.	W.J. Hines	1904-1910
W.J.O.	W.J. Ober	1904-1906
W.L.B.	William L. Bates	1870-1879
W.L.B.	William L. Borden	1844-1854
W.L.C.	W.L. Crowl	1898-1902
W.M.	William Maynadier	1838-1863

W.M.F.	William M. Folger	1861-1898
W.M.L.	W.M. Lyndon	1898
W.M.M.	W.M. Mills	1894
W.N.	Walter North	1831-1863
W.N.J.	W.N. Jeffers	1840-1878
W.P.	William Page	1863
W.P.	William Prince	1875-1877
W.P.P.	W.P. Pulcifer	1896
W.P.T.	William P. Taylor	1862-1864
W.R.	William Rich	1862-1863
W.R.	William Richardson	1808
W.R.	William Russell	1808
W.R.S.	W.R. Shipley	1898
W.S.	W. Syrett	1904-1906
W.S.	William Smith	1828-1843
W.S.W.	William S. Wood	1862-1863
W.T.	William Taggart	1838-1860
W.T.	William Turnbull	1843-1851
W.W.	William Walters	1862-1864
W.W.B.	W.W. Bartlet	1899-1904
W.W.K.	W.W. Kimball	1879-1889
W.W.S.	W.W. Street	1874-1875
Z.B.	Zadock Batt	1862

U.S. ARMS INSPECTORS WHO HAD THEIR OWN SHOPS

Samuel Alexander
Oliver Allen
Thomas Annely
George Flegel
Joseph Morgan
Henry H. Perkins
Joseph Perkins
Daniel Pettibone
H.K. White
Marine T. Wickham

APPENDIX B

Armorers to the Pennsylvania Revolutionary War Navy (Made and Repaired Ordnance and Edged Weapons)

Armorer	Date	Ship
Daniel Bollard	1776	Armed boat *Hancock*
Peter Barkley	1777	Brigate *Convention*
John Connor	1776	Armed boat *Warren*
Arthur Conway	1776-1777	Armed schooner *Lydia*
John Dawson	1777	?
William Farley	1776	Armed boat *Ranger*
Matthew Ford	1777	Armed boat *Dickinson*
John Garland	1776-1777	Warship *Montgomery*
John Haye	1777	Armed boat *Chatham*
Hamilton Hazleton	1776	Warship *Montgomery*
John Keys	1779	Warship *General Greene*
Charles Knowles	1775	Armed schooner *Delaware*
William Mayberry	1776-1777	Warship *Effingham*
John Patton	1776	Armed boat *Argus*
Joseph Richards	1777	Armed boat *Chatham*
Joseph Roberts	1776-1778	Armed boat *Hancock*
John Sansfield	1775	Armed boat *Congress*
William Smith	1776	Armed boat *Congress*

APPENDIX C

U.S. Cavalry Practice Swords

1840
Practice sabers first used.
Probably an oak stick (round) with a wicker-basket hilt.

1872
Single stick (cavalry officer).
Used to practice for the use of the new M1872 cavalry officer sword.
Shown in Capt. J. O'Rourke's manual, *A New System of Sword Exercises for Use in Instruction of Officers of the U.S. Army*.
Round 38-inch hickory or ash stick with a leather-covered hilt and leather guards tapering up from a disc-shaped bottom guard to the top of the stick.

M1891
Practice saber (trooper).
Flat blade of hickory, ash, or beech with a 6-inch grip.
Sheet iron or leather guard.

M1891
Single stick (officer), 96 inches long.
Disk of sheet iron or leather (6-inch diameter) attached to stick 6 inches from end.
Lengthwise hole on grip end of stick for lead shot or weights to be added for balance.

M1891
Single stick (officer), 1904 variation.
36-inch stick with wicker-basket hilt.

M1908
Experimental practice saber.
Tapered steel blade with tip cut off square.
Hilt padded with buckskin.

1912
Experimental practice saber.
Steel blade.

M1913
Used for practice in the use of the new M1913 cavalry sword.
1. Flat 36-inch wooden blade with a thumb groove on top. Steel guard screwed to the end of the blade and attached on the bottom with two screws.
2. Same wooden blade with wicker-basket guard with two holes (one each side) for blade to slip through.

M1913
1915 variation.
Flat wood blade with a shaped grip and rounded pommel.
Sheet steel guard riveted to the pommel and retained with a round roll pin 6 inches down the blade.

M1916
42-inch steel tapered blade, cut square at the point.
23-inch center single fuller.
Wide tapered ricasso.
Steel-bowl-shaped disc guard with sheet-steel knuckle guard fastened from bowl to pommel.
Maple grip slightly curved and tapered near the pommel.

Known U.S. Production of Cavalry Practice Swords

1897	U.S. Rock Island, IL, Armory 150 M1891 Practice Sabers 150 M1891 Single Sticks 500 M1891 Practice Saber Blades
1903	U.S. Springfield, MA, Armory 100 M1891 Practice Sabers
1913	U.S. Rock Island, IL, Armory ? M1913 Practice Swords ? M1913 Practice Sword Blades
1916	U.S. Springfield, MA, Armory 279 M1913 (1915) Variation Practice Swords
1920	U.S. Springfield, MA, Armory 50 M1913 (1915) Variation Practice Swords
1923	U.S. Springfield, MA, Armory 75 M1913 (1915) Variation Practice Swords 14 M1916 Practice Swords
1924	U.S. Springfield, MA, Armory 62 M1916 Practice Swords

www.ingramcontent.com/pod-product-compliance
Lightning Source LLC
Chambersburg PA
CBHW080723230426
43665CB00020B/2588